TRAUMA SPONGES

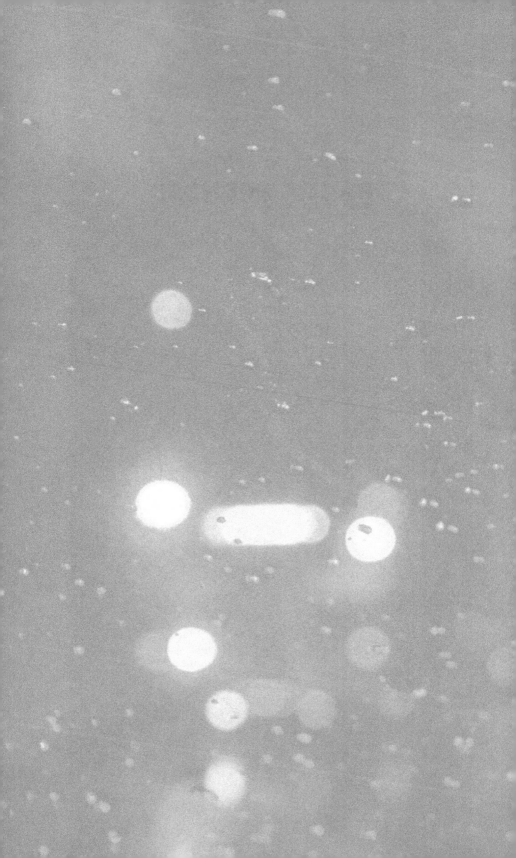

TRAUMA SPONGES

DISPATCHES FROM THE SCARRED HEART OF EMERGENCY RESPONSE

JEREMY NORTON

University of Minnesota Press
Minneapolis
London

The publication of this book was assisted by a bequest from Josiah H. Chase to honor his parents, Ellen Rankin Chase and Josiah Hook Chase.

Quotation from James Baldwin, "Notes of a Native Son," reprinted with permission from Beacon Press, from James Baldwin, *The Price of the Ticket: Collected Nonfiction, 1948–1985* (Boston: Beacon Press, 1985); permission conveyed through Copyright Clearance Center, Inc.

Excerpts from *Begin Again: James Baldwin's America and Its Urgent Lessons for Our Own*, by Eddie S. Glaude Jr. copyright 2020 by Eddie S. Glaude Jr.; reprinted by permission of Crown Books, an imprint of the Crown Publishing Group, a division of Penguin Random House LLC; all rights reserved.

Quotation from "Kid Gloves," by Dessa, reprinted with permission.

Published by the University of Minnesota Press
111 Third Avenue South, Suite 290
Minneapolis, MN 55401-2520
http://www.upress.umn.edu

ISBN 978-1-5179-1418-9 (hc)
ISBN 978-1-5179-1582-7 (pb)

Library of Congress record available at https://lccn.loc.gov/2023287603.

Printed in the United States of America on acid-free paper

The University of Minnesota is an equal-opportunity educator and employer.

30 29 28 27 26 25 24 23   10 9 8 7 6 5 4 3 2

for all the girls
and
for Hank

He bears witness for those who cannot because they did not survive, and he bears witness for those who survived it all, wounded and broken.

—Eddie S. Glaude Jr., *Begin Again: James Baldwin's America and Its Urgent Lessons for Our Own*

I get nervous at parties but I'm like bedrock at hospitals.

—Dessa, "Kid Gloves"

CONTENTS

TERMS AND ABBREVIATIONS

AED	automatic external defibrillator
BIPOC	Black, Indigenous, people of color
bus	ambulance
BVM	bag valve mask
CVD	Covid
durgan	rank firefighter; slang for runt pony of the team
EBD	emotionally/behaviorally disturbed person
EMS	Emergency Medical Services
FEO	fire equipment operator
FFR	firefighter
FMO	fire motor operator
GFS	George Floyd Square
HCMC	Hennepin County Medical Center; also referred to as County
IAFF	International Association of Fire Fighters
ILI	influenza-like illness
MFD	Minneapolis Fire Department
NFPA	National Fire Protection Association
NIOSH	National Institute for Occupational Safety and Health
OSHA	Occupational Safety and Health Administration
SATs	oxygen saturation levels
SOB	shortness of breath
tramp	A junior or extra firefighter who is moved around per shift to cover staffing shortages; to tramp is to cover open spots. The tramp bed is the forlorn spare bed at each station.
17s, 14s	Station 17 or engine 17 (or 14) in MFD parlance

INTRODUCTION
This Is Not the Minneapolis *Backdraft*

A FUNNY THING HAPPENED ON THE WAY TO WRITING A MEMOIR ABOUT FIRE-fighter/EMTs, the street-level realities of health care, and the punishing cold weather of Minneapolis. A few things, actually.

And none of them was at all funny. But there you go, and here we are.

Twenty years into my career, twenty years of collecting experiences from work toward a book that addresses cultural issues in emergency response, the Covid-19 pandemic crashed our world. Soon after that, four Minneapolis police officers killed another Black man, slowly, in front of a crowd. My crew and I responded to that call—with no inkling that the world was about to erupt.

In the aftermath of these twin events my work and personal life shifted, but less than one might suspect. A great many of the societal and sociological elements have long been apparent to those of us in this world (those who are paying attention). Writing helped me process my complicated responses to the pandemic and the killing of George Floyd. I have disinterred buried or smothered feelings. I have discovered pockets of raw woundedness, reactive anger, and sustained worry. I've met wonderful, brave people and learned a great deal.

//

The book I had been writing prior to 2020 was an examination of EMS response, which is the health care system at its lowest level: the raw truths of living, dying, and illness; the often-ignored factors of race, class, and gender on responders and patients; and the ill effects of compulsory machismo on society and responders alike. Then the pandemic hit: so much noble sacrifice and tender care swamped by selfish behaviors and malignant denial. In late 2021 (between delta and omicron), I began to edit my early writing on Covid. There were such fear and loathing dripping from every sentence, the result of nearly two years of suppressed and sustained worry and anger. I was exhausted from keeping sane while managing the crazed disconnect between what we experienced and how larger society was handling its end.

The killing of Mr. Floyd by Minneapolis police occurred in front of a store where I had experienced a "near miss" of poor policing three years prior. I'd written about it in 2017 but was pooh-poohed for making rash accusations (by people who had never seen the police overreact on calls, never witnessed them body Black men out of phantom menace). *Past is prologue.* I was trying to raise attention to how blindly our system churns along, how individual responders act out ingrained scripts that are created by yet denied by the system, leaving only spurious accounts of how yet another unarmed Black or brown man ended up dead shortly after being accosted by the police.

The 2020 uprising and reaction were very much the language of the unheard. Except, I suggest, it was more accurately the language of the ignored. Our status quo absorbs the peaceful protests, the principled speakers, the anguished and bereft families of those killed extralegally by the system. The machine rides it out, banking on short attention spans, the revolving news cycle, the next issue, the next scandal, the next "tragic incident."

This time, it was a body too far. Within the pandemic's lockdown fishbowl, millions of people watched simultaneously, and the supersaturation of Black deaths and white indifference reached its tipping point. The heartbroken, angry, and exasperated crowds finally turned their fires outward, toward the domains of white folks accustomed to watching *other* neighborhoods burn.

After the spasm of anger and upheaval in the wake of Mr. Floyd's killing, white America briefly attempted to consider the plight of our Black citizens. But, wow, that was *hard.* And so *much* to untangle! And people were *angry!* And we had to listen, and apologize, and then there was talk of *reparations! I mean, I feel bad for, like, centuries of ingrained and legislated inequality, of financial injustice, of property denial, of sub-*

par education and health care, but can't we just put a sign on our lawn and call it even? Not surprisingly, many white people fatigued of the effort rather quickly. And many others refused this opportunity to look clearly at what we have wrought, retreating instead to the fiery embrace of white victim complex, further balkanizing the nation.

Through all that, my coworkers and I did our jobs, carrying the stress and worry of the next potential flashpoint—because it was apparent to me, terrifyingly so, that the police had learned no lessons, that the city was run largely by tyros and the inept, that nothing had truly changed. And there was still Covid, except now it was both a medical and a political virus.

I am grateful that it's taken so long to write and publish this book. Five years ago, this book would have been interesting and vibrant and full of relevant points about life, death, and dying. The past three years have amplified my observations—and, frankly, provided me with a unique perspective from which to guide readers who might otherwise miss the poignant, interrelated connections of race, systemic inequalities, and compulsory machismo that shape so much of our society.

//

There's a firehouse saying: No one ever called 911 when they did something smart.

This is a book about my twenty-two years as a firefighter/EMT for the city of Minneapolis—twenty-two years in which I've had an intimate view of the 911 emergency medical system and the almost unfathomable reality of what passes for the social safety net in this country. From birth through death, people dial 911 and we respond. Actually, *before* birth (given prenatal issues and miscarriages) and *after* death (sometimes long after life has departed the body).

Few people understand what firefighters actually do. It bemuses me to explain, yet again, to 911 callers (let alone to police officers or my relatives) why there is a fire truck outside when someone "just wants a ride to the ER." We explain that the ambulance is not merely a fancy taxi: the paramedics are skilled professionals trained to do advanced prehospital care. We are not simply burly firedudes who break doors and squirt water. If you call 911 in Minneapolis at three in the morning for a minor issue (especially if you say any of the magic words: *heart, breathing, chest pain*), you will find one of our big red trucks right outside your house faster than you expect. Because if you are, in fact, dying, you will need *all* of us working hard to give you a chance at survival.

As a captain—the company commander—I am responsible, first and foremost, for the safety of my crew, and then for the delivery of our services on every call. I must assess, decipher, interpret, and take action within seconds. To do this well, I have to be skilled at reading situations and people. The complexities of the job are the complexities of human nature. We do not diagnose illnesses: we interpret signs and symptoms. We read the person, listening and observing critically. If we don't know—or don't care to look past the surface—we fail to see what's really going on. Not every captain can or is willing to do that.

What I have to offer the reader here is more than just a collection of "scary fire stories." I am not your representative fireguy. I'm a Gen X, punk-rock and rap fanatic, a book nerd D.C. native; philosophical, cynical, yet fiercely idealistic. I bailed on the family path of lawyering, electing instead to teach literature before becoming a firefighter. I cannot ignore how life's tragedies and triumphs, its grand epics, occur on an individual scale: highbrow and lowbrow are not so different.

I am a unicorn in this profession, an assessment that would bring rare agreement between my fans and detractors. Typically atypically, I considered the fire service only when I moved to Minneapolis in 1994 and connected with Jen Cornell soon after she completed rookie school. Jen is another DC expat, a high school acquaintance. She joined the Minneapolis Fire Department at twenty-three, thinking it seemed like a cool challenge, with good pay, health benefits, physical and honorable work. Being one of the first women also appealed. She promoted up through the ranks, encountered vast misogynist and homophobic hostilities at every turn, earned advanced degrees in public health and law in her spare time, and left the fire service. She is now a successful and highly regarded lawyer. She misses the goofy mayhem, and me, but little else about the job.

I was fascinated to listen to Jen and the clutch of second-wave fireladies talk shop. The work was wild, interesting, dangerous, noble. But what stood out was the encompassing and persistent hostility the women faced: chauvinism, misogyny, homophobia, racism. The job—and the mass of its workers—was resistant if not antagonistic toward women's participation. From the gear not fitting to structural gender incompetence (open dorms, urinals, *firemen*), to being ignored or given the silent treatment, to being actively harassed, to verbal and even physical abuse—the few groundbreaking women were treated with open contempt by many firefighters. The first women endured levels and layers of mistreatment. Jen was young, educated, very smart, self-confident. She had not gotten the memo that she should feel guilty and ashamed for taking up space in the Brotherhood. Some men were supportive, but they were the exceptions. To hear these women discuss work was to learn the myriad forms of micro- and macroaggressions, outright bullying, and vast male blindness.

They couldn't simply learn to be good firefighters; too much time, effort, and emotion were spent battling widespread resistance and undermining. Coming at it via the underdogs and outcasts, my appreciation for the nontraditional firefighter—as well as skepticism of the traditional narratives—helped me see through a lot of the default macho posturing. I started out mistrusting the clichéd *fireman* essentialism. I was the first, and sole, male member of the MFD's Women's Association, which earned me no love from the firedudes.

I marveled at how pervasive the backhand, sexist dismissal of EMS work as "nursing" and not-real-fireman work was, despite its comprising 80 percent of our actual job, despite its offering the greatest opportunities to serve the public and save lives, and despite what I came to understand as the striking distinction between how we see ourselves and what we actually do: all those treacly narratives of the He-Man's Woman Haters Club, er, the Brotherhood . . . a lot easier to call bullshit if you can see clearly what bunk it is.

//

Trauma Sponges is set in Minneapolis, Minnesota, literally anywhere within city limits: on the streets and in alleys, in homes and apartments that are spacious and well-kept or cluttered or barren, on bridges and along the riverbanks. Firefighters witness the full range of human behavior and the complex dynamics that shape our society, but our view comes amid chaos, horror, and absurdity.

The existential nature of our profession may be what cuts deepest. We cannot force anyone to change their habits, their influences, their beliefs. The systemic solutions that should exist do not. There is no protecting emergency workers from the effects of daily immersion in others' suffering. The job is, by definition, a traumatic experience. We operate in a state of high alert, trained to respond and react. How we live with it, how we manage to continue to do the work without cracking up, or how we crack up: those stories are the B sides to the depths of woe we witness. This could be *The Things We Carried*, EMS version.

The corrosive effects of this work on the people who do it are exacerbated by the enduring macho firehouse culture. This book seeks to challenge that culture and its deadly consequences. In my line of work, hypermasculinity and desperate denial have pushed the incidences of PTSD, stress, and suicide to crisis levels. This mythos of machismo is ingrained from rookie school, reinforced by relentless peer pressure. It provides a performative identity that many coworkers cling to at horrendous personal and cultural cost—physical and emotional trauma, depression, and the burgeoning rates of PTSD and suicide.

Throughout my career, and as I've worked on this book, revisiting old calls, sifting through details, I've been shocked by the number of my peers who manage to ignore the human aspect of our work. Some of my coworkers cannot remember a single detail from incidents we experienced together. I recognize that the depths of sorrow and pain I have experienced vicariously are not healthy. Many other coworkers carry unresolved grief and guilt that weigh on them, eat at them, haunt them. Even writing about it, while I feel better purging some ghosts and hard bits, I find myself steeped in the mire. But then, remaining open to what I see, both the beauty and the horror, reinforces what it means to be deeply human.

I feel heavily and take seriously the weight of racial discourse. I am an educated, straight white man. I do not presume to explain Black experience to anyone, certainly not to any Black people. I am writing specifically *against* white supremacist culture. I seek to break through the walls of rationalization and denial, dishonesty and delusion that we white people hide behind, prop up, and fight to maintain. I hope to explicate the ways our artifice and denial-scarred cultural fictions shape American society. Because what we see, both explicitly and indirectly, in emergency response *are* the effects of generations of structural inequalities and their consequences. A person does not suddenly wake up poor and trapped; neither does another person suddenly wake up wealthy and protected.

I feel it is both my duty and my privilege to examine what I encounter and to speak up. My tone can be brusque but my aim is true, as one Elvis said. If I see the world with a peculiar clarity, and if I see too much silence and avoidance layered over our perspectives, I should speak up. As Eddie Glaude Jr. writes of James Baldwin in *Begin Again,* "He bears witness for those who cannot because they did not survive, and he bears witness for those who survived it all, wounded and broken." As witness to so much death and suffering, and with a rare perspective on the crushing systemic wheels, I find myself a midwestern Ishmael or Ancient Mariner, reporting what happened to me and mine. I feel determined to speak for those who cannot, and to speak to those who might not listen otherwise. A note: I refer to a generalized, collective "we" throughout: white folks, white men, or male firefighters, generally. If you are white and male and a firefighter, and you feel besmirched by my broad brush, I apologize. Those of us who rise above shouldn't feel threatened. Here: #notallmen.

//

I promoted to battalion chief (BC) from captain in 2015. I was the ranking officer of a battalion, or district, in charge of running fire and hazmat incidents, administratively overseeing the stations and personnel in my district. BCs do not respond on medical calls. They do very little hands-on work. I have a decent mind for command, for strategy and tactics. I have an outlier's appreciation that there are better ways to be an administrator than simply barking at one's subordinates. I found myself at odds with many of the old-guard BCs and deputies, and my allegiance was to the firefighters in the stations. I am stubborn and contrary, when pushed by bad leadership. There were conflicts and headbutts.

Significantly, I no longer interacted with or served the public directly when I toodled around in my sporty chief's SUV. I roamed my district, alone, and I did not get my hands dirty. I didn't mind the solitude, but the citizens? I missed that part. For me, that is what the job is about. After two years, I voluntarily demoted. I could—and can—serve the public and lead my crews from the captain's seat of an engine company. I felt clear in my decision and have been far happier at work

99 percent of the time. It is harder on my body, and I get less sleep, to be certain. It would only be "career suicide" were I to care about higher promotion and departmental politics. I do not.

I've gleaned a lot of material in this book from experiences that occurred after I demoted. I would have spared myself a bunch of rough, heavy calls had I remained a chief. I accept that. I gained clarity and understanding of the bigger picture when I was no longer participating in it. The distance I had as a chief confirmed my belief that EMS is the core and heart of our job, and I made connections that have deepened this understanding.

I want the reader to come away better informed: about personal health, human behavior, the dying process, death. I want people to increase their compassion, challenge their denial, and appreciate the depths of trauma and suffering many folks carry with them. I am not writing for shock value, although some of this material is inescapably visceral. I am writing to make the reader truly consider what it means when there are no alternatives, no other options, when it is not possible to look away or skip out on something hard. Our cultural passivity, abetted by profound denial, leads to a great many of the problems I confront at work.

Everything included here happened. I have changed and obscured identifying details, of course, to respect the people I've served while honoring the truth of their experiences. There are some items of public record and official documentation. Otherwise, all real people have been concealed, blended, altered. The names are fake, and there are composite characters: I am grateful for the opportunity to serve this public, and never wish to violate anyone's privacy. I am one captain on one rig at one station in Minneapolis, Minnesota. We have three shifts and divide our lives into six-day rotations. There are twenty-six other captains working today. At every station, every single day and night, my peers are responding to situations similar to what I share here. Across the United States, in big cities and small towns, a version of this human circus continues eternally. We are born, we live, we die: in crisis, someone must respond. Me and mine are that someone. In your city, it's just another version of us.

If Samuel Beckett were a firefighter/EMT, he would feel at home in the absurdity of this system. *You must go on. I can't go on. I'll go on.* As with Beckett, there is abundant wry humor amid the misery and squalor. We laugh to keep from breaking. Other times, we laugh because there is little else to do. The panoply of human behaviors is fascinating, exhausting, heartbreaking. The calls keep coming, lives altered and ending. This book is my attempt to share the human piece, the weight of responding endlessly to dire situations. The cost of immersion in others' suffering and pain and loss. It is not trauma porn. It is a compendium of sorrows. They call; we respond, always and no matter what. It is our job.

I give deep appreciation to all the good cops, medics, and firefolks who daily show up and do right, who honor the badge and the profession, putting their lives into the pot as ante for the well-being of their fellow citizens. May we all find our way home safe.

1
911 IS NOT, IN FACT, A JOKE

I'M A MINNEAPOLIS FIREFIGHTER/EMT. SINCE THE YEAR 2000, I HAVE GONE TO work for twenty-four-hour shifts, donned my lustrous blue poly cotton uniform, arranged my bulky firefighting gear beside the massive red fire truck, done my chores around the station, participated in perfunctory training or boundless chatter and gossip (mostly the latter), all while waiting for the alarm to dispatch my crew of three or four men and women to some type of emergency.

When the alarm comes in, we stop eating, put down our phones, drop whatever we're doing, jump up from the Murphy bed, pinch off a poop, slip out of the shower and scramble to dry and dress, and hustle out to the rig. In any shift, the vast majority of alarms arrive with the signature up-down, up-down, up-down tones of a medical call. We heft our bunker gear—the reflective, fire-resistant turnout jackets and pants, the thick boots, all heavy and arranged for swift donning—up onto the fire truck and roll out the big bay doors. The rig rumbles through the streets, its vibrations setting off car alarms and rattling windows, flashing red lights and sirens and thundering diesel engine causing civic disruption.

In all weather, at all times of night and day, no matter what we were doing moments prior, we speed toward the address, dodging panicked or distracted drivers and pedestrians, in order to arrive as swiftly and safely as possible. We park just past the address—to allow access for the ambulance, as our rigs clog most residential streets—don our medical gloves and safety glasses, grab our clunky bags of equipment—oxygen cylinders, blood pressure cuffs, bandages, defibrillator, and more—then stride purposefully to the door. We are taught not to run on the fireground: it causes or reinforces panic, they say. EMS calls are similar: swift, steady forward movement.

We enter and handle whatever we find. Actually, strike that: we *arrive* and handle whatever we find, wherever we find it. For our patients are everywhere: on or under the porch, on or crumpled beneath the roof, in garages and cars and alleys, on stairs, in attics and basements, and, all too frequently, in narrow bathrooms. Sure, many we find on the sofa in the living room, or in bed, but so very many people have bad times while they're in a cramped bathroom.

And that becomes our initial work site.

I am a firefighter, but most of my job involves providing some type of EMS care to citizens. We are emergency responders who happen to fight fires occasionally. Very occasionally. Most shifts, we respond primarily to 911 non-hazardous-emergency medical calls. Not fires, not building collapses, not hazmat incidents: EMS incidents. And "emergency" is always relative, no matter the type of call. So, while we're always prepared for a fire, a car crash and extrication, a gas leak, the majority are medicals. The big red truck, the hoses and ladders and tools and water, my cumbersome turnout gear, the self-contained airpacks and iconic helmets: all of that is superfluous for more than 80 percent of my work.

But you're firefighters!

Weird, right? We drive the fire truck through our little patch of the city to whatever 911 call Dispatch has received. Our job has changed as culture and society have. The number of fires has dropped each decade since 1980, and the scope of our job has expanded. We provide "emergency services" to the people of Minneapolis. It's a broad phrase that doesn't begin to capture the range of our work. In the 1980s, fire departments across America—with varying levels of resistance or acceptance—began pairing with local ambulance services to respond in tandem, as a complement to the more skilled paramedics.

There are nineteen fire stations and twenty-six rigs in Minneapolis, located strategically to provide rapid emergency help to all citizens throughout the city. We can get to most places in our response box within four minutes. The paramedics who serve Minneapolis cover a wider area, spreading into the suburbs, with fewer ambulances. They have higher skills, more training, and better equipment and medications. They can provide advanced life support while transporting patients to the emergency department, or ED. On most EMS calls, they arrive with us or within a few minutes—if they're responding from afar, a *long* ten minutes after. Firefighters do the basics and the essentials, which include confirming that someone is or is not dead, picking someone up off the floor, helping them breathe, stopping their bleeding. On critical calls, we can keep a person breathing and their heart pumping until the ambulance crew arrives to treat and transport. We arrive, evaluate what is actually happening, address what we can, and, if appropriate, radio to Dispatch to give medics more info and a better sense of what to expect and what is needed. Our dispatchers then send the information to the medics' Dispatch, which then sends it to the medics. There are unavoidable time gaps with this—and sometimes human errors—but we must remember and anticipate the delays. If I scream, "I NEED MEDICS RIGHT NOW!" it might sound impressive, but it's a hollow, desperate gesture. Anticipation and logical approach are more effective.

Once medics arrive, we are their support staff. Having firefighters respond to EMS calls provides the citizens with faster response times and access to care: when seconds count, a difference of several minutes is literally the gap between life and death.

For the same reason that we need enough skilled firefighters to complete multiple simultaneous tasks if your house is on fire—thus the thundering herd of rigs converging in a riot of sirens and lights—if you are having a life-or-death crisis, getting trained technicians to you as fast as possible, with skills, equipment, and steady hands, improves your chances of surviving. A true medical emergency is time sensitive and labor intensive. We take immediate measures, if that is what's needed, and we assist the medics doing multiple essential tasks in rapid succession. Neither paramedics nor firefighters diagnose anyone. We respond to how the patient presents, and we address the critical issues as we can. The signs and symptoms (and our honed experience) can point toward what is likely happening or the causes, both solvable and not.

The naked truth is that fire departments, firefighters, no longer do what the name states—not with any regularity. On one hand, that is great news for our citizens: the decrease in fires means an increase in homes and people not being on fire. But it does put the fire service in a quandary. Minneapolis is like most cities in the United States, where the full-time firefighters respond as a medical unit to the majority of their calls, wearing the very large tires off their very heavy fire trucks for respiratory complaints. Or else they sit idly inside the stations, waiting for fires that seldom come. I much prefer to get out and help people.

Many of my own friends still do not truly comprehend that we primarily respond to EMS calls, and even those who do, don't grasp the range of our responses. They think *firefighters* and imagine New York Fire Department (FDNY): six brawny guys with their iconic helmets and turnout gear and glorious mustaches fighting rollicking blazes day in and night out. I understand that misconception and confusion. Too many of my peers, from rookies to the top brass, clutch at the idea (delusion?) that they are *Firemen!* (*Fireladies! Firepeople!*) rather than multiskilled emergency technicians. The fire service is deep in the throes of a paradigm shift, an existential crisis, an obsolescence verging on oblivion. Fires will always occur, but advances in public safety and technology have driven the exponential decline of working fires, vastly curtailing the frequency of firefighters fighting fire. If the idea is that we need X number of firefighters spread around the city to swiftly and aggressively stop fires from burning houses, buildings, neighborhoods, yet we only have Y number of fires daily (weekly, monthly, yearly), what is the actual number of firefighters the city needs to pay to work each day?

In the 1970s, before widespread smoke detectors (and home security systems, nanny cams, and cell phones), a small fire on the stove would spread in the kitchen and possibly to the rest of the house before someone smelled or saw the smoke and called us. Now, smoke detectors catch fires in the early stages. Now, we have sprinklers in new apartment and office buildings. We also have deadly toxins in all the plastics and petroleum-based products in our lives. A single laptop computer produces more noxious chemicals than an entire 1970s living room. The contents of modern life make every fire far more dangerous and volatile. They just are stunningly infrequent. This contributes to some of the nervous posturing by firefighters, consciously or not: we need to be needed, and the threat that efficiency experts will cut our numbers even further scares us. Conversely, we can get too comfortable in the unexamined presumption that fire's ubiquity guarantees our unchanging existence. We glorify and romanticize a John Henry–type of atavistic approach, going mano a mano with fire, even as technology and progress leave us behind.

There are far fewer fires and far more 911 calls, whether medical issues or public safety concerns, than ever before. My point, as you will see throughout, is that there is a perilous aspiration to be what we wish we were: *Firemen!* To ignore the evolving realities of the profession, we put ourselves at a disadvantage on many levels. Because it is the most reactionary of professions, we, like the dinosaurs, refuse to acknowledge the deepening snows of the already descending Ice Age.

//

The essence of the Good Samaritan principle is that people call 911 for real emergencies, in dire need of help, and emergency crews come quickly with the intention of saving lives. Seconds count. In reality, people dial 911 for more reasons than I can tabulate. Firefighters are the default option for emergency and unknown events in the city. Essentially, anything that is not clearly a police call will justify a fire department response—because someone has to respond.

For many people, 911—the phone call and the emergency system—is the place uncertainties get sent: an unknown car outside your window; funny odor in your basement; stranger on a bench; weird feeling in your chest (*chest* can stretch from tongue to bowels); smoke or steam coming from a house.

Dispatch will receive a phone call from someone in Minneapolis—or from someone out of state asking us to check on a relative or friend in the city. From their isolated location four stories beneath city hall, the dispatchers will scratch their collective heads at the randomness or uniqueness of the call, and then send us to check it out. Whether it's to investigate a weird smell, a weird person, or a weird house; a strange puddle or bottle or truck; a mess on the sidewalk, whether blood and brains or foamy soap or spilled casserole: if a citizen calls 911, the city must address the issue. Dispatch has us on speed dial, first and last option. And so we go.

No one at Dispatch disputes, challenges, or qualifies what you say when you call: they take you at your word. That is the social contract.

Some people call 911 because they want a ride to a hospital's emergency department to be "checked out." Paramedics are skilled prehospital emergency technicians, not Uber drivers, but there you go. What this means is that Emergency Services get deployed for a wild, near-inconceivable range of issues, a great many not emergent at all. But still we must go. That is also the social contract.

We cannot control what we get. No matter what we are dispatched to, we must show up and address whatever the actual issue is. Sometimes that is saving a life; sometimes it is resolving a traumatic injury. Sometimes it's providing assistance until the person can get to the hospital; sometimes it's being calm and reassuring. Sometimes, it is holding in our laughter at something so deliriously goofy and dopey, a situation so far removed from *medical* and *emergency* that it's galling. Except that is our job: to respond and investigate someone's perceived emergency. And, some calls, we must look someone in the eye and say, "I'm very sorry. Your [person] is dead. They are beyond help." It can feel like a ceaseless, brutal, futile grind. As Roger Huder writes in *Gutter Medicine,* "I was supposed to save lives. Instead, I seemed to be some highly trained witness."

We cannot fix 911. And, frankly, we are powerless to effect true change in human behavior. We show up, again and again, for chronic human issues, acting as lifts—physical, emotional, and transportational. Paramedics burn out because their skills and training are squandered on incessant transport calls (and reams of insurance- and hospital-mandated paperwork).

Some shifts it seems as if all we catch are "nothing" calls. Granted, for many citizens, their issue might *feel* like an emergency, and that's where our calm and perspective can be of service. But three such calls consecutively, five, ten: a night's sleep stolen, the next day ruined in the fog of sleep deprivation. We get slack, our wits and reflexes floppy. And then we catch something that demands our utmost: a multiple-casualty incident, a heart attack to work in front of a boisterous crowd, a shooting victim barely alive, a horrific car wreck, a house fire with victims needing rescue and then treatment.

A majority of us are adrenaline junkies to some degree and we are always up for a good catastrophe, so, even at zero dark thirty, exhausted at hour 18, 41, or 68 of a set of shifts, we can kick it into high gear at a moment's notice. I recently had a fire call that came in at 5:30 a.m., starting off as a report of "a chair possibly on fire on a porch." That sounds like a minor call, maybe an ashtray smoking. Two minutes later, we turned onto the block to see the entire front of the house on fire, and there was a victim, unresponsive and trapped behind a wall of smoke and flames. I had to make a lot of decisions in very quick succession. We cannot afford to be indecisive or flat-footed. Our lives, and those of the citizens, demand vigilance. We charge hard on every call.

//

Several years before I joined the MFD, I sliced open my knee on a corrugated metal door. I limped to the nearby station, where Jen Cornell, the woman who got me interested in this job, worked. "Hi," I said, when she answered the door. "Check *this* out!"

She grimaced. "That looks nasty! You probably ought to get to a doctor."

"That's why I'm here!" I said, triumphantly.

A couple of her crew members sidled up to check out the idiot dripping blood on their floor. They looked at each other, laughing. "We've got some duct tape," one offered, shaking her head. "But why? The hospital is three minutes away." A lanky, bald white guy shook his head. "Last thing *I'd* ever do is let any of these clowns come near me with a needle."

I was baffled. "You don't do stitches?" They all laughed grimly. "But why not?"

Jen looked at me funny. "Because we don't. I can give you some bandages. Or a Junior Firefighter sticker." More laughter. I was the butt of a joke I did not understand. I was surrounded by people speaking another language. Jen hugged me. "But, seriously, Jer: go to a doctor. You need stitches."

Folks who don't know what exactly is wrong or what might be wrong, or who are clouded by some form of uncertainty and worry: they call 911, Dispatch sends us, we arrive. In the intervening time, the baby has stopped crying or the smell has evaporated, or the caller has taken a moment to calm down. But now we're crowded into the room, and the caller is abashed. Or, they research WebMD, get concerned, and call the nurse line. For liability's sake, the "nurse" always recommends the person call 911—*just to be safe.* Which they do, and Dispatch sends us and an ambulance, and sometimes the police. We all arrive and stand around a living room with a person who now feels silly.

But that's the job. Sometimes, citizens show up at the station with a question, a concern, a bag full of anything-under-the-sun: batteries, loaded guns, homemade *maybe-it's-a-bomb?*, vials of meth, human bones, classroom cleaner . . .

The truth is, it is up to me and mine to figure out what's what. We are Jacks and Jills of general skill, trained and ingrained to solve emergency questions. We aren't MDs, PhDs, snake charmers, or alchemists. My extended family generously presumes I'm part orthopedic surgeon, part nuclear physicist, part mechanical engineer. I'm flattered but quick to tell them to call the real pros instead of texting me with questions about significant injuries or electrical issues.

When we pull up at a fire or hazardous emergency, the captain must decipher what is pertinent information while sloughing off the extraneous, the irrelevant, and the distracting, in order to safely assess what the true issue is and how we can best mitigate it. This process, the size-up, happens in seconds. It happens despite noise from the rigs, from the radios, from the screaming public. It happens at three in the morning or at noon, whether responders are wide awake or groggy, whether it's hot or cold, sunny or snowy or pissing rain.

It is my responsibility to figure out how to save viable citizens and not let my people get killed. I must make smart inferences immediately. I have mere seconds to assess and decipher the situation, locate the true dangers and fundamental needs, and make a plan, while filtering out everything else besieging my eyes and ears. I look at the scene and ask myself as we're moving into the fray: *What have I got? Where is it going? What do I need? What is my plan?* (credit to former MFD chief Ulysses Seal for sharing this four-step process; origin unknown). Then I must cue the radio and give a clear, calm transmission to the world.

For EMS calls, we have a similar, albeit less dangerous, process. We arrive, assess what is actually happening—parsing the info someone gave Dispatch as well as what someone on scene might be shouting, muttering, or babbling, as well as whatever we're looking at—and decide what needs to be done. This happens fast, while we're moving forward. It is fascinating and difficult. How someone answers the formulaic patient-information questions can be far more informative and relevant than what they say.

I was reminded the other day, returning from a benign but weird call, that the majority of our work is, on a human level, disturbing. My crew enters apartments and houses and public spaces for citizens whose "normal" is decidedly at the far edges of social norms. We stand there, amid dangerous clutter, detritus of excessive drinking, psychological torment, and we treat each patient, accepting in the moment their reality without question or quibble. We treat what we can, taking it all in stride. Only afterward do we pause and say, "What the hell did we just see?"

And, beyond, in addition, and despite all the non-emergency calls we catch, we are who respond to the sudden, the emergent, the tragic. Rich, poor, everyone in between: bad shit happens and we show up. No one plans to have their worst day ever, yet they do. And that is our workplace.

//

Most published writing about emergency response focuses on a newbie's descent into hell, the struggle from nervous beginner to seasoned vet. Many such books end with the writer having burned out after a few years, having suffered the adrenaline junkie's moral or mental collapse, then retreating to safer shores (generally law school or an MFA program).

Many people's first thought when they think of EMS writing is *Bringing Out the Dead,* Joe Connelly's fictionalized version of his few years as a New York City paramedic (well, the Nicolas Cage amped-up film version). Or TV's *Emergency!* with Johnny Gage and Roy DeSoto working for Los Angeles amid all the natural disasters of the 1970s: earthquakes and quicksand and flammable polyester. For fire rescue, most of us think of *Rescue Me,* Denis Leary's hagiographic treatment of the bad-boy martyrs of FDNY. Or the inane soap operas for dudes like *Chicago Fire* or *Texas 911 Fire Hunks.*

I could focus on my tremulous early shifts, the nervous struggle to learn how to help people and fight fire. How weird and scary things were.

But that isn't what is truly important. I have lost that early earnestness, the *Wow!* of intense situations. Over twenty years, I've witnessed thousands of tragic things, and, more significantly, uncountable variations of human behavior and biology. I've come to understand the limits to the systems: fire service, civil service, public health, public safety, social services. And I've seen how humanity operates outside, and despite, the best-intended plans of experts and lawmakers. Denial plays a disproportionate role in end-of-life care (in)decisions. When denial's flimsy curtain falls, there we are, standing over a very sick, or very dead, person.

Our normal workday includes death and dying, the dead, suffering, visceral trauma, emotional and psychological anguish, multiple forms of self-inflicted wounds, economic and social injustice, race and class issues. These are facts. Life, by definition, includes a terminal point. Imagine what that means, to normalize so much death and suffering—because it is normal, routine. People are always dying. And someone has to see the bodies, touch and move and clean them.

A journalist friend argued that my job, our work, this profession, is profoundly unhealthy and objectively not normal. I considered her statement and largely disagreed. "I think it is essentially normal—which might be the problem," I replied. "We see all the very real, common, normal consequences of living and dying, life and death. It is all part of the natural process. I find very little of it abnormal."

"Which is my point," she countered. "Your normal is completely fucked up."

"Well, if not me, it would just be someone else. Right? *Someone*—plural, actually—must attend to the dying and dead. It's just life, or just death, life's end. Right? It's as normal as it can be."

"But it's a career of horrors."

"True that," I conceded readily. We also see life's rich pageant, as REM called it. The scrappy humanity, the goofy and the absurd, the raw humor. But one must be able to handle the brutal to appreciate the sublime. My rookie classmate and friend Doug Gilbert observed, as we were talking about the rise in traumatic-response cases among our peers, "This is a shitty job. There's no other way to say it. From childhood, people read *Clifford Fights Fire*, or *Curious George Saves a Cat*, or Richard Scarry's *The People in Our Town*, and think of firefighters as local heroes. We grow up thinking the same things, then we try out for the job, and the hiring process is so long, twisted, and frustrating that we simply want to get on, no matter what. Then in rookie school, the training captains are shouting at us to be tough, that we need to prove ourselves against the Red Devil. But no one talks about all the rest of it."

Doug is right: it is a shitty job. The recruiting posters and news articles don't cover this part of it. I don't want "Clifford Extricates a Dead Family from a Wreck" or "Curious George and the OD'ing Man in the

Yellow Hat." But consider how we "sell" the idea and identity of firefight-ers. We are told we are daring to fill the boots and turnouts of *real heroes*. We are carrying that weighted expectation before we start our first shift, before we've ever seen a fire (or worked a dying person). Throw on that uniform, climb on the big red truck, and the public looks on with rever-ence. Not only that: the public expects great things from us, whether it's our first shift or our last. That pressure is real.

No one warns us of the depths of what we will experience over and over. They say, "You will see bad shit," but nothing of how to handle it. Nothing about how much, how varied yet frequent, how unresolvable the forms of trauma we will be immersed in. This takes a toll on any human. It cuts deeply into each of us, whether we recognize it or not. The thing is, we don't simply need wizened, battle-scarred dispassion-ate brutes to do this job. Because there are humans attached to these traumatic scenes: victims, family members, bystanders. We need to be compassionate, caring, patient, and understanding—which requires empathy, tenderness, vulnerability. Which often are the Trojan Horses through which the pain and trauma invade *our* psyches.

//

Trauma Sponges is my attempt to share what we do, how we do it, and what is happening behind the doors, within the apartments, on the bathroom floors all around you. I worked most of my first decade in my own neighborhood, and I saw the ways my friends and neighbors were living—and dying. The texture of our lives is far more complicated than most of us care to acknowledge. Entering people's homes time and again, I've seen intimately how things are going. It's very often heartbreaking.

I see this book as having two parts, what I think of as "Songs of Innocence (Lost)" and "Songs of (Scarred) Experience." The first ten chapters address the basics of EMS work and the culture of emergency response and firefighting; the realities of who and what we encounter; the roles that race, class, and gender play in shaping responders' atti-tudes; and the curdling effects of compulsory machismo on all of the above. The second half starts with my reflections on Covid-19. Then, what I consider the heart of this material: an evaluation and discussion of mental health crises and emergency responders' perilously uncriti-cal engagement with individuals requiring care. I share an essay about police and Black men, written in 2017, that is both unsurprising and prescient in its parallels to the killing of George Floyd. I reflect on the aftermath of the uprising. And I return to the fact that, no matter what is happening in the big picture (Covid, civil unrest, politics, inclement weather, personal issues), the tones go off and we respond to other people's calls for help.

I want to cite two works that have shaped my thinking profoundly in recent years. Laurence Gonzales's *Deep Survival* offers incredible insights into human behavior, systems failures, gratuitous risk-taking, and the disproportion of avoidable factors in catastrophes. Reading *Deep Survival* clarified my understanding of our unconscious behaviors and the cultural habits and mentalities firefighters persist with, at great peril. Eddie Glaude Jr.'s *Begin Again,* a meditation on James Baldwin's writing and life, provides a deep read and discussion of Baldwin in historical context and an adept lens to understand America in this era. The former book improved my understanding of my profession's avoidable risks, as well as the predictable paths humans take to find themselves in a catastrophe. The latter increased my understanding of the tensions of race, class, gender, sexuality in our current cultural chaos, and how to perceive them in historical context as well. I recommend both heartily.

I have read an array of books related to emergency response, health care, death and dying, grief, and a range of cultural issues. Many of these proved to be more helpful and nuanced than the blood-and-guts action writing. Specifically, Sunita Puri's *That Good Night*; Terrence Holt's *Internal Medicine*; Daniela Lamas's *You Can Stop Humming Now*; and both of Frank Huyler's ER memoirs, *The Blood of Strangers* and *White Hot Light.* Physicians Michele Harper's *The Beauty in Breaking,* Thomas Fisher's *The Emergency,* and Damon Tweedy's *Black Man in a White Coat* each addresses the poignant role and effect of race in the U.S. medical system.

There is a key difference between those thoughtful, searching physicians' work and what I'm after. Paramedics and firefighter/EMTs work *outside* the sterile and supported hospital setting. It is two medics and three firefighters in a tiny bedroom, trying to restart a heart, delivering compressions and shocks and ventilations and meds, then ferrying the body out to the ambulance (a cramped ER on wheels) and working while zipping through traffic until we deliver the patient to the expert care of the ED staff. It is just us. We lack the sterility and reinforcements of the emergency department (I use ED and ER interchangeably). We find you where you fall, and we work you amid the rubble and chaos. Angry dogs; hysterical, screaming families; random children; broken glass or dirty dishes; a backyard, an alley, a busy street: that is our operating theater. Anthony Almojera, an FDNY paramedic, wrote *Riding the Lightning* about his years working emergency services in New York, including the devastation of the Covid pandemic there. It is a powerful read, chock-full of colorful New York characters and the big-city diversity that Minneapolis lacks.

What's funny (or tragic) is that from the very beginning of rookie school, we are immersed in a culture that continues to celebrate and champion a desperate nostalgia. I am stunned, though I shouldn't be, that even now, as a profession and department, we continue to undermine the significance EMS plays in the essence of our job. We privilege these hypothetical, mythical fires that will test our mettle, the *infernos that will forge and reveal the true firefighters,* while ignoring the actual work that fills our shifts, allows us to serve the public, and costs us a piece of our health. It's gobsmacking.

There have been recent studies and a growing awareness of the human cost of this work. Firefighters, paramedics, police pay for our proximity to and immersion in chaos and suffering. Consider that every single firefighter, paramedic, and cop is guaranteed to sustain a potentially crippling PTSD diagnosis; 100 percent of the workforce will experience traumatic–emotional harm. For decades, the response was hard-bitten stoicism and booze. This continually does not work out well, yet this culture is tightly wrapped in its own folklore.

I've lost coworkers to injuries sustained lifting heavy people (knees, backs, and shoulders are what claim most medics and firefighters).

I've lost coworkers to unresolvable alcohol abuse (too much downtime off-shift, alone with ghosts and a bottle).

I've lost coworkers to recreational drug use that became vocational, and then devoured their health, minds, money, and jobs.

I'm losing coworkers now to emotional trauma, burnout, and stress.

When things finally become too much or unsupportable, there is a depth of compressed trauma behind whatever the precipitating incident is. The term *PTSD* gets thrown about, for better or worse, a lot now. Better: it is good to acknowledge the hard effects of traumatic exposure.

Worse: it's applied overbroadly and without clear understanding. More recently, a clarification or mutation has emerged for emergency workers: complex trauma syndrome (or, alternatively, traumatic exposure response). It isn't just one bad call: it is a career of bad scenes.

This book should be among the front wave of a cultural shift in the discussion and debunking of performative/compulsory masculinity. And while I approach the topic from an archetypically macho profession, directing my thoughts and insights toward my coworkers and peers in emergency response, the truth is that this is a reflection of the same behaviors that are widespread in the United States.

The discussions and slowly evolving ideas about masculinity have been nearly absent from the fire service, a culture about as aggressively atavistic as one could find. This quotation from *Backdraft* was lifted from Chicago Fire Department lore: "One hundred years of Tradition, unimpeded by Progress." It's still bandied about as both stale cliché and prideful defiance. We used to be rough and brusque, brooding and insensitive, as defense, default, and well-honed personae. We are grudgingly recognizing that the *suck-it-up* ethos solves very little. Without productive coping skills, we will perpetuate our collateral damages just as surely as our frequent flyers will be calling us again next week, cigarette in hand, complaining that their emphysema is acting up.

I've long insisted that this cultural machismo is contrived and counterproductive. A growing movement has reinforced this idea, in part because, despite being a hermetic and proudly reactionary profession, we are not immune to the rules of time and gravity. More so, as we have witnessed so many peers burn out, bail out, or immolate, the best minds among us have taken up our health and longevity as a worthy cause. I concur.

Beyond the iconic gear, shiny rigs, and bushy mustaches, there are a lot of nervous folks faking it, more terrified of asking for help or admitting to vulnerability than of making a fatal mistake—because a fatal mistake ends with a hero's funeral. A workable assessment of the fire service: ego and insecurity wrapped in empty boasting, panicked fumbling in the dark, defensive avoidance of reflection or introspection. I'm far more interested in discussing the troubling implications of male behaviors than in arguing about Fantasy Fireman Fight Club.

I am a middle-aged, straight white man with two college degrees and a background in teaching and cultural studies. Some coworkers say I have no business being on the job—that I am too bookish, too much an outlier. I strongly disagree. There are many skills that contribute to being excellent firefighters.

Perhaps a messy childhood broke the narrative of happily-ever-after. Perhaps my particular upbringing primed me to question and challenge everything. Perhaps my blended Irish, Anglo, and Mormon forebears shaped a genetic affinity for human suffering and endurance. But at some point, it made profound sense to me that the mainstream narrative was specious and selectively, self-servingly flawed. The perspectives of people of color on their own experiences were more accurate than those of a bunch of white guys looking in a mirror. Ditto for women: an amazing amount of truth can be discovered if you don't simply take the word of those who most benefit from cultural imbalance. One doesn't need to have read Adrienne Rich on compulsory heterosexuality (although one should) to fathom how slanted our gendered narratives have been. That awareness has helped me negotiate a great many of our sociological issues that are either screamingly obvious or utterly invisible (if one is not inclined to look or think). I am forever grateful for those who have taught me, tolerated me, and showed me the deeper, richer truth.

//

An earlier version of this book included a panorama of medical calls, episodic scenes to give the reader a sense of the wide, weird range of our work. One of my literary friends read it and wondered, "What happened to that person? Or that other person? Or *that* person?!" He wanted a traditional dramatic arc, a denouement for each call.

"That's the thing: we generally don't find out anything afterward," I countered. "We fix what we find as best we can, then we leave."

We show up to something that's in progress (frankly, something that has already happened), do what we can, then drive back to the station to clean our equipment before the next call. Sometimes the patient is forgotten; sometimes they are seared into our psyches. But infrequently do we receive follow-up or end results. We do not get tidy resolutions, and 95 percent of us have no idea what *denouement* is. That's the nature of it.

There's a sticker on my station's workbench: *It was already on fire when we got here* . . . I don't mean this glibly. We encounter people in horrible, tragic, painful situations: that is our workplace. We do what we can, and we move on. If we perseverated over or became emotionally and mentally invested in every call, we'd crack up before dinner. But if we erect too much of a wall, we become dead-eyed, unsympathetic brutes. I discuss this throughout: fighting to protect the sweet spot between heartbreak and disconnect, caring and callous.

There is no "solving" human nature. Before I started and long after I'm gone, people will be calling 911 for help. Life doesn't stop. (Well, all lives stop eventually. But the human process is ceaseless and inexorable.) Every single shift, I come to work with no idea of what I will experience during the next twenty-four hours. Whoever happens to be working catches whatever calls come in. Our lives get altered with no advance notice: a benign call goes sideways, and we're left scarred by it, both literally and figuratively. A job where there are precious few victories, no means to force people to change their human habits, no way to get the system to reboot itself for the better: that is a job that refuses the narrative arc.

I truly hope this book will help some readers make connections to their own lives and habits. Some valid advice: Stop smoking. Exercise more. Drink less. Eat less. Wear a seatbelt. Wear a helmet. Crack, crank, heroin, and PCP remain bad for you: don't trifle with them. Walk your dog. Complete your advance medical directives. Have a DNR/DNI not just on file but signed and stuck to your fridge. Be brave and have the hard talks about illness and dying with those you love.

This is a book about emergency medical work, about human behavior—how people live and die—and about our systems. And *the* system: race, class, and gender shape so much of what happens, to whom it happens, who responds, and how they respond. I have been an eyewitness to some extreme situations, and I've seen the shapes of structural and systemic inequalities. I am trying here to share that, to start larger conversations.

Smart, visionary people are fighting to reshape or fix or obliterate the stuckness of the system. They are outgunned and undermined by corporate power, lawyers, and lobbyists at every turn, as well as by petty despots and control freaks and a legion of naked emperors. I feel that true advancement with understanding and purpose evades us in our present societal model. And yet, but still . . . Citizens continue to get sick, get hurt, give birth, fall down, overdose, die. And there we are, up to our elbows in someone else's innards.

This is also a book for and about those of us who respond, day and night, week by month by year, to the cries for help from our citizens. Sometimes we save lives. Sometimes we rescue people. Very often we cannot and do not. Nearly always we are trauma adjacent. Whether we are carrying someone small or frail to a safer place, holding the hand of someone scared and hurt, or standing witness to a person's dying breaths, we are immersed in the rawness of suffering.

All of us carry the memories with us, consciously or smothered in some hidden place. In that manner, this book in itself is a testament to trauma immersion. My coworkers have their own memories and perceptions. I'm inclined to look at the human piece in the mayhem. In retelling the calls, I'm trying to give a sense of how and what happened, as well as connecting with a larger human and sociological narrative. I have come to understand that this process of reflecting, examining, and writing helps me process the things I've seen, purge the poisons and sadness from my heart, to let me breathe freely and return to work day after week after year.

//

I spent my first several years working Southside, mostly on Engine 5 (Twenty-Seventh Street and Bloomington Avenue, about as desolate a stretch as Minneapolis offers). I returned there as a new captain after a few years Northside. I worked Engines 17, 5, and 8 between 2008 and 2015. In 2015 and 2016, I was a battalion chief. Then in 2017, I returned to helm Engine 17, where I remain.

I know this patch of south Minneapolis well. The streets and houses are haunted with former calls, random scenes spliced together into an endless roll. The years blur and blend, the crews I've been fortunate to work with become composites. The dead and stricken remain vivid. Sometimes my memories feel like a popcorn popper, the furious exploding images spilling out over the top, one replacing the next, all of them hot and insistent.

Writing has been a means to understand and express how the job has affected me. I started before I ever stepped onto a rig, detailing the bizarre civil service hiring process. Then rookie school, where noble dreams die from absurdity and poor management. Then the fright and fluster of rookie life. Then the cluster of years where I gained experience, learned how to do the job. I'd call that the sophomoric phase: we are no longer shaking rookies and we've seen a few things, so we think we know a lot. The cockiness and posturing are a cultural currency and a means to fit in. Everyone acts like a badass—because we are seldom truly tested. Sometimes that posturing gets exposed in brutal, deadly ways.

This project has been in progress since 1998, essentially. Yes, I'm a slow writer. But the past three years have forced me to alter the structure of my text, largely to encompass issues of contemporary significance. The specter of the police killing of Mr. Floyd hangs over me in multiple ways. The factors that brought about his death have been present in the country since its inception. I had written about similar situations already in earlier drafts of this book. Mr. Floyd's killing distilled and amplified those. I will not treat his death as a marketing angle or a mere talking point, but, for once, white America paid attention when yet another unarmed Black man died in custody. It was the most widely seen example I can use—even as I insist it remains poorly understood by too many.

//

I've said that we don't pick what calls we get. We receive no warning which ones will change our lives. We show up and the die has been cast.

Imagine sitting around the station after dinner on a warm May night, early in the pandemic, trying to teach the rookie some fire stuff while socially distanced and masked. Not even a chalkboard, just talking—strictly Fantasy Firefighting. The tones click for a Code 2 (non-emergency) response. The rig computer says only "one with a mouth injury." We get no further information in the six short blocks, the two and a half minutes, it takes from dispatch to arrival.

Imagine stepping off the rig and seeing neither ambulance nor patient, passing some police officers who offer no information. Imagine walking through a small crowd of distraught young people saying, "They killed him. The police killed that man."

There is no patient, only the people crying out. You look around. *Who? Where? What is going on?*

Dispatch tells you to redirect four blocks northwest, that the medics need you, Code 3. Imagine zipping away from the scene, confused, getting no further information. Imagine pulling up to the ambulance, stepping inside, looking at the paramedics' flurry of activity, the lifeless body, and finding yourself on the brink of American history.

2
YOUR FRIENDS AND NEIGHBORS

"I didn't call the Fire Department! I called for an ambulance.
Nothing's on fire. I want a ride to the hospital!"
—Folks who call 911 at zero dark thirty
complaining of "chest pain"

I OFTEN FORGET THAT MOST PEOPLE HAVE NO IDEA WHAT FIREFIGHTER/EMTS
actually do. It is so ingrained and normalized for me that I gloss over the
details of our job, or else I plop some horrific story on the dinner table
when someone asks, "How was work?"

Filling the hours between our sporadic fire calls, the smoke alarms,
the beeping CO detectors, the car wrecks, and all the ordinary mayhem
of life and gravity, are a wide range of emergency medical calls. I wrote
before that for nearly anything that is not an explicit police response
(often we go on those too), Dispatch sends the fire department, either
alone to investigate and handle, or with the paramedics.

For clarity, let's separate these into three broad categories: urgent
and severe emergencies; minor emergencies or routine maladies; maintenance and neglect non-emergent calls. The first group would be acute,
life-threatening emergencies. They are what this system was made for: to
swiftly bring skilled responders to people in dire straits, to begin treatment on the spot, and to transport to the hospital. Routine maladies
contain a wide expanse of issues: broken bones, severe illnesses, open
wounds, potential heart or lung issues. Some of these require immediate treatment; others, while painful and uncomfortable, are not critical. And then there is the deep well of the non-emergent, not critical,
noncrisis.

We are called when people are having the worst—sometimes the last—day of their lives. (For some, we are called *after* their final day.) We enter their homes and are witness to the raw intimacy of people's fear and pain and loss. For the first two categories, all of us have bad days. Gravity and biology are always at work. I understand if most of you reading this have called 911 after your parent fell down the steps and cracked an ankle, or your kid did not stick the landing from the roof, or your partner fainted, or, unfortunately, the horrible day a loved one had a heart attack. These are true medical emergencies. Most people call 911 only for these emergent situations.

However, a plurality of the calls we get in most parts of Minneapolis carry not simply the additional but often the *fundamental* weight of sociological issues. We respond and engage with people who seldom catch a break, whose existence would break most of us. We see so much hardship: Desperate loneliness. Bad living. Neglect. Despair. Alcohol and drug abuse. Domestic troubles and violence. Mental illness. Hoarding. Factors of race, class, gender, sexuality, mental wellness, disability, and many more, shape and inflect our calls and interactions. There are layers, there are connections, there are echoes. Throughout this book, I use the word *sociology* to encompass this range. I argue it is pervasive but too frequently ignored.

People who have health insurance and money call 911 far less than those who have neither insurance nor money. The people who rely on 911 and a hospital's emergency department for their health care are people who aren't doing well in this, or any, economy. They exist at the bottom margins. For Minneapolis, like much of urban America, this means that in our responses we disproportionately encounter the poor. More people of color here are living in the lower bands of the socioeconomic strata, and their health, wealth, education, and self-sufficiency reflect these deficits. Reflect and often reinforce: it is a brutal cycle. While Minnesota, especially the Twin Cities, keeps winning awards for "livability" and "healthiness" and "urban grooviness" and "most miles of incomprehensible bike lanes," the area racks up numerous other distinctions: "most racially stratified," "worst urban Native poverty," "biggest achievement gap between Black and white students," "highest urban income disparity between races," and "worst place not in Alabama to be a Brother or Sister." The ongoing and surging tensions since May 2020 certainly reveal the depths and complexities of this iteration of America's blood sin, but the conditions have been present for decades.

With so many trapped in cycles of poverty, uninsured risk, and poor health, we are the first contact for the struggling multitudes of our society. Chronic maladies such as failing hearts, high blood pressure, diabetes; respiratory dysfunctions such as COPD (chronic obstructive pulmonary disease), asthma, and emphysema: these are our standard calls. Decades of poor eating habits, lack of fitness, smoking and drinking drag humans down, becoming chronic issues and creating spiraling disabilities. Minor medical problems that aren't emergent and have little solution become daily "emergencies." Limited opportunities exacerbate the constant tension, frustration, worry, stress, and despair; the bad habits and maladaptive coping persist; the cycle continues, spinning ever downward. These folks exist in constant states of discomfort. They dial 911 to go to the ER in hopes of being fixed there.

I do not want to diminish the genuine acute medical emergencies that we—firefighter/EMTs and paramedics—respond to and the help we provide. I state here, and will emphasize throughout, that the 911 system does not distinguish, and, in addition to all these emergencies, EMS workers are overwhelmed not simply by non-emergency calls but by intractable repeat callers.

What we see on the job can, if taken uncritically, reinforce base stereotypes. I've changed from what I've experienced. Not less liberal but less abstractly liberal: I'm impatient with the airy platitudes and theoreticals of my pie-in-the-sky (liberal) white friends just as I aggressively refute the reductive, unrealistic bootstrap cant of my conservative coworkers. The well-meant and awkward, strident and self-conscious attempts of many white people after the riots—to show *they were not the bad whites,* that *they were the good ones*—meant that we spent June through November 2020 negotiating enormous and fragile white guilt on calls in public involving a person of color. White folks "witnessing" and "holding space" and "allyshipping" by inserting themselves into any number of routine street calls with BIPOC citizens. It was the essence of white privilege, ironically. Karening on behalf of Black folks for once: *I need to see your badge! I am recording you! I am not leaving this person's side!*

The majority of these white people seemed to have awoken on

June 1, 2020, to the horrible fact of American racism, and by gosh, they were going to *do* something about it. They were going to post all over their social media accounts, they were going to share the same five articles, they were desperately seeking some BIPOC folks willing to befriend them (without making them, you know, uncomfortable or *too* guilty), and they were damn sure going to stand in the way as I tried to assess and treat Black patients.

Thank you for your service, Earnest Whites.

I'm jesting, slightly. For too long, white people have enjoyed our privileged ignorance. Having responded on the call for Mr. Floyd, *and* having been on multiple other scenes with bad interactions between police and nonwhite men, *and* knowing that many of these suddenly crusading white folks had not given much thought to the racial and economic disparities outside their window prior to the streets erupting, I am skeptical and bitterly bemused. The sudden, forced awareness of systemic inequalities and injustice was *shocking*—to many of us. Some have been aware of and awake to it for years. Too many remain determinedly in denial, no matter what video proof they are given.

Firefighters benefit from the public's goodwill. Most folks are happy to see us and have positive regard for us. We are not the police: we don't enforce laws. We attempt to fix the consequences of lawbreaking and physics (speed, drugs, violence). We try to improve people's bad days, if only by treating patients with courtesy and respect, by providing steady hands and calm minds to panicked human beings. During the summer of 2020 when our crew visited George Floyd Square, which the police and conservative media declared a *No-Go Zone!*, the refrain we heard on the street was *We love Engine 17! You're all right with us. There isn't a song called "Fuck the Fire Department," is there?*

I'm a Southsider, having worked at my current station since 2017, and at stations within a mile for another decade-plus. Having engaged and caring crews who know their response area is a very good thing. Familiarity with the buildings, the residents, the nuances: this allows us to provide better public service. We can establish trust or rapport or simple facial recognition, and, when people are struggling or scared or angry, having that human connection can help de-escalate and provide calm. I think it helps to have emergency service workers live in the cities they serve. Unfortunately, economics and personal choice don't support that idea. When the majority of us are residents and voters, we have a loud voice in local politics as well as actual experience with the abstractions politicians banter about. Conversely, a lot of public safety workers take an oppositional regard for their work environments: rather than having pride in serving the city, too many firefighters, police, and medics consider Minneapolis a *dangerous wasteland*. They commute in from the suburbs, exurbs, or rural areas. That is their right, of course, but the disparaging mentality cannot be separated from racial and class dynamics.

There's something else, too, about our job. We see you. Even if you were expecting company and have tidied up, you weren't expecting *us*. You might be naked or in last Tuesday's drawers, on the toilet, in the bath, half-dressed, wearing dirty sweats, your wig off: *Here we are!* While we are there for a purpose, in glimpses while we are working, or in the moments waiting for you or the medics to decide whatever happens next, or tromping through the wreckage, we *see* your world—those of us who remain awake to it. We take in the furniture, the clutter, the meals half-cooked, -eaten, or never-to-be-completed, the forlorn kids, the mess, the order, the underwear, sex toys, drugs (so many drugs and sex toys), empty bottles, medications, homework, bills, trinkets, figurines, all the usual flotsam and jetsam of domesticity and humanity.

And the photos. I love seeing people's pictures. Chronological history, literally. Generations assembled on the walls, captured in and out of time.

It's a kick in the heart to be working an old person, someone withered and fragile, and look up to see this person's earlier incarnations, their younger selves, captured in photos on the walls. It's the human condition, our one-way journey. Seeing it arrayed like that, suddenly, without context or footnotes, can be jarring and sad. I see the patient's elapsed youth looking down on us as we wrestle death for them. In other homes, we witness good people trying to create good lives, making do with little. We see not-so-good people who might have the same basic photos on their walls as the good ones. Everybody loves their babies—some folks struggle to do it healthily . . .

We go to work in lots of very sparse apartments, filled with nothing but heavy air and the residue of despair, sorrow, fury. Damaged walls, broken furniture, no furniture, meager possessions looking more meager in the barrenness of the rooms, clothing spilling out of the garbage bags used to haul their lives from one shitty place to the next whenever the landlord evicts them. The weight of economic and class struggle is brutal and smothering. How can people pull themselves up when they have nothing to stand on?

It's an intimate glance at raw humanity, and often far more than a glance. Keeping sight of the people, the real and vulnerable humans, amid so much struggle: that is the profound challenge for us. Especially in a culture that is not inclined to look past a surface appearance, or to hold contradictions and nuance to see clearly what is happening.

//

So, what do we actually do? you ask. What is an emergency medical technician? What is the difference between a firefighter/EMT or a fire-fighter/medic or a paramedic? Firefighters without EMT training would be first responders, like police officers: trained to recognize medical emergencies, able to use bandages and perform adequate CPR and use public AEDs. But we need repetition, the daily or monthly deployment of these skills, for they are perishable. EMTs who take the class and pass the registry exam can't really "practice" on the street. There is little market for freelance EMTs to ply their trade.

We assess someone, take their vitals, distinguish what their primary and secondary issues are, provide oxygen, assist with medications, help set up IVs and nebulizers and other accessory tasks for the paramedics. The medics have advanced training, able to provide medications, read EKGs (electrocardiograms), insert IV (intravenous) lines.

I cannot interpret an EKG and I am not licensed to stick you with a needle. I can do CPR on you pretty damn well. I can provide oxygen, ventilate your lungs, and help the medics. What I have gained from twenty years responding to medical and other emergencies is a sharp, swift parsing of information, context, cues. I can recognize both what can be done in the moment to address something deadly and anticipate what must come next. I can create a plan for my crew to lift and carry you from where you fell to a better spot for all of us to surround and try to revive you. We move a lot of bodies through cluttered spaces. At its basest level, our work involves brute strength, but physics and planning and logic must be applied to do it well. A common jape from a medic to a firefighter: *Aw, cute, my compression device has an opinion. That's sweet.*

And the riposte: *Gee, the ambulance driver is still salty he couldn't pass the fire department test.*

//

The cornerstone and the bedrock of American public health care and emergency response are quite simple: the Good Samaritan principle—and the fear of litigation. We joke about "job security" that comes from our citizens' myriad and ongoing bad decisions. The range of why people call 911 can be astounding. When I describe the calls we catch, people can be aghast and incredulous. *They* would never call 911 for something so obvious or preposterous. Likely so. Many folks, however, do call for things that, from an inch outside the moment, are ridiculous. Not ridiculous, but clearly not emergencies. Hangnails, buzzing fluorescent lights, a single bump on the skin, a swath of bumps, a cough, a runny nose, a vague sensation that something might be wrong.

Again, I am distinguishing between acute emergencies, routine maladies, and using 911 as first- and last-choice medical option. One early favorite, still top-tier audacity: a man called 911 because he'd incurred a thumb cramp during a marathon session on his children's PlayStation. He said his arm tingled, he couldn't feel his hand. Dispatch sent us to "one having a stroke, possibly a heart attack" for a grown man with a thumb cramp from monopolizing his kids' video game.

It's emblematic of a culture that has somehow ceded autonomy and a culture that demands others solve all problems. I generally hint to people, "Well, if it were *my* house [cat, child, bloody nose . . .], I'd let it be." I do not say, "I certainly wouldn't call 911 for this nonsense." Because, at the root of it, people want to be reassured.

The trump card is "concern." We get called to check a phantom "gas" odor. It is nothing. Perhaps something on the breeze, or a burp from the sewer, or burned food or moldy laundry forgotten in the basement, but no hazard and nothing dangerous. We use our monitor to check for the range of bad things we can check for, we use our noses, we look at their pilot lights, then their furnaces. "All clear," we say politely. They will insist that they still want the gas company to come—just in case.

A kid is playing with her friend and trips on the sidewalk. She has a bruised knee and a scraped elbow. There is no loss of consciousness, no open fractures, no blood from her ears. The child speaks coherently and is crying appropriately. But the parents will ask (demand) that we treat and the medics transport the child—just in case. And the thing about exploratory investigations—like going to therapy too much—is that if you keep digging, you will find (or create) something that *might* be a problem.

The emergency room or department is intended to rapidly treat people experiencing urgent, life-threatening conditions. The majority of its clientele are there because their regular clinics are closed: people called 911 instead of scheduling a routine appointment or visiting a clinic. The ED staff will cover the bases and do their best to ensure you are not dying of some imminent cause. Beyond that? They'll recommend you make an appointment to see your regular doc in your regular clinic.

//

A stunning percentage of 911 calls are generated due to failures of communication and comprehension. What? How? There is a fundamental breakdown between how a great many citizens view the 911 system and what it actually entails. More pointedly, there is a gaping difference of context and understanding between the caller and the call taker. A fast and dirty explanation would be that people call 911 because that is where all curiosities, concerns, and questions go. Civilians dial 911 unaware that there is no discretion, no "just curious" option. Your concern will be treated as an emergency *because* you have called the emergency line.

Dispatchers are incredible. They are near clairvoyant, taking panicked and jumbled phone calls and translating people's unfiltered emotions into a coherent response plan. They hear the desperate screams and cries of citizens in peril and pain. They talk people through giving CPR to babies, parents, and partners until we arrive. It is a tough job, and the good ones make all of our jobs and lives better. Given budget cuts and "efficiency" hucksters, however, there are fewer dispatchers than before, and to cover the reduced numbers, information-management software systems are often used. The EMS dispatchers now follow a rigid flow chart of questions, and depending on the answers, further and different questions dictate who gets sent on the call. The seasoned dispatchers' skills with inference and deductive questioning were shelved in favor of the rote algorithmic flowchart.

The 911 call takers ask their scripted questions; the folks in

Dispatch relay what the call takers enter into their computers, sending the info to our computers. All of us, firefighters and paramedics (police too): we have no choice but to go and go hard. Time is precious, and we must rapidly respond *as if.* Why? Because the system is predicated on the assumption that someone *might* be dying. We respond excessively, redundantly, for many calls, but that's because we will need this much and more on those actual critical cases.

It is all well meant, but over time, we have lost the ability to critically engage; passersby call over trifles, without pausing and investigating at all. As responding agencies, from 911 Dispatch to EMS to fire to police, we respond too literally, as default, with slight logical analysis. Like Ron Burgundy in *Anchorman,* we will read what-*ev*-er is on the screen and take it as gospel.

Is it wasteful? Yes. Is there another way? Certainly. But the fear of low-balling someone who then dies—exposing all involved agencies to litigious liability—beats common sense, practicality, pragmatism, and financial wisdom. So, we respond to each call *as if* it is as dire as its generic category states: "possible heart attack"; "respiratory distress"; "severe bleeding"; one unresponsive.

I don't blame the people who are scared or uncertain or confused, who call 911 and answer the call taker's questions literally. They don't know what to do, or what they're being asked. Semantically, they and the call takers are speaking two different languages. "Chest pain" translates as "possible heart attack" even if the caller is just saying his ribs hurt. They don't understand that their call for help, or guidance, is triggering a massive response machinery. Some common examples:

A guy was seen in the morning for a kidney stone—which is incredibly painful, yes; it's not a swift passage—and then calls 911 at 4:00 p.m. because he's still in pain. I express my sympathy for his condition, then ask what he hopes to accomplish going back to the hospital. "It just hurts, man," he says. *Ah, I see.* This is not out-of-the-ordinary pain: it is the unfortunate status quo for a kidney stone. He told 911 that he was in *severe pain* and that *he could not breathe.* We were sent, with the paramedics, to someone "in severe respiratory distress." He was not "drug seeking," as cynics say. He was in pain and bummed out. He wanted relief—right now.

A woman calls us for SOB (shortness of breath). We arrive and are told she is in pain. We see hospital discharge papers, a sack of meds, the huge personal belongings plastic bag Hennepin County Medical Center issues. "When were you last seen at the ER, ma'am?" She tells us she got back from the hospital two hours ago, but she doesn't feel better so she wants to go back. Except she wants to go to a different damn hospital since the first one didn't fix her. Dispatchers gave us "one possibly unconscious. Severe chest pain. History of heart attack."

There are so many variations of "I can't breathe/I'm having trouble breathing/I can't catch my breath/my chest hurts," which Dispatch must record as "respiratory or cardiac emergencies" and send firefighters and medics charging to the rescue.

Dozens—no, hundreds—of "caller passing by thinks there's something wrong with the person sitting/standing/lying on the bench. Possible unconscious or unresponsive person. Caller has left area."

A person calls 911 after thinking they heard someone or something yell by the riverbank. They tell Dispatch, "Maybe someone jumped or fell into the river?" This will be entered as a "river emergency." Our default response is to send multiple rigs, the heavy-rescue team, two chiefs, an ambulance, MPD, and Park Police. All for a random "I think I maybe heard something." Same for a person looking suss along a bridge railing: someone calls in a "possible jumper," bringing more police (here, again, the conflation and confusion of police roles: are the officers there to write a psych hold or to prevent the hypothetical jumper from taking us all with him into the Big Muddy?), plus our six rigs, two chiefs, a boat or two.

Minneapolis Fire does not have a dive team. We do not even make distinctions between one of the city's lakes (round and deep and without current or hazards) or the Mississippi River (turbulent and treacherous) or a creek (generally swift but shallow). Eight to twelve rigs, every time.

All this after someone called who thought they *might* have heard a cry for help, or thought the person staring at the river while smoking was possibly going to jump. They did not look over the edge and see a person in distress. We might spend an hour investigating this call, which is difficult because there is no victim. The absent victim could be anywhere, literally. And we can't just not search, no matter how ludicrous. We must answer the call. Emergency services are a reactive force. Think about the adrenaline surges, the noise and upheaval of the big rigs rumbling like tanks through the neighborhoods, the sheer waste of fuel.

In the aftermath of the killing of George Floyd by Minneapolis police officers, there were local and national calls to alter the 911 system as part of addressing overmilitarized police forces. *Don't call 911: handle it among ourselves,* people say (and by *people,* I mean well-meaning white folks). Or they call 911 and demand that no police officers be sent on certain calls.

That's not how the system works. If a person says X, or Y, or Z to the 911 operator, Dispatch must send A, B, and C. If you demand no police, Dispatch will add extra police because you sound suspicious—and EMS rigs will stage until police arrive and declare the scene Code 4 (safe for EMS), delaying the patient's access to help. (To stage is to remain outside a scene—and there is no clear distance, just "safely away" from whatever might be dangerous, generally a block or two. The idea is that there is something potentially violent occurring, and we need the police to control the scene before we can enter. It is a well-meant concept but problematically understood and applied.)

If you call 911 and say, "I found my friend bleeding all over the floor. I don't know what happened," you think you are saying that your friend stepped on either a piece of glass or a nail sticking up—not that your friend was assaulted by a foot-stabbing armed maniac who is still in the room. But you haven't said that. It will be entered as "unknown circumstances" and the flowchart will decree "Unsafe scene. Possible crime." Dispatch will send a fire rig, an ambulance, and a police squad. The medics and the fire rigs will stage until the police declare the scene Code 4.

You don't know what Dispatch's charts demand: you just want some help for a cut foot. Meanwhile, your friend continues to bleed. In the weeks and months after the riots, Minneapolis experienced incredible delays in police response times due to officer shortages and an increase in calls. So, there might be a wait of from five to forty minutes for a squad to arrive. All the while, your friend is still bleeding and we are sitting in our rig up the block.

Why are we sitting there, staging? For *safety.* What does that mean? Good luck getting a cogent answer. It is a valuable concept deployed blindly.

When the police do arrive, they are not there to help your friend medically. They are there to confront and neutralize a "threatening" situation—one inferred and created by Dispatch. No one on your end has suggested that any of this is dangerous. People who don't want the police jamming into their house, or who have had bad interactions with the police, will be upset, surprised, defensive, scared, and angry. We sometimes enter a scene of chaos that has nothing to do with the original injury and everything to do with subsequent police interactions. White people get their feelings hurt, Black people get killed. Afterward, there is no one actually responsible for what's happened. *We were all just doing our jobs.*

Additionally, when a caller is (appropriately) distraught, the rote questions from the call taker can flummox or agitate the person. People call 911 when something has happened that is bigger, scarier, bloodier than they can solve. Affluent and educated people can get haughty or indignant with the litany of questions: "I do *not* have time for this nonsense. Just send an ambulance, *now!*" People with less social clout or agency can get defensive with the questions (many they do not have answers for), which amps up their emotion and creates a point of conflict or tension with the call taker. These dynamics lead to Dispatch sending police because "the caller is noncooperative; there is yelling in the background; caller is cursing." Followed by, "Engine 17, stage for police Code 4."

The 911 call taker's misreading of a caller's emotion can have significant consequences. Police respond to quell a "threat." EMS stages. Tensions increase, as do the delays. The patient gets no help while things get sorted out. This dilemma is an example of the profound unintentional and unexamined consequences of our public safety system's automatic actions. Who is responsible for this? None of us are empowered or encouraged to challenge the system—the anonymous, faceless "It" or "They." And on it grinds. Again, *we were all just doing our job . . .*

If I am having a hard time, and you call 911, worried about my acting weird, my chest pain, my bloody nose, my depression, anything, an "Emergency" will be generated, even if I am wholly lucid and fine. But everyone—police, Fire, medics—will show up in good faith, according to protocol. If I am curmudgeonly and pissy about the spectacle (and I will be), I will be seen as noncompliant or even a threat. The medics will feel pressured to bring me in for examination "just in case"; that is, to avoid being sued by you, the well-meaning busybody who called in an abstract concern. Think about that: the medics or police might force me to go somewhere against my will because you were worried. No one investigates or examines the validity of your concerns.

Concern is the bane of modern existence. Every cookout-narcing Karen is concerned about the gathering of "suspicious" Black people sitting around a grill. Every random odor causes concern that it might be a fertilizer bomb, not a fetid wheatgrass smoothie. Concern about my friend's bloody nose, or the neighbors' graduation party, or that car on the block.

The 911 system gets these "unknown hazard" calls and sends forth the agents of the city.

Again, add race, testosterone, class, gender to the mix, and, well, we know where it goes. It goes down.

//

The fire department does not charge people for our services. We show up for everything, and we do what we do for free—in terms of citizens' payments. The ambulances and hospitals charge the hell out of them, but we don't. We're a huge drain on the city budget, and everyone (but the city payroll people) loves us.

I wish I had a solution. Well, I wish I had the *power* to effect change . . . but the corporate hospitals and the insurance companies call the shots. Since the 1970s, when both well-meaning activists and cynical budget "efficiency experts" briefly found themselves on the same side of the reform debate about mental hospitals, and the resulting changes "freed" the mentally ill from state hospitals—ostensibly to live happily at home or in smaller facilities (many of which were never built, because there weren't funds to do so, something conveniently missed by the "experts")—the epidemic of homelessness and unchecked mental illness has metastasized every city's EMS costs. With the reductions in social services, we see a great many citizens struggling to control their mental illnesses. They run out of or forget or don't have access to necessary medications, let alone psychological support, and they begin to struggle. We get called; they get transported; they get meds and are released back into the wild. The cycle continues.

A social worker could solve more of their problems than the unmerry-go-round ED trips—and vastly reduce their cost to the public health deficit—but that would require forward thinking. To dedicate the money to preemptively help someone challenges the business model of the health systems that can ignore statistics and continue to feign surprise that the same person continues to call 911 for the same complaint monthly, weekly, even daily. It has not yet happened tomorrow, so administrators can pretend it might not happen (and save money from budget line items). Of course, it does and will happen again.

There's another type of call, or patient, and these occupy both the routine trivial and the urgent emergent: all of our citizens who do not have health insurance, who are poor, who are isolated. For this wide, varying, often hidden (until they're not) section of society, the 911 system is primary care provider, local clinic, and social worker. For people who have no support network, no health care, no home, no options, they get by as best they can—until they cannot. When things turn dire, we respond to their severe and immediate health crises.

These folks are survivors, one way or another. They're generally proud, self-sufficient, if self-defeating (by circumstance or autonomy). We try to find a common ground: respect their independence while exhorting them to accept medical assistance to keep them alive and somewhat healthy. People without insurance lowball themselves, which often leads to greater, deeper, more significant health issues. I recommend Victoria Sweet's *God's Hotel* on this topic. She spent her career as a physician in San Francisco's last charity hospital, serving the poorest and most in-need patients while witnessing the devastation that privatization wrought. Also, Thomas Fisher's *The Emergency* provides a trenchant examination of the long-term effects of racial inequality on communities, written from the perspective of a Black doctor who works where he grew up.

It's not a crime to sleep on the streets. We get called for "one down" throughout the year. Winter temperatures make exposure risks dire, and we're called out nightly, mostly by drivers on cell phones who see someone curled inside a sleeping bag under a tarp. They call it in but will not stop to investigate themselves. We arrive and the person says he doesn't want to go to a shelter. That he prefers to sleep outside, unhassled by rules and authority. We state the obvious: that it's perilously cold outside. He'll stare at us, hard eyed. He knows how cold it is. The best we can do is echo the medics' offer to give him a ride to a shelter, if only until the cold snap ends. Generally, it is to no avail. Sometimes, we'll offer a spare pair of gloves or extra fireproof hood.

There is a significant connection between decades of cuts in treatment facilities for citizens with mental illness and our vast homelessness issues. Pharmacology can help treat symptoms, but with no support or network, we end up with a large population of folks with brittle stability. When people run out of or go off their medications, within hours, days, or weeks, significant physical and mental issues arise. At home, at least, there might be a context to glean in the form of empty bottles, meds lists, housemates. In public, it can be difficult to gain a context for their presenting behaviors. The cliché of the "crazy homeless person" ignores the multiple factors that have put the person on the streets and out of reach for continuing, necessary care, especially mental health medications and treatment. If the patient is homeless, we find them when they're far sicker, far worse off. When the issues are mental illnesses, going off their meds causes social as well as medical consequences. These people need help, many forms of help, and they're generally struggling on their own, without any support scaffolding.

Too, there remain profound biases in the medical system—ingrained, and embedded, in the unconsciousness (and consciousness) of the workers: staff who cannot see beyond the race or culture or gender of the person, and who ignore or dismiss the patient's complaints. The consequences of unexamined and unchallenged racial, gender, sexual identity, and xenophobic bias and devaluation are stark and comprehensive. A system built on exclusionary principles must do a lot of work to debug itself. The effects of such biases continue to play out in EDs and clinics across the country. These occur outside our purview, often, but we are the ones who catch an earful the next time the frustrated, aggravated, anguished person calls 911 for the recurring or incessant pain. The disproportionate ill effects of Covid on the Black, Native, and Latino communities were testament to layers of sociological issues: access, health care, finances, baseline health, and comorbidities. The wariness of the Covid vaccine in the Black community, in particular, had deep roots in American medicine's historic mistreatment, dismissal, and active hostility toward Black patients (and, oh yes, the Tuskegee Experiment).

//

The jokers in the pack aren't merely the horrible unexpected calls, the ones that take a chunk out of our hearts. Those truly emergent calls continue to occur: car wrecks, heart attacks, bad falls, violence. These require rapid emergency response. That is who we are and what our mission is. Yet too often these get swamped in the miasma of non-emergent calls, which eat time, energy, and resources. There is nothing we can really do for the chronic callers, and we cannot force people to help themselves. This is the "minute clicking of little wheels," as Faulkner wrote, that grinds us to the breaking point.

Day and night, night and day, we run non-emergency calls. This explains the high burnout rate paramedics experience, as well as the jaded disposition many of us develop. We are powerless within a broken system. We *have* to treat people's complaints as if they were real, and the medics *have* to transport them. All the while, any other call in our vicinity—including genuine emergencies—will be covered by another company, with delays for the added travel distance.

This unsolvable stalemate is the root of the callousness and brusqueness many veteran emergency workers present to the world. We are firefighters who seldom see fire. We are medical personnel who respond to unnecessary calls a significant portion of our shifts. We who pride ourselves on being able to handle problems are ultimately powerless against human nature and bureaucracy. But most responders don't consider that: instead, they grouse, "People are dumb." We fight the frustration and simmering resentment when responding to the same patently not sick people over and over again—it's empathy exhaustion. Even the most compassionate must have a purge valve, a means to off-gas the accumulated tensions and frustrations.

Many of us are able to maintain a compassionate buffer, but that often comes with a protective shellac of humor, most of it quite twisted and gallows-inflected. In the privacy of the rig or the station, we vent and make horrible jokes; we have casual, wildly inappropriate discussions. That kills stress. But it can also reinforce a cynical narrative.

We get so accustomed to our hermetic world that we forget normal citizens do not think or act as we do. Then we open our mouths in public or with cameras rolling, and there are problems.

The sheer weight of immersing ourselves in sorrow and suffering and poor living can be overwhelming. Many of us put up a wall: *They are not Us.* Emotional calluses become emotional callousness. Years of this alter how we see the world, how we engage with others, how we treat our families. These ill effects are what lead to the high percentages of divorce, addiction, and burnout in emergency service workers.

I learned something important from several very gruff and crusty old medics. After decades on the streets, these guys had become so frustrated by their inability to change human nature, so impotent against a system and against humanity, they calcified into ornery, impatient grouches. Whatever noble intentions had sent them into EMS were long gone. They were brutally caustic. I understood that profound frustration, that helplessness, but I did not want to be like them.

I did not know any of this when I tried out for the MFD. I might have had a better sense of what was to come, thanks to the time spent with Jen and her cohort, but most of their shoptalk was about dealing with the endless misogyny, homophobia, and racism of dunderheaded men. Still, what they spoke of told me it was a world far removed from what I knew. Even after rookie school, I had no inkling. None of us do. And this is one of the savage twists of emergency response: the things that eat at us, the hard and unsolvable dilemmas are not in the job description. No section of our training manuals deals with the amount of suffering, poverty, and dysfunction we will encounter, or how to deal with it. That is the reality of our job. I remind our rookies, as I was reminded years ago: The citizen's emergency is not *our* emergency. It is our workplace. Do not meet their panic with panic of your own. Handle it with grace, aplomb, and humor. Save the snark until we're back on the rig. Treat people well. Make people's bad days better, even by your mere presence at their side as they suffer. Take it all in, remain open. Do right, be kind.

3

EXILE IN FIREVILLE

If you destroy the culture this department has, that tradition this department has, you destroy a very basic part of this department, and we become just another city agency. I don't think that when you have a department whose men and women are expected to be ready at any moment to put their life on the line to go to the aid of a stranger, I don't think you can pay people to do that job. There has to be something beyond money that makes them do that, and I think it's the culture of the department.

—Interview with FDNY chief William Feehan,
shortly before the September 11 attacks that took his life,
discussing FDNY's poor history with women and minorities

FIREFIGHTERS HAVE LOTS OF DOWNTIME. WE SIT AT THE STATION BETWEEN calls, waiting to be summoned to help someone. It is a culture shaped and perpetuated via oral tradition: we while away the hours rehashing past calls, romanticizing our awesomeness, giving horrible relationship advice, one-upping each other with Scary Fire Stories or Gruesome Medicals. We bitch and backbite as if that were the currency of our paychecks. There is a nice communal feeling, though, spinning old stories about kooky calls back in the day. Because of our shift work, we might share an incredible day or even a single, momentous call with a crew, then not work together again for a decade. When we reunite, the first conversation will likely be whatever crazy shit happened that one time.

Many of us are good storytellers (well, we *think* we are), skilled at embellishing or seasoning with juicy details. Someone says, "This one time . . ." and off we go into the past. The litany of weird, gross, smelly, sad, funny (so many funny, so many horrible *and* funny!) incidents recounted for the crew gathered in the dayroom, or at the dining table, or rolling around town in the rig.

Driving a neighborhood can bring back years of calls, a blur of blended or overlapping memories. Half-awake and sluggish at zero dark thirty, we show up for a "patient" standing on the stoop conspicuously not-dying; we walk them down the steps to greet the medics, they shrug and bring the person aboard, we all drive away. Another Code 300-A (nothing) run, the patient forgotten before we get back to the station. This block, that night? Or that block, this other night? Details escape us. Other times, the details are seared into our deepest chambers: long-dead faces, slivers of horror, intimate tragedies known only to the victims, their families, and us. We tell our stories to the crew, to share something, or just to set some of these hard memories aloft in the night air.

We show up at the station each morning wearing a clean (clean-enough) blue uniform, put our turnout gear by the rig, and begin the shift by checking the inventory to see what equipment might have wandered off on the opposite shift's watch. We mop the floors, scrub the toilets, wash the rig, eat, read the paper (an anachronism; for today's youth: we scroll our phones), talk, and wait. Alarms come in and off we go. We return to quarters to continue whatever we were doing when the bells sounded. All day, all night: that is my job. We wait for people to call us, and we go address their problems.

One day we might have seven runs. The shift before we had twenty-one. Three of our seven that first day were critical or fatal cases. None were fatal the shift before. It depends. EMS responses for chest pain, heart attacks, breathing issues, falls, depression, medication issues, loneliness, self-harming, locked-out of house or car, locked-in a bathroom, substance abuse, withdrawal sickness. Also, car wrecks. Smoke alarms. CO alarms. Fires. Some of these; many of these; none of these. It depends.

In between calls, we are together: on the rig, in the station, training, errands, shopping for meals. We get to know each other pretty well over twenty-four-hour shifts. That can be a lot of social interaction. We generally have poor boundaries, no filters, balancing gradations of vanity with a holy determination to take everyone down a peg. Some crews become tighter than family, forging deep and close bonds. They travel together off shift, help each other with construction projects, go drinking, play sports, stand up at each other's wedding. Other crews are icy strangers white-knuckling through the endless hours, or simmering with pass-agg rage and resentments. Ego and insecurity propel too many of us and shape far too much of this job. Mostly, though, we are social creatures who fill time gabbing, laughing, sharing, teasing, working out, playing games and pranks. Even our busiest stations have oodles of hours of small talk, bad ideas, unchecked rantings. The social hierarchy that favors the senior guys—and those with the most clout, not just the ranking officer—means there are a lot of one-sided soapbox disquisitions. These topics range from how to lay a hoseline up the stairs to how the admin or union or city is out to get us, to why it used to be better in some vividly cherished but abstract yore—or why Ford makes better trucks than Chevy. Stations with functional behaviors achieve a great deal together. Dysfunctional crews have twenty-four long hours to be horrible to each other, but mostly to the lowest person of social ranking.

This is a workplace like no other.

Minneapolis has nineteen stations, nineteen engine companies, eight truck companies, and one heavy rescue squad. Fire stations are massive. People think each station contains an entire department, dozens of firefighters at the ready. Often, the cavernous buildings hold just three of us. A single-engine station houses an engine company, which, due to perennial staffing shortages, is three people. A captain, who is nominally in charge. A driver (in Minneapolis, that is the fire motor operator, or FMO; other places, it is the FEO—fire equipment operator—or chauffeur or engineer) who is responsible for getting us safely to the scene and operating the engine's pump to get us water. The third person is the rank firefighter; in Minneapolis parlance, the durgan (runt pony—from when horses pulled the steam engines). When (if) we have enough personnel, there would be a fourth firefighter. Engine companies carry water and a lot of hose. We are the primary EMS units, thus derisively labeled the Band-Aid Brigade.

Truck companies have four members. Their rig is the long one—with the hundred-foot aerial ladder. While the engine companies "just" squirt water, the truckies perform multiple fireground tasks: climbing ladders, chopping roofs, searching for victims, pulling apart ceilings and walls to expose hidden fire. They are quartered with engine companies in what we call double houses. Most of the time, the engine companies take the medical runs; the truck crews get them only when the engine is already out. Fires, car wrecks, hazmat incidents: both rigs go together. Movies, TV shows, and images in the popular imagination depict a double house (and one with full staffing), so eight or more men and women eating together and rushing to the rigs pell-mell. At my station, and most of our engine companies, it's just three of us playing hide-and-seek in the vast, empty space.

Minneapolis trains its firefighters to be interchangeable. We are all expected to be able to perform truck and engine tasks, but given the unequal number of rigs, most of us end up doing engine work. With few working fires and inconsistent review and training, a person might get through the first decade with scant working truck knowledge. That person—me—might decide that a focused skill is preferrable and remain an engine punk for the rest of his career.

The captain is essentially a player coach. I am a supervisor, responsible and accountable for daily operations, safety, documentation, station upkeep, training. I respond with my crew and am responsible for putting together our safe operational plan on every call.

Our crews might not be family, but there can be something special shaped by this work, by our time together, through our shared experiences. Our workplace is more intense than most, and we develop blithe bonhomie despite—and within—human horrors. That juxtaposition is essential, really, and it's connected: we encounter situations that are foul, are tragic, are strange, are unpleasant, and we have to deal with them. There isn't a "No, thanks" option, so we square up and handle it. Together. Our shared suffering and toil bond us. Together we drive to and from the event. At fires, we work in pairs. We lay lines and pull hose and throw ladders: together. Together we chop roofs and walls, pull ceilings, carry and work victims. Afterward, we catch our breath together, then pick up the dirty, heavy wet hose, together. It is together that we clean our helmets, hose, and axes. Together that we decon our medical equipment, scrub the blood and flesh off our shoes. Together that we sit afterward and finish our meal or the chores or our card games.

The dependence on one another ranges from cleaning the floors to saving our own lives. It is the fundament of the job. Shirkers, half-assers, selfish pricks, incompetents: they are protected by the civil service's generous buffer, so for decades, peer pressure shaped group dynamics (for better and worse).

The job can be delightfully and deliciously crazy fun. Almost everyone loves their firefighters. We get thanked constantly and kids love us and some sweet young ladies mistake us for heroes and future ex-husbands. It is nearly criminal, sometimes, how much fun we get paid to have. It is likely tragic, oftentimes, how much hardship we share together. The bonds help us survive what we experience. The laughter helps dissipate the ugliness and powerlessness we experience on too many calls.

We laugh gravely and deeply. We laugh to keep from crying, sure. But we laugh because that is a barrier against despair and fear. A brusque, lacerating *Fuck you, Mr. Death.* And then we continue on with our shift, awaiting whatever call comes next. Not always, and not everyone. Some crews are stones, cruelly cold and indifferent. Far too many rookies have been aced out by our atavistic pecking order and tough-guy bravado. And too many of us thus have never learned to say when it's too much. We have nothing but our caustic laughter sometimes.

//

Shifts used to pass with the crews sitting around a table playing hours of cribbage or poker, first drinking and smoking, then just smoking, and then simply throwing cards. Crews would have elaborate woodshops in the basements or major car repair projects on the apparatus floor. The long hours permitted and encouraged big projects. And deviously intricate pranks. The essence of the job's interpersonal dynamic is to toughen hides and sharpen wits. The glory days were back when "things were wild and fun. When we could do anything." The remnant witnesses describe abject cruelty, inventive and cruel psychological torture, and deviously brilliant tricks with the same fond indifference to propriety my ex-Mormon grandfather showed when he described what can only be deemed child endangerment, abandonment, and abuse back in the zany old frontier days.

Any perceived weakness—whether ego, insecurity, vanity, or personal peeve—becomes the wound that never gets a bandage. An entire shift might be spent constructing some gotcha, whether running a hoseline into the dorm, setting buckets of ice water precariously above every doorway, putting pennies between the door and the floor (until the door is pinched shut, forcing the person to climb out a window or cry for help). Leaving one's badge shirt out demands that someone or everyone will find the smallest possible container into which to cram the shirt, until only the badge is showing, then wetting it down and sticking it in the freezer.

"Kid, if you're *not* getting hazed, you better watch out: that means they don't like you."

Uh, sure. I guess that sounds—normal?

Bullshitting, backbiting, and pranks. This is not a normal office. A coarse and very funny populace, but an HR nightmare. As with many stressful professions, firefighters goof off boisterously, rowdily, loudly. We fuck around a lot, frankly. There is science behind it, a healthy coping mechanism for the deep tides of unhealthy experiences. Certainly. But this is not a demographic known for moderation or judicious discretion. Thus the risk of saying, "Well, *some* acting up is fine—just don't push it too far." All we know is *too far.* Our baseline is extreme; thus our excesses are dangerous, illegal, fireable offenses. And then we cover it up—lie, deny, bully, and bribe the victim or witnesses—and admin fumes, and the civil service is horrified.

We once were brawny rogues, impish of spirit and noble of deed: The Guys! But the acclaim that our good actions earned us also concealed and abetted our dysfunctions and some widespread, atrocious behaviors. This false equation of cruelty and hazing with team building and morale persists even today, embraced by all those who feel cheated by being born too late to enjoy the lawless good old days. The refusal to accept that what had once been "OK" (i.e., tolerated, overlooked, ignored) had never actually been right and led to harassment, lawsuits, bad publicity, ruined careers. A defensive nostalgia impedes the progressive, right-minded efforts of many leaders and workers.

Because culture, inside and outside the fire station, has changed. We got cable TV and bigger recliners, and people spent more hours staring at the ever-widening screens. Then came high-tech video games, then wireless consoles, and people would scatter to play online warfare against their station mates or strangers around the world. Then came smartphones, and now we're all just staring down at our palms.

//

Imagine sleeping about as well as possible on a lumpy, narrow institutional mattress you share with the firefighters on opposite shifts, in a dorm surrounded by two to seven snoring bodies, and being jarred awake by the pop of the station speakers, the overhead lights snapping on. "Engine 17, 4455 Woebegone Avenue for a possible heart."

Imagine stumbling to the sliding poles, willing yourself awake as you drop twenty-five feet to the apparatus floor, getting onto the rig, racing through the night to an address where someone has called 911 for a heart attack.

Imagine hustling through the night air—be it sweltering and dank with summer humidity, or humorlessly cold, or windy with arctic daggers, or dumping rain: weather doesn't matter, we always respond—crossing the lawn, quickstepping to the front porch, knocking forcefully and announcing "*Fire* Department! *Rescue* squad!" (to prevent getting shot at the wrong address), entering, and finding . . .

Someone clutching his chest, eyes watery with panic, terror etched on his face. "Help," he gasps, then falls to the floor, where you kneel and attempt to revive him.

Or, someone unresponsive on the couch or floor, or in bed, or in the bathroom, with a panicked family member frantically trying to follow the 911 dispatcher's guidance for performing CPR.

Or, an unresponsive person, with the family member frozen in shock.

Or, someone who won't put out his cigarette complaining his chest hurts, while a passel of children sprawl on couches, chairs, the floor, stupefied by the six-foot flat-screen TV.

Or, several drunks, fighting. The less belligerent one shouting his heart is exploding.

Or, a dead person. *Clearly* dead.

Or, a person whose drunk friends are screaming, "He's dead! Do something!" when (a) we can't raise the dead, and (b) he is, in fact, just drunk and sleeping.

Or, someone off their meds and wanting us to do something about the aura coming from the lights and the noises from the sink and, also, their heart feels like it's moving all over their rib cage, you know?

Or, someone who woke up for no reason but worries there *might* be something wrong, maybe a heart issue or something, and they checked WebMD, which said it could be a heart attack, so now they want a ride to the ER.

Or, someone complaining their heart isn't beating (it is). Who says they are having a heart attack (they aren't). Who adds, belatedly, that they have been smoking meth since Tuesday (there you go: cause and effect).

We assess the person, go to work if they're in an emergent condition, while filtering and parsing out the extraneous background noise. Frequently, we find no actual emergency, simply someone who doesn't feel well. We escort them down to the arriving ambulance. We perform a brief information exchange with the medics, wave at them as they load the patient, and we climb back on our big red truck and roll slowly back to the station and our perhaps still-warm beds.

Until the next call, which might be a car wreck, a car on fire with people trapped, a car over a wall and into a house or down an embankment or on frozen, cracking ice. Or a shooting at a house party, multiple people injured. Or a suicidal person, at home or on a bridge. Or another heart call, with a warm body, or a cold body. We don't know what is coming, this call, the next, or the one after that. We get no warning about which calls will be routine and which will take everything.

//

We endured the many waves (as of this editing) of the Covid-19 pandemic, working among the sick and infectious, watching people struggle to breathe, to survive, to lose family, or to die—while worrying about getting sick ourselves. There was significant denial and foot-dragging at the outset, then bureaucratic concerns about sick leave and mask counts. Meanwhile, as administrators tinkered and adjusted and changed protocols, we walked into homes with sick people, and latently infectious people, and dead people. Far too many of my coworkers refused to take the pandemic seriously. Rather than seeing it as a public health duty, we got caught in personal-preference battles: firefighters have a shitty track record with those. Covid was no exception. A workforce whose purpose is to help and serve the public but who will not do what is necessary to protect themselves and the public: where is our compass? A nation that feels a mask is emasculating needs some serious therapy.

Similarly, men ignore our weight gain, our chest pains, the moles sprouting, the lumps and nagging coughs, because we're afraid of what it means, the underlying decay. Much can be handled safely if we are willing to do something about it. Or we remain in denial until we're shocked to find ourselves quite incontrovertibly dying. This is true for many of my male coworkers despite witnessing the consequences of persistent denial over and again on calls.

I extend a smidgen of sympathy for the old guard. The men who existed in an all-white, all-male workplace for generations. They inhabited their artificial environment, believing it was the rightful and natural order of things. They put out fires, had throaty drama and petty intrigues, bickered and yelled and fought, sat in companionable or seething silences. It was a man's man's man's man's world. They didn't necessarily *do* much to make it how it was: they applied for the job, tested, trained, worked. Essentially, *they didn't make the rules.* But: the mass of them were concertedly hostile toward anyone else's attempts to join; they made life miserable for the rare nonwhite men; rampant chauvinism and racism and homophobia were pervasive.

The system worked well for them (many of them). Their confusion at the regular world's demands that they change, that they bear some responsibility for their unjust status quo, is "understandable." They were not inclined to evaluate or examine their own biases, their own "normal." That they did the job and handled it well is not the point. The exclusion of everyone else created this false normal. Letting others in is simply fair. It isn't radical; it's basic equity.

What is misunderstood, I believe, about cultural change is that the traditions or habits we must replace are seldom the *essence* of the thing. A great many Americans feel they must defend tackle football and keep the fighting in hockey, lest we "ruin" sports and manhood—despite all the evidence of traumatic injuries, physical ruin, increasing instances of chronic traumatic encephalopathy due to repeated blows to the head, ingrained violence. If violent headfirst tackles and fistfights are the beating hearts of football and hockey, what are we even talking about? Those are extraneous attributes, adrenalized offshoots, developed over time and accepted as custom, ingrained as essential. They are public diversions, hyped for our media-dependent minds. But they are not essential to either sport. Not the core, not the essence, not the "real." Firefight-ing does *not* require antisocial drunken bullies, or blind aggressive ma-chismo. The job is not even what most of us think it is, certainly not what we claim or wish it were.

Other largely unchallenged, past false equivalencies: "If we let women on the fire trucks, the cherished Brotherhood will be no more." "We had to let those Black guys on so we wouldn't get sued. They're all quota hires, can't do the job right." "They're *ruining* this great job!"

Well, any "Brotherhood" that exists by aggressively and consciously excluding women and people of color from its ranks is neither noble nor natural. Refusing to adapt doesn't end well. The impassioned—I'll call it *hysterical*—cry of the reactionary traditionalists is *We have lost the essence of what it means to be a fireman with all this change and safety talk and diversity.* As if there is either a qualifiable, quantifiable, or an esoteric Truth to the job. The actual core work—dealing with fires and alarms, running EMS calls, and helping the public—has no real connec-tion to those defective defenses. Mixed-gender and mixed-race crews can still put out fires, help people with asthma, and laugh at fart jokes. The next step is to create and elevate a false distinction: *Well, that part is just the job. Anyone can do that. But the craft of firefighting is different. It is rare and special and not just anyone can do it.*

Similar disingenuous arguments are being deployed currently against the growing discussions about safety and sensible risk manage-ment. *These new guys are afraid to go into a building! No science is going to show you how to crawl low through the bad shit to make rescues! If you're not willing to face the devil, you shouldn't even be here.*

There are now webpages dedicated to #Firemanship. Get a grip, boyos. I challenge this because it reinforces the mindset and behav-iors that impede health and productive learning; because it perpetuates macho bluster and keeps us stupid, frankly.

//

A common refrain in the emergency response field is "You've gotta be crazy to run into burning buildings, only a nut can deal with all the mayhem. We are not normal!" We embrace and internalize this so that it becomes a truism for us: "Well, we're all a bit screwed up, what do you expect? This job attracts damaged people."

I call bullshit. That's a sloppy glorification of maladaptive behavior. Excusing bullying and crass, mean-spirited dysfunction does a disservice to all the thoughtful, caring firefighters who choose not to be assholes. We mistake rashness for courage, cruelty for manliness. We are threatened by compassion and vulnerability. "Crazy" people are liabilities on scenes. They can turn a situation dangerous by their impetuous actions.

Here's the bigger twist: I argue—steadily, angrily, lovingly—that many of us do not even understand the "truth" of our job, neither the essence nor the risks, when we start. And for those of us who carry formative scars or the weight of loss and suffering, we can find greater meaning and healing in connecting with, in helping, in seeing those before us who are sick, scared, hurting, and scarred. That is not crazy. That is a better side of the human condition.

Let's pretend the #firemanship claims are true, that there is some magical essence of this job. The reality is that most firefighters never understand more than task-level basics: *Put the wet stuff on the red stuff.* A firefighter might retire after three decades grasping little more than the grunt work: spray water; pull ceiling; chop on roofs. From the outset, we are too adrenalized and too nervous to learn, study, or understand the *why* of tactics, let alone strategy and purpose. We might become "senior guys" without even knowing what we don't know. We blindly charge or stumble through smoky buildings, doing tasks out of habit or impulse without regard for the structures, conditions, or situations. We bemoan the lack of experience but maintain unhealthy denial about the true paucity of working fires.

The impressionable take this noise as gospel. They want so badly to fit in that they parrot the empty bravado and refuse to think beyond the clichés. The pressure to fit in smothers the openness to understand fire and human behavior, physics, strategy, and tactics. Seeking peer acceptance over personal knowledge is a risky gambit. And that's how we spawn another generation of insecure bluffing fireboys. As Laurence Gonzales writes in *Deep Survival,* "The word 'experienced' often refers to someone who's gotten away with doing the wrong thing more frequently than you have."

We continue to survive dangerous situations—without evaluating or examining how or why. We fool ourselves with the belief that our survival is proof of our skill. Until one day our fraudulence is exposed cruelly and starkly, people die, and we are left decimated. And, dear reader, I remind you that what these throaty firedudes call the "essence" is the equivalent of championing helmet shots and fighting as the essence of football and hockey.

The second critical misunderstanding is that, rather than examining what our mission as public safety workers is or should be, rather than accepting and emphasizing the EMS component of the work, we fall in line to get baptized by the grunting gods of fire, keepers of the sporadic flame. We dismiss and give short shrift to 80 percent of our workload. *Eighty!* All this hype and hyperbole and flop sweat and posturing for the scant few fires each of us will attend per year—and those, I emphasize, we too often flail through and strenuously resist learning from.

I am heartened that many more of the new hires are computer literate, flexible in their thinking and learning, and frequently seem to recognize empty boasts when they hear them. Newbies can now research and learn on their own rather than dumbly swallow the meaty declarations from some guy sitting at the table. But peer pressure remains heavy, and the illusions of skill and security are tough to lacerate. When a rookie is told, "Look, kid, fire will kill you *unless* you follow Ol' Smokey Jeremy's lead. He's been doing this awhile. He's seen some fire. He knows," it is hard to find a true north.

We are not lost, but we will lose a lot until we recognize the futility and harm of chasing a chimerical past.

//

Because we encounter immigrants who are unfamiliar with American, and Minnesotan, customs—including the medical system, the fire service, household maintenance—some of us regard them contemptuously for not knowing what we were taught as kids, or think their lack of knowledge is deliberately wasteful or hazardous. Not all of us, but too many. It's the threat or consequence of provincial homogeneity. Rather than appreciating how far afield these folks must be from their birthlands and the complexities they are negotiating, we revile and mock them. It might not be simple racism, but it seems awfully like that in its expression.

We can easily misread a patient's presentation or description, making false assumptions, haughty judgments, or knee-jerk reactions. Or we lead with our biases, and presume what we think fits, rather than what is actually the issue. We can be callous, brusque, rude, sexist, homophobic, racist, classist, xenophobic—without consciously "meaning" to be any of those things. Some of us adopt a blank neutrality toward people "other" than ourselves, but that dispassion verges on indifference. And many of us really do find pleasure and interest in meeting strangers and, in our brief encounters, glimpsing a slice of global humanity.

Responding to the routine problems of our poor, disenfranchised, and struggling citizens, as well as catching the truly emergent calls, our job is good and hard and punishing. The intimate proximity to physical, mental, emotional, psychic suffering takes a toll on us. But there's resonance: we contribute to the public welfare. We help those who need help. The positives often, or generally, outweigh the negatives.

In this regard, we often serve as social workers or counselors, with little official training. Over time, with effort and guidance and reflection, we can learn to read people. Some calls come in as medical emergencies or as public disturbances, which also bring the police. The cuts to the mental health system for years now, the reliance on meds, the dual issue of criminalizing mental issues and enforcing the superficial status quo ("safety" concerns triggered by someone who's just talking to himself, the pigeons, or God): there is no good or easy way to address the range of humans trying to get by.

I am not being phony when I'm with patients. I am present, listening to and seeing them. Most of us do a great job of this. We offer human connection and contact and witness and respect. I truly believe this *is* part of our job. My understanding and approach have deepened over the years. Possibly this is because I now feel the weight of mortality on my own head. I can see myself in that hospital bed or wheelchair or crumpled on the floor. I see my parents in the elders we respond to; I see my siblings in the families struggling with their parents' decline. A variation on Tolstoy's line about unhappy families, I think. In illness and decline (moribundity), we each suffer uniquely and in isolation. I am grateful this job has allowed me access to such a wide array of humans and the ways we live and die.

My elder daughter is in nursing school. We've had discussions about her learning process with patients, the struggle to extend compassion and empathy—things that aren't textbook but are essential to care—while not burning out. I tell her it is something that cannot really be taught, not in a classroom setting, as much as learned through experience. To be present and compassionate with each person, and to let it go when one's duties are done. We will not save a fraction of the dying people we encounter. They deserve our respect and witness and compassionate treatment, but we must go home to our families with some humanity remaining—because we need to buckle up and return tomorrow to do it all again.

This is not a job for earnest people. Having a roaring tender heart is great, but there must be a measure of grit, some grim clarity about the human condition. Blind idealism will be disastrous; hoping despite reality will be disastrous; see(k)ing only the good in people, no matter what, will be disastrous: these tendencies will trap you in cognitive dissonance, or you will be overwhelmed. Being coldhearted is not a path through: treating others as if their suffering or dysfunction is contagious is also disastrous. It will leave you isolated and broken.

That is the tension: to remain open to each person, to not get bitter or jaded or coldhearted—while also not getting emotionally exhausted or brokenhearted. We get scant guidance, or support, and we must walk that line, between losing ourselves or losing human connection. Because if one omits the unnecessary non-emergent EMS calls, we'd just have the horrors, which would break us to pieces in weeks. Frank Huyler describes it in *White Hot Light*: "When the eye is too cold, when it's down near zero, it looks through everything, and everything seems the same. This life, or the next. This man, or another. This woman, or another. This child, or another. *But everything is not the same, and you have to see that, too*" (emphasis mine).

The simple truth is that being kind is its own reward. It gives me more energy to be nice to people, to expose a sliver of my heart to them. I feel happier with the world, better connected, even in the despairing futility of what we see.

//

I am incredibly fortunate that I have had friends, teachers, mentors, and adversaries who pushed me to examine and rethink all the ways in which I was born, raised, and live in privilege. That I am a cynical idealist has helped me question the status quo, but without those people—women, queer folk, people of color—whose existences are made far more complicated by the very things that render mine comfortable, I would likely not have learned to question and challenge social "norms."

I have tried to educate myself, and had my presumptions and perspectives challenged and obliterated by smarter people, incisive teachers, and great writers. I am quite flawed. It is hard not to revert to form, given that America reinforces the white supremacist, the heteronormative, the misogynist narratives at every turn. Fortunately, my learning and growth are ongoing.

A seminal example: My good friend Hank Lewis encouraged me to come teach with him in Chattanooga in 1990. Hank had been recruited and was the first African American faculty member at a very conservative school. He had been one of the first Black students to attend this school, a groundbreaker and student leader in his time. I rolled in knowing very little about the Bible Belt and white evangelicalism—except what I'd read in books, and neither Faulkner nor Hurston helped much with that. We were young, opinionated, engaged (and enraged). We felt like agents for change, but really we were pains in the ass to the administration and especially the all-male, otherwise all-white English department.

I watched Hank struggle to get our fellow teachers to acknowledge a long list of racially problematic issues: representation, course materials, the fraught history of the department itself, the literary canon, the school, the town, the nation. He was polite, respectful, patient, reasoned. He got nothing. He pointed out, still politely, the hypocrisy or problematic dismissals. He was instead seen as radical and disruptive, unstable, unreasonable. The department "valued" his diversity but not his honesty or his perspective.

Yet who *but* him was in a position to speak to the ways an all-white, all-male traditionalist faculty might not see their ingrained biases?

Watching and listening to Hank struggle, seeing the barely coded language and nonverbal expressions that iced him out, dismissed him, delegitimized his complaints and the truths of his experiences: I saw how the system—white male America, patriarchy, unexamined racial bias, classism, all of it—chugged along paying lip service to good intentions and no one wearing a hood.

After my first year, I secured a grant to do research on ways to diversify the curricula of the English department. This was in 1991: pre-Google. The gentlemen did protest too much about the terrible dearth of "alternatives" to their beloved canon. *Goodness! Where, oh where might we find these things? Show me a Black version of* A Separate Peace *and I will happily teach it!* Ah, yes, the venerable Black New England prep schools of the 1940s . . .

I found a few American studies bibliographies from northern colleges, researched women's lit, African American lit, Latino and Native American fiction and essays, a range of queer and cultural studies. I bought a couple of cases of books. My stipend allowed me to rent a room in the Colorado mountains and read all day. I made copious notes, found connections and allusions and analogies and comparisons to our very traditional reading lists. I typed up a thorough report, suggesting easy ways to broaden the bibliography and teach more inclusively.

I was smiled at, thanked, and my report shelved.

//

I get away with a lot because I fit in superficially. I can raise a lot more hell than Hank, and others like him, in dominant culture settings—explicitly *because* I am a white man. I owe it to myself, my friends, and everyone, to speak up for the very same reasons. I have continued to study cultural criticism, gender and race relations, and the narratives of people of color and feminists. I learn by reading, by thinking, and by applying it to the world around me. The more I listen and observe the systems that shape our world, the easier it is for me to call bullshit on them.

This is not radical. I am not special. I have to check my biases and privileges constantly. But the more I question myself, the clearer it is how deeply rigged the culture is. It is the simple fact that dominant systems seldom give up power willingly. I'll spare us the MLK quote here (but heartily encourage readers unfamiliar with it to read "Letter from Birmingham Jail" as soon as you put this down).

Applying this realization to the fire service, where middle-class, suburban, white men are the mainstays of EMS response in poorer, racially mixed communities, there are bound to be breakdowns in understanding and communication. Studying how the world works improves my ability to find connections and context. I am never "just" Jeremy when I stand before someone, and they are never "just" a person in need. We carry the bloody American legacy within us. The street-level interactions allow me to take the theory I've studied and apply it to real life. I also am able to give thorough, research-based information when I challenge the received assumptions that flow freely through our culture.

As I examine throughout this book, the caustic effects of our wrongheaded chauvinism are found in every aspect of our work. Men who cannot or will not ask for help for fear of appearing weak, who never learn to ask for help, who are taught not to say they need help: when they're trapped in a building collapse or under the weight of depression, PTSD, addiction, they are incapable of asking for help. Men who shout, who hit, who shoot—rather than think, reflect, and respond with heart and mind.

The gruff old-school guys are gone. Their legacy has seeped into the culture, but it is diminished. I do *not* need a crew of untethered berserkers to fistfight a burning house. We need grit and hustle, but we need brains and heart too. The challenge, which no one explains, is that we must find a way toward grace, healthy acceptance, compassion, while not losing ourselves in the world's suffering.

4
THE LAYING OF HANDS

WHEN WE WERE ROOKIES, OUR EMT TEACHERS WERE BOTH GRIZZLED FROM twenty years as paramedics. Bill S. was a cross between midcareer Bill Murray and a less stoned, less Canadian Seth Rogen. He's the one who instilled in us that "if you don't have airway, you don't have shit." He also told us that he went ten years without a successful CPR, "and not because I'm a sucky medic, either. It isn't magic, not like they show on TV: '*Thump, thump*—hooray! You saved him! What a hero!'" Twenty-plus years in, my success rate isn't much better.

Sandy Y. was a bony, birdlike woman with frizzy brown hair and the raspy voice and corrugated skin of a heavy smoker. She had a tattoo, she told us during our section on advanced directives, right above her heart: *DNR & DNI*, with her doctor's signature copied in ink. "Lest there be any confusion what my final wishes are," she added dryly. (Reader: Such tattoos are neither legal nor valid. Get your paperwork completed properly.)

Both were good-hearted people and good teachers. Both personified the personal hazards of the job: Bill admitted he'd had a heart attack and nearly died. Knowing his coworkers would see him scared and in peril, he refused to call 911. His wife made the call for him, and he got help, but it wasn't a large window of time he was messing with. Sandy's smoking destroyed her health, her skin, her lungs; it cut years from her life. Both acknowledged they were stellar examples of the bad ways one might cope with the job.

The first months of cadet school were about learning the EMT basics to pass the National Registry EMT exam. A surprising number of my classmates were shocked that they had to learn medical "stuff." Because, you know, they were *firemen* and what the hell did they need to learn all this medical crap for? And the veteran captain in charge of our class didn't help much: "Just pass the test. All we do is take a pulse, slap an O_2 mask on, drag them to the ambulance."

Be that as it may, there was a lot to learn and remember about physiology, bones, medications, proper methods of doing many things. It was a rushed but thorough education in the human system. As many standardized tests are, the National Registry's questions weren't about ensuring we would do a good job on the streets, as much as about whether we could answer specific questions in very specific manners.

Eventually, we all passed.

The transition from textbook to "real world" or "street" happens in many professions. Touching strangers; kneeling on their dirty or spotless floors; filtering out the noise of bystanders, family members, distraught patients—that's what we learn through repetition and immersion in real time. The newness, the awkward self-doubt, feeling overwhelmed by the realness of it all. Learning as we fumble, trying to do right while realizing there are seldom textbook patients and that it's a lot harder to take a blood pressure or stop a bleed on a massive, combative person trapped in a small bathroom. A captain should help the rookie overcome his or her nervousness, beginner's mistakes, feelings of incompetence. *Should* help: not all do. Many still subscribed to clichéd toughen-up sternness. Patience, encouragement, calm: these are great attributes. "Next time, try turning the oxygen on. Relax, kid. *You* didn't kill him . . ."

As a rookie, unless one has previous emergency medical experience, the jolts of adrenaline, uncertainty, nervousness, and immersion make for stressful shifts. We were learning how to apply what we learned (or didn't learn) in cadet school, but doing it in decidedly nonsterile, noncontrolled circumstances. The instructors had always warned, "You're practicing on your classmates here. Most of you are in pretty good shape. Once on the streets, I guarantee you, dollars to doughnuts, you will have a very fat person in a very small car."

Sure enough, my first auto extrication, on my second shift, was a very large man wedged into a very small, inconceivably junk-filled car. None of the meager skills I'd learned in rookie school helped much for a distraught, uncooperative human. As I wrestled my fingers between the seat back and his turgid, sweaty skin, I chuckled, thinking, *Well, they weren't joking. Big man, small car. No shit.*

The actual, concrete skills we learn are not very difficult. Baseline vitals, scrolling through the endless mnemonics for a patient's symptoms and medical history, providing oxygen, doing whatever the medics request. Even CPR, while crucial, isn't complicated: squeeze the bag valve mask (BVM) every six seconds, do rapid and deep compressions in the center of the sternum, attach the AED and follow its prompts. If only it were so simple and clean in practice.

The rookie's job is to learn the job at the macro and the micro levels. Within a few weeks, tasks that once seemed difficult and fraught don't merit a pause (for most of us at least—for some, the process takes longer, and a few never "get" it). With repetition, the rookie learns to parse the initial comments from Dispatch, read a patient's presentation and description, and understand the gradations of emergency. The stumbling blocks disappear. There will be mistakes along the way, which is why the captain is there (and, when there was full staffing, why a good senior firefighter was an invaluable mentor). The lessons will be gained via citizens' suffering. Unlike paramedics or ER docs, our scope of practice is relatively small and safe. My failure to get a good blood pressure is not on the same scale as a medic's misjudging how many cc's of a medication to inject—or shooting the wrong drug into the vein.

The training videos we watched could show the range of calls we might encounter—and even more so now with high-def cameras everywhere, though back in the prehistoric days of beta and VHS tapes the quality was mediocre—but nothing prepared me for the sights, sounds, and smells that are the essence of our work. I use the word *intimate* to describe this job: physical proximity—touching naked strangers—as well as witnessing the raw and exposed parts of someone's life. There is little privacy when we are involved.

People scream in pain, in terror, in despair. They scream from the bottom of their heart or from the edges of a broken soul. They scream in fear and fury. They wail in sorrow and pain. We enter a scene and are right beside them as they void every torment. It's all close quarters: examining a patient, lifting and carrying a patient, working the patient inside the ambulance. There is nowhere for the screaming to go that does not wash over and into us.

Same for the sights: Morbid obesity. Bloated morbidity: festering, decaying, rotting flesh. Papery old skin that tears at the slightest touch.

Flamboyantly bruised flesh, both young and old. Burned skin and flesh. Open wounds, whether from penetrating trauma: knives, gunshots, metal poles, glass shards, tree limbs, anything else that slashes through our flesh. Or from illness: the ravages of diabetes, MRSA (flesh-eating bacteria), amputations, infections, untreated small issues growing worse, cancers, unknowns.

Broken bones, broken bodies: *deformities* is the technical term for body parts that have been forced into unnatural positions. Open fractures, when the jagged bones pierce the bloody flesh. Or viscera: gut wounds where the innards spill outward.

Coupled with all the oddities, there are the deviant natural issues. Meaning: Two shattered heels aren't normal, but they are the natural consequence of falling off a balcony onto the cement patio below.

And then there are the smells.

The odors are brutal—because we don't get a warning, unlike with the visual and audible. Deep-seated ammoniac tang from months peeing through the adult diapers or not-so-absorbent pads onto the couch. Putridity of human decay. Gastrointestinal infections: vomit, urine, diarrhea, regular shit. When it's your own puke or poop, it's pungent, but when it's a stranger's and you're stepping over or through or (worse) *in* it, that ain't no picnic.

Much the way we gain experience on the fireground, with concepts we've studied made real through practical experience—and much the way there is a tension between textbook ideals and the actual chaos of fire scenes—we learn that, although the ABCs (airway, breathing, circulation) are the basis for everything, their dry protocols sufficient when dealing with lab rats or hypothetical patients, the reality is complex and messy. We are walking into other people's upheaved lives. They don't know or care what the National Registry says is the appropriate way to obtain patient history. They don't care that I'm a nervous rookie. They do not care that this is not my usual crew, or that Dispatch entered the call as a cough, not a cardiac arrest. They want help *right now!*

Although EMS calls are the majority of our work, the threat of fire, its unknown and dangerous and chimerical chaos, awaits us. For rookies, it is a lurking monster. We will be proved, or revealed as lacking, in the forge and crucible of fire. The rookie's uncertainty and nervousness about facing a fire stew and simmer, the fear of danger tangling with the insecurity about passing muster as a firefighter. Except, as I say, the proportion is so skewed at this point, we ought to be called catastrophizers, not firedudes. While we might don our turnouts to chase fire *alarms* daily, the ratio is something like one hundred–plus EMS calls for one working fire, at best.

This is true, and why I encourage us to take more seriously the role EMS demands. Otherwise, we mistake it for a distraction. With each non-fire call, the what-if stress about fire compresses onto itself, creating diamond-hard doubt. *Now? Now? Now?* Meanwhile, off to the next possible heart attack or respiratory distress or GI bleed, and then the next one, and the next after that. On and on, running EMS calls while anticipating fires that seldom come. And most of us carry some degree of profound fear of fire—especially when we are inexperienced and don't know what firefighting actually is. The specter of burning to death is understandably fraught. Worrying about dying in your first fire is human. The truth, though, that there will be so much fumbling and hectic, semi-panicked flailing in the smoky dark, isn't expressed well to cadets. We think *FIRE!* when we should think *TOXIC SMOKE!* And none of it is concrete or literal until months, if not years, on the job. This paradox is the core of the firefighter's existential crisis—as well as the cognitive dissonance that obscures a realistic assessment of our profession. We are not what we think and claim we are supposed to be: a firefighter. Yet we are, still.

By the time I'd get into the rickety tramp bed most nights in my rookie year, I'd be bone weary from the constant adrenaline surges running calls all day, *and* worried that some horrible event was brewing in the night, one I'd be woefully unprepared for. We wait and wonder and worry. *Will I prove myself? Will I perform? How will I fuck up?* It is a haunting weight. With no objective means of resolution, because we never know what will come next. *Sweet fever dreams, kid.*

When we're new, it's all terrifying and foreign and weird. I've had several rookies struggle with the concept that we are allowed to walk into people's homes and touch them. Not only allowed but expected to. Our badges—our big red trucks, really—are all-access passes into the homes and offices of the citizenry. These newbies keep hesitating, as if they're waiting for the real medical professionals to arrive. "Better get to it, kid," I'll say. "Nobody's coming but us."

Reading people and scenes swiftly and accurately involves complex skills, not always quantifiable, not necessarily teachable. Being present and calm helps a whole lot. Engaged captains teach their rookies to stop fumbling, remember to breathe, learn to touch people, and cut through the extraneous distraction to find the truth of each call. Demonstrating efficient treatment, compassionate engagement, coolheaded disposition: that's leadership. Notice I omitted bullying, shouting, demeaning to "toughen-up the worthless babies."

//

We aren't skilled like paramedics, whose scope and training far exceed ours. They bear more responsibility on EMS calls, from evaluation to transport. We can be skilled assistants, or we can be road debris. When we work well together, we provide the advance guard, evaluating, assessing, addressing the essentials, translating prearrival info into usable details. We have a different outlook too. Trained to evaluate catastrophes of many forms and any situation, we develop a broader approach that can transcend the more focused, and thus more limited, technical approach the medics require.

I had a rookie recently who joined the fire department after nearly a decade as a paramedic (with several years as a paramedic training instructor). I was overjoyed to have a smart, capable crew member; a rookie who was aces for the 80 percent of our job that requires touching people, asking them personal questions, entering their homes, and knowing how to treat them. Plus, he's another quizzical nerd. He outranked and outstripped me medically, even if my decade-greater experience provided me with a different, possibly deeper perspective. My previous several rookies had done fine, but we spent a lot of time in this comfort-and-comprehension phase. I was giddy to have someone who could teach me medical things on every call. And I, in turn, was able to push him to examine macro issues, tactical approaches, big-picture concepts.

One thing he told me, a few weeks in, was that he noticed a difference in how we approached scenes, as opposed to the medics. He described it as a difference in overall awareness, a holistic evaluation of a scene. We have more things to consider—more hazards, different issues than the given medical complaints, larger safety perspective. He appreciated that these are more variations on emergency response than any notion of better or lesser.

The medics are highly skilled, but they have exponentially greater turnover and burnout rates. I have more than fifteen years over the majority of their staff now. So even though they've had more schooling, many of them have less actual experience when they hit the streets. We can provide insight from experience and practice that adds to the success of a scene.

The good paramedics are incredible. They do advanced prehospital care for anyone who calls them. They are trained to intubate, secure IV lines, push drugs and medications, and more. They do it on dirty kitchen floors, for victims trapped inside crushed vehicles, in the tight confines of the ambulance while it bounces down rough city streets. They work fast and efficiently. At the ER, there are machines, staff, multiple doctors, multiple nurses, all those other people in scrubs and sensible shoes, more machines, armed guards, med techs, chaplains, translators. In the streets, it's just the two medics, and us.

//

When I started in the stations, I kept a run journal. Jen encouraged me, saying that I would witness and experience so much in those first weeks and months that it was important to write down details and reflections before it all blurred together. To record my memories before the uniqueness of both the incidents and my perspective was lost. She had five years on at that point, and she said she couldn't remember what it was like to see and feel things as new.

So I made notes for each run on my first one hundred-plus shifts. I would write down the crew, the rig, and shorthand notation for what I responded to, as well as a brief commentary or reflection. I established a list of Firsts, with space to enter dates and details for each: first car fire; first house fire; first CPR; first CPR save; first baby born alive; first dead baby; first DOA; first shooting, stabbing, hanging, maiming; first amputation; first burned body. First line-of-duty death (LODD; coworker killed on a call).

It was a catalog of tragedy and mayhem, frankly. Other than "first baby born alive" and "first CPR save," it was nothing but loss and death. Some of the items did not get checked off for years. Others were done in the first month. Some, I'm still waiting for: I'm yet to deliver a baby. I have not lost a coworker on a scene.

I looked back through those pages a decade later. Some calls felt so far removed, they might have been another person's scrawled jottings. But many were etched within me, even inconsequential calls: the small details of a dirty kitchen, a gaggle of cats, the color of the walls, the lady with the severed ear. A mental Rolodex of images, of faces, of rooms, light, sounds, odors. Some blur together, others remain striking. I carry them all. And I add to them with each shift.

I do remember how nervous I was, how everything seemed so strange. We would walk into strangers' homes, confront their unique crises, trampling notions of privacy in the name of *emergency* and *rescue,* and spend three to thirty minutes trying to rectify or stabilize whatever was going wrong.

As cadets, we weren't given much prep for the impressive spectrum of death we would encounter. The straightforward or the ghastly, the miserable or the transcendent end to biological existence. There might be one door between worlds, but it's a wide, wide door.

We were told we'd see dead people, but that is like saying you'll see the Grand Canyon.

Words fail.

The stillness of a room where a corpse lies. It's a psychological, existential trick: I *see* a body, but it is a body without life. Most of us expect, presume, a body to be alive. Anyone not rotting or decapitated gives the impression they *might* suddenly move. My first DOA, I stood there, staring at the body. *She's dead,* I told myself. *That is a dead person.* Even though my captain had checked already for pulses and breathing and declared her DOA, I made myself kneel beside her on the floor between the worn, dirty mattress and a stack of boxes. I touched her arm, pressed at the base of her wrist. No pulse. Her skin was dry and not cold—it was summer and the apartment did not have air-conditioning—but not warm. *This is a corpse. This is death.*

It didn't scare me or freak me out or make me sad. We had gotten called because someone was reportedly experiencing shortness of breath and walked into an apartment and found a dead person on the floor, appearing to have died overnight. The family found her as she lay. They spoke her name, quietly then insistently. They poked her, trying to rouse her. She did not respond. They called 911. *Something was the matter,* they thought. They did not know what. The obvious was not in their realm of possibility, not yet. My captain could tell from the doorway she was dead. I didn't yet know enough to see it clearly. It was weird: the stillness, the discrepancy between a body and nonlife. And we cleared and returned to whatever we were doing at the station when the call came in. In my case, that was mopping the floors badly.

My journal entry said: "First DOA today. Shitty apartment. She was old-ish, but way younger than she looked (before being dead, I mean). Hard living. Hard life. Family stunned and standing around. They wanted us to do something—either bring her back or remove the body, since it was fucking up their morning."

Now, twenty-plus years later, I expect everyone to be dead.

//

The learning curve also occurred between calls: negotiating the multiple personalities on each rig at each station on each shift. Trying to learn each station's daily duties and assignments, as well as the myriad unwritten rules and customs. It was all new and arcane, varying by station, shift, and crew. Learning to deal with chaos, while operating within chaotic situations. Seeking good guidance, learning to read the bluster and rhetoric while gaining insight, understanding, and appreciation for other firefighters' good (and bad) actions. I encountered a range of captains and crews. Some bosses were hands-on, some directive, and some barely got off the rig.

Those early months were where I also learned to parse the rhetoric and hype, the received wisdom—a.k.a., the dense clichés—of this profession. *Get some time on, kid. Shut up and listen. We will tell you what to think. Those guys know their stuff. This job ain't for everybody. We've got job security because some people don't know how to live. Every fire is different. Bread-and-butter house fire, no biggie. Don't overthink it, kid. Put the wet stuff on the red stuff. That crew fucked up—they don't know what the hell they're doing. Do it our way, you'll be fine.* The density of these trite, empty phrases protects many of my peers from feeling the breeze when they've dressed themselves in the Emperor's New Fire Clothes.

I gleaned a bit of this before I joined, from listening to Jen and her cohort of female firefighters. But experiencing it daily, and seeing how fatuous it was, how tumescent and contrived but fiercely embraced— *wow.* If one has not worked this sort of job, it is difficult to describe the sort of meta machismo that underpins and overlies the social fabric. Excessive, nearly preening, performative humility that is dripping with vanity. Vicious slashing of others' achievements and (perceived) egotism. The well-manicured tone used to describe various imagined slights, failings, politically correct travesties. It is the voice one hears from shock jocks and sports radio and wingnut talk shows: deeply male, scabrous toward all the insufferable weakness and softness that affront their virtuous existence.

The best guys on the job are witheringly self-deprecating: they mock themselves as much as everyone else. They bring a twinkling rogue bemusement to almost every situation. But too many invest desperately in creating an Us versus Them dichotomy.

These attitudes are reflected in the response to recognition and awards. The gold standard responses are incredulous, disgusted, indignant: "An award? For what? Just doing their jobs?" Or, "Everybody gets a ribbon now. When I was a rookie, we did our job and were grateful to be paid."

Clint Eastwood would be proud. The truth is, most of these guys have scrapbooks and mancaves clogged with their firedude memorabilia. But they will never admit to wanting recognition or acclaim. It's a phatic social response: anyone who stands out "thinks" they are special. By implication, too, each of the scoffers has done *multiple* impressive, daring rescues that were ignored by the administration, so they just suffer in silence. "My brothers' calling me a good fireman: that is my award."

Similar calls with different crews would reveal vastly disparate approaches and treatments. I'm grateful I found sharp, dedicated mentors who demonstrated competent and caring EMS work and encouraged me to get in there and learn. I will say here that we, as many fire departments tend to do, have distinct shift identities. Many of the purported differences are nonsense, but, because we pick (by seniority) our shifts, stations, and crews, there are some distinct personality types evident along shift lines. There are folks who pride themselves on doing the job right: they are (self-appointed) guardians of the flame of Tradition, and they follow the letter of the law. Their counterparts would be those who do the right thing: they are ambivalent about strict rules but dedicated to the spirit of the service.

My greatest mentors have fallen in the latter group: captains who were a bit rogue about our quasi-military sensibility, but who performed awesome, beyond-the-requirement service for the citizens. More compassionate, more helpful, more willing to go the extra distance to solve someone's problems.

Some of us are rule-bound and police-like; others, roguish adrenaline junkies. I often said that I preferred being the most uptight captain on the A-shift to being the least formal one on the B-shift. When I returned to the rigs from battalion chief, I went to the C-shift, the land of bizarro misfits.

//

Three weeks out of rookie school, I had a swell Saturday, one that encapsulated the wonder and randomness of our job. My first parade, my first overdose, my first shooting, all in one afternoon. We polished the rig before riding in the annual Aquatennial parade, rolling down Hennepin Avenue in the sun, waving and smiling at all the happy parade-watching folks. Grinning joyously, I thought, *Holy shit, I'm actually riding a fire truck, in a parade, waving to the crowd. This is my job!*

Later that afternoon, fancy dress uniform stowed in my locker, we had a drug overdose, my first one (I'd seen lots of people on crack, but no heroin ODs): a small, wiry, sweaty guy sprawled on his stoop. I kept looking at him, wondering if he was alive or dead. He had a pulse: not dead. I got the BVM ready and started breathing for him. (The bag valve mask looks like a purple Nerf football. We squeeze it and push oxygenated air into the patient's airway, "breathing" for the unconscious person.) We breathed for him until the medics arrived. (MFD didn't carry Narcan until 2016, so we depended on the medics to revive the ODs. Then, as now, our ventilations kept them alive and fought off respiratory failure but wouldn't reverse the drugs.) He popped up, was squirrely, denied anything had happened, tried to convince us we were mistaken— that he'd totally *not* been unconscious on his stoop. The cops arrived and he glumly submitted to the hospital transport.

It was all so exciting! *We saved him!* Captain Kath rolled her eyes at me: "Sure we did."

Next we were called to the bathroom of KFC for a drunk drifter smacked on the head, bleeding everywhere, mumbling and crying—which made me sad, seeing a grown man weeping, bleeding, and lost. Trying to clean himself up, he'd splattered the bathroom walls, floor, sink, and toilet with his blood. He was sweating, which diluted the blood and spread it all over his face and neck, soaking into his dirty clothes. Soused, he kept asking, "Why'd they do me like this? What did I do? Why did they hit me? What did I do?" I had nothing for him. I patched his head wound, tried to wipe off some of the gore, and rubbed his back.

The shooting call came in while I was cooking. I had another epiphany: *Wow, this is just like* Emergency! *We're trying to make dinner and the tones sound again and again.*

We ran that call and several more over the night. It was a poignant feeling: the excitement, the adrenaline, the mayhem, the sorrow, riding a rig and being an icon in a parade, then getting splattered with several people's blood, sweat, and, yes, tears. (And notice: no fires.)

Many shifts weren't like this, not the ratio of excitement to boredom. My rookie season was spent getting comfortable encountering people in a variety of bad ways, learning to read situations and people and narratives, deciphering station house gossip and histrionic histories and folklore, and, occasionally, putting out fires.

Jen was right: the feeling one has when it's all new, strange, awkward; that magic is fleeting. The other part is, we don't have clear progressions, nothing that graduates us from innocence to experience. We accrue the experiences, the situations, the sorrows, the traumas. Then one day, you find yourself standing on an island far from what everyone you know considers normal.

//

Not long ago, my crew responded to a home early in the morning, for a man who had had a heart attack in bed—a case of literal heart failure. His wife was awakened by his final, agonal breaths, tried to rouse him, then tried to pull him to the floor (following the 911 operator's instructions) to do CPR. We entered and found our patient half on the bed still, half on the floor, with his wife straddling him, panicked and stricken. I could tell we weren't going to get the man back: he was simply too large. His size indicated profound systemic health issues. His heart had quit.

But there was space in the apartment, we were right there, the wife was standing beside me, begging us to save him. We began working him. Doing compressions on someone that massive is brutal work. The medics arrived. We did CPR and ventilated him while they pushed their standard set of drugs. Their monitor never indicated a shockable rhythm (again: his heart had expired). He was too big for the Lucas compression device. We fought hard against his girth, trying to make that crucial muscle work. My crew took turns, spelling each other every two minutes. The wife stood beside us, encouraging us, speaking to her husband, fiercely focused. Only when the medics called off our sweaty efforts, after forty minutes or so, did she collapse into sobs. She thanked us for all we did, and she fell to the floor in heartbroken grief. (People's default and reflexive politeness is amazing.)

Afterward, my junior firefighter asked if we thought there was something odd about the scene. I asked what she meant. She thought the woman's behavior was suspicious. We talked about it. I realized the rookie had only one or two fatal calls, and, while she inferred from the jump that we were likely looking at a dead man, she did not yet understand all the very human ways that people exist in denial. Also, she had a law enforcement background. "She seemed calm, too calm," the rookie muttered.

I explained that, until the medics had said, "Stop CPR," the wife was fully able to believe that her husband was about to regain consciousness. Because what else is there? This was her beloved and he had gone to bed alive. Until that final moment, when reality cracked her apart, she could resist death, could remain in the world where he was still living. As long as we were working him, there was still, to his wife, a chance. "I didn't see anything suspicious. Just human. All too human."

We discussed all the ways people wrap themselves in denial, refusal, obliviousness. "And," I pointed out, "you saw her collapse when we stopped. She'd been holding all that back, keeping the fear and sadness at bay, hoping against hope there was something to be done."

I thought of all the similar questions I'd asked Jen twenty years ago, as a curious, inexperienced rookie. *You don't know until you know.* I have long forgotten how strange it all felt. I remind myself that death isn't a normal occurrence in most people's routine. Remaining open to the mysteries of the world keeps me from losing sight of the humans I'm honored to serve. Keeping connected to our shared humanity prevents callousness and sloppiness in my treatment of our patients.

//

I leave you with this: Police officers join the force with notions of law and order. Paramedics want to perform prehospital, advanced lifesaving treatments. Firefighters want to, well, you know, fight fire and shit. We are public safety responders who have simplistic job descriptions that expand (explode) to encompass a vast array of complex, messy, intractable social issues—few of which we get training on. We all want to help people, but we get little true instruction for what that means. The hands-on and on-the-job training we receive is often random and bumbling, without formal or sanctioned context and follow-through. Often the inculcation of cultural mores carries more weight than applied learning. Meanwhile, we are the ones tasked with helping the sick, scared, sad, violent, and desperate in extreme and acute moments of crisis. We confront and are confronted with radically unstable, volatile people and situations. Lives hang in the balance. It is an incredible honor and a thorny challenge. We owe ourselves and our citizens our best and brightest minds.

5
THE HEART REMAINS A
LONELY HUNTER

THE FIRST TIME I RODE OUT-OF-RANK AS CAPTAIN FOR A SHIFT, WE RESPONDED to a call for shortness of breath. We marched through the house until we found our caller, a lady in the upstairs bedroom. She was propping her husband against the wall with her body, holding the phone to her ear with her shoulder. She said he'd been complaining of not feeling very well. The man looked at me, his eyes bulging with panic. He managed a few garbled words but was unable to respond to my questions coherently. Within seconds, he went limp, then unresponsive. I dragged him from the bedroom to the hallway floor, knocking over a linen hamper and an end table, and we began to work him.

We did CPR for forty-five minutes, with the wife right next to us. She alternated wailing for him and imploring us to stop death. The man did not rise again.

It was early September, a warm day, and I was sweating while we worked. I sweat a lot. The poor woman kept interrupting her cries to offer me a towel to wipe away the sweat. That day, and many others since, my gloves filled with sweat as I did CPR, sweat ran down my face and dripped onto the patient's chest and face, sweat rolled down the trench of my spine into the crack of my ass, pooling in my drawers. I felt it whenever I shifted. I lifted my arm to adjust the IV bag, and rivulets of sweat rolled out of my gloves and down my arms, splashing the patient. There is little grace working a patient in the field.

At the end, when we loaded him onto the canvas and maneuvered down their narrow stairs, through their house to the stretcher, knocking furniture everywhere, fighting hard to keep ourselves upright and the patient's wires attached, then bumped down their walk to the ambulance, and worked him all the way to the STAB (pronounced "stayb," short for stabilization) room of the ER, we had kept him biologically alive. That is a small victory. He wasn't dead, yet.

But: he had said his final words—to me, incoherently, in their bedroom. There would be no recovery. He was no more. Two kids were returning from the third day of the new school year as we wheeled their father to the ambulance. The mom and kids and whoever else in the family circle would be able to gather around his bedside, amid the expensive machines doing essentially the tasks we had—filling the lungs and pumping blood—and they would talk, pray, cry, then say goodbye to him. He would likely hear none of it. Certainly, he wouldn't respond to any of their words. He was alive, but gone.

We had forestalled death enough for them to watch him go. For that family, this was the slim solace we could offer.

//

If I have a heart attack while typing this, I'm a goner. I'm alone at home right now. Later today or tonight, my family will find me sprawled cold across the keyboard, the dogs looking guilty. This is a crucial distinction: if I have been down (without a pulse and without respirations, no oxygen to brain, blood, and tissues) for even a few minutes, the chance of functional recovery is slight. If I have been down ten minutes or more, I am a corpse. When I discuss working people or calling them dead in this book, these distinctions are, for us, implicit. We can tell that, empirically, someone is beyond return, but we might still perform CPR if it's possible—for the family, as an intercession between living and dead.

If I have a heart attack when my family's home, they will call 911 (and begin CPR, I hope). I've tried to foster an anti-panic reflex in my daughters: *You are allowed ONE scream, then figure out what you need to do. You can't save yourself while you're screaming. Shit happens: adjust and respond to it.* I hope they would stay focused and whale on my chest until a fire truck and an ambulance both responded. The rig will likely arrive several minutes ahead of the ambulance (unless the medics happen to be driving nearby: timing and chance are always factors).

The firefighters will assess me, find that I have neither pulse nor respiration. If I'm not cold and stiff, they will drag me bodily from the couch to the floor—shoving the coffee table away and knocking over the stack of bills I intended to get to—and they will begin proper CPR. The crew will take turns doing chest compressions and ventilating me, three men and women crowding over me, while a fourth—in the uncommon chance we have full staffing—will search for identification and medical information, or try to calm my family while obtaining pertinent medical info. Most shifts, two of us do the work while the third gathers information, or all three of us work and then we try to collect information later. While one is pressing hard against my chest like a piston, up and down, the other will insert a long plastic tube to secure my airway, then attach our BVM and supplemental oxygen, squeezing the bag every six seconds to get oxygenated air into my lungs, bloodstream, and brain. If I have choked on food or vomited or my throat has filled with blood or bile, they will have to address that, too. They will attach the defibrillator and shock me—*if* the machine finds a shockable rhythm. If no shock is advised, they will continue manual compressions. The medics will arrive and attach their EKG monitor.

If I threw a clot or had an aneurysm, or the wrong type of heart attack, there will be no rhythm to grab. I will be done, despite everyone's best efforts. If I have a viable heart rhythm, the medics will inject a range of drugs into me while the firefighters continue doing CPR and/or using the AED to shock some sense into my heart. The three primary IV drugs, besides saline solution, which keeps the volume up in the bloodstream, are epinephrine (increases blood flow to vital organs), sodium bicarbonate (lowers acidity in the blood), and calcium chloride (helps the heart beat more powerfully). These push and prod the system into motion; then offset or counteract the gasses that build quickly in the bloodstream when one's blood stops moving through the pipes. "Heavy blood" is not a good thing to have.

At some point, if I seem credibly not-dead, the medics will make the decision to move me from my floor down to the ambulance. I'm not a large fellow, but it will take three to five people to maneuver my limp, dead-weight body through the turns and stairs of our house. It's not as simple as throwing the patient over your shoulder and running. Unlike at the funeral where I might soon be the centerpiece, carrying a patient out of most places does not afford six pallbearer-like helpers. One at the head, one at the feet, one trying to stick closely behind, holding the various machines and wires aloft. This is why we work with the paramedics: many tasks must happen concurrently during a cardiac arrest, too many for just the two of them, and certainly more than one can do while the other drives the ambulance.

To get me from the floor of whatever room I collapsed in to the stretcher and ambulance, they will have to work hard but delicately. Someone will carry the oxygen bag and guard the cannula snaking from the O_2 cylinder to the mask on my face, while also trying to keep my intubation device in place. Someone will also have to control the medics' bulky, heavy, and essential monitor. Further, the multiple wires connected to the EKG's twelve leads cannot be tangled or pulled loose. The IV line will be tucked somewhere to prevent it from getting ripped from my arm as they move me. Someone will have cut my shirt and pants apart to expose flesh for the EKG's sticky pads.

It's likely that in the efforts to manipulate my unresponsive body around corners, over furniture, down or up flights of stairs, the IV and the O_2 will be pinched off at some point. If they get tangled or dislodged, I won't receive brain-saving oxygen, or the medics won't be able to see if I still have a rhythm. And I'll bleed profusely from the open hole in my arm.

Also, someone will be trying to continue CPR as they lug me through my house.

It is a crowded, clumsy, and delicate process to get an unresponsive person from place to place, even before we confront the daily mess of people's lives, the piles of kids' toys and laundry stacked on the stairs. If the family is present, there's the added aspect of their emotional response, their fears and worries and panic and questions. We try to minister to them as best we can, but we tend to give terse, brusque updates while working the patient. Often, we are providing the mitigating barrier between the old life (the patient was alive and seemingly well) and the new one (patient is unresponsive and might never come home alive). This brutally disorients the families as the event unfolds. And we do our best to revive the patient no matter what is happening behind or beside us.

So, if I am the patient: Out in the ambulance, they'll run more tests on me before heading to the ER. All the while the firefighters will be doing CPR and breathing for me. The window for functional survival is small. There is much that can and *must* be done before driving to the hospital. Explicitly, if the medics simply chucked me in their bus and drove me to the hospital to "save time," that 10 percent per minute loss of brain function would reach its limit: *tempus fugit et vita brevis.* So, we work our patients on the floor, then in the ambulance. Generally, if I'm going to come back, the first rounds of compressions or the first shock or two will do it. Then, I'll be very brittle—literally dangling between life and death—and they'll have to continue breathing for me. Even if I regain a pulse, I may never recover actual consciousness.

//

Cardiopulmonary resuscitation keeps circulating good, oxygenated blood to the brain; chest compressions move the blood and ventilation keeps oxygen in the body. CPR is literally using my hands from the outside of your chest to simulate the heart's beat and keep the blood flowing. If the blood flows, the brain keeps its oxygen level closer to stable, fewer tissues die, and the body has a chance. Every minute a person is down is a 10 percent deficit against their functional recovery. After ten minutes without blood flow or breathing, the chance of regaining vitality and consciousness is essentially nil. There is a large, often horrible, expanse between living and dead.

Performed correctly, CPR does violence to the body. For elderly patients, it is standard to break multiple ribs—one of several reasons CPR is not recommended, and frankly not intended, for the aged. Old people whose hearts stop have generally reached the end of their allotted time, or there are too many illnesses working against an aged bodily system. It is not the same as a correctable cardiac issue for a forty-year-old. This is why I continue to encourage everyone to have end-of-life discussions. I have done futile, gratuitous, near-sacrilegious compressions on so many frail old people because their families could not and would not "upset" them with a frank planning discussion. For many reasons, people avoid honest last-stages conversations, or frank planning discussions for the eventuality of death. It *is* scary and hard to face an imminent or unknown demise, but once we accept someone will die or is dying (as we all must do), we can help them articulate what they want at their end; we can be present with them and help see them off, with clear albeit teary eyes. Fighting against the inevitable robs us of grace. Denial sets us all up to suffer.

Because it will happen, death. And then you'll call us, we'll show up, there will be a warm body and no DNR/DNI. And so we must start our very intrusive (very futile) ministrations. It feels like we are violating their corpses, and it spares no one any pain. Denial is the beast that bites twice: it makes you avoid what you fear, but spares neither of you, then haunts and taunts you for falling for its con.

Even for younger men, the force of an effective compression will cause a tangible "snap" of rib cartilage or the ribs themselves. Sustaining a life at one hundred compressions per minute for ten to thirty minutes in the room where we find the patient, on the floor where we've dragged them so we can have a (somewhat) open work space, and while the medics run a rapid gamut of tests and meds on the patient—that's hard, violent work. Stiff back, straight arms, fingers overlapping in center of sternum, pressing down two inches with the heel of the hand, then releasing to allow for better chest recoil: that's CPR.

And it works, or can work, provided the person's had the "right" sort of heart attack. If there's an embolism or a chronic blockage or simply a wrong electrical failure, the person is dead. If there's internal bleeding, all we do by pumping is hasten the blood flow from arteries into the body cavity. But for the correct electrical failure, CPR can and does work.

With a heavy person, we have to exert more force to get through the girth, both muscle and fat, to reach the heart, but to do that we also have to overcome the poor angle we're working at, the massive body and limbs, the thick neck. There is so much bulk and heft that absorbs our compressions that we can barely squeeze the heart at all. Given how taxed the heart is from keeping an enormous person going, the chances are paltry that we will achieve a positive outcome.

With a baby, it's the opposite: such a tiny little body, using just the thumbs to tap-tap-tap away. Pressing firmly but gently on the frail chest, its ribs like twigs.

"Hands-only CPR" is now recommended for the lay public. It makes sense. People are understandably squeamish about putting their lips to strangers. Press hard in the center of the chest, repeatedly, and the blood might continue flowing until an AED arrives and the medics can ventilate and aggressively push their battery of drugs. Also, over the past twenty years, ongoing research has found that patients were getting *over*respirated during significant events. The person doing the compressions was pulsing up-down-up-down over and over, one hundred per minute. The BVM person was only supposed to ventilate every six seconds, but working in proximity, there was a tendency to speed up the respirations, triggered by the pneumatic chest-thumping fifteen inches away. Think of the kids' game of patting your head while rubbing your stomach: proprioceptive confusion. We would overinflate their lungs, causing air backups and infections. *Simmer down with that oxygen, folks* was the gist of the protocol change.

//

I have walked into calls where someone *is* having "the big one." But because they recognized the pain, responded to their own distress (or let a partner call for them), and were lucky to be in a city where responders (when called) can arrive promptly, we found them in grave distress, started oxygen, carried them out to the ambulance, and helped the medics start IVs, medications, and stabilization attempts. Some of these patients have waited even a few minutes too long, and, despite our attempts, they died right in front of us. (Like the man I described at the outset.) I've had others: someone talking to us, clearly in significant distress, who insists on walking himself out. He stands, the change in position drops his blood pressure, he looks stunned, briefly, and falls (dead) to the floor in front of us. And we go to work.

After the first time, when the medics let the patient walk out and then frantically called us to help them mid-transport, on the side of Interstate 35, to do compressions and ventilate and assist with suctioning, IVs, and the rest, if I see someone showing the hallmark signs of an imminent cardiac arrest, I take it very seriously. I don't let them stand and walk; we carry them; we are prepared to start working them; it is a critical call. If I'm wrong, no harm. When I'm right, it has meant the difference in keeping someone alive. The textbooks try to describe the signs, but until it happens, it's abstract and conceptual. When it happens in front of you, it snaps you to attention. I can tell which of the newer medics have witnessed it and which have not, by how seriously they take the nonverbal cues.

//

My first CPR came my first month on the rigs. It was a friend's grandfather. The old man, his wife, and their adult granddaughter were having dinner when he dropped at the table. We found him on the kitchen floor, his wife and granddaughter standing over him, frozen in shock. We dragged him from under the table into the living room. We checked him for a pulse, respiration, reaction. Nothing. We began doing CPR. Several minutes into the cycles of compressions and breathing for him, I glanced around the room, taking in details, seeing family photos all over, then coming back to one picture in particular. It seemed familiar, but no, I thought, lots of kids look alike.

I kept doing compressions, trying to get a steady rhythm, then looked around the room again, back at the little boy in the photo and remembered why the photo seemed familiar: It was my buddy's son. I'd seen the same school portrait at his house. I studied the gray, slack face. So this must be his grandpa. Crunched ribs, air in stomach, boatload of meds shot into his thickening blood: the revered grandfather who had been a prominent Black civic leader in Minneapolis. Dead beneath me. No shockable rhythm. He'd had "the big one."

We worked him hard nonetheless, with his granddaughter and his wife standing right there, and my buddy's son staring down at us from the wall. I wondered if they knew too: if they could tell that this was the end, that there's no negotiating with death like this? Or if it's such a shock that they just wanted him to pull out, since that's what we hope—despite a deeper sense of truth, we hope for miracles. I was so new then, I understood so little.

I identified profoundly when I read Michael Morse's lines in *EMS by Fire: The Making of a Fire Medic*: "Our patient remained pulseless during transport, and we continued CPR all the way, truly believing that we would get her back. It was the first and last time I did CPR on a newly deceased person, thinking without a doubt that she would regain respirations and a heartbeat, walk out of the ambulance, and hug her husband . . . She was declared dead at 8:30."

So it goes, and goes, and goes. I hesitate to say how many people have walked out of the hospital after we have attempted resuscitation:

it would be a grim, small number. The positive spin is *Wow, we were able to give even these few people another chance!*

//

A month or so after that first CPR, we were cleaning up after a car fire when we caught a call for a baby not breathing. Those are calls everyone hauls ass for—driving near-recklessly to get to the child. The family was Hmong and spoke no English. The distraught mom was holding the limp little girl, perhaps eighteen months old. A cop had arrived ahead of us and was trying to do mouth-to-mouth, frantically and awkwardly, while the mom clutched her daughter. The child's lips were stained blue. We stepped in, taking the kid from mom and officer. His lips were also blue-stained, fainter than hers.

No one could give us any relevant information on her, so we raced down the stairs and jumped into the ambulance as it arrived. I can't remember whether we spoke or if I just grabbed the child from the mother and officer. It's been twenty years. The medics had my back-seat partner and me continue compressions and ventilations (not mouth-to-mouth . . .), while they tried to get the IV going and figure out what was going on. Healthy children don't just die, certainly not from cardiac arrest. So, possibly, choking or some respiratory issue; or accidental poisoning. Perhaps whatever was tinting the lips blue was the root, but she was in a ceremonial outfit, and none of the pantomime and communications gave any indication that the family found her lip color disturbing or unexpected. Maybe an attempt at a cultural remedy for an illness. There were no signs of trauma. Her round face wasn't distended or discolored. She was small, warm, and lifeless.

It was a tense, crowded space in the back of the ambulance. Little kids have such small veins that the medic had to use the intraosseous gun. The way he fumbled, it was clear he hadn't used it much. And this was an infant. I'd never seen one deployed, but I was right there as he drilled the needle into her tiny shin bone. Once it was in, they had IV access and pumped a range of meds into her, without success. The cop popped his head in, now concerned he'd poisoned himself giving mouth-to-mouth. The language barrier with the family didn't assuage his worries. The medics told him it didn't look like poison, but he could follow up once we reached the ER—and in the future to use a mask.

We continued to work her down to the STAB room, with no change or improvement in her condition. The ER staff took over and, within seconds, we were dismissed. We stood idly on the periphery of the growing STAB team, peering over shoulders and around backs to see the tiny figure strapped onto the full-sized gurney. It was a horrendously absurd contrast. Then, not being lost, with things yet to do, we turned away and returned to our world.

The ride back to the station was somber. The utter absence of details and information was vexing. Before the captain could follow up with the ER staff, the red phone rang. He hung up and said, "Hey, kid, you know where Station Fifteen is?"

I nodded from where I was on my knees, restocking our med bags. "Well, get going. Fifteen's lost one and you're going there for the rest of the shift."

And so began my first tramp. No warning, no preparation: one minute, we'd been washing hose and airing out our turnout gear, then we were flung into this tiny apartment where no one spoke English and I took a dead child out of her mother's arms. We immersed ourselves utterly for thirty minutes, gaining no purchase against death. Then the ED kicked us clear and took over. Before I could restock our supplies and wrap my head around the details—blue lips, ceremonial outfit, freaked-out cop, nervous medic with a bone drill, the small round kid motionless and flaccid—I was sent out to cover at another station. I was a body for the department, detailed wherever the city was short.

Station 15 was largely a retirement station then, the crews on both Engine 15 and Truck 7 quite veteran and salty. It was very slow, a staid residential neighborhood; very unlike 5s. I sat amid the old men, ignored, and pondered the call. No one at this station knew or cared about the dead child. I had no one I could talk to, no one to share my feelings about the baby, the scene, the prickly details. I was alone with strangers. Then the shift ended and I drove home.

The kid didn't make it, and we never learned more than that.

I add a coda, as several early readers have struggled with this vignette. What I am trying to share with you is not simply the sad call. A baby dying suddenly is a brutal tragedy. I am not wondering if we could have done more to save the child. We worked hard and well together. We did all we could. This is a vibrant (tragic) example of what this job puts us through: not simply the hard call, working the tiny dead child; not the details of distraught family and crowded ambulance and raw intimacy of fighting death for a human body; not the jarring contrast between what tragedies are occurring in an apartment or in the ambulance, then stepping out into daylight and everyday living.

I'm asking the reader to consider what it's like: to carry the weight of that lost child and her family, with no resolution, no positive outcome, and to continue my work shift, then to find myself alone among a crew of jaded strangers who are more concerned that I kick in five bucks toward a dinner I don't eat than learning anything about me. And I go home to my family in the morning, hold my young daughter close. What can I say? Some shifts, we see multiple deaths. Most every shift, we encounter suffering, grief, fear, pain, loss. How can I explain to anyone what this job does to us, when one single call is too disturbing for some readers to bear?

//

The first successful CPR save I had was vivid. (Spoiler alert: this is also not a happy tale.) A nice man dropped in front of his whole family. It was a birthday or anniversary, everyone was gathered. We got there and worked him, and worked him, and worked him. The medics kept furrowing their brows as they studied the monitor. I don't understand the EKGs enough to know which peaks or valleys are hopeful and which indicate fatality. All the while we worked: CPR and the AED delivering one, then two, then three shocks, then more, a fourth and a fifth. More shocks than I've ever done on one patient. We had the airway inserted in his throat, we were breathing for him. It felt like forever. We had to swap out O_2 cylinders. And the family was right there, forming a wall of stricken faces around us. I couldn't tell if we were doing placebo ministrations: providing the family a brief delay before the horrible reality that this beloved member of the family—husband, father, uncle, brother—had taken his last breath. But the AED kept telling us to shock him—there was an actionable rhythm there somewhere, and so we worked him, CPR punctuated by shocks. The medics kept staring at the monitor, trying to decipher what the bouncing or still electrodes implied.

And then, *Bing!* We had a faint pulse. The medics shouted with surprised glee. We kept breathing for him, hustled him out to the ambulance, and hauled ass to the hospital. He was trying to breathe on his own when we left the STAB room. We'd succeeded!

It felt awesome. *Fuck you, Mr. Death!*

Our next shift, we followed up to check on his recovery, and when the EMS director called back, we learned that he'd done so well that the hospital had moved him out of the ICU.

Hooray! We were joyous—for the family and the dumb luck of finally having a successful save.

Except: He'd come out of sedation without someone monitoring him, had started gagging on the breathing tube, had extubated himself, then, essentially choked to death on his own secretions. "Complications from heart attack" is likely what the official report said. No one at the hospital would say different. It happens. That was a kick in the throat. Poor man; poor family.

And poor us. The profound range of futility, failure, frustration we experience—even on "good" calls—can put a dour filter over our perspectives. Doctor Terrence Holt writes in *Internal Medicine*: "There is a pure and uncomplicated pleasure in taking a patient who is minutes away from death and dragging him out of darkness into light . . . The problem, of course, is that sometimes you fall short of that goal. Too often, we're able to rescue somebody from death, but can't quite bring him back to life. People get stuck in that horrible twilight in between."

This hard truth can leave us jaded, self-protectively cynical, or resigned to ubiquitous death. Again I suggest this is the crux, the sweet spot, the essence of this job: How can we open our hearts to so much relentless loss and not be lost ourselves?

Since May 2000, I've done CPR hundreds of times, with scant positive outcomes. That's largely because only certain types of cardiac events can be reversed by compressions and shocks and medications. We still try for everyone we can. It is as incredibly intimate as it is rote. Several—the majority, actually—of my successes have been due to a patient's respiratory failure, not cardiac. Meaning, even though they present the same—unresponsive, no pulse, no breathing—respiratory arrests have better chances of being reversed, and CPR provides the oxygenation and stimulation to restart the respiratory system, which restarts the cardiac system.

I once had an argument while working someone with my dear friend and former captain, Rita Juran. This was right across from Station 14, and we arrived within a minute of the call. There had been a domestic incident and the adult son had stepped in. Someone had been shot, and now there we were, trying to raise the dead. I kept whispering to Rita (she was the boss; I was her durgan), "We don't work traumatic deaths." And she kept responding, "We don't *know* for sure. *Maybe* he had a heart attack. We want him to have a chance." Away we worked, ventilations, compressions, back and forth we argued. I pointed at the blood spreading from his chest: "He got shot at close range. His heart got attacked—by a bullet." Rita shook her head. "We don't know. Maybe the bullet missed the important organs."

The man was dead. The bullet had ripped through his insides. Nothing could revive him. The only thing to save him would have been avoiding the argument. We are trained and inclined to give everyone a fighting chance. We enter, find a warm body, and we go to work. Both are true: he was dead; there was no harm in trying. It is often futile, but we try. Degrees of dead matter: a warm body versus a cool body versus a cold body. Type of death: sudden cardiac event or systemic failure from disease or illness. Witnessed or found later. When in doubt, we work the person. Deciding not to can be more difficult, actually. Because doing compressions and breathing into a corpse gives us a sense of purpose, an action against futility.

We have had people who presented as dead who were actually "just" deeply unresponsive because their alcohol intake had shut down their respiratory system. There wasn't a shockable rhythm when the AED evaluated the heart's electrical currents, or the medics scrutinized their monitor's readings, because it wasn't a heart issue: they'd drowned themselves in booze, essentially. With enough forced ventilation and cardiac stimulation, the person's system fought through the alcohol's depressants and the person came back. From "dead" to awake and talking . . . We might joke about a faux save, but the truth is, had we not worked these unresponsive, pulseless people, they would have remained dead.

//

I recently pulled a man from a house fire. I can't say I saved him, because he never regained consciousness. It wasn't a "win." The toxic smoke and severe heat took him in seconds; he was pulseless and unresponsive when I grabbed him from the bedroom floor. But: we knocked down enough fire for me to find him and get him out. The truckies got him to the front yard, then performed aggressive CPR. They helped the medics load him into the ambulance and continued breathing for him. Together they worked him furiously to the hospital. We got his pulse back, but the effects of the smoke and heat were too much. He was brain dead, never to improve. He died the next day.

His family, though. We allowed them to gather by his bedside and say goodbye. And, while I'm bitter we couldn't save him, I understand he was already done in by the fire. It *does* matter that we preserved enough life for the family to be there with him. Too many families never even get that.

One of my former coworkers quit smoking after decades. He had a heart attack two days later and dropped in his backyard on a nice spring day. Fortunately, his wife was also a firefighter and their teen daughter was a level-headed kid. Both were home and heard him collapse. They did CPR on him until the nearby engine company arrived—ironically, with his brother in charge. Together his firefighter brother, firefighter wife, and his daughter, plus the rest of the crew, worked him. Prompt and efficient CPR, quick access to AED, the "correct" type of arrested heart, swift paramedic response—he got lucky, or, the system worked well for him that day, or it simply wasn't his day to die. I don't know. I do know that he is a retired firefighter who has happily lived twenty years after coming back from the dead.

6

THROWING ROCKS AT GOD

I HAVE WRITTEN SO FAR ABOUT THE HEAVY LOAD OF NON-EMERGENT MEDICAL issues and the dearth of fires. So it goes. This is the job, no matter how many packs of matches we scatter in the alleys . . . The stark reality is that we often operate within the shadow that death casts. We walk into a room and find horrible or banal deaths. I want to provide an understanding of what this work truly entails. Because, if I can help the readers recognize their own very human denial and avoidance of the inexorable facts of dying and death, I hope that will help all of us embrace the living *and* the dying. And, to understand the realities of illness, dying, and death is to begin to wrestle with how those of us who are immersed in it might carry—and struggle to carry—it.

Dispatch might initially say, "One with SOB" [shortness of breath] or "Difficulty breathing," and, in the short time it takes to load onto the rig and pull out of the station, updates it to "Caller says patient is unresponsive," then "Caller is afraid to go near the patient," then "Caller says they are cold to the touch," then "Caller refuses to touch the patient. Will meet responders outside."

These brief emendations provide an approximation of what is to come. (Nothing good.)

The details will vary, but absent a contributing factor like alcohol or a pinched larynx (or a penetrating trauma from a bullet or a sword), people who spontaneously stop being alive generally have something very wrong with them. The number of people whose cardiac issue can be resolved by CPR and the AED (defibrillator, "heart start" machine) is pretty small. We don't know until the medics attach their monitor, so we work everyone who might be viable. A precious few come back. Others, who might seem "better" or more recoverable, never do. Many have regained a pulse but never full consciousness. They are *alive* in a technical sense, but nothing resembling the people you know and love. They will spend time on ventilators until the family can say goodbye, if that.

I have also participated when a person was sinking into death, and we were able to drag them back to the living. We've responded to people who called for help literally with seconds to spare. We arrive, assess that they're about to die, and help the medics keep them living while hauling ass to the ER. If they're lucky, emergency surgery for stents to clear blocked arteries will cease the imminent death situation. If not, this wasn't your day—or, it was your day, your final one.

I have on several occasions looked into a person's eyes as he struggles to express a sudden terrified, desperate recognition that something is terribly wrong with him—the circle of consciousness is closing swiftly—and as his eyes widen in panic, and maybe he fumbles a few words, inside, his heart stops pumping and he promptly drops. And we go to work on him right there. Most of those calls have been fatal—the "Big One" from which there is no recovery. (And it is most often a *he*, as men tend to ignore or deny their growing health emergencies.)

I have had many, many fatalities. Hundreds of the dead: on floors, in beds, couches, bathrooms, living rooms, basements, attics, cars, garages, freeways, sidewalks, backyards, woods, restaurants; anywhere; everywhere. We stand before death—the dead—and absorb the details, the somber facts and the tragic nuances and the mildly absurd. As a captain, I make the declaration when someone is dead. DOA. Unworkable. The official requirements for "Obvious death" are rigor mortis or lividity; cold and stiff; decay; decapitation or vivisection. If it's borderline, we'll work the person until the medics arrive, but once we start, we must continue with the process, no matter how futile.

In some cases, the person's respiratory system rebounds with an advanced airway and a few blasts of air. Others, all the winds in the world won't fill their sails again.

We also can lose focus on the human aspect of these scenes. That sounds odd, but it's true. Our focus is on our patients, and secondarily (tangentially, peripherally, belatedly), on those around them. Someone calls 911 in a panic; Dispatch sends us hustling to help; we arrive, rush into the room, and find—someone quite dead. The paramedics join us. We look at the deceased person. We look at each other. There is nothing medical or mechanical for us to do. Either we cut the medics loose, or they clear us. Procedurally, one of us must notify and await the police. The others simply turn and leave.

But the witnesses? People whose family member or beloved partner has just been discovered dead? These people are in shock. They might be literally confused and are certainly psychologically and emotionally in upheaval. Smothered in denial, because the alternative is unfathomable.

None of the medical, or the biological, facts matter to someone who finds a friend, lover, parent, auntie, grandparent, or child unresponsive on the floor, stiff in bed, slumped in a chair. It does not compute. Humans exist in the realm of the living. The sudden presence of the not-living resists synthesis. It's existential: no longer *is* but *was, were.* It will seem unreal, surreal, like a very bad dream. The mind might be processing what it is seeing, but the emotions are several steps behind. This lag time exposes our human vulnerability like almost nothing else.

"Save my child!"

"Save my husband!"

"Save him!" the person wails.

"I'm so very sorry," I reply. "He is dead. There is nothing we can do."

"SAVE HIM!"

"I'm sorry."

"Please help. *Please,* save him!"

Save. We often recognize there's no hope, but the bereft person does not know that—cannot yet accept it. The human factor on these calls: the desperation, fear, tremendous emotional upheaval, panic, uncertainty . . . it's a lot to confront, particularly while making a clear-eyed assessment of the patient. We become the recipients, the targets, of the bystanders' panic, fear, anger, and grief. We are grief eaters.

Decreeing someone dead is less cut and dried than it seems. Even *dying* is rooted in the fleeting present and still-living. We are not playing god by any means, but it's a weighty statement. The complications arise from the immensely grieving family: they demand we do any- and everything to recover their beloved. It is not the deceased who is in limbo: it is their family. Their helplessness in the face of sudden death is brutal.

"Do something! Do something! Don't just stand there, damn you: *DO SOMETHING!"*

Dead is dead.

"I'm sorry."

It is easy—very human—to erect defensive walls against that cha- otic emotionality, resulting in a broken connection to the very human scenario playing out before us. Meaning, we walk in, see a corpse, and say flatly, "She's dead." It's true: this person, a stranger to us, is no lon- ger alive and will never rise again, no matter our efforts and intentions. Our inaction is a rupture of hope, a declaration of finality, a savaging of denial.

"Do something! Help her!"

Dead is dead. "I'm very sorry."

Maintaining the balance between compassion and fact is the challenge.

There are times we all know the person is not coming back, but we work the call as a comfort for those left behind. As long as the corpse is somewhat warm and there's a way to do so, we will work the person. Whether palliative or placebo, I don't know. If we choose to work some- one who is clearly dead, if only to provide the family with a buffering illusion that reality is not what it seems, there is no true harm done. (Essentially, we're there; the body's right there; we won't make it *worse*, not any *more* dead. We'll provide the compassionate distraction of ac- tion.) But there are rules, especially for the paramedics. Once we start the process, we have to see it through, and they have to justify the use of resources on a clearly, objectively, biologically nonviable corpse.

Maybe they might surprise you? You never know. Miracles happen.

Sure, but the equation flows the other way: seldom, very seldom, do people come back. *Dead is dead* with very few, rare exceptions. Of course, we each hope our dear person will be that exception. Too, most civilians only know "emergency medicine" from TV, where all manner of ludicrous revivals occur every episode. For a medical emergency (respiratory or cardiac issue, stroke or embolism) we refer to the *na- ture of illness.* For a traumatic emergency, we consider the *mechanism of injury.* I understand it matters little to you how or why your person stopped breathing, but for us, there are significant differences between choking on a piece of steak (frequently resolvable), having an unwit- nessed stroke (less resolvable), going unresponsive from a medication or drug (depends on dose and time down), or a gunshot to the head or chest (generally deadly), or the violent internal trauma of a high-speed collision (also deadly).

//

A man was reclining on his couch, watching TV and enjoying a bowl of fresh raspberries. He choked. His partner found him unconscious and called us. We worked and worked, but we could not overcome his clogged airway. We did compressions, we used all manner of suction devices, but he was beyond our grasp. Our compressions jolted his body, sending the liquid in every direction. As the minutes passed and the futility loomed, I kept staring at the reddish juice spilling from his mouth, the small, viscous seeds. It was nearly incomprehensible. *Berries,* I kept thinking. *Fucking berries.*

We will work someone when we can, as I say, but we cannot ignore the likely causes and the consequences. Someone who died overnight is clearly deader than someone who died an hour ago. Both are dead. Neither is coming back. For the family, I know, it is horrible and profound to see the sudden mask of death covering your dear one's face.

The presiding doctors and administrators have perfect vision from the safety of their plush rooms. They are not standing before the distraught families. Too many calls we simply cannot and do not work. It is very anticlimactic, for us, and horribly, almost cruelly, jarring for those experiencing the fact of bereavement.

Sometimes, though, I'll see a clearly dead body on the bed, or chair, or floor, and turn to the person trembling at the doorway to confirm, to inform—or to lacerate the hope and denial—by stating, "I'm sorry. He's dead. He's gone. There's nothing to be done."

It is abrupt, and final. This is not easy. I have been a captain since 2007, responsible for decreeing *Dead.* I am the face and voice of death. There is no getting around it. I say the word, *Dead.* I manifest it. I breathe death into their world. And then I stand there, dumbly, while they sputter, scream, and cry, and the body of their person lies between us.

And while the survivor's shock racks them, I might be very aware that the person has been dead since before we even started our shift, that we're burning whatever we were cooking because we rushed to this call and neglected to shut off the stove. Our lunch is ruined and that won't bring the deceased back.

But I'll stand by, stolid and quiet, absorbing their grief, witnessing their sorrow, until police arrive and take over. Our lunch will wait.

I will express condolences.

I will ask if there's anyone they want to call.

I will hold them as they cry.

I will not join their distraught wailing. It's horrible and tragic for the survivor. It is not so for us. Many now-dead people have been sickly, ill, actively dying for a while: we can see that from across the room. The discrepancy between the survivors' shock and what we are seeing can be jarring, disturbing, and frustrating (for us). We are less than strangers, and our shift continues after this call. It isn't good or bad, it just is. There aren't enough tears, our skin and souls aren't thick enough, to cry for every death we encounter. And we get plenty that take a piece of us with them into the grave.

Michael Morse writes in *EMS by Fire*: "I have learned through experience that giving in to their wishes against your better judgment does more harm than good and simply prolongs the pain and suffering of the living while disrespecting the remains of the dead. By acting professionally, with compassion and authority, the worst moments of a person's life need not be spent in a state of confusion, helplessness, and rage."

//

The people we encounter on our calls, the bystanders and family and friends: they are not clueless, not daft, not oblivious. They are fighting against something devastating, horrible, and unsparing. Death is permanent, and we cling to life so desperately. Humans traffic in hope and denial; we go to profound depths to maintain them. People blindly bet on hope, a sliver or a miracle, something, anything—really, they fight against the permanent stillness, the other side of that last breath. Most people believe the finality of death must be resisted, must be fought—as an expression of their love for the person, as well as the foundation of their lives. And then here we come, sudden brusque interlopers: "He is dead. I'm sorry for your loss." We were—we are—that finality.

Sometimes our steely resolve is armor against the messy, explosive grief of the newly bereaved. Will it kill me to humor their denial, their panic, their desperate clutching at hope? Of course not. But we are seeing and experiencing very different realities. And I have to keep working. My crew might have an even worse fatal call just around the corner. This is the tender balance. These are raw, complicated, emotionally fraught interactions, with a vast array of permutations and configurations—how the bereaved respond, as well as how we do. I said earlier that once I became accustomed to responding to "possible heart" calls and finding corpses, my default was to expect everyone to be dead. Roger Huder captures this in his fine memoir, *Gutter Medicine*: "I figured I was seeing someone die every time I went to work. Every third day of my life, I saw someone die. No wonder it was so easy to lose perspective."

When we bring critical cases into the STAB room with the paramedics, I like to hang on the periphery to watch. The staff is professional and very focused, controlled. Each new patient is a body on which they practice medicine—in both meanings of the verb. That is how the residents and interns learn. It is all in the service of the greater good: for one day their years of practice on unsavable patients might allow the "miracle" saving of some lucky person. Unlike the ED staff, we find people in their homes, surrounded by their interrupted lives, with distraught family, and we go to work right there. It is far more emotionally loaded. For us, we must balance the same cold clarity of the emergency room staff with a compassionate diplomacy for the family surrounding us.

We are trauma sponges: call after call, shift by shift, week by month by year, we absorb the boundless sadness and fear, the abuse, the blood and viscera, the sights and sounds and smells of tragedy and loss. There's no relief or release: it's just dying, death, loss. I get paid to help people. Do I get paid to absorb the survivors' sorrows? Do I get paid to inhale the first molecules of decomposition as I do superfluous compressions? Libraries have dozens of books and poems about the weight of a soul. What is the weight of grief?

//

We were returning from something abject late one night—a heroin overdose in a derelict, menacing household. Every adult in the place was scarred by decades of abuse of drugs or alcohol or both, no one appeared sober or functional, small children were neglected. There was also a long police call sheet for ODs, fights, threatened violence and assaults of neighbors, drug dealing, domestic abuse. The minor OD was the least disturbing thing going on in that house. On our drive back, we heard another crew across town catch a reported hanging.

It was quiet on the streets as we rumbled along, the rig's lights throwing brief sharp shadows along the lawns and houses. We weighed the range of suicides we'd had, calls where someone had slipped down to the basement, or up to the attic, out to the garage, into the bathroom, and stepped off the earth while his (the majority of these were men) family was unaware.

"That's cruel," the junior firefighter said. Taunting the survivors forever with the futile regret that *if only they'd found him . . . if only they'd opened the door, checked on him sooner . . .* the brutal weight of survivors' guilt.

We discussed the suicides who snuck away and died in private, those who left notes or just ghosted their dear ones. Which was worse, in terms of pain for the survivors? Reeling from the haunted knowledge that he died in another room while you were cooking, or that he was alone and sad and scared as he took his final breath? It is forever in one's heart and mind, this sorrowful unanswerable searching. Our consensus: it doesn't matter. None of that hairsplitting matters—one just cannot see that yet, not through the torrents of loss and pain.

Lives are obliterated. Death is death. As we backed the rig into the station and I looked out at the quiet, cold street before returning to my bed, I pondered: We just had a ten-minute conversation about the nuances of suicide, all the varieties we have encountered, and we objectively discussed these gradations and distinctions. There is no point in saying, "Suicide is bad. Don't do it!" because that's not how our job goes.

People *do* it. We get called. We enter the room or garage or basement or woods, and find whatever the aftermath may be. Sometimes we try to work the body, sometimes we simply turn away. Sometimes it's quiet, still, empty. Sometimes there is a spouse or entire family screaming and crying and shouting (at us, but not really *at* us: at the deceased, at death, at God or the devil. We're the ones in uniform, the ones tasked with solving problems. There are no solutions here).

I thought of the various suicide notes I've found, on both completed acts and foiled or self-aborted attempts: how the note is better than nothing, but the note is nothing of substance. Some letters are manic and incoherent, desperate and unhinged. Some are direct and contained. All fail. For nothing can explain the truth, which is never even true, just the momentary embrace of despair.

But those who leave no notes? They leave the worst mystery, the haunting *WHY?!* to echo for years and through lives. The act is the act. A permanent conclusion to a temporary problem. No words will explain away Thanatos sufficiently, but no words at all leave the bereft grasping after an eternal, illusive *Why.*

I didn't share that with my young crew. One firefighter had seen just one suicide, the other had three, the driver maybe five. Only one body of all of those had they worked, a gunshot that hadn't (yet) done its job. I wasn't sure how many I'd seen, how many I'd worked, how many more I'd stood over, staring at the damage and the cold body. Enough that only some of the bad ones stick? Enough that they bother me only occasionally? Enough that I don't give them too much thought? Enough.

This is our work. What we share, what we see, what we can talk about together. It is not a conversation I can have when I collect my kids from a sleepover, not a casual discussion with the other parents between gluten sensitivities and college fretting: which form of suicide seems *least* or *most* damaging to survivors.

Looking at my young crew that night—and on similar calls other shifts—I realize how protective I feel of them. I've been responsible for the lives and health of my crews for fifteen years now. I know they will continue to catch these calls; that they will sit in my seat at some point. I will be long gone. And they will be the ones who have lost track of the number of dead they'd seen. The circle, unbroken.

//

Early on, I worked for a captain who had completed his master's degree in social work and was soon to leave the rigs to be the department's counselor. His tone and demeanor suggested a socially awkward mortician, but he deeply cared and did yeoman's service for us. Our crew that year was two mid-forties men (one white, one part-Native, both straight and married) with nineteen years on; a mid-thirties white lesbian; and me, late thirties, white, married. My second daughter was in infancy, so most days I was a zombie from overnight feedings and diaper duty. No one else had kids, although we all had dogs and/or cats. "Furbabies" are not real children, but I humored them. I picked this rig in this area deliberately for the year after my daughter's birth, anticipating sleep dep on the home front and desiring a slower schedule at work.

It turned out to be one of the most productive and interesting EMS years I've had. We were in an affluent area, almost everyone had insurance, the "regular" calls that crews ran elsewhere were largely absent. The realities of class and comfort stood in stark contrast to what I'd seen at Station Five my first few years.

One particular morning, our rig was the Grim Reaper's caboose: four DOAs before noon, all natural causes. The shift started with a call for a person having trouble breathing. We arrived to find a young woman on the couch, where she'd been watching TV with her kids the night before. Her husband worked third shift and, upon returning, had assumed she'd fallen asleep in front of the tube. Her kids were lying on her, watching cartoons and eating breakfast, when one of them noticed she wasn't waking up.

And wasn't moving.

And was cold.

Mom had died in the night. The kids were playing on her body as if she were just napping. She was cold and stiff, dead for hours. We could do nothing for her. We remained in the house, mostly wrangling and distracting the young children until MPD arrived. We herded them away from the living room—away from their dead mother—and tried to sustain the illusion that the worst had not just befallen them. It seemed important to stall, buying them even a few more minutes before their worlds collapsed. The father was disconsolate, devastated. He rushed to the back bedroom—away from the kids—and we could hear him wailing and punching the wall. The oldest kids were awakening to what had happened, but the little ones were still unaware.

We stood in a line, making small talk and trying to distract the children, who were, naturally, curious why we were there and why their mommy wasn't waking up. Uncertainty and sleepiness gave way to rapidly spreading concern, fear, then grief. We tried to block her body from their view. Their father's shrieks and crying went unanswered, loud, raw, guttural sounds filling the awkward silence up front.

The police arrived and our captain briefed them: what we found upon arrival (dead lady on the couch), had we moved her (only her arm when we checked for pulses), did anything seem suspicious (no, just tragic). The father came into the kitchen and pulled his kids to him, telling them their mother was gone. He excused himself and ran to the back of the house. A door slammed, and we heard his screams, his wailing, his fists again punching the walls. We stood with the children for a few horrible minutes. The father came back, tears soaking his beard, and knelt before his children, his arms wide and shaking. They were huddled and crying together when we left.

We had just pulled back into the station when the tones struck. We raced out, our coffee and newspaper still untouched, and arrived to find an old man taking his final breaths. We stood by with the family as he passed. He had terminal cancer and his paperwork was in order, but one of the family had still dialed 911. We stood by, along with two paramedics, trying to be inconspicuous in that nakedly vulnerable room (another living room converted to a hospice suite, another rented hospital bed incongruously, horribly, stuffed into a room intended for hospitality and socializing). Another family facing the essence of human biology: life's process trumps gestures of faith, hope, denial; obliterates all by ending.

Returning from that call, we caught one to a house where an infant was found unresponsive. Calls like that, we fly. Race from the rig up the sidewalk and into the yard. From the curb we heard the young mother's wailing. We rushed up the stairs, through the living room, back toward the bedroom, following her sobs. She lay curled on the bed around a tiny, still, bundled child. The mother's face was distorted in naked, total loss. Inside the small house, her cries were searing. In the next room, a four-year-old son and the kids' father sat stonily on the couch, hugging each other and staring deep into the television screen. The dad was crying silently, rubbing his son's head.

An ER doc on the way to work had heard the call on his radio. He was first on scene. He indicated the baby was dead, mouthing "SIDS" to us grimly. Three police squads responded, clogging the street with their vehicles as they also raced up the steps and lumbered into the entry. The ER doc left. We explained to the cops what we'd found, that the doc said it didn't seem suspicious, and they cleared us to interview the mother and notify the medical examiner. Their son looked at us dumbly, then retreated into the television while his father silently sobbed, stroking the boy's head like a talisman.

As we drove away, the crew was silent. Not much to say. Then the captain looked around and asked if anyone wanted to debrief. (It was a new term in the fire service; he was trying to model good mental health. It was of course like having your grandma ask if you were getting laid.) We all shrugged. He asked again, looking at me, then added, "You know, I mean, it must be hard, harder for you, having kids and all . . ."

I stared at him. "We've had a dead mother, her kids literally *crawling* on her, a dead baby—the old guy with cancer was the *good* call! I don't think it takes having kids to feel that those were fucked-up situations . . . Dead dogs, dead babies—aren't those always B-A-D?"

The two senior guys were so inured to death, so jaded from twenty years of seeing it, that they did not have any connection to what we had responded to. It's a safety mechanism, a survival and mental health reflex, but it's also eerie. Their disconnect seemed like disinterest. Many veteran firefighters have echoed that: the less you see, the better. When we're new, it's always a big rush to get into the mix, to be right there in the heat of things. Plus, there is such pressure to prove we are studs, that we've got what it takes—that we are not afraid. We plunge in blindly. After a few years, the damage and trauma get wearying. Many senior guys won't go in if they don't have to. They *know* what's behind the door. Too, you can end up with senior guys chatting about vacation plans in the midst of a family's tragedy.

As Laurence Gonzales writes in *Deep Survival*: "Survival means accepting reality, and accepting reality takes a hard heart. But it is a strange kind of coldness, for it has empathy at its center." I hold this tension, this balance, deep in my heart and mind. Editing this book, I have more than twenty years on, too. I am scarred in similar *and* different ways from those two former senior guys. But I still go in. I still stay hands-on. In part, I like to walk the margin of adrenaline and chaos. But I believe in the job, in the weight and responsibility of leadership. Many of the old guys became slack or indifferent—or burned out. They hid behind their seniority and avoided engaging. I am fighting a battle in my head and heart against that mentality. I try to lead by example. I also try to protect my junior firefighters from the sharp horrors that await us. I reject the notion that we should toughen our newbies by shoving them into the fire (literal and traumatic).

//

The official phone rang as I was finishing our interrupted daily chores. A few minutes later, the captain came out of his office, shaking his head. It was the police, he said. They were suspicious about the husband of our dead lady. *"He wasn't grieving right"* was the thrust of it, so the cop asked if we'd noticed anything else suspicious.

"Else?" we asked, incredulous. The man's anguish had been crushed by the needs of his children. He had swallowed his grief, fear, and devastating loss in order to be present for his kids. This was the hardest moment of a person's life, yet it was seen by the cops as something else, and they went right to suspicion. Sure, many domestic fatalities are femicides committed by the husband or male partner, but there was absolutely nothing suspicious on that scene. A Black man's grief in the eyes of white cops was "suspicious." I was glad he had the alibi of being at work, or else the cops' "suspicion" and "instinct" could have led to the children's being taken away, made him a suspected murderer, cost him his job or life.

An hour later, we worked a full-code nursing home resident. The staff wasn't sure how long she'd been unresponsive or if she'd been ill or complaining of anything. She was a dead lady in a light blue gown in a nursing home. We pulled her onto the floor, started compressions and breathing for her. The AED did not find a shockable rhythm. The medics arrived. We rotated through multiple rounds of compressions while they injected the meds that could help, were she not beyond help. There were scant personal items in the room, not even photos taped to the institutional walls. We didn't know her name. This was an unresponsive elderly white lady with displaced dentures, pale and frail. She was gone before we arrived and never came back. We never had a spark of hope, of vitality. There was no circle of anguished family, no one begging her to fight, no one calling her name. She was frail and alone. She'd slipped away, unnoticed by anyone.

We worked her, rotely. There was no reason she did not have a DNR/DNI completed—other than denial and procrastination by the family. We were abusing her frail dead body, cracking ribs, intubating her. All of it: useless and gratuitous. There was blood, and saliva, and piss, and shit, and torn skin cooling by the minute. The medics called it finally, and we rose stiffly from the floor of the nursing home, packed out our bags, and returned to quarters.

I don't remember the rest of the shift, only how hard I hugged Annie and the kids when I got home the next morning. My love, gratitude, hunger, and fear for my family felt all-consuming. A dead baby should depress anyone with blood in their heart, but having a baby at home starkly reinforces how awesome and awful the game of life is. I couldn't put into words the submerged, throbbing emotions. I felt for that small family with a dead infant. I felt for the man dying of cancer, at home surrounded by his loving, heartbroken family. I felt for the old gal in the faded blue nightie, dying alone in the institutional machine. Most of all, I felt for that poor widower and his orphaned kids. The world will break us all.

7
BOYS DON'T CRY

EARLIER, I SAID WE FIREFIGHTERS ARE JUDGMENT-FREE ANGELS OF COMPAS-
sion and mercy, and—well, I didn't say that. Because we aren't.

We see people committing horrific crimes against their own humanity, mistreating themselves and, worse, their families. Particularly
their kids. We help people up from the gutter knowing full well we're
assisting them back to a cycle that ends in the gutter. We try not to make
judgments about how people live. But we see it. We go into houses,
rooms, apartments, cars, and we witness what is going on (or the consequences of what has been going on). We are official interlopers in the
everyday madness of humanity.

In our brief encounters, there often isn't time to get full context or
backstory. We find whatever we do and attempt to treat what we can.
Many folks are trying to get by, but they're struggling or failing. Some
people are profoundly screwed up, with no support network, no access
to or inclination to get help. There are myriad cultural, sociological,
chemical, and economic complications.

The ability to quickly make coherent a disparate, chaotic jumble of
sights, sounds, and characters is invaluable. Parsing a person's narrative
for pertinent, actual info requires a blend of sharp scrutiny and dispassionate empathy. Inferential acuity is not something the city tests for,
unfortunately. So, we show up, see what we see, and (try to) keep our
opinions to ourselves.

We definitely have opinions.

On scene, we muster a professional facade when confronting people's messes. (Saying "Eeeewwww! That's gross!" isn't encouraged. Nor
is "Why did you do *that*?!") The nature of the job is to be problem solv-
ers. Many of us act, or pretend, as if we have all the answers, which

is ludicrous. Mistaking decisiveness for omniscience is a simplistic and inaccurate conceit, too common in our work. It is instilled from the very start: *There is no one coming but you! Figure. It. Out!* This "decisive" mentality breeds a simplicity of perspective. *I would not do that. I would never find myself in this situation. You are in bad straits because of who you are.* And *If it's unfamiliar to me, it's flawed, incorrect, sinful.*

The persisting emphasis in emergency response on being "manly" and macho rewards, even demands, a certain type of person—not because these are empirical values but because that is the culture we have created, inherited, reinforced. Being aloof and stoic, being seen-it-all jaded: these defenses are not mutually exclusive to being caring and compassionate, but sometimes—too often—the aloofness either calcifies into, or is caused by, indifference or repulsion. A fear of others.

What we do not ask ourselves, frankly, is what props up *our* "normal." We don't examine what cultural components allow us to stand where we do, rather than on the other end of the interaction. Many of my coworkers who have come up through hard times, who aren't firefighters from the typical demographics, have a deeper understanding and appreciation of the complexities of life. But the vast wide middle: the white, male, and straight? They can absorb uncritically the most reductive stereotypes and never look beyond, or question, the superficial images.

When people who weren't white or male attempted to join the fire service, their outer differences were the first barriers. Wait, let's clarify: the racism and misogyny of the white firefighters, the administration, the union, and the civil service were the barriers. Was it merely superficial, the difference in "skin color" or gender? I argue that it was not. But in systems where conformity is emphasized and demanded, the limited understanding of sociological issues became a secondary barrier.

Can a crew of white men walk into any situation and objectively do the job well? Absolutely. Can these white men have done work to understand the historical, sociological, and cultural complexities that shape our society? Absolutely. Is it *likely* they have? Nope. There is very little incentive in America for the dominant culture to critically question its myths and construct.

Would a crew of all women, or of men and women of color, provide better treatment, solely based on race or gender? Nope. Might there be a better engagement, a swifter human connection, if the representatives of the city shared some resemblance to the people encountering those in uniform? Absolutely.

In the late 1990s, our former chief, Rocco Forte, pitched a vision to the mayor at the time, Sharon Sayles Belton (Minneapolis's first African American and female mayor), when he was negotiating to start hiring again, to get the department out from under *Carter v. Gallagher,* one of the longest-running federal hiring injunctions. If she would let him hire more firefighters, he would curb the ballooning overtime costs and diversify the department.

A word about Mayor Sayles Belton and the MFD: when she first met with the firefighters' union while campaigning, the greater number of those in attendance turned their backs on her as she spoke. Literally. *What can a Black woman say to us?!* She won the election. We earned her rightful scorn for years. I cannot exaggerate how petulant and contrary this profession has been.

A word about the MFD and its intractable racism: Beginning in the 1970s, because the MFD could not *stop being racist,* we (they) were not trusted to run the hiring process any longer. Due to this ingrained bias and recalcitrance, the department was placed under a hiring freeze as well as heavy city restriction on its hiring practices. Beyond the delusional dogma—*This profession is not for everyone: only the select few, those who do it correctly. Any change weakens the force*—the enduring hostility of white men on the job toward "outsiders" made it hard for diverse applicants to get hired. Again, the MFD had the longest-running federal hiring injunction due to the persistence of bias. Our profound resistance to equality cost us in myriad equally profound ways. More specifically, this was a job where women weren't *allowed* to apply for generations, and men of color were first barred from applying and then their applications were jetted into the trash. When only white men's applications were considered, guess what the workforce looked like?

A brief history lesson: In 1888, a formerly enslaved Black man, John W. Cheatham, joined the Minneapolis Fire Department, rising to the rank of captain. In 1907, he was in charge of (former) Station 24 in South Minneapolis. The brigade there was composed of Black men (because no white men would work with them). Actual segregation was the rule, and few Black men were hired over the decades. In 1944, a Black firefighter, Payne Calhoun, was fired as a probie—for wearing the wrong color of shirt. An investigation by the city council found multiple white men at stations around the city wearing noncompliant shirts but facing no discipline. The uproar forced the chief, Earl Traeger, to reinstate Firefighter Calhoun, but Calhoun declined, fearing he would be abandoned by his coworkers to die in a fire. From 1944 until 1971's court order, no nonwhite men were hired. In 1971, U.S. District Judge Earl R. Larson ruled that the MFD and the Minneapolis Civil Service Commission had violated both federal hiring laws and the equal protection clause of the Fourteenth Amendment in its discriminatory hiring practices (the city had essentially been siding with white firefighters who did not want to work or bunk with Black, Asian, Latino, or Native men).

Due to *Carter v. Gallagher* and the subsequent 1979 consent decree, the revamped civil service took over hiring from the department, and a priority was made to improve diversity (racial percentages). Affirmative action hires, quotas of various forms: none of these are bad if they produce positive results, especially if redressing historical inequalities. This department has made profound strides. And yet, but still . . . Many white men bemoaned these changes when I was a rookie, telling crybaby diversity "horror" stories—without acknowledging the definitive role *their* bigotry and cheating played in losing control of hiring. White men's tears fuel Fox News, but that's a mile away from realistic discussion of impact, equity, and justice.

People of color come to work not to "steal jobs" or to get free cable (no more than the white dudes do) but to do their jobs. They don't have an endgame of faking a workers' comp injury or fabricating a racial bias lawsuit. They don't expect or deserve to find horrific slurs scrawled in their boots or a noose in their locker.

But they did.

Women come to work not to wreck marriages or chase boys or husbands or fake injuries for payouts, but to do their jobs. They don't want, and certainly didn't sign up for, sexist banter; misogynistic attacks about incompetence, weakness, and cowardice; juvenile sexualized obsessions; being harassed, groped, or assaulted; finding vile obscenities written in their lockers.

But they did—and still do. In terms of active or aggressive resistance, my sense is that misogyny trumps racism, but parsing that is a three-way tie for last.

Note: I removed the actual epithets from this manuscript, although there is something compromising in not showing the actual malice of the specific words used against our coworkers. Suffice it to say that whatever the vilest, most racist, misogynistic, homophobic slur you can imagine is, *that* is what the fireboys scrawled in cowardly anonymity.

Beyond, or in addition to, these grievous personal assaults on dignity and workplace safety, there are the comments, the free-flowing discussions (separate from the closed-door ventings, when the [white] boys are safely "among their own") in which incredibly ignorant, ugly, ill-informed, wrongheaded comments are offered noninsultingly. Meaning, folks whose majority position allows them to never have their perspectives challenged struggle mightily to acknowledge the realities of others. And the lone person of color or woman in the crew must reassure the "team" that their casual racism and/or sexism is fine, or face more ostracism and retaliation.

In September 2022, Minneapolis—the MFD and the city itself—recognized the thirtieth anniversary of the 1992 all-women crew on Engine 5, the first in MFD history and possibly in the nation. These were tough, talented individuals, to be sure. I learned from and had the honor of working with all of them before they retired. But their "achievement" reflects far more about the benighted work environment and culture than their own sheroic powers. They came together because, after Jean Kidd became the first female MFD captain, no men would pick her rig, opening spots for Bonnie Bleskachek, Mary Mohn, and Vicki Hoff to join her crew. Much like Captain Cheatham running Station 24 in 1907, they did their job despite individual and systemic resistance. They faced open hostility, aggressive bullying, abusive undermining. They were simply trying to do their job, despite massive interference from the men alleged to be their "Brothers in Fire." The more the men threw at them, the harder they worked. The Ginger Rogers "backwards and in high heels" line doesn't feel quite apt, given our clunky fire boots and heavy turnouts, but I think the "breakthrough" achievements of minorities are often merely examples of individuals finally getting a previously denied opportunity and then persisting despite the hostility and bias of those who enjoy profoundly unjust advantages.

A few years ago I recognized a depressing parallel between the stories I heard Jen and her pals tell back in the mid-1990s and what I heard around our dinner table in the early 1980s. My parents were both lawyers; Amanda took the D.C. bar exam when she was nine months pregnant with my brother, then joined her first firm within a few weeks of giving birth. This was one trap the second-wave feminists got snared in: the notion (and expectation) that they could do it all. Our dinner table conversations were often dominated by Amanda venting about her workday. Not that law was hard or that she didn't have the innate skills to be an attorney, but the sexism and sexist bullshit she and her female peers had to fight through just to exist at the firm were endless. The tedious male chauvinists and the aggressive sexists and harassers, the comments, the groping, the condescension. This was the other trap: whether by legal edict or grudging yield, women who broke out of the glass basement still found themselves involved in a guerrilla war of sexism. *You've come a long way, baby!*

//

Now, back to 1998: To finally fulfill (or escape) the consent decree, Chief Forte offered to build a diverse workforce and strive to populate the rigs with a representation of "how the city looks." A woman, generally white; two men, one of color, one white. It wouldn't resolve the historical cultural problems, and the proportion of white men was too great to not outnumber everyone else. It was aspirational, but it was positive. For a while, our rigs did have some racial and gender diversity. I noticed it when we were in public and on calls.

After the court orders and Chief Forte's hiring gambit, the MFD had one of the highest per capita percentages of female firefighters nationally. Briefly. And even at its highest, it was under 20 percent. For all the carping that *diversity ruins everything,* all four of the thirty-plus-cadet classes of my list were predominantly white and male. Our collective hiring was derided as nothing but a diversity stunt—despite so very many honky dudes to the contrary. *But then . . .* in the mid-2010s, we had five rookie classes with only two women hired out of seventy cadets. The attrition rate for female firefighters has been massive. There are no studies, no exit interviews, to learn why so many women have left. But nearly every woman with whom I've spoken has said she never felt genuinely welcomed, never felt she would ever be seen as equal, never felt less than an intrusion. Many never felt safe. "They might *tolerate* you, if you're one of the lucky ones," one woman said. "But you'll never really fit in. And don't you *ever* forget that. Because as soon as you let your guard down and relax, they'll screw you over."

I do know why Jen Cornell left the job to become a lawyer. She told me she came to understand that not only would she never receive fair recognition for her talents or contributions, but she also recognized it was the sort of workplace where telling someone they did a good job was anathema, and that was something important to her. "Look, Jer," she added, "it might not be as important to you—this external validation— but you haven't been rejected and dismissed out of hand. Even as an outcast, you're still a white man. You can afford to be indifferent. I can't spend a career feeling like that."

She was right, of course. We all face a degree of withering scrutiny, but adding racial and gendered hostility makes it all the more complicated and undermining. I suffered for being out of step, but that was a consequence of my choices—not a fundamental rejection of my right to do the job. When we talk about the MFD, Jen says she misses the excitement, the chance to help people, and a few of the good firefighters. The rest? Tedious, wrongheaded, fixated on the wrong issues: gladly done with all that. I share some of her sentiment: I truly love a great many of my coworkers, and I love the work, but the city politics, department dysfunction, and ass-backward mob? No thanks. And, as we learn with any job, you can't slice out the bad to keep the good.

//

The court-ordered diversity advancements were very good for the department, even if the core membership resented and resisted the change. Let's be very clear: this profession remains a challenge for women and people of color, due to the deeply ingrained traditional mentality, generations-deep demographics, and personality profiles of the general workforce.

Our Black firefighters faced parallel resistance, incomprehension, blatant and unspoken judgments: a person's skin color guaranteed that the person would be regarded as a token, a quota, someone who "stole" the job from some "deserving" white dude. Because we respond to a disproportionate number of impoverished and struggling Black citizens, the Black firefighters are often charged with answering for (on some level, *apologizing* for) these unrelated random strangers. We don't demand that white firefighters answer for the poor whites or obnoxious rich whites we encounter. I'm not saying anything groundbreaking, but I see how it plays out with the demographics and sociology of our emergency response.

The hostility toward women's incursions into this previously "sacred" all-male space has deprived many, many qualified female firefighters and potential leaders a fair shot at a good career. The misogyny ran deep and wide. It has prevented all of us from benefiting from the skills, wisdom, and perspectives of potential female leaders. If the majority of my best crew members, captains, and mentors have been women, what would it mean had more women been allowed the opportunities to learn and then to lead?

The depths of ignorance of this atavistic culture would stagger contemporary sensitivities. The essence was *How dare these women even dream of competing with men?* At every turn, too many of the men, from durgans to top brass, waged war on the women's attempts to simply learn and do the job. Lesbian indifference to (straight) men bought them some space (unlike the straight women, whose "fuckability" remained the obsessive topic of prurient gossip, whose physical weakness, on one hand, and sexual seductiveness—the "distraction" canard, blaming women and girls for man-boys' inabilities not to sexualize them—on the other, were the preoccupations of rank firefighters and administrators). But it did not spare them the added homophobic misogyny, the layered resentment of women daring to compete in a man's space.

For people in normal jobs, this might sound preposterous or extreme, and this is exactly why I am pushing it. The galling privilege of white men bullying everyone who threatens our timid minds. Men control women through violence: verbal, implied, and physical. For a grave example, look up Nicole Mittendorff, a Fairfax County, Virginia, firefighter who took her life after vicious gossip, slander, and cyberbullying from her own coworkers (on private but widely shared Facebook groups). Grown men spreading an orgy of salacious, juvenile lies about their coworker. The gynophobic calumny is fodder and fuel for firedudes' bonding. And then we turn around and impugn their abilities: "I wouldn't go into a fire with *her*! She'll get us all killed."

As for gay men? When I started, there were none who were out. And the honest, unselfconscious response by many of the "Bravest" was "A faggot on my crew? Fuck that. I'd let him burn in a fire."

For real. I heard a version of that several times in my first months. It was all posturing, tough talk, and empty words. The fear of contagious queerness is so profound among tight straight dudes that even allowing the *idea* of a gay man undermines heterosexuality. And with no openly gay men, the notion of a "faggy fireman" was spectral, a gossip's boogieman. But it was vicious, damaging, and moronic. Statistically, and factually, there *were* gay men on the job, just deeply closeted. So those men endured fear and doubt and the weight of reinforcing their closet doors, and the homophobes never had to confront an actual human who challenged their raw, hysterical fear.

Culturally, things have improved. Our union leadership changed around 2010, bringing in fresh and progressive individuals who sought to improve relations with the mayor, the city council, and constituents in every walk and corner of the city. Their leadership reflects progress, and their recognition that we do not exist in a cloister, that we are part of the city's fabric, has brought a lot of positive changes.

And yet. We are who we are. The social currency of homoerotic machismo and dick jokes remains strong in many stations. At most retirement parties, there was sheet cake (perhaps more a midwestern thing than just a firefighter thing) and the hoary offering: "Welcome, boys. We've got two things on the menu, cake and cock—*and we're all out of cake* . . ." To which the response is a knowing laugh and vapid grin, and then everyone repeats the joke at the next event. *Sorry, boys, we're all out of cake!* Har, har, har.

You know the delicious, campy irony of the Village People, their powerfully gay embrace of the butchest, nominally straightest icons? The construction worker, the sailor, the cop: macho, macho men. I presume the fireman's costume was too bulky to dance in, because we boys at the fire hall really are a Tom of Finland drawing come to life. The obliviousness to how deliciously homoerotic our butch identities are amuses anyone who can read symbols and signifiers.

In the aftermath of the uprising that started down the street from our station, and as a blow against despair on multiple levels, we decided to create a new mascot for Engine 17 ("we" meaning: largely *I*, with the encouragement of Tracy Terbell and Brian Michor). In a sea of dragons, devils, bulls, skeletons, bulldogs, stallions, and reapers, we went with a sparkly unicorn. "Engine 17: Southside Magic." The new administration accepted the logo (which never would have flown anytime earlier), and now we have a magical unicorn on our duty shirts. Kids love them. People do double takes and grin. To fight the Covid doldrums, I made T-shirts with the logo to sell for charity. They were wildly successful. Wu-Tang is for the children; so is Engine 17! It was also a mordant litmus test: a lot of my macho-but-not-scaredy coworkers bought a bunch of shirts. It's a lark, a way to poke fun at the derivative posturing and our silly machismo. The best of us, as I've said, have a lusty sense of humor about almost everything, including ourselves. A *lot* of dudes were shook, though (not a surprise). *I'm not down with that fruity unicorn. Get me a bulldog or reaper.* Exactly: F minus.

//

The racist, sexist, and homophobic sleights of hand are societal in a microcosm, played out in a hermetic, reactionary subculture. It does a disservice to all the people of color and white women who show up to do a job but must fight endless petty, vicious battles. We are *finally* recognizing that this macho white default culture is killing *itself.* These fundamental behaviors and mindsets contribute to the raft of issues (white) men are facing: depression, drug and alcohol addiction/abuse, cancer, PTSD. Not only have they violated any genuine notion of bravery with generations of racial and gendered hostility, they also have poisoned themselves in the workplace they claimed was special.

Very often in my first few years, I was just another nameless white-guy rookie. I was taken at face value: man; white; white man. The other guys would feel free to speak openly with me—and not just speak, but performatively reclaim their space: "Damn, it's nice to have a *normal* crew, just *us*. No worries about saying the wrong thing or *offending* someone." The others would nod and chime in. *If she's offended, you're suspended!* Har, har, har.

These poor souls felt severely oppressed by the few women and nonwhite men sprinkled in their midst, making them half think before saying something stupid and sexist, or stupid and racist—or something stupid, racist, and sexist. An all-male, all-white crew, just like it used to be: these hero firemen could once again speak freely, express their truth, without the damning oppression of Them. From what I witnessed, their truth was frequently racist, sexist, misogynist, homophobic, xenophobic, put-upon, insecure, entitled, reactionary, victimized, and astoundingly comfortable with their shallowly smug self-certainty.

To suggest that the guys were part of a flawed larger system was viewed solely as an attack on them. No nuance, no reflection. Just hyperbolic defensiveness. Which gets tiring to confront. And it is tough to witness dudes embodying the things you're trying to discuss, while they deny these things exist. Tim Wise writes in "Imagine for a Minute": "This is what white privilege is about. . . . It's the ability to channel racialized rage and hostility . . . suffer no consequence, and yet still perceive yourself as the victim." This deceit occurs in many places, but few jobs allow so many hours of uninterrupted gasbagging.

Soon, the word spread. I was friends with female firefighters. I was unperturbed by the lesbians, so I was probably gay. I would challenge the racists and I argued in favor of affirmative action. I was buddies with Black people. I'm from out East, a college boy. I challenged anyone who floated the whiny reverse-racism balloon. I would launch into crazy antiracist arguments, citing books and intellectuals and studies. *Books!* And, because it's the fire department, parallel rumors started among some of the Black guys that I was a white supremacist. Even after I worked with many of these guys individually, and as crews, and they saw I was not, in fact, a racist skinhead, it was easier or more compelling to keep the rumor afloat.

That's the job: never let facts interfere with a good rumor.

For all the chest-thumping machismo, these brawny fireguys can be some of the most wet-lipped gossips imaginable. Hysterical rumors spread like, well, wildfire. It's a breathless game of macho telephone. Volume trumps veracity, and we do worship a loudmouth. So, the word spread: I was queer, liberal, educated, not to be trusted; maybe racist, maybe reverse-racist. I definitely wasn't one of the Guys. For a decade, I existed in that limbo: eyed warily by some; dismissed by many of the old boys and Haters; feared and reviled by others.

I did myself no favors. I *am* brusque and bookish, verbose and opinionated, pugnacious and contrary. After listening to Jen's and the Women's Association members' tales of ongoing misogyny and male hostility, and then witnessing for myself the boys' club, I saw it was useless to make milky appeals to the Brotherhood's better nature in hopes of starting a productive discussion or gently encourage them to rethink the long-held biases. I should use my privilege to fight my ilk on behalf of all those who cannot afford to, or who are worn out from doing it on the daily.

After enduring tedious, dead-on-arrival rationalizations about *Now just isn't the right time to force radical change* (i.e., to rethink fossilized false beliefs), I saw that the Emperor's New Clothes was too apt an analogy. The facts, the truth, the reality: it was already here, readily in front of us. Solely by massive collective denial could anyone persist with the empty claims that only white men can take blood pressures and spray water on burning things. And that's what we have: a massive collective denial, one that prevents so much easy, good, necessary growth just to comfort the lazy preferences of a few naked emperors.

//

This mentality is not restricted to the Minneapolis Fire Department. Most fire departments remain deeply white and male, homophobically hetero male, and chauvinist. The hermetic nature of the profession has unduly protected us from outside influence and reality. We might joke about everything, and claim we tease everyone equally, but the added blades of racialized, gendered, and xenophobic bias reveal our well of ugliness.

My argument has long been that the narratives we spin to reassure ourselves of our machismo are the very webs that fatally entangle us. Maintaining an aggressively macho posture, refusing to examine our own biases and outmoded traditions: these lead to collective illness. The fire service fights several battles now: obsolescence, identity crisis, leadership vacuum, generational disconnect, poor health of its members, inexperience on scenes, failure to train realistically, defensiveness, and denial.

We die of heart attacks, reckless driving, cancer, overextension into buildings we shouldn't be in at all. Depression and suicide are claiming more of us. Our collective cultural identity is what puts us most at risk. We ignore what's obvious in our adherence to false principles. It's a matter of profound identity (and denial) for many of my peers. Guys who would rather die from a heart attack on scene than take a cardiac stress test and do something about their shitty health.

More firefighters died nationally in 2021 due to Covid-19 than in the first year of the pandemic. Despite the vaccine, the clearer information, the abundance of masks, more firefighters died than when we didn't know much. And these deaths were *not* from work-related infections. Those who died were people who refused to wear masks and refused to get vaccinated, who contracted Covid out in their lives (and risked spreading it to family, coworkers, and the public we serve). This indicts our general health, too. How many of these guys had ignored or undiagnosed compromised health, significant comorbidities? Too many. It's a shame.

So many guys who do not get challenged, who get a free pass, are also unmotivated to think critically about the entire framework—just as long as they skate under the withering gossip and barbed jokes, right? But a world run on insecurity and posturing is not good for one's heart, mind, or spirit. That is a different closet, if you will. Equally confining and mirrored with self-loathing. A lot more guys are now succumbing to the effects of suppressing their fears and feelings. Accumulated and chronic traumatic exposure is taking out more and more firefighters. The weight of this work, coupled with the absolute aversion to functional emotional processing, means that many guys suffer from toxic masculinity in the form of compulsory machismo. Men who have never really had to fight for anything—without recognizing all their privilege has provided them—have poor coping habits when they need to be vulnerable and resilient. Acting tough isn't actually a good life skill.

Fortunately, there is a growing movement to address this disastrous cultural identity crisis. I am not alone in pointing out these issues and suggesting alternatives. A lot of good women and men are lighting torches against the darkness, but we are still fairly isolated, lone flashes in the night.

And during this slow evolution, or battle against stasis, we come to work and the tones sound, and off we go to help the public.

We aren't angels, despite some good days, but I titled this book *Trauma Sponges* for both literal and figurative reasons. We wade through our patients' blood and guts, of course, but we absorb their sorrows, terror, and despair. I think some firefighters develop—or some might already possess—a superstitious barrier between themselves and the people we serve. There but for the grace of God and all that.

In rookie school, we had five new captains running our training, promoted "young" at their five-year mark (because of Vietnam-era retirements, the racial-discrimination hiring freeze, and staffing shortages) and one twenty-five-year senior captain. The newer captains were nominally progressive about the reality of a more professional workplace and interpersonal relations (*nominally*), but the old salt was gruff, funny, irreverent, and wildly impolitic. Assigned to teach a unit on infection control (*Whenever possible, don't get stuck with dirty needles. Don't kneel in blood. Don't do mouth-to-mouth. Don't stand in front of someone who's puking*), he rambled on about how medical calls were a necessary, unavoidable imposition—*but that didn't mean we had to like them!*—and then closed with this: "Look, guys. There's a lot of bad stuff out there. Really bad stuff. So be careful. You owe it to your wives, your kids, your crews, you owe it to yourselves: Stay clear of the bad stuff. You'll see people who are sick, and hurting, and in a bad way."

He paused, scratching his poorly shaved cheek. "Look, you got to remember that whatever they've got, whatever they're suffering, *they* did something to put themselves in harm's way. If they've got hepatitis, AIDS, or something like that, they brought themselves to that point. It's between them and God. You don't have to take that on." He shrugged and shook his head. "We're firemen, not faith healers."

We were stunned. There were six women in our class of thirty-five—and this 17 percent was considered a shit-ton, a clutch, a murder of fireladies, rather than a paucity—but still: "guys ... wives ... firemen." After months of being told "Respect everyone, treat everyone decently, don't judge or blame folks," here was a very veteran captain telling us that those folks in misery were experiencing God's judgment and will, and who were we to interfere?

//

Having worked as a battalion chief, I can state that the focus on EMS—again, more than 80 percent of our work—gets negligible focus by the command staff. The frankly confounding anti-EMS bias persists from the top down. The chiefs see themselves solely as fire-suppression supervisors, and many rejoice at "never having to touch another patient." Many newer durgans have either started with or quickly learned a similar mentality: "I'm a *fireman*. Put me on a truck so I can work my craft!" Easy there, *Backdraft*: our entire department goes to maybe three hundred working fires in a year, and many of those are just bad cooking calls. I can't blame the rookies for imbibing the cultural liquid: this joint runs on peer pressure and conformity. But, listening to our cultural discourse, what gets bandied about at every station, every training, I'm stunned by the cognitive dissonance between the actual fires we fight versus the hours in the day, the days (weeks, even months!) between fires, and all the calls we run between fires.

I have saved significantly more lives as an EMT than rescuing people from fires. But we still see ourselves as smoke-eaters and salty dogs, born and bred to fight the devil at the gates of hell. I am grateful for every senior person who takes the medicals seriously and demonstrates professionalism and compassion. That is a legacy worth sharing with the next generation.

There is something wonderful about the many ways my coworkers find to help people, be the friendly, unflappable presence that reassures the public that things are not as bad as they seem. We don't get training for this because these are human skills, not textbook items. But the majority of the people I've worked with and for, the firefighters and medics across this city and in every town in the United States, are quite good at showing up and helping out.

I wrote at the beginning of this chapter that we see people who have made bad decisions on a micro level and on a macro level. We encounter many people who lack—and have lacked for many generations—health, education, and welfare. To the uncritical—or judgmental—it is *their* fault they are this way, because *we* don't have the same problems and don't make the same bad choices. From positions of relative wealth, health, employment, education, it's easy to ignore the structural underpinnings of society's inequalities. That is a challenge for my coworkers: to really consider how our systems press down on people.

Another aspect is that we see so many people truly suffering. We see sick babies and toddlers with painful ear or lung infections, screaming themselves raw without comprehension. Kids with broken limbs, fatally wounded children: these are emotionally brutalizing calls. We respond to people mangled and dying, or mangled and facing an obliterated life. People suffering, hard. We try to help them. When we can do little to fix the crushed bones or the psychological breaks, we stand beside the patients, taking in the force of their grief, fear, and anger.

And when the next call is someone with a splinter or a stomach ache, it can be difficult to ignore the comparisons, hard not to resent the whiner. These juxtapositions are hard on the spirit.

I ask again: Are men better at this because we compartmentalize, putting aside emotions to get to the necessary work? Are women better because they connect with patients on an emotional, personal level? Neither cliché is accurate. Doing this job well requires compassion, compartmentalization, pragmatism: all of which are gender-neutral and can be learned, or approximated. Feeling too much can break us. Walling off our feelings can, too.

Emergency responders in general are action-based folks, thrill seekers, adrenaline junkies, risk takers. One must be a bit bent to take a job whose essence is to put oneself into dangerous situations. But that doesn't—or shouldn't—mean we throw ourselves away. Our duty is not to die. A building is already on fire when we arrive. Nature, gravity, and physics are not impressed by our cool gear and beefy mustaches. Firefighters have perished, and will again, in buildings there would be no saving, buildings that had no victims to rescue. It isn't fear that should keep us out of a deathtrap but professional assessment. Running in just to show we aren't afraid is a different cowardice.

Likewise, we cannot blame ourselves when someone dies despite our efforts. We mustn't preemptively give last rites to anyone who sneezes, but we cannot bury ourselves with patients whose day was today, no matter how much we want to save them. The space between these two is quite gray.

We are best when we're a bit like a troop of flinty Boy and Girl Scouts who have spent time in the French Foreign Legion: eminently capable, calm and skilled, and seasoned or worldly enough to take anything we encounter in stride. A Gallic shrug gets one pretty far.

//

Cultural change has seeped into the fire service. Most changes have come from external pressures—lawsuits, diversity, budget cuts, increased range of responsibilities. A very few have come internally: bastions of tradition seldom change willingly. Some changes seem unavoidable, by-products of cultural shifts. Fewer people are skilled in traditional trades; fewer firefighters have carpentry, construction, manual crafts in their backgrounds. Military veteran points ensure each applicant class remains composed primarily of vets. But even vets are arriving with different skills and mindsets than previous generations did. Old guard folks like to bemoan the millennials, but I've found the majority of "young people" to be capable and adaptable, and—importantly—able to use technology to learn.

This last is antithetical to the traditional hierarchical teaching and power dynamics of the fire service. Senior people talking down to the rookies: "I'll tell you what to think." Now, especially in the absence of repetitions and coordinated education, many departments drift rudderless on folklore and received wisdom that offers little substance. Because it's a top-down system, the typical senior folks have no sense that they should come down from the mountain (or, that they are not, in fact, the mountain). New hires are adept at internet research, and many of them spend their time online, studying whatever fire training they can find.

Competent crews who resemble and respect our populations, and who are able to engage with them on human levels, is the essence of successful public service. That truly is neither heroism nor rocket science.

What I find amusing and telling is that the old guard, who bemoaned our softness and lack of grit, was talking to a lot of people raised in the 1970s, with steel-and-asphalt playgrounds and coaches who yelled, belittled, kicked us in the asses. Water breaks? *That was for ladies' tea parties, not football players!* I've said about my upbringing that I don't begrudge or resent the spankings I "earned," but I dead-ass remember the ones I didn't deserve: you lash out in your anger, the victim sees your weakness. Same with the fireground where a great many roaring chiefs and captains were screaming to make the fire go away. They learned from screamers, reacted to screamers, then replicated the behavior when they took command. Most of the time it's a measure of a person's fear or insecurity. I'm bemused by all the "this new generation is weak and worthless" declarations. *Every* generation fails the test of an idealized past.

8
ANTE UP

I AM THE LAST MEMBER OF OUR FIRE DEPARTMENT TO DO MOUTH-TO-MOUTH on an adult patient. No pocket mask, no plastic barrier: straight-up lips to lips.

It was Christmas Eve 2001 and we were called out to "one unresponsive" in a car in a garage. We arrived in front of a house festooned, like many on the block, with flashing holiday lights. Our flashing emergency red-and-blues blended with theirs. At the end of a well-shoveled driveway was a man waving frantically from the attached garage. I beelined toward the wan yellow light and whirling mist of exhaust. The car was still running. There was our patient, slumped against the car's half-opened door. He was youngish, under forty. I turned off the engine, pulled him from the driver's seat and onto the floor between the car's rear tire and some yard tools. No pulse. Not breathing. Inside, I could hear the noises of a Christmas family gathering. No one but the adult relative who found the guy and called 911 knew what was happening. He was begging me to help, begging the patient to be okay.

With the distraught family member standing over me, and my sluggish crew members seeming miles away with the O_2 and AED, I began breathing for him. Pinched his nose, tilted back his forehead, puffed two breaths into his mouth. I knew it wasn't protocol—that, in fact, it was considered highly risky due to the possibility of infectious transmissions.

But I had to do something.

I gave a few breaths, checked for chest rise or pulse, and started compressions. Pressed down hard and firm in the center of his chest fifteen times, then pinched his nose, adjusted his head, put my mouth on his, and blew two breaths. I did several rounds of this before the crew assembled and we used our proper tools. We worked him on the floor of the garage for a long while. Slowly the noise from the Christmas party died out. Soon, there were family members crammed in the service doorway behind us, their wailing and cries mixing with the holiday aromas coming from the kitchen.

The man didn't make it. The family's Christmas joy (and many subsequent ones) was obliterated by his death. I didn't get infected with anything. I haven't done mouth-to-mouth since.

And nor should you.

Secondhand respirations are pretty ineffective in getting oxygen to a person's brain—and a great way to suck in poison or infectious saliva. Compressions are the key to freelance CPR.

This was long after mouth-to-mouth was prohibited, mind you. I was rightly chastised for it, a few shifts later—by a captain who cared enough to pull me aside and read me the riot act.

"But"—I began my righteous defense—"he was down, and the others were so slow, and his poor family was standing right there. I *had* to do *something!*"

The captain shook her head. "Nope. Good intentions with bad actions are not how we do our job. You endangered yourself."

I tried to argue that my noble intentions made it all right. That the guy *needed* my extraordinary efforts. That it's our job: taking risks to help others. I puffed up: *I'd do it again because it was the right thing to do.*

All of which were wrong.

The salient points are *How* and *Why* I put myself at unnecessary risk. I was no longer a rookie but lacked perspective and wisdom. I was sophomoric and headstrong. Confronted with a problem, one with fatal implications, I felt compelled to act: I *had* to do something. So, I did *something.* And that's how I ducked under the safety rope and launched myself off a cliff in the DANGER: AVALANCHE HAZARD area of a mountain. Anything bad that occurred subsequently—as a direct result of my dumb action—was entirely predictable. I proudly, defiantly, wielded the invisible mantle of hero: "I'm trying to *help* someone! This is my job! I'll risk my life for another!"

In the moment, I wasn't thinking, I was acting—acting without clarity of purpose. And that is precisely the danger. Our duty is to protect life and property: to risk a lot to save a lot; and, importantly, to risk little for that which is already lost. A suicidal (dead) man deserves help, but my putting myself at risk to deliver essentially useless breaths for him helps neither of us. Grandiose, futile gestures should not be part of any operations manual or any organization's unofficial culture. In fact, it is our active refusal to use relevant contextual information—not applying lessons learned in the past, science, sound tactics, and clear assessment of what we are facing—that puts us in pointless danger. When we persist with unnecessary, unjustifiable, risky behaviors, and when those actions produce predictably dire consequences, we fall back on the Heroes' Sacrificial Duty: "That's our job!" Which is bullshit.

Firefighters employ an unspoken, likely unconscious rationalization: that *because* we help people, we magically accrue good karma. That because we put ourselves out there, into the fire and catastrophe, helping strangers, we are paying indulgences against our own foolishness and mortality. As if our good works will balance the ledger against our own foibles and risky chances. Thus, when an emergency responder falls—to bad decisions, unjustifiable risks, gravity—we collectively shudder and cry, and the news anchors drop into their very-somber-inflection voices: "Tragic news out of Fireville today, a forty-five-year-old firefighter fell through a hole in the clouds. He was base-jumping in a hurricane. A shocking, unexpected tragedy. Things like this shouldn't happen. He was a *firefighter*, after all."

It is not based on anything—no guarantee from God or payroll or the union. Nowhere in any of our contracts does it say that "for every seven shifts worked, member will be granted .33 of an extra year of life." But we, a bunch of thrill-seeking, risk-taking, adrenaline junkies, seem to believe that our good works offset our sins and protect against the forces of nature. Your number, my number, everyone's number comes up, eventually. In the same way many of our patients are truly surprised that something has happened to *them*, we're surprised that nature and the laws of physics—gravity in particular—aren't swayed by our badges and swell mustaches.

As Laurence Gonzales writes in *Deep Survival*, "It is a common human reaction to do something foolhardy and even life-threatening while trying to help others." You might see by now why his book spoke so deeply to me. Gonzales cuts to the bone of our unexamined behaviors. Other than sports movies and dead dogs, the funerals of coworkers are about the only sanctioned places we can cry. It's as if we are more comfortable crying over one dead "brother" than forcing all four hundred of us to examine our habits, beliefs, and actions.

//

For years now, the two largest killers of firefighters have been vehicles and our own faltering hearts. Firefighters crash responding pell-mell to calls (many of which are not even actual fires, and fewer still have victims to save). Firefighters get struck on roads and highways operating at motor vehicle collisions. The shock to our overweight, sedentary bodies when the alarm sounds, when the crews go from sleeping or chair patrol to full-bore activity, causes heart attack after heart attack. I repeat this, incredulous and furious: a disturbing number of Covid-19 firefighter deaths occurred *after* the vaccine was available, due to infections sustained elsewhere than emergency scenes. These are *preventable* deaths, "lifestyle" choices. Habits and behaviors matter.

Off duty, too many of us leap into macho stress-venting: partying hard, doing extreme sports, forgoing safety precautions (whether seatbelts, bike or motorcycle helmets, sober drivers, backup ropes) because to admit our vulnerability to gravity and risk is to acknowledge the flaws in our mentality. "Blowing off stress" becomes blowing off a hand, blowing through a stoplight, or getting blown off a mountain. Then we shake our heads; speak big, empty, heroic tributes at the funeral; and turn away, eager—desperate, even—to put mileage between the one who fell to earth and the rest of us high-flying tough guys. On duty, too many of us refuse to take basic safety protocols seriously, because acting tough and impervious to fear (and reality) fits a contrived self-image. We escape serious consequences time and again (until we don't).

As more information becomes available, journalists, family members, and insurance companies discover that, often, we have no business doing the things that cause grievous harm. As in, *we were not doing our jobs correctly.* But those discussions occur in the aftermath of a line-of-duty death, where emotions and sentimentality and psychological defenses all run high. Just as the actions of police officers have gone unquestioned until enough body-worn camera evidence became irrefutable, for too long, firefighters' actions were presumed noble, heroic, correct—and anything to the contrary was lost in the smoke. Science and technology are dissipating those obscuring red and blue lines. That can, and should, be a good thing—for those of us interested in learning, changing, and improving. For those who want to do whatever they want, unchallenged and unquestioned, it's an imposition.

The International Association of Firefighters created a great training program titled "Fireground Safety and Firefighter Survival" that included a manual with examinations of line-of-duty deaths, as well as hands-on training for recognizing, avoiding, escaping, and surviving Mayday situations. The physical training was great, if brief and rushed (as most things are). The manual was a revelation for me. In addition to the safety and tactical pieces, which included numerous grim and informative case studies, the authors quoted Laurence Gonzales's *Deep Survival*. Intrigued, I bought the book, and his two sequels, and my understanding of human behavior grew profoundly. His work isn't for or strictly about firefighters but rather human behavior. His research and discussions are enlightening and terrifying. I have given copies of his book to my daughters and my nieces and nephews for graduation gifts, as well as my past several rookies. I recommend it to anyone and everyone who might ever go outside, literally. Gonzales writes, "If you find yourself in enough trouble to be staring death in the face, you've gotten there by a well-worn path. Your first reaction might be: 'How could this have happened? What rotten luck!' But if you are alive afterward and bother to examine what happened, it will all seem as orderly as the Cajun Two-Step."

He continues, quoting another writer/firefighter, Peter Leschak, who writes in *Ghosts of the Fireground*:

> We were normalizing risk: We'd been through a similar situation and had emerged just fine . . . [T]he mental path of least resistance is to assume it was your skill and savvy that told the tale . . . Head-lines . . . would scream that it was just a "freak accident." It was not. It's a very common one, repeated over and over on numerous mountains.

It is hubris and dumb luck, ego and insecurity, that propel us down the familiar risky paths, and each time we escape unscathed we think we did something right, ignoring the flop sweat and the screaming obviousness of chance and peril. And we then tell our rookies to shut up and do as we do, because *We have seen some shit.*

//

My parents were less than thrilled when I became a firefighter: *The risks! It's so dangerous! Why not be a paramedic? Paramedics don't run into burning buildings. Why not do that!?* (Because medics have worse schedules, make less money, and burn out way faster.) I try to explain that we aren't battling infernos each shift, but, really, I can't pretend it isn't a dangerous, risky profession. My job description entails direct engagement with literal dangers.

In fires, hazmat leaks, car wrecks, river rescues—the true life-or-death situations—we put our lives, our bodies, into the pot as ante for the chance to save people in distress and danger. That is undeniable. We should make a calculated assessment of whether the person inside the bad place is credibly savable. If so, we *will* put our lives on the line to give that person a chance at survival. That is real.

What is also real is that there's often no distinction between the above and launching an emotionally blinded or desperate suicide mission into an empty or untenable situation, just because *we had to do something.*

We talk about training as the antidote to risk, and it is very true that good training can prevent many avoidable errors and risky actions. As a profession, we have improved, slightly, with better hazard assessments of burning buildings, and the culture is slowly shifting to internalize that there is no glory chasing ghosts in a vacant, fire-ravaged structure. I mean: there are papers written, and the outliers are now gaining traction. But the general population of many stations cling to the outdated mentality.

Why? Because, men. Honestly.

A distressing number of firefighters continue not to wear seatbelts—even as they get ejected in crashes or sail face-first into some inflexible part of the rig's interior. An overwhelming percentage of fireground deaths have happened in lost buildings with no victims reported or present. Meaning: firefighters enter unsafe buildings without regard for a victim profile—just because there is that mythical vagrant who *might* be hiding in the attic. But many of these structures are clearly unoccupied.

Which means these firefighters have died for burned property, chasing a notion that it's "real" to be inside the furnace going one on one with the Red Devil. And then a ceiling or floor or wall collapses on them.

I feel we do not make adequate real-time safety assessments on the fireground, and that leads to danger and harm. Suggesting this, I run afoul of a lot of the macho chest thumpers: *We FIGHT fire! Do your job or quit! "Safety" is for cowards. Roar!*

As more sensible firefighters explore better approaches to risk management, there has been a reactionary backlash. Computer cowboys claiming that science and millennials and safety nerds are ruining this great job. Faux-nostalgic meatheads fighting loud battles against Straw Men who are too chicken-shit to enter any building. This indignant self-righteousness is akin to all the NRA pawns who screamed for eight years that President Obama was personally coming for their guns. It was utterly untrue but felt really good to crow about and rage against. The problem is, lots more impressionable, insecure young men (a.k.a., the mass of mortal young men) are swayed by the braying bullies. These chaps try to earn approval by parroting such canards. They fail to learn what they should about tactics, size-ups, risk management, and fire behavior, and they push deep into lost buildings for no damn reason at all.

Hear me: I *love* the adrenaline and juvenile kicks of taking (moderate) risks. It *is* fun to rush into the maw and traipse amid chaos and destruction. The thrill of the rig pounding toward an incident, the destructive power and beauty of fire, the teamwork and hard effort to fight the fire, wandering through the wreckage: it's stimulating fun. If one is calm and clear and judicious, it isn't necessarily dangerous—until it is. But the endless litany of unjustifiable firefighter deaths reinforces that we clearly are poor judges of risk and safety. So, I have no patience for the retrograde claims of *firemanship*. It's empty phrasing and disingenuous hype.

My job is dangerous, but not all the time. I am rarely scared or nervous. I have occasional shudders of grim imagination. But, truly, reasonably, I carry neither a death wish nor tumescent fear about my neck—though I am selectively superstitious, wearing both a Saint Florian and a Joan of Arc medallion. When one spends this long responding to people in every conceivable walk of life who definitely did not plan to find themselves on the ground looking up at us with desperate eyes, it is hard to think any place is safe. People who live moderate lives, take no risks, eat their veggies, still find themselves in dire straits. And there we are.

We enter homes with impunity, and, surprisingly when one considers it, only very rarely do citizens object or challenge us. They might not always be happy about it, but our good-deed vestments get us by. There have been rare attacks on firefighters and medics on EMS scenes. There was an assassination, deliberately arranged, by a man in upstate New York who set his house on fire, hid behind a berm, and shot at the fire crews when they responded to fight the fire, killing two and wounding several. A crazed man knife-attacked two fire medics in California while they were treating someone on the street, stabbing one badly. A disoriented older man in Maryland opened fire as soon as the crew stepped through his door on a welfare check. (The man's adult son asked Fire to check on his dad, who, in his senility, mistook their calling out for him and banging on the door for hostilities. He shot two firefighters, killing one. He was not charged. Because, guns and castles.)

More recently, a heroin overdose was revived at a transit station in Appleton, Wisconsin. He pulled a gun on the crew as they tried to calm him. He killed a firefighter and wounded a police officer and two civilians. That cut deep. Too easy to imagine a similar situation here.

//

When I was a teacher, in the depths of my otherworldly first year in Chattanooga, there was a shooting at my school. You haven't heard of it, I'm confident. There was no national coverage. It was pre-internet. Also, for whatever reason (and many of my peers there ascribed it to heavenly intervention), the student reversed his plan, killing himself first rather than after slaughtering as many other students and teachers as he could. "Just" a suicide, rather than a bloody rampage.

The young man was an international boarding student. Everyone thought him weird but never menacing. I was a dorm "parent" for the underclass residence, one of three adult men charged with monitoring the adolescent males living a spartan and moderately-to-sublimely homoerotic existence (all boys, all male teachers, social conservatism, religious-based misogyny, near-hysterical, pervasive gynophobia: it was Boystown!). The boy, Felix, lived in the senior dorm but would visit students in ours occasionally. I was new to the school and stuck out more than he did. I was a Yankee with a weird haircut (a hack job done by my own hand), a decidedly not evangelical-Presbyterian disposition, and a Siberian husky named Watt (after both Samuel Beckett's *Watt* and the legendary bassist Mike Watt, not after Reagan's grim secretary of the interior). I spent many late nights irately chasing that fucking maniac dog across the campus, hissing furious, impotent threats after him.

It was a very traditional school, with the usual strictures and narrow perspectives of the type. Plus, it was Chattanooga, the Buckle of the Bible Belt. A portion of the boarding students were international, largely the white sons of white southerners working in Saudi Arabia for Aramco, and a few truly international kids, foreigners to the scions of Dixie. The misfits were drawn to me, whether the outliers or awkward types or nontraditionalists or angry youths banished from their homes.

Felix had spied a tattoo above my ankle and commented approvingly. I replied with what I always do: "Vanity of vanities, eh?" (Quoting Flannery O'Connor doesn't endear me to either the misfits or the cool kids, but I persist.) He asked me directly, "Why are you here?" emphasizing the *why,* the *you,* and the *here* with equal incredulity. I tried to walk the outline of the party line: "It's a good place to teach. I needed a job."

He scoffed and told me that, were he me, he'd be off in California chasing girls and never putting on a tie again. I shrugged. He wasn't entirely wrong, about the desire to travel into mythic lands and about how poorly I fit in the school's mold.

He was troubled in the sort of way too many kids are: an outsider, shipped off from his family (rejected literally and figuratively), a stranger in a strange land, keenly aware of and chafing against the stringent social gradations around him. He was disaffected, resistant to the rules and regulations of high school, especially a former military academy. I found him tedious and unpleasant in that surly, curdled teen way, and I kept our interactions brief.

The weeks before the shooting, spring of 1991, it was fully light by 5:30 a.m. Bright enough for Watt to decide it was time to go out. I'd been enjoying our predawn meanders, the breaking spring, the air and light redolent of vernal magic. The campus was quiet, and Watt and I roamed its paths freely.

The morning of the shooting, I woke to light rain and gray skies.

Nope. I rolled over. Watt hopped on the bed, snout poking me. I played dead but failed to convince him. *What is time to a dog?* I threw on my rain jacket and we walked through the light mist, the soft dawn muted in the overcast humidity. As we approached a small building in the center of the campus, I saw one of the cafeteria's cooks standing on the other side, hand to his mouth, eyes wide. I approached. He put his hand toward me, shaking his head. I slowed, eyes tracking his gaze. On the stoop between us, I saw a pair of sprawled legs, sneakers with no socks, bare hairy legs. I started forward, thinking a student was hurt. The cafeteria worker hiss-whispered, "No!" (Even there, even then, we yielded to the predawn propriety.) I saw the hem of his shorts, his arms limp across his lap, a bandolier belt of ammunition, and the barrel of a gun.

The man said he'd found the body and told his coworker to call the police, who were approaching now, squad cars' lights flashing as they bumped up the long, oak-lined driveway.

It was Felix, and he'd shot himself in the head. He was heavily armed: AR-15, hunting knife, enough ammo to wipe out everyone on campus. My first thought was of his roommate, a very nice, quiet Indian kid who had been paired with him in the typical logic that two foreigners would naturally get along . . . If Felix was here, dead by his own hand, I feared for his roomie, and then, as the implications of this clicked, for the entire dorm. He hated everyone.

In that moment of stunned clarity, I realized his contempt for his classmates would have made exterminating them first a logical choice for him. This was before Columbine and the weaponizing of alienation and the study of such kids, but my reaction was raw and it was true. I envisioned a dorm full of blasted corpses, blood running down the burnished stone stairways.

I told this to the police officers, who sent someone to check the dorm. My stomach was knotted and roiling. I stood in the growing gloomy daylight, light rain falling against my face. Watt's fur sparkled with mist. The police told me to move on as they stretched their yellow scene tape. As we walked away from the scene, I was told the senior dorm was unharmed, his roommate safe in bed.

The school went into defense mode, declaring this an aberration, the sick tragic act of an alien mind. And that was it. One assembly spent in generalized prayer—but this school prayed for everything: sports, weather, my dumb dog when he started a fight with a pack of feral strays. "Felix was not 'of' us" was the thrust of the prayers and official speeches. Implicitly and explicitly, a foreign body. *Do not ask WHY this happened, boys. There was nothing anyone could have done. Only the Lord knows.* (Do *not* ask if your ceaseless xenophobia and incurious ostracization might have driven him off the edge. Only the Lord knows.) Some vague prayers, a lot of reassuring contextualizing of Felix as Other, and "we/us" as blameless, then we put it behind us as fast as possible.

The moment I saw the weapon and bullets and knew it was Felix, I couldn't shake the wonder-worry of timing. Had it not been gray and rainy, I would have been out there as I had been every previous day. We likely would have crossed paths. And then?

I don't know.

I don't believe my life was spared that day for a higher purpose. Timing worked in my favor, and I got lucky. But, while I wonder whether he would have shot me on sight, or if we could have had a decent conversation, or if I might have talked him out of any killing at all, I recognize there is nothing but chance. Call it destiny if you wish. I don't. The wheel of fate? Dumb fucking luck.

Lots of people end up in exactly the wrong place when a minute on either side would have spared them. Then, as we are digging through the wreckage, wading through their blood or blocking their corpse from traumatized coworkers or family, we hear "If only . . . ," "But he said he'd take the next train," "She was supposed to go home an hour ago," and all the rest. It is a form of grief, of denial: *If only I had called him! If only I had answered her call! I could have saved them!*

If our time is truly predetermined, that appointment in Samarra is not going to be postponed. Our wishes mean nothing to what's already in motion.

This is not to say I am particularly reckless, flaunting my vitality, my privilege, my existence, taunting fate. I was more than marginally young and dumb when I was young and dumb. Surviving that, I realize we only have so many chances—and never know when the joker will be played. I love my life: my kids, Annie, my friends and family, my dogs, nature, breathing and thinking and fucking and laughing, all of it. I will be sad to leave this world. I try to live so that no one will doubt how I felt about them or what I thought, in case I die suddenly. But I don't fear dying at work more than I do biking or driving home on my off shifts.

The fatal shooting of the Appleton firefighter shook me, however. I have been on calls like that many, many times—closer to hundreds than dozens—where we approach someone who isn't in their right mind, whether due to sickness, mental illness, drugs, or booze, and we try to help them. People who come to, are disoriented, and find themselves in a strange position—on the ground, in an ambulance; a clutch of firefighters, medics, and police looming over them—can have myriad reasonable responses. In their mind, whether addled or loopy or delirious or psychotic, whatever they are doing makes sense. *We* are the intruders. The person's response may not be rational or safe or legal, but to them, it is what it is. Unfortunately, many of those reactions are problematic for us: fight and/or flight, in particular. We cannot treat every unconscious person as a potential threat, even if each truly can be.

//

I find it striking that, in the aftermath of the uprising in 2020 for racial justice, there's been a heavy use of the word *safety* on EMS calls. As in, "We won't put our people in danger on the streets—for safety." *Safety:* vague, amorphous, emotionally weighted. It sounds serious, like necessary diligence. As if there is a clear and direct danger to us on every call on the streets. In the months (months!) after the riots our bosses kept saying, "It's a *safety* issue. Period. I'm not risking *our* people [for *them*]. Let the police take care of things."

What things? I asked. Never got an answer, because there weren't active threats and because the true issue was elided: Black people, formless, faceless, generalized. During two of the nights of unrest, a few protesters or agitators threw things at the fire crews fighting the conflagrations. We don't know who threw things, but the implicit presumption was that it was "BLM radicals." It was as likely some wilding white youth, but that possibility is lost in white fright.

In the days of and directly after the riots, many crews were afraid—despite genuine reassurances from citizens on the streets, even very angry and vociferous protesters, that the Fire Department was cool by them, that MFD was *not* MPD. Too many of my peers on the job—and a great many of the paramedics—made a blanket assessment that any area with a largely Black crowd was de facto *unsafe*. EMS would not enter without police escort. There is a racial, if not racist, generalization at play in this formation, whether conscious nor not.

Over two years later, we (too many of us in emergency response) were still treating the vicinity of Thirty-eighth Street and Chicago Avenue as a hostile war zone. I explore this tension later in detail, the use of *safety* as a coverall, and the undeniable connection between Black citizens in peril and EMS waiting for the police.

None of these safety-conscious bosses recognized that it was the presence of the police that exacerbated tensions, so in waiting to enter a medical scene until the police mounted up and rolled in heavy, the EMS crews were failing to help citizens in need *and* allowing tensions on the street to increase due to the citizens' prolonged frustration, suffering, and pain.

If we cannot distinguish between the uncomfortable (and, frankly, self-conscious) and the unsafe, we aren't making good or clear decisions.

I tell my reactionary bosses, "My job is to get my crew and myself home safely after *every* shift. I *constantly* make safety assessments. If I go into a scene, I have made a conscious decision, and I keep evaluating throughout. I *am* taking safety into consideration. And I'm looking at what is *actually* happening, rather than preemptively saying, *No.*"

Because of this, I feel clear and comfortable about which scenes are safe and which might be marginal. That is more concrete, and engaged, than throwing a blanket concern for *safety* at anything remotely complicated.

//

While I say that our work is not very much more dangerous than anything else—I spend my shifts responding to people in far less dangerous jobs who have come to need our services—it is true that we are exposed to many hazards. Despite all the crazy violent calls, the deranged and damaged people, we don't carry that much worry with us. Nor do we carry guns or wear Kevlar vests. We trust that our red trucks and blue uniforms will buy us enough goodwill to stay safe from harm. *We cannot be afraid of everyone.* Not if we hope to do our job and remain sane.

With the firefighting part of work, our macho posturing is our biggest risk: showing—whom, God? our inner children? fate? mostly, each other—that we are brave men who don't need air packs when fighting a measly car fire (yet everything in a car is toxic when on fire). On hazmat calls, with chemical substances we don't even know to be afraid of, we stomp about impatiently to show we aren't ninnies. Both situations are far more dangerous for us than a crowd of racial justice protesters. Which do we treat as the threat, though? And why?

We have guidelines for making hard decisions and taking big risks with relative safety. We simply do not learn them well or follow them. Human nature, especially male insecurity, plunge-ahead machismo, fear of emasculation by showing thoughtfulness, Emperor's New Clothes syndrome: these lead us to step far into the unjustified-risk realm. And when we fall, or the building collapses on us, or the speeding rig rips into a building or a car, in the aftermath, the default rhetoric protects us, badly. "He died doing what he loved." "He gave his life protecting the citizens of Fireville." "What a tragedy."

There's another aspect here, I believe. The seduction of adrenaline gets into one's core. The phrase *adrenaline junkies* is apt. The surges of cortisol and the *Boom!* of excitement when we launch into the unknown: these are intoxicating. While I recognize the perils my peers face in escaping the emotional, mental, and physical trauma with alcohol or drugs, there's another group of us who will acknowledge the dirty side of the blade. For those of us who have opted out of drugs and booze as coping mechanisms and escapes, the adrenaline kicks and sleep-deprivation fog are the closest we come to the old embrace of Morpheus. Studies have shown that the effects of driving while exhausted are equivalent to driving while drunk or high. The fuzzy-headed slurriness I feel after a beat-down shift leaves me sluggish, addled, lost in my own buzzing mind. The jangling nerves after a big call or crazy scene or dangerous response: all too familiar.

I quit drinking in 1989. No booze, no drugs, no smokes. The world is a better place for it. I was a sad–mad drunk, plunging ever deeper into the bottle to drown familial pain and anger. I unleashed a malevolent surliness on those around me; I hurt myself; I was emotionally unreliable. None of those are good qualities. Sober, it's just me. I deal with my shit on steady ground. Do I miss being fucked up? Certainly, at times. It's tempting to abdicate duty and responsibility, right? That's how people jam themselves up.

But the effects of sleep-dep have offered a day pass into the Land of Nod. As with everything that is seductive and entrapping, several of my friends who have had their own battles with the bottle or drugs have pushed too far into the madness that comes with work's constant chaos and prolonged sleep deprivation. Several have gone off the rails— without actually relapsing. The lack of sleep for weeks and months, without recovery of balance, broke them down in the same manner as a bad bender. And several others have said "Fuck it," and uncorked the jug or hit the pipe again. Talking to them in the moment has had no effect, just as with someone on a bender: "You need to get some sleep. You need a break from this rig."

"Helllllll noooo! I'm fine. It's all good. This is how we do it!"

And then, once they take—or are forced into—a break and catch up on their sleep, they emerge to survey the wreckage with the same hooded eyes as one sobering up in a trashed apartment: "What the fuck is all this? *Who* did *this*?"

And we start counting once again. One day clean and sober, and rested.

//

As we fight fewer fires and find ourselves consciously and unconsciously wrestling with existential and epistemological identity issues—*If we seldom fight fire, who and what are we? Fire-seekers? Fire-hopers? Smoke-detectors?*—the reactionary defense clings to this noble, fated martyrdom.

We also deploy scapegoat rationalization like a magic cloak. Here's the thing, though: as long as firefighters are dying in other cities, we can puff ourselves up and assert how *risky* our work is, how *necessary*. When other firefighters (whether in other departments or our own) get caught out making bad decisions—we all make bad decisions, only some pay the price for them—it is reflexive, essential even, to put some distance between those individuals and us. *They* screwed up: that's why they got hurt. *They* made poor decisions: that's why they were in that collapse. *They* don't know how to do the job right: that's why they were burned in the flashover. Essential, I say, because the alternative would require us to examine our own behaviors and see that we are no different, no better, than those who caught the bad call. It simply hasn't happened to us (yet). But we will use their deaths to remind the public, and ourselves, that we are big brave heroes. It is psychologically dishonest and self-defeating, but it is true.

Minneapolis Fire has had bad injuries and multiple close calls. Departmental response has been par for the course: denial, avoidance, rationalization, scapegoating. No comprehensive lessons learned; no investigation of system or culture. Sadly, our human tendency to avoid the ugly truth about ourselves remains stronger than our desire to make genuine, productive changes—because those will come at the expense of our self-concept. David Dodson and David Griffin, two leaders in progressive fire service improvements, have each written about the challenges of paradigm shift in this industry. Although they come from different regions and have separate approaches, both have essentially stated that fire departments will not make necessary cultural improvements unless one of three events occurs: a death in the line of duty, which brings with it an alphabet stew of investigative agencies that *mandate* changes; the "dying off" and retirement of the old guard—with progressive leaders replacing them; or, least often, a visionary veteran chief who steers the organization forward. This last is a rarity.

In the same manner we look at the rough-living, self-destructive, struggling patients and draw an illusory line between *them* and *us*, we manage to twist reality and logic to somehow abdicate our own flaws when essentially looking in a mirror. I near-obsessively read NIOSH, OSHA, and NFPA line-of-duty injury and death reports. At this point, with each subsequent event and examination, the investigators state there are about ten common factors that *continually* lead to these generally avoidable catastrophic events. All are human failures. I return to Gonzales's *Deep Survival* here:

> The design of the human condition makes it easy for us to conceal the obvious from ourselves, especially under strain and pressure. The Bhopal disaster in India, the space shuttle Challenger explosion, the Chernobyl nuclear meltdown, and countless airline crashes, *all happened in part while people were denying the clear warnings before them, trying to land the model instead of the plane.* (emphasis mine)

Human behavior drives them all. For police and EMS, that can mean treating every "one down" as "just another drunk" and accosting him roughly, starting a process that can lead to death, lawsuits, riots. For firefighters, that can mean running into the building fire without studying the actual conditions. That fire, the one before it, the two before that one: *They're all the same. Why should this one be any different? We do what we do!* This cultural defect fills me with dread: we allow ego and insecurity to exploit the truly noble virtue of putting ourselves at risk for others. And then the roof collapses on us, or we fall through the floor and burn in a fully involved basement. We lose people in staggeringly unoriginal ways. I do not believe I am any better than anyone who had the worst day possible. The need to plunge in, posture up, act blindly will send us into indefensible positions yet again. Eventually, our luck fails. As Gonzales emphasizes, "Gravity is on duty all the time." All I can do is hope I remain clearheaded. Hope, as we have seen, is *not* an action plan.

9

THANATOS IS A MOTHERFUCKER

The suicide takes his secret with him, and it's easy to get caught up in a monomaniacal search for the Answer, pinning your painfully vast hope to a single Idea. . . . You believe the person who killed himself took the ultimate truth, and life afterward often feels like a sorrowful search for that last, unknown key to life, which will explain everything. The paradox is that this hope or need for certainty seems to make the world less stable. The belief in a single Truth leads to doubt about everything.

—Charles D'Ambrosio, "Salinger and Sobs," in *Loitering*

ONE OF THE REALLY POSITIVE WAYS THAT EMERGENCY RESPONSE WORK has changed during my career is the approach to self-harming patients, which has improved by 1,000 percent, at least. When I started, with suicide attempts, the cops and EMS crews would often treat the distraught, despairing person as a pathetic whiner: *It's nothing. She's being emotional. This guy's just looking for some attention.* And the very sad, deeply hurting person would be brusquely hauled to the ambulance, taunted for bad nerve, bad aim, bad luck.

A slow but substantive recognition of the futility, if not abject cruelty, of treating a despondent, suicidal person like a criminal has brought many police officers to a more compassionate baseline. The police are called because Dispatch received info about someone harming, or threatening to harm, himself or herself. Any (potential) threat to the public requires police intervention; the threat to self requires police intervention. The former for safety; the latter is procedural.

However: (A) Sometimes, more so in the past than now (but it still occurs), the police would shoot the person while trying to stop them from self-harming. (B) Not all suicide attempts are violent. (C) *Very* few suicidal people are threats to others. But, in the name of precaution, a self-harm call brings the police along with EMS. (D) From a legal standpoint, there are administrative reasons: Minneapolis officers are the ones who write the psychiatric hold on the patient. If the officers exacerbate the scene's tensions, or harass or kill the person in crisis, they're neither keeping the peace nor protecting the public.

Gradually, we have recognized that the person in distress, in despair, is someone who needs our help in the form of compassion and gentleness, almost as much as the medically ill person needs oxygen, CPR, or insulin. I have responded to more noncompleted suicide attempts than fatal ones. They give differing levels of sorrow.

//

We respond to an apartment building for a check-welfare call. A young woman hasn't answered her mom's calls or texts. A police officer arrives, too. We get the keys from the security box, but the apartment's rotating ownership hasn't updated the master keys, so we knock hard for a few minutes, listening for noise inside, banging on the door and calling out, then we kick through the lock. The apartment is messy and quiet. The officer leads us in. Shades are drawn, dim shadowy light coming through the southwest-facing windows. We see her legs first, then the rest of her. Young woman slumped against the closet door. There's a belt noosed around her neck that snakes through her hair and is secured to the doorknob.

Her face is discolored but there is no rigor or decomposition. She is still, so very still. It's always surreal. We loosen the belt and she tilts over. We guide her to the floor. We check for pulses, looking for chest rise, a gasp of breath, a beat, anything. It's a formality. There is pooling already, her skin is cold to my fingers. This is a dead person. But we still check.

We know better, but still must do it.

Her mom and brother are behind us now, screaming. There is nothing for us to do for the young woman, and protocol requires we leave her as she is while the police investigate. The family wants to hold her, to cover her, to protect her dignity. We are not certain, as we step away from the body and assess the room, that it's a clear-cut suicide. The mess could be the usual disarray of a sloppy young person, or the aftermath of a domestic battle, or what seems normal to people on drugs. Nothing is definitive, except the dead girl on the floor.

The family's grief fills the room behind us. They are crying and screaming, raging about her scumbag boyfriend, and heroin, and how she'd been doing better but he was a snake and a killer. Again, we survey the apartment. It looks neither suspicious nor above suspicion. We are not police: we don't investigate. Whether it was suicide or a covered-up OD, we had nothing official to do. The officer asked us to escort the family to the hallway so he could document the scene. They were contaminating a possible crime scene. My crew guided them out. I stood near the broken door, blocking the family's view and giving the officer some company (and a witness, in case, in their grief, the distraught family claimed he'd done something wrong). Twenty-two years old, dead by her own hand, a needle, or some asshole.

The juxtaposition is difficult and inescapable. We try to comfort an inconsolable family as they wrestle with the abrupt fact of the dead young woman. The corpse of their beloved lies sprawled without dignity on the floor. They are smothered in grief, anger, and confusion. There's nowhere to go, both literally and figuratively. Adding to the tension, the clunky, dispassionate formalities of the police investigation stand between their vulnerability and their dead loved one. They want to hold her, to cover her, to know with certainty what happened, and, above all, to have her sit up and not be dead. None of which will happen, now or ever, and we—we stand there, an imbecilic blue wall between them and their girl.

Another squad arrives and we're cleared. We offer more useless condolences to the family and depart. The shift proceeds. We catch calls, some actual emergencies, many minor or routine. The dead girl recedes into the memory bank of my existential curiosities. We're called back to the apartment hours later. The officers have done whatever investigating they'll do, the medical examiner has removed the body, and they now need us to secure the door we broke down. There's the usual yellow **Police Scene: Do Not Cross** tape X-ing the doorway.

A different police officer greets us, impatient to leave. He has no reliable updates, repeating cheapened versions of what we heard initially.

They've processed the scene and didn't find anything to suggest homicide. The sad fact was she killed herself; how she got to that point, a mystery beyond our knowing. I feel for the family. Answers are illusions: she's dead and whether it was depression, despair, junk sickness, heartbreak, it doesn't change their loss. "Knowing" might give something to hang their *Why* on, but it's not going to solve anything. Nothing but sadness.

We go to work quietly (it's well past midnight), trying to secure the door.

A few late-night residents wander up and watch us work. "What happened?" each asks. We demur and evade. As we're finishing up, the girl's mother returns. The contrast of the police tape and our fresh-cut plywood against the dark door frame cause her to stumble and gasp, as if she'd perhaps thought it was just a bad dream. She asks if she can go in, just to be in her daughter's space. I weigh the options. We're not supposed to. But the investigations are done, and she is her mother. Even if she "steals" her daughter's journal or drugs or money, none of it will bring the girl back, and the police didn't regard this as a murder. Grief is grief. We unscrew the screws and reopen the door. Two of us stand obtrusive but silent at the edge of the room, while the mother kneels and leans on the dirty single mattress on the floor, almost in prayer. We leave her to her thoughts. After what feels both too brief and endless, she walks out. We wish her well and reseal the room. I never learned more about the girl's death, which means it was ruled a suicide.

//

I've been to a fair number of completed suicides (the word *successful* is accurate but bothers me). Sometimes we arrive because the family has discovered their loved one in the final embrace of death. Others, the neighbors hear the gunshot, or the person has made a call or sent a goodbye text. Others, it's been a while, and someone notices their absence—or a neighbor can't ignore the smell. Dead is dead, as we say. The actual and implied torments of the deceased can be haunting. Dying all alone seems so lonely (versus *feeling* alone and killing yourself while your family is out of the room), but lonely people also die of natural causes. Despair weighs heavier in our minds, I guess.

With the stigma attached to suicide slowly being reconsidered and replaced by attempts at understanding, a lot of formerly "unknown causes" are now acknowledged as suicides. That's a good thing. For too long, the various religious prohibitions on suicide have redoubled the anguish and suffering of many pious people, who lose a loved one and then are bereft of both their person *and* any community recognition or cultural ceremonies. Reducing the stigma, opening up conversations, allowing for frank remembrances: all are positive changes. And yet. I am troubled by how many people are pulling the plug on themselves.

The number of both attempted and completed suicides has grown significantly since 2010, and in fact has been increasing yearly. Economic reasons underlie many suicides; more people in poor health have chosen suicide over pain or crushing medical treatments (and bills); older people have taken their own exits rather than facing a powerless, slow decline; younger people have yielded to adolescent fear and despair; enduring racial, gender, and sexuality biases have claimed too many people. The layers of cultural disconnect, isolation, and anomie during the past several years, from politics to social isolation and Covid stress—there has been a lot that weighs fatally on people. There has been a surge of suicide among middle-age, middle-class white men. That is some of what I'm writing toward here: the obvious failure and insufficiency of compulsory machismo—of *suck it up* and *get tough* and *be a man*—are apparent in the soaring rates of depression, despair, and suicide of the group this society has coddled and privileged for generations. What must it be like for others, and isn't this reason enough to try something different?

I do *not* believe the increase in suicide attempts is caused by, or a reason to retreat from, the improved discussions and acknowledgments of suicide. I worry that the reduced stigma gives more despondent individuals a quick solution, but I don't want a return to the shame and silence.

Depression is brutal and cruel. I hate that there's so much weight on people that the spontaneous gesture appeals—and I wholly understand its sinister appeal. I hate it. I'm threatened by the idea that depression is so comprehensive, so prohibitive, that there seems no other choice but to kill oneself. Despair is separate from depression, and it is a multiplier of torment.

A rash or impulsive or planned action to lacerate the temporary pressure on the mind and soul, suicide seldom allows a do-over. It's a permanent solution to a temporary problem. It sucks. It destroys those left behind. And those who feel so low, so down, so despairing, of course, cannot fathom that they're solving nothing but spreading pain and regret. It might feel as if it's their only way out, their only choice to end the pain, but that's the chokehold of Thanatos on their hearts and minds. I can't solve it. I am terrified by it.

People desperately seek a note from the deceased, as if there will be a clue to the inexplicable. I've read numerous notes by attempted and completed suicides. They are striking in their despair and struggle, incoherent and rambling and panicked. There is *never* a good reason. And yet: the lack of a note causes exponentially more pain in the uncertainty and mystery for the survivors. Even though notes fail to explain, they are something. The absence echoes into eternity: *Why? Why? Why?*

Tim O'Brien's novel *In the Lake of the Woods* addresses such perilous mystery:

> This is how it was. You go about your business. You carry the burdens, entomb yourself in silence, conceal demon-history from all others and most of the time from yourself. Nothing theatrical. . . . Betray the present with every breath drawn from the bubble of a rotted past. And then one day you discover a length of clothesline. You amaze yourself. You pull over a garbage can and hop aboard and hook yourself up to forever. No notes, no diagrams: you don't explain a thing. Which was the art of it . . . that magnificent giving over to pure and absolute Mystery. It was the difference . . . between evil and a bad childhood.

//

Early in our relationship, likely on our first date, Annie and I bonded over a shared understanding of the tragic vagaries of life—we'd each lost a parent young—the skewering of *normal*. Over time, we half-jokingly made a pact: I wouldn't commit suicide; she wouldn't get cancer and die. (There may be truth in jest, but for many of us, there's jest in truth.) I think I got the easier end of that bargain, genetics being what they are. And yet, but still.

I've never suffered from depression. I've been down and struggled with feeling overwhelmed by the world, scared by my powerlessness to solve personal issues, but never the soul-deep tarpit. When I was nineteen, I was running fiercely toward a wall—or a cliff. I'd started drinking with purpose and edge at thirteen. Unable to address or resolve family issues, I instead dove deeper into alcohol abuse—doubling and trebling my precocious teen debauchery. Sotted constantly at college, with sharp blades of rage springing from my eyes and mouth, I was drowning myself. A nadir occurred, ironically, standing on the tall hill of Tufts campus, winter exams, 1986. I'd just made the heroic decision (*ahem*) not to participate in the group cheating during an astronomy final. I'd barely attended the class, never studied, hadn't bothered even to take it pass/fail. That I might fail a class—let alone a really simple one—was galling to me. That it became a matter of fallen honor versus desperation (cheat to pass but risk the humiliation of getting caught) was absurd.

The bigger problem was the pressure in my head and heart—the profound feeling of being trapped by the sorrow and anger connected to family issues. There was no solution at hand, which meant the trapped feeling seemed permanent, as did the futility of running from it. The squander and squalor of heavy drinking did nothing good. I was bloated, scared, morose. I stepped out of the exam into a crisp, starry December night. I felt minuscule in the universe, and miserable. I wanted to cry: *Pity, pity, pity the sad, confused boy who knows he has abundance everywhere but within.*

The night was cold, clear, and stark. I had a panoramic view of the sky. I looked off the hill at the Medford neighborhoods surrounding the campus, all lit up with their gaudy, unironic Christmas decorations. I looked upward again, feeling overwhelmed and scared. My eyes were watering from the sharp wind, and the hot tears mixed with the cold on my cheeks.

I thought: *I can't do this. I can't solve this. I have failed* (myself, my family, my friends). I was scared more than anything else, but in the moment, the desire to escape this trapped feeling was powerful and dreadful. The feeling of being overwhelmed, at a loss, trapped: it flattened me. If I'd been standing on a bridge or a ledge . . . I don't know which direction my next step would have been.

Oddly, I thought of my aunt Lindsay, and her laugh, and her constant positive spirit despite her own losses and her work with the dying and doomed. She is my dead mother's younger sister, someone I saw only a few times until I was an adult. But there was something about her, a light, a spark, a connection. I don't know what it was. We weren't close then. It was enough to get me off the hill and back to the dorm.

I didn't attempt to take my life. The sun rose. I felt raw but alive. Grades, school, holidays: they were blips along the way. Over time, I found a path through, and over more time than that, I gained a measure of understanding, and of peace.

But here's the thing: four years later, I was staying with my family in Washington, D.C. between teaching jobs, and it became clear—belatedly, once it was upon me, or I was mired in it—that the past was neither dead nor past. The same problematic, painful dynamics remained. I struggled to reconcile the emotional work I'd done on my own, away from family, with the ongoing dynamics and issues at home. I had stopped drinking and partying a couple years prior, and generally had a decent handle on my life.

And yet.

The old scars, the ingrained dynamics, the ghosts of the past, all of that swirled over me. I found myself deep in the old, specific despair. Which felt so strange, having been away from it for a few years. One day, I had that familiar, smothering sense of being trapped by a dynamic I could not solve or beat. I felt crushed. And as I walked across one of the bridges over Rock Creek Park, in a moment, a sharp, swift instant, I thought—or, heard myself think—in response to some inner voice: *Jump.* Because jumping off the bridge would end the feeling of inescapable entrapment. Because leaping would end the pain, frustration, fear, sadness. Because I could not fly. I would exit this life. Because grabbing the railing and launching myself was one thing I could do against the welled-up powerlessness.

I caught my breath. *Where the fuck did that come from?!* I was shaking. I eased myself off that bridge. I sat on a bench for a few minutes, trembling. It was as though the voice had always been there, but also, it spun itself out of some whirling ether. I wasn't depressed. I wasn't suicidal. I wasn't hopeless. Yet suddenly, a bridge, a leap, an expanse of sky and trees and blurred air, then the finality of the earth. I'd never considered killing myself, let alone jumping to my death. But the profound, long-term issues with my family did feel crushing, and, in a moment, the open door to escape beckoned. Subconscious ideation? Fuck if I know.

I seldom cross a bridge on foot without musing about that seductive impulse: solve all your problems by removing yourself—leave the problems, and your death, for others to handle. Had I leapt, the shame and sorrow over the mistake I was making, the immediate regret for all the life I was squandering—that part would have ended quite soon, upon impact. But the reverberations, the literal aftershocks—my family, my friends, my dog: the horrific *Why?*, the emptiness of one fewer soul in the world, the terror at the unknown despair and self-negation—would have echoed a long, long time. Now, thirty years later, I'd be a pause, a missed face, a memory. No kids, no adult relationships, no life lived. My friends' and family's lives would have continued, albeit altered, scarred, punctuated. You would not be reading this book.

//

With social media, I'm finding the circles of lives overlapping more often than not. We'll go on fatal calls, see what we see, then later I'll read the social media version of the event (or the result). Two younger men killed themselves within a month, one by hanging and one by gun. There wasn't much overlap in their social groups, but I knew both crews who responded, and I knew many friends of both men.

I witnessed how the man who hanged himself—how his death—echoed through the community like a bullet ricocheting through a marble hallway. Everyone felt gutted, felt as if they'd failed him, that they'd missed something that might have saved him from himself. In the weeks afterward, the sorrow mixed with guilt and then a resolve to reach out to anyone else who might be suffering, who might be considering suicide. He'd been at work, seemed in a good mood, made plans for a weekend he never reached. Then he was gone. And their lives continued, without him. They sought reasons, replayed minutiae of conversations, examined the import of glances—but found none.

The guy who shot himself was praised for doing it "out of the way" in one of the skyway's dead-end hallways. Social pages were full of tributes to him for "going out as he lived," in a fiercely independent blaze of misbegotten glory. His graffiti tag was posthumously splashed around town (and across the country: I found one in Oakland a year later). "He decided he'd had enough, and he ghosted this earthly party." I understand the defiance: *Death, be not proud, you motherfucker.* To sing the praises for a punk-rock angel, to celebrate his idiosyncratic life. *He died how he lived, by his own code.*

But: some unsuspecting passerby found his corpse, the gun by his side, hair and skull and brains against the beige wall. The first people on scene saw him: the firefighters, cops, and medics had to kneel beside him while someone checked for a final pulse (despite the incontrovertible damage). And some poorly paid cleaners had to scrub down the wall hours later, after the investigation, the photographs, the medical examiner's removing the body. The human contents had soaked into the industrial carpet. All of it had to be cleared with elbow grease and antiseptic.

That is *not* a cowboy way to go. It seldom is. I am not being crass or coarse: suicide is a tragic act. But our culture ignores or elides the gritty facts of life—and, here, death. In that elision, that polite discretion, we ignore the hard parts, the ugly images, the brutal truth. And the young and callow romanticize being "punk rock" and "taking the cowboy way out." I'm here to call bullshit on that.

A friend of mine has had hard times of mental struggle and has made several suicide attempts. I'd categorize them as cries for help rather than deliberate, dedicated attempts, but there have been a couple with room enough for the rescue plan to fail. We were talking in the psych ward after one attempt. His mind was addled with hysterical fantasies about God, angels, heaven. I listened politely and consistently refused to buy into his squalid escapism. The truth was, he'd felt off most of his life and the stunting of his engagement with the world was a sad, tragic thing. He kept saying he would be a better daddy to his young kids from up in heaven. There was such profound sadness and confusion and desperation in his voice.

"Look," I interjected. "Think for a second. I know you're hurting. You're scared. You're sad. I'm so sorry. I'm here right now with you, and I'll tell you every day that I'm so glad you called for help. That you're still here. But the important thing is, you are not a failure. Your kids love and need you."

We argued about this a bit. He returned to his parenting-from-heaven idea. I stopped him: "Hey, dumbass. When was the last time you spoke to your mom? When did she drop in to see how you're doing?"

He looked at me blankly, eyes flighty in the reddened sockets. "What do you mean?" he asked, as if it were a trick question.

"Your mom killed herself. Cancer got my mom fast. We are motherless sons. We have carried that shit our whole lives. Right? You have. I certainly have. Have you heard a single fucking word from your dead angel mom? No? No shit. Because that's not real. We are here. This is it. Dead is dead. So don't start any bullshit about being a better parent from heaven. You will be *gone*. You'll *never* see them again. They'll spend their lives in anguished grief over your abandoning them. Just like you carry for your mom."

He was staring at the floor, shaking his head in half-hearted denial or refusal. "No. No. It's different. I'd be there for them."

I rubbed his shoulder. "We both know that's shit. You'd be gone, and that would be a shame for all of us, and for you. And you'd pass on that family curse. You can help them by living. By *not* following your mom."

Over time, with meds, he grew more comfortable, slightly, in this earthly existence. The suicide attempts stopped. I've seen enough folks depart to know that the seductive temptation remains nearby, always. The legacy of a parent's suicide, of course, increases the likelihood of an orphaned child's later taking their own life too. Finding a way to break that cycle, reroute that legacy, that is a dire challenge.

//

I have revived many, many people over the years from opioid ODs. I have pulled some from fires and car wrecks, have been calm in the face of panic, desperation, despair, and great pain. I am proudest of the single, brief action I took one night, ironically as a battalion chief rather than a working crew member. During the 2016 Super Bowl, crews were dispatched for a report of a possible jumper. I arrived first in my chief's SUV. A young woman was perched astride the outer railing of a bridge, a long drop over the Mississippi River. A passerby had seen her and was now holding the woman's hand, terrified. The small Samaritan, one arm linked through hers, was pleading with the young woman not to jump. The woman on the rail was sobbing, abject, also terrified. The two were shaking. It was early February, the temp solidly below zero. The night was clear, the sky stark, the wind biting exposed skin.

I pulled over, radioed Dispatch what I had, and hopped out of the car. They were standing one hundred feet over the water, a thin, short, cold steel barrier keeping them topside. The young woman was wrestling with whatever drove her to the edge of the bridge, the pressure to leave it all behind. And she was leaning, teetering. The Samaritan was trying to hold her. They were swaying, precarious against the night sky. The wind had force. Gravity is neutral about suicide but not about physics.

I jumped the guardrail, and quietly approached from behind, staying in their blind spots to prevent any sudden, panicked, fatal lurches. They were small women, and I wrapped both of them in an embrace, quick and hard. I pulled the young woman back up and over the rail, onto the bridge deck.

I carried them backward, putting enough distance between the rail and us so that the desperate woman couldn't just hop over if my grip slipped. I said, "Hi there. We're all okay," or something. I reached the divider between the sidewalk and the road and leaned against it. I let the terrified Samaritan out of my grasp. She was shaking and pale. "Nice job," I told her, and turned my focus to the jumper. "You're all right. It's going to be all right. My name's Jeremy."

I had my arms and legs wrapped around her to ensure she didn't wiggle free and leap, but, once back on the deck, she wilted and sobbed brokenly. I loosened my grip, uncoiled my legs from hers, and told her she was a good person and I was very glad to meet her.

I sat with the young woman until the ambulance arrived, enveloping her as she wailed. I only let her go when the medics took her gently by the arms and escorted her into their bus. I'd tried to learn what caused her to try to jump, but she was too distraught, too sad. I just held her and repeated, "It will be okay. You are here and that's what matters. Nothing else matters. You are here. I'm so glad."

The medics took the girl away for evaluation. The police cleared the scene. No one ever identified the Samaritan. It was deep winter, and she was bundled against the cold. I tried to give a description but had seen only her wide, terrified eyes. I wanted her to receive recognition—and therapy. It's shocking to stumble into unexpected proximity to death.

I looked up to ask her name, but she was a small shape disappearing into the cold night, out of range of my voice. Just like that: gone. I briefly wondered if she'd been a literal guardian angel—or if she, too, had jumped. Neither: I spied a tiny form exiting the far end of the bridge and disappearing into the night.

I was alone on the bridge. I stood a few in the icy air, looking down at the dark rolling river below. It's chance. We live and die by chance.

I got in my SUV, turned the flashers off, and drove back to the station, where the crew was watching the Super Bowl. My hands were raw and aching from the cold, and I shivered from within for a while. No one else knew how it went, since I'd arrived and handled it before the rest of our crews reached the bridge. I had made a difference, perhaps the most significant of my career. I never learned the girl's name or anything else. I wanted to talk about it, not to brag on myself, but to unload the weight of that suicidal girl, the jagged hooks of the despair I saw in her eyes, heard in her voice. But I was alone with it.

//

A year and some months later, I was on a call and Sam Erickson, one of my favorite paramedics, quizzically asked why I wasn't a battalion chief any longer. I shrugged, said something coarse and clever, and we laughed. He's a great paramedic, a good man, and union leader for the medics. We share a gimlet disregard for admin. "Good to have you back," he said. "I haven't seen you since that girl on the bridge."

I didn't remember which medic crew it had been. "Yeah, Super Bowl night—the girl on the bridge over the river."

"Nice job," he said. "You saved her."

I said the girl was saved by the stranger who stalled her long enough for me to grab her. He flicked my shoulder. "Yeah, sure. Who pulled her off the edge?" I nodded, then shrugged. *Fair enough.* (Firefighters and medics really are allergic to acclaim—we know it's generally a matter of chance, which crew, which shift. Nothing else.)

He told me the story they'd learned from her, a depressingly familiar tale of family torment and despair. It brought back the girl's tears, her broken voice, and profound anguish. I had nothing to say. I was glad we'd given her another day alive, and I deeply hoped she'd gotten help, found peace, and understood she wasn't the problem. But I didn't know.

We don't know on so many calls. We get our flashes of adrenalized action; the patients get transported, and we go on to whatever's next. People ask, when I talk about work stories, *What happened to that person? How did they end up like that? Did they make it?*

There is so seldom any closure. The person might die, or survive—in some form. We might see them again, but generally not. We might see their family, in passing, or face-to-face (suddenly, shockingly—for both of us) on another call. We will see the houses as we drive around our area. Some of the crew might remember. Others weren't there that shift, weren't even on the job yet. I have flashes of memory, look around, and recognize I'm keeping company with ghosts and phantoms.

10

FATES AND FURIES

FOR TWO DECADES, I'VE FELT PEOPLE DEAD BENEATH MY FINGERS. I HAVE found them freshly dead and worked them to no avail, or I've found them decidedly dead and turned away. Twenty years responding to people dying slowly and horribly from terminal diseases, or rapidly and horribly from terminal injuries. I have been present for some peaceful, natural deaths—but those, while sublime and moving, are very rare for us. And the surviving families, the bereaved, they are still devastated. I see dead people and dying people as a matter of course. We will all join them, eventually. It is life, finite by definition.

People may debate the existence of atheists in foxholes, about which I have no firsthand experience, but in peacetime debacles, I see multitudinous prayers lofted skyward.

Answered prayers? That is harder to assess.

It is a brutal form of humility, the abject impotence when a traumatic or medical catastrophe has occurred to someone you love. When tragedy happens in front of you, I should say. We often go to work amid the pleas and screams of unrelated bystanders, people whose lives crossed paths with the stranger beneath our hands. Again, the killing of George Floyd is one poignant example of this: the lasting, collateral damage to the young witnesses.

Few people are too proud, or too hardened, to call out for help—for divine or magical intervention, for peace or comfort or their mom—in the face of death itself. We arrive on a cardiac arrest or a shooting, a suicide (attempt) or a car wreck, and as we go to work on the patient, the bystanders—whether family or friends or random folks whose day was interrupted by this incident—will call out toward both the heavens and us:

"Save him!"

"Please, Jesus: save her!"

"God, I'm begging: please save this little kid!"

"Lord, please help these firefighters save our Johnny!"

"Jesus, we need your hand in here. Steady *their* hands and help them save our auntie!"

When we regain a heartbeat, or pull someone out of a burning building, or a car wreck, or from the river, the initial "success" cheers the onlookers, who give praise and thanks. I don't argue with the public. The reality is, many of these victims never regain consciousness. Looking down on the unconscious or burned/broken/drowned person, I again feel the striking dissonance: *This is a miracle? This is God's magic?*

Beyond the emotion and uncertainty of the moment, I foresee what will follow, whether a few days in the ICU before the family pulls the plug, or years of persistent vegetative state. It's a hard silence I keep in those moments.

When we correct a potentially fatal issue: unclogging a windpipe, stanching blood flow, arriving in time to remove someone from a wrecked car or burning house, there is joy and rejoicing. Some citizens see us as the hands, the agents of God and Jesus, calling us angels and such. I again say nothing. I do not see divine fingerprints on these bodies, because then I would see them on all the corpses I encounter, the dead babies and young cancer patients and shit-luck fatalities. It's either all, or none. (I wish I could share more happy stories in this book, but that is not how the job goes—which is one of my points: how to survive a career so short on "good" outcomes. The mirth is generally of the gallows variety.)

If the rare saves reward faith, I marvel that the multitude of not-saves does not douse people's piety. I also balk at the rationale offered when things go the way they tend to (poorly, fatally): *It's God's plan. Who are we to question his wisdom?*

If the devil is in the details, we really dance with the devil a lot, since the details of who lives and who dies are all we've got.

I'm all for the comfort that faith, or philosophy, brings a person. I understand and appreciate how a belief in something larger than us helps people. What I find troubling is the ways that faith gets inserted in the spaces where biology or physics are. It is fine to pray for your auntie, but she would feel better with morphine. Looking toward the heavens while ignoring what is happening in the sickbed beside you serves no one.

Peter Leschak wrote in *Ghosts of the Fireground* about his own lost faith and the lessons he learned from studying a preacher who saved dozens, if not hundreds, from a Peshtigo, Wisconsin, wildfire in October 1871:

> [The preacher] believed good and evil ultimately emanated from the Deity, and since the universe encompassed both, the Creator must be responsible for both. You should not praise his sunsets then curse the hurricane; if you celebrate birth, then honor death; if pleasure warms you, then snuggle up to pain.

My experience is that most humans are surprised by unsurprising, causal events. Too many years making bad choices catch up to a person. It's distressing for family and friends, but it is seldom an objective surprise. Biology is a wonder, but it is capricious. Healthy-seeming young people catch terminal diagnoses, women still die in childbirth, heart attacks drop fit folks. In traumatic incidents, I see people escape relatively uninjured from absurd violence, or they die from something "minor." When a person is on the receiving end of a bullet or a car or a piece of steel, the difference between survival and death can be milliseconds or millimeters. *Who* is in the details, again?

//

The four years I spent in Chattanooga, Tennessee, teaching at evangelical Presbyterian prep schools, were an education in the range and gradations of Christian faith *and* the problems with a religious social structure. I was twenty-three, a freshly sober, liberal, and bookish Yankee, feisty and antiauthoritarian. I was far afield, trying to forge a better path, to find meaning and feelings without the escape of booze. I was zero-for-seventy applying to teaching positions when Hank Lewis called to say they were looking for a new literature teacher. The school was in the Bible Belt. It was a job; I was broke. I readily agreed.

I had no idea what I was getting into. I wrote "Gothic" in the slot for "Church Preference" in my application. On my contract, I had to sign that I "accept the concept that Jesus Christ is sufficient for the salvation of mankind." I shrugged. *Sure, I could "accept" lots of concepts.* Once employed, I realized it was not a hypothetical or philosophical statement. They wanted, expected, a *literal* acceptance.

This was an immersion in an entirely different environment from any I'd known. Purity culture and Young Life (a Christian organization whose activities struck me as horny teenagers playing in the woods, using Bibles as cover and prayer as contraception), odd internecine Christian quibbles (nine flavors of Baptists versus the Methodists versus the Presbyterians versus the God-in-Christs, everyone united against the Catholics), unselfconscious anti-Semitism, raving homophobia, "scriptural" misogyny, unquestioned arch-conservatism, faith healing, prosperity gospel, xenophobia, evangelical literalism. It was a lot to fathom. There were prayers galore. We prayed before school, during school, in the cafeteria and on the playing fields before every meal and game.

So many prayers . . .

Mondays and Fridays, there were compulsory sports and faith assemblies; the middle three days would have structured prayers, with people offering devotional testimonials. Largely these were adolescents striving to make sense of their faith, which was interesting if as underformed as most teen philosophies are. But a great number of adults spoke. Frequently, they were visiting preachers or else successful people (pro athletes, wealthy businessmen, and—actually, that was it: sports or business as gateway to prosperity), men who flashed their gilded exceptionalism. They thanked Jesus and credited their faith with getting them where they were (rich, successful, powerful). The very few Black speakers were men and either sports stars touting for Jesus or preachers—definitely *not* liberation theologists. Black or white, the men spread litanies of problematic assertions fashioned as God's natural order, "his Word." I cannot remember any female speakers—maybe a couple of "notable wives" who pitched the party line of *A woman's place is behind her man.*

I was learning how to teach, how to convey information, how to solicit thought and articulation from my students, wading through massive cultural dissonance. I met many good people; I learned about life, teaching, and faith from lots of folks. But none of it was singular: I gained deep insights from non-Christians as well. The rigid explicitness of Jesus *is* Lord, the widespread implications that those without

Jesus weren't simply lost, or unfulfilled, but *morally* lacking, did not jibe for me.

Hank recruited me to Chattanooga, knowing I was desperate for a job and wanting an ally for himself. He was a friend from college—though not my college. I had been lonely at Tufts and often visited Steve Belber at Trinity College, in Hartford, Connecticut. Hank and Steve were friends. Hank and I became friends. He was raised and schooled in Chattanooga, well versed in, if wary of, the cultural dynamics. We would drive around town in his convertible, and I'd witness the pressure and constant threat from police and security guards; the frequent "unintentional" harassment from coworkers and parents; the aggressions, micro, macro, passive, *and* explicit. A Black man always had to watch himself lest white people became dangerously uncomfortable. That was the true and deep education for me: the gaping chasm between what American culture claimed it wanted (demanded) from its Black citizens, and how it treated them.

A funny thing happened on the way to salvation. As a proctor for chapel/devotional, where I would monitor my three rows of assigned students, I was a captive audience. Four years of this provided me with ample reflection. The more I pondered, the more I had serious, searing questions. Not about faith, but about the humans and systems deploying the faith language. I listened to the speeches and prayers, then witnessed how people lived their lives. They were merely human, flawed and conflicted and contradictory. Just like the rest of us. As a nonbeliever, I did not condemn anyone to eternal hellfire. The same was not true for a striking number of the Prince of Peace's posse. Low-hanging fruit? I don't think it is.

I looked around at an elite, all-boys school, an all-male and all-but-for-Hank white faculty, listened to what was being said, what was conspicuously unsaid, and I started asking deeper questions. I could not fault the school for being true to itself: an avowed evangelical Christian private institution. But the myopic privilege and utter failure to consider others' beliefs, as well as the implicit and often explicit certainty that *any* other beliefs were wrong, invalid, sinful: this obliterated the cultural monotheism for me. I emphasize that this was a white-dominant chapel, school, cultural construct. I would expect a far different liturgy were it a Black Baptist or AME school. As Dr. King wrote, "The most segregated hour in Christian America is eleven o'clock on Sunday morning." (Although, on many progressive social issues Black and white evangelicals share a dim view.)

A repressively homophobic school that claimed there were neither gay students nor gay faculty, despite living (silenced and closeted) proof to the contrary. A place that was throbbingly homoerotic and championed the absence of women's interference, while maintaining the necessity of women for breeding and homemaking—their "civilizing" influence reinforcing compulsory heterosexuality—but wouldn't let female students compete with the boys in the classrooms. A place that had barely begun allowing Black students in and was in the process of running its lone Black teacher out—yet the maintenance, custodial, and kitchen staff was composed of primarily of working-class Blacks: it was either the natural order, or it was a reflection of a very slanted playing field.

As I wrote earlier, I took the summer between my first and second years to self-educate on all the things our English department "couldn't" manage: Black writers, female authors, Latinx and Asian stories and essays; cultural criticism; race theory, queer authors and theorists. The more I read and heard from those whose voices were constantly excluded, dismissed, and silenced, the more sense they made. The more I read and thought and examined the status quo *and* the excluded voices, the more I balked at what we ("we") claim to be normal and natural.

An apocryphal tale: a year or two before I arrived, Ted Turner, the media mogul and an alumnus of the school, made a substantial donation. At the ceremony, rather than thanking Jesus and the school, in that order, for making him the success he was, Ol' Ted told the full house that he didn't think too highly of the school's rigors and self-importance. Further, he declared, "I was only freed in my heart when I stopped believing in God." They were *still* talking about the blasphemous horror of it when I arrived. Given Mr. Turner's well-documented personality, I could not see why folks were either surprised or scandalized. *Who did you think you were inviting to speak?* They still cashed his big check and built a new building with it.

Why am I dragging my readers down memory lane? Because my struggle for understanding led me to see through the surface of American identity to the human workings, the men behind the curtain. I questioned the "articles of faith" I encountered because I had to: too much was incongruent, inconsistent, illogical. This forced me to challenge the default presumptions of American identity and history. Chattanooga *was* America in a condensed, regional version. As much as Chattanooga seems a punch line, an apogee of proudly regressive backwardness, I learned that it was a great blueprint to understand our country's essence. The issues of race, class, gender, and power had southern accents, but it was *profoundly* American. That I was witnessing the vice grip of cultural insanity on my dear friend Hank, a Black man trying to play by ever-changing, never-upheld rules, forced a clarity concerning the rigged game. Moral suasion is a con, I saw. My privileged impunity demanded I stand against all that we call "normal."

I was Hank's assistant at the nascent African-American Students Association. I was the only white member that first year. Other faculty members "supported the idea" but never felt willing or comfortable enough to cross the threshold, despite Hank's weekly open invitations. Some "traditionalists" objected, claiming a *special* identity group was *exclusionary*. But those relativists abound, growing like mold in their festering rot. They reject any movement toward equity or equality, object to any honest appraisal of past and present, and offer nothing but staunch adherence to what works for them.

The Black students were welcoming, if wary. I experienced the humbling gut check of being the *only* for once. I shelved my positional authority to listen to and learn from all the young members. The "discomfort" was a profound self-consciousness about my conspicuous whiteness, something most white people are spared in the majority of our social and work lives. We all got past the surface initial dissonance of my presence, and I think the guys were able to speak freely, to drop the mask.

My time there coincided with the first Gulf War, Sinead O'Connor ripping up the pope's photograph to protest the Catholic Church's aggressive role in the widespread abuse of children by its priests, the Rodney King beating and the easy exoneration of the violent officers, and the Los Angeles riots. Pre-internet, these cultural moments were all covered on TV. I watched them with the students in our dorm. Spike Lee's *Malcolm X* was released, and police officers patrolled the mall cinema: *fear of a Black audience*. Witnessing our Black students wrestling with these issues, the implications and history that shaped each, listening to their anguish and layers of struggle while we gathered inside one small room amid throngs of oblivious, or hostile, white students and faculty was profound for me.

Many of the aggressively racist students would peer through the classroom door and make faces or laugh. Several came up to me once in the parking lot; one grabbed my hand and pretended to examine it. "Well, shoot," the ring leader said. "He *is* white after all. We thought you had a secret you weren't telling us, or you got a head injury and forgot who you are." He offered to introduce me to some good country people who would teach me the difference between whites and Blacks. This was a fifteen-year-old without a sliver of self-consciousness.

What I saw, or learned, in the evangelical halls of Chattanooga, was to question the narrative. Not simply the conservative Christian— although definitely that one. But I realized that straight white men ran the banks and businesses, shaped the rules to serve themselves, called the shots, and then tricked everyone else into fighting for peanuts. It wasn't so much that I suddenly "saw" Black people, or women, or gay folks: I saw how fundamentally *we* (white, male, straight) benefited from the con and how we propped up this disingenuous, slanted power dynamic.

So, my battle wasn't with Jesus. It was with those who wielded his name to cover their unexamined or selective biases, their warped world order. But that was also the essence of American cultural identity: telling ourselves what we have is *natural* (if not ordained)—not something achieved brutally, at the expense of a great many others. I would question, pointedly, the inconsistencies, the problematic illogic, the sleights of hand that rigged the cards against so many. The answers I received, if I got any, did little to placate me.

Hank left for graduate school, and for the next two years, my boon companion was David Feldman, a vegetarian, Jewish atheist from New York City with a lesbian mother, a profound intellect, and absolutely no connection to Dixie. He'd been recruited to teach science and math, and this was a lark for him—a few years teaching high school before going for his PhD. Some lark. Imagine how many "opportunities" he had to be rejected, condemned, insulted while at chapel. Likewise, how fatuous the cant seemed when his very essence refuted and disproved it all. Dave was brilliant and bemused, too wise for my incandescent furies. He put in two years then left, earning his PhD in physics at UC Davis.

The Taco Bell along the commercial strip was the only place open past nine that served "vegetarian" food back then. We would grab bean burritos and grade papers, incredulous that this was our life. While David was well schooled in jazz, our soundtrack consisted of Consolidated's "The Sexual Politics of Meat," Michael Franti in Disposable Heroes and Spearhead, Henry Rollins's *End of Silence,* and Fugazi, "Angry Music to Quit Your Shitty Job To . . ." We shared endless hours of mirth and frustration, keeping each other sane while wondering what type of fish we were to be so far out of the water and still breathing.

I am comfortable with ideas of faith, but I object when their articulation causes or justifies the oppression of others. I see quite clearly the too-human aspect of a man-made apparatus. So, on the many emergency calls where we hear and see religious utterances, desperate cries to the heavens or quiet, determined affirmations of faith, I understand. Having a calm center is a good thing, a clarity or reassurance.

Kathryn Schulz captures the heart of my view in *Lost & Found*; she won the Pulitzer Prize, so I trust her to be more articulate than I:

> Questions about goodness and justice, suffering and evil, the origins and ends of the universe, the nature of the self, how to treat one another, how best to live our brief lives while we have them: all of these are of passionate interest to me, but I have never found satisfaction or solace in any faith-based answers to them. By constitution, education, or both, I am profoundly skeptical of religious authority, and although I am deeply interested in the many fathomless mysteries of the universe, I do not believe that an omnipotent creator numbers among them.

Perhaps that is the essential meaning of *skeptic* or *nonbeliever*: I can be awed by the Grand Canyon or the birth of a baby or the wizened skin of a 105-year-old, and that is enough. Our losses and our joys come from Life, and that is holy to me. I don't need to connect it to a Heavenly Father, a divine human-esque creator. I am comfortable here, and now. If I believed, mind you, I would likely be a roaring Old Testament prophet, a Cotton Mather or Jonathan Edwards type of humorless absolutist. But I don't, so I'm not. I appreciate the irony, y'all.

If you can endure being ostracized, the misfit's life feels purer than smothering your integrity to fit in. I accept my path. The crusader in me has little patience for the false idols and empty words. I witness close-mindedness and shallowness and petty judgments, and I call them out. I am a stubborn, self-righteous, persistent contrarian. I have no beef with God. I know nothing of God. I believe none of us do. God is by definition unknowable. Inscrutable. I have many issues with those who claim to speak *for* God: their messages seem skewed toward selfish ends.

Ironically, or perhaps unsurprisingly, my time in the Buckle of the Bible Belt solidified my contrarian nature. This skepticism and critical engagement put me at odds with the Brotherhood when I joined the fire service. A bunch of white guys carping that Others were *ruining* their sacred existence? Legal remedies to generations of malicious exclusion were seen as *unfair*? All that self-serving and deceitful folklore. Same game, different fields. Being a good, moral human does not require a cross; being a good firefighter does not require a mustache.

//

I was not born a skeptic. My tendencies toward being a crusading zealot and skeptical curmudgeon come honestly: my maternal lineage goes deep into the Mormon canon . . .

My mother died of pancreatic cancer when I was very young. She was diagnosed in September and died in October, three months before my third birthday. She'd had "back pain" for a couple of months, but everyone chalked it up to my sister's recent birth. When they finally discovered the cancer, she was done. There is no cure for pancreatic cancer, just attempts to slow its inexorable fatality. She didn't even get that. I had thirty-three months with her, although the final weeks were not great. My sister had four months.

So, from toddlerhood, my sense of Happily Ever After or Nuclear Normal was obliterated and rewired. It's been said that by age fifty we should make sense of whatever shitty things happened in our childhoods and stop reacting as if we were freshly wounded. I concur. Experiencing profound loss in one's formative years alters the presumptive and unquestioning expectation that all is well in the world. That deviation from "normal" explains a lot about my disposition, outlook, and psychological framework. If we consider Piaget's "object permanence" developmental stages from the age I was when my mom died, no wonder I'm skeptical: I've been searching for that missing central person since 1969.

Recognizing this in myself, I can understand the profound and complicated forces at work on a great many of our patients. Am I drawn to suffering, or merely better attuned to it? When I taught high school English, I saw through many adolescent facades to the deeper, truer issues besetting the students. In her incredible memoir *That Good Night*, Sunita Puri writes, "There is no script, no training course, that can teach you how to sit in silence, how to listen to them. You either have a deep well of your own suffering—your own intersecting, interlocked circles of loss, grief, anger, fear, sadness, regret—to draw upon, or you have a well of suffering that you have not recognized or are not ready to draw upon. We all have our suffering. Whether you can use yours to connect to the suffering of another is a separate matter entirely."

Did I seek out the macabre in applying for the fire department? I *truly* did not know what lay in store, and, back then, there was negligible discussion about EMS and the effects of human suffering. When I listened to Jen and her friends talk, I had no inkling how much trauma was involved, how it would affect them and me. But, yes, I believe having a cracked compass can point us toward the true north of human connection. I have little patience for dissembling pleasantries, decorous small talk, hope or wishful thinking as action plan. I struggle with "appropriate." The heart is a lonely hunter, after all. Relentless and lonely, it seeks its truth.

//

My dad is a stand-up guy, a reserved, hardworking man, raised with five brothers and no sisters. He was, to put it mildly, unprepared for my mother's intense, complicated family. And then she died. He experienced this rapid, colossal loss, and found himself widowed at twenty-nine with an infant and a toddler. He did not ship us to the New England Home for Wayward Youth. In 1969, there was little in the way of bereavement leave or grief counseling. He was a new lawyer, expected to put in long hours. He would come home from the office, see us for dinner and bed, then return for more hours. The presumption, of course, was that there'd be a wife at home to handle "all that childcare stuff." Except she was dead.

Even before he lost his wife, my dad has said, his faith had wavered. Raised in the traditional Boston Irish Catholic cultural faith, where church, mass, prayer, and shame were ingrained into daily life, he said he'd begun doubting before leaving home. Then at college, he stopped attending mass. He said there was a passage in Dostoevsky's *The Brothers Karamazov*, in the "Grand Inquisitor" section, that cemented, or articulated, his loss of faith. Essentially, "If God is God, he is not good; if God is not good, he is not God."

The theodicy strikes again.

I can't imagine watching his young wife die swiftly and finding himself widowed with two squalling kids improved my dad's relationship with God.

The night my mother died, her schizophrenic brother locked himself in a bedroom and played the Mormon Tabernacle Choir's rendition of Handel's *Messiah* at full volume for hours, over and over and over, until my bereft dad had to break down the door, physically remove the record from the turntable, then wrestle his hysterical brother-in-law to the ground outside on the front lawn.

That's not a good sort of bonding. And my dad, true to his background and the era, conflated my uncle's homosexuality with his mental illness. Gay = crazy; crazy = gay; one caused the other; mutually inclusive, both sicknesses. My other maternal uncle had abandoned the family in his teens and was an early hippie vagabond. Around this time, a car wreck when he and his pregnant wife were driving from the southwest back to Salt Lake City resulted in the deaths of his wife and their unborn child. He was a hurt, angry, antagonistic man. He and my dad had no common ground.

My mom's mother came to D.C. to help out in the weeks after her death, but she was beset by her own emotional traumas—and alcohol. Her volatile instability only added to my dad's stress. She returned home, then her own cancer was discovered. She died within the year.

We flew to Salt Lake City to see her before she died. The rented hospital bed was in the same place in the family room as it had been for my mom. That must have been devastatingly haunting for the immediate family: two women dying a year apart. For years, I *thought* I remembered seeing my mom in her sick(death)bed. I hitched my emotional grasping to the *idea* that I remembered her final days. Because that was one of the few memories I had. I was likely remembering my grandmother dying. In truth, I have no concrete memories of my mom, just stories I've written myself into, gauzy dreams.

After my mother's death and my dad's remarriage, we didn't see my maternal family much, and talked about them seldom. My dad said very little (almost nothing) about them. He's a quiet man, steady and staid as can be. An emotionally arid fellow, his alpha and omega after he remarried was to suppress anything that would distress his wife. I was instructed not to mention my mother, as it was upsetting to our new mom. Putting the weight and responsibility of an adult's insecurities on a five-year-old kid is, well, bullshit. The depths of unknowing, curiosity, hurt, desire: they are profound. Of course, making my mom verboten only deepened the aching wonder and desire. Class genealogy projects were fraught, asininely complicated.

I didn't spend much time with my mother's family while I was young. My dad's terse summary was "Well, your mother was the most stable of a family of tragic and strange people." That's not quite true, but it's not untrue, either.

Half of them were wiped out in that brief span, my mother and grandmother, cancer, 1969 and 1970, respectively; my uncle, 1976 (cause unknown: either murder, suicide, or very rough "natural" causes—the effects of mental illness and drug use; the coroner's report was inconclusive. San Francisco police didn't expend much effort investigating dead gay men then). I did not see the surviving uncle until my grandfather's funeral in 2005. Three times between 1973 and 1987, my grandfather Tom and my aunt Lindsay flew to D.C. for a thirteen-hour visit (ten hours of which were spent at a hotel). We would eat a brief, semi-awkward meal, and they would depart the next day.

I've had people say, "It all worked out for the best. These losses were not for nothing: there was a reason, a purpose. God had plans for you." As if God needed to unceremoniously snuff out my mother to bring me to faith. Or that my lovely life is a consolation prize, the divine purpose of sticking my mom with a treacherous pancreas. I'm not Job, first of all. And I hope God would have resolved that stupid argument with Satan by now. It's been millennia. But, even as an analogy, Job's story makes no sense at all. His family, his wife and kids and cattle, they were collateral damage in the bar bet between God and Satan. According to the Bible, it was all to show Job how powerful and inscrutable God was (to show the devil, really). Once beaten into submission, Job receives a brand-new family and more cows. But what about his first wife and kids?

Same with that absurd cant "God has special plans for you. Your suffering and loss are for some bigger purpose." But my dad's suffering? My sister's existential confusion? My mom's devastated family? My mother's shitty premature death, the vicious final knowledge that she would not see her kids grow up and not be there for us?

No. Cancer sucks. *Dead is dead.*

In addition to having a mother-sized hole in my heart, I've never lost a fatalistic sense of the world's tendency toward the tragic, the fatal. I would have apocalyptic worries when someone was late (before texting and cell phone ubiquity). Of course, the worst might-could happen: I had hard proof that it does and did happen. It's no surprise that I bristle and refute the *Good God: Good Plan* bromides.

//

I sought out my aunt as I got older, and the connection we formed saved my life. Lindsay was the youngest child and lost half her family before she was twenty-six. She was largely alone in the world. Her remaining sibling had run away from home at sixteen and was estranged (and strange). Her dad, like mine, was spectacularly unemotional and dry. She turned her losses into a life's mission of sorts. She became a nurse, then specialized in hospice care. She has said she became a nurse to understand and fight against death, spurred by her own losses. Through the depths of the AIDS crisis, Linds worked in Los Angeles, tending to dying young men. Then, as the demographics shifted, she worked with the homeless, the addicted, the mentally ill. Similarly, she said, her focus shifted toward mental health, to address the damages wreaked by mental illness in her immediate family. She radiates a deep joy and kindness, yet her humor is earthy and deliciously perverse. She walks with light, carrying her darkness in a hidden pocket.

It was a lifeline to connect with her, hear her hearty cackle and see the twinkle in her eye, and recognize kin. She has inspired me to be more gracious, patient, understanding with people. I try to emulate her pleasure in human foibles, her skill at finding joy and meaning with people who are on the margins.

My grandfather wasn't big on visits, or emotions. He was a hell of a raconteur, though, telling lively gothic tales of our Mormon forebears. Neglect and tragedy were fodder for blithely kooky anecdotes. Everything was hilarious: everything was extraordinarily dangerous. (It's not unlike firefighters laughing it up over horrific calls, when I think about it.) As I pressed him for info, for memories, for *something* of their side of my family, my bloodline, I felt the same affinity I felt with Linds: mordant wit, dry perspective, scant emotional reflection. He and my father were both stunningly rational, men without emotional depths. Aunt Linds has suggested that, on her side, at least, the endless misery and deaths of the Mormon settlers inculcated a fundamental hardness—not just hardiness, but to survive all the mortality on the frontier, people saw death and loss as much a part of their lives as the vast skies, the stunning landscape, and the constant duress of existence.

I met Annie when we were twenty-nine, and one of the first common things we shared, other than attraction, was the loss of a parent at a young age. Her dad killed himself when she was seven. She, too, had a hard time believing in Happily Ever After. As a couple, we managed to overcome attachment and intimacy issues, largely, and throw the cosmic dice, conceiving and raising two daughters. A miscarriage between Flann and Lux wasn't devastating. We both understood biology and the grim odds of the universe. When the kids were young, Annie's strong concern that the plane would crash caused intense tension when we traveled: should only one of us fly, so the kids would have a surviving parent? Should *none* of us fly—but then, what about car wrecks? If the plane went down, she would want to comfort the kids as they plummeted. Nothing could reassure her it was unlikely to happen.

It's hard to convince people who have lost someone catastrophically to relax and trust the process, or God, or physics.

And yet, I think of Linds, the baby of the family, who lost half of her family in stunning succession. I see how she has turned her losses and her grief into something positive. But the darkness and the light are there, together, in her. As Ayn Rand wrote in *The Fountainhead,* "No happy person could be so impervious to pain." For many years, Linds was a theist, and we would have long discussions about faith, humanity, and notions of God. She wasn't keen on formal religions, though she studied a great deal of them, to little satisfaction. She focused on what mattered (to her): human connection, the innate wonder of humanity, resilience. Her perspective, having seen so many people suffering and dying, has been a good touchstone for me. I figure, if she who has seen thousands of final moments can say there's a holiness within us all, I should trust her and look for it more.

Life tends toward ending, death is natural—and imminent for a great many of us, whether we accept it or not—and my years on the job have reinforced this. My immersion in it gives me an appreciation of all that I have. If we only get this one shot at life, we ought to launch into it bravely, openly, honestly, daringly. If there's a heaven ("above"), well, I'll see about that when it's my time . . . The formative bending of my horizon toward death likely forged my saturnine disposition. I see not the worst in people, but the human in people. I see denial spread over everything—and that is what I rail against. That which does a disservice to our better natures and our integrity.

I know I don't know what God is, but I also know from the ceaseless stream of hard deaths, painful dying, long-term suffering—as well as the millions living in poverty, want, loneliness, fear—that the general tale of an immaculate, immediate God is too, too human a figment. I still have that furious, hurting little tyke within me, searching for his mom, taking umbrage at bromides and heavenly promises. No wonder I bristle when I hear "God is good: All the time." Faith as meditation and comfort, I get that. Nature is wholly separate from our anthropomorphized versions of a deity. I don't buy into the good versus evil dichotomy. Many "good" people have done bad things. Many "bad" people do good things. Does that make them good, or bad, or simply human? I fear I'm being too general or abstract. I am trying to write this without the hard details. I have seen parents who killed their children; men who have killed their partners; drunk drivers who killed innocent strangers; men who lashed out in a moment of furious insecurity and shot someone (strangers and enemies alike). Teachers and preachers and coaches who abused students—and the systems that protected them. Police officers who killed those they were intended to help. Good and bad are porous concepts. Too often we get caught on the surface and superficial. Bad people get away with doing bad things, and worse, they do it in God's name. That alone should give the believers pause.

My elder daughter worries for my soul and asks me about my concerns for an afterlife (*the* afterlife, in her scheme). I believe our job, task, purpose on earth is to make sense of ourselves, connect with others, do right, and help each other as we can. Are "broken" people drawn to emergency response because the chaos feels like home? I don't think so. In the best of ways, I hope it is more like what James Baldwin describes in "The Artist's Struggle for Integrity":

> You must understand that your pain is trivial except insofar as you can use it to connect to other people's pain; and insofar as you can do that with your pain, you can be released from it, and then hopefully it works the other way around too; insofar as I can tell you what it is to suffer, perhaps I can help you to suffer less.

I take that as a challenge, a core belief, a compass for living. This broken world is imperfect and worth fighting for. I do not look to the heavens, but to each one of us. As Craig Finn sings, *We are our own only saviors.* Just as I must guard against complacency and cynicism, and my duty as a captain is to set a good tone for my coworkers, I challenge myself to remain open to the mysteries of life—and death. Certainly, a great many of the people I respond to are dying faster than the general population, but sometimes they surprise us. Whether that's God, or fate, or dumb luck, or human resilience, I do not know. I'm just happy whenever someone gets to see the sun also rise again.

(Deep thanks to Flannery Enneking-Norton for doing battle with an early, rough-hewn version of this chapter.)

11
WHAT WE TALK ABOUT WHEN WE TALK ABOUT COVID

WHAT FOLLOWS IS MY PERSONAL REFLECTION ON THE PANDEMIC. AS EMTS, my peers and I danced over the hot coals of uncertainty and perilous threat from the very outset. We lifted, carried, held the very sick and infectious, shouldering the duty of risk and care when nothing was yet known or certain. This has given me—forced on me—a sharp perspective to ponder and scrutinize the larger social catastrophe Covid-19 has caused. The truths about our country revealed by the pandemic reflect nearly every aspect and criticism of our sociology: health, wellness, class, race, gender, information and education, the limits of the health care system, the risks when those who are paid to protect you are hostile to your existence.

All of it. Covid showed our best and weakest humanity.

April 2020: All Roads Lead to the Contagious Hospital

In the earliest days, as the sickness—and fear—spread across the United States, I kept a journal based on our shifts on April 7 and 8, 2020. Andy Mannix, a reporter for the *Minneapolis Star Tribune*, excerpted some of it for an article published April 24, 2020. This first section is my contemporaneous recording and reflection of the Minneapolis Fire Department's response to the early stages of the pandemic.

Looking back as I wrote the manuscript for this book in early 2022, I marveled at the distinction between the immediate intensity of unknown and comprehensive fears, and the blurred and blurry equilibrium we reached. From the terrifying unknowns to the aching tedium of a still-contested, wildly destructive virus. Almost a year later, approaching the final edits, I have trouble accessing what it felt like in the beginning stages. I'm glad I kept notes, but even they feel remote. The human ability to filter out hard experiences is stunning. Or maybe through the tedium of repetition, it all became a foggy blur.

Tuesday, April 7, 2020

0515. Thunderstorms passing north of the Twin Cities jolt me up before my alarm. I bike to work in the wind and rain. It's nice to be out in the dawn, a good chance for quiet and reflection. By the time I'm on the back stretch, the rain has passed and the sun is climbing the sky. I see four other humans on my ride. I swing wide and nod hello. We exhibit wary, confused regard toward each other. No one knows who might be contagious or how much distance is *enough*.

//

0710. Starting the shift. I clarify to my crew that we are officially adopting social distancing and protective masking in the stations: no group meals, no sitting together on the couches, no clustering around a single computer; masks on at all times. I have a good, thoughtful crew, but this is an odd adjustment. The time spent with each other between calls is not solely about joking or training. It serves as a bond to process the difficult things we encounter; it protects against isolation and depression and emotional trauma. It breaks the tension.

I've spent my off-shift days reading the evolving suggestions and guidelines for PPE and patient treatment in emergency response. Information keeps coming, the gravity of the virus intensifies, our attempts to catch up are frantic, chaotic, floundering at times. The implications are monstrous. We are getting updated warnings and protocols weekly, if not daily, as more is learned or guessed about the virus. My thoughts are on the practical application of theories. The human factor, as ever, is the wildcard.

Our official direction from the administration has been to emphasize symptomatic patients exclusively, the direction being to *Limit exposure whenever safely possible.* No specifics, just general guidelines, ideals. These are best-practice plans, commonsensical, but anathema to the fire service realities. Because the virus is invisible, there is no way to tell if we are successful—nor what mistakes we make. No way to know if we are standing in a miasma of infectious droplets. At this point, we do not even know how it is transmitted. Through the skin? The eyes? Ears? By touch?

I have a rookie on my crew, Jenn Hall. She's brand new and untested. Her class has the singular fate of beginning their careers in this pandemic. Hard to provide solid hands-on, face-to-face, real-life training when we are social distancing, minimizing patient exposure, and restricting all regular nonessential station activities. I remind my crew to read the longer updates and studies I have sent them. My goal is to improve understanding about the various exposure or infection threats we face, and to increase buy-in for mask use and decreasing vectors.

In a job that has chaos as a constant, this feels ludicrous. As captain, I feel the duty to protect my crew. I've been going solo on all medicals. If I can assess the patient and escort them out to the ambulance, I do. Fresh air, fewer people exposed, less time inside: it all helps. Many of the sick folks cannot walk alone, so I lift, escort, or carry them out. That is a lot of direct contact. If the person cannot walk even with my help, or is in acute medical need, I'll have my crew join me. Mostly, I do it alone. I feel for my rookie, whose formative weeks are spent standing on front lawns, waiting for direction or dismissal.

We are told that simple surgical masks are sufficient for anything but Covid droplets. There are varying reports of how deep Minneapolis's cache of N95 masks is. Administrators and budgeters look at stockpile and surplus numbers and reflexively try to protect surpluses. For those of us working the streets, we want to be protected *now*, not reassured that there *will* be masks for some hypothetical future event.

The proffered solution is to wear simple masks, but if a call turns out to be "more" than just a basic EMS response, we should stop, back out of the room, and upgrade our PPE.

For those of you who don't do this job, that might sound reasonable and clear.

It is not. Lots of theories crash into reality during the pandemic.

When Dispatch hears anything remotely ILI-suggestive (influenza-like illness, before they switched to "positive screening") from the 911 caller, they announce it to the crews via radio and rig computer, and we are instructed to upgrade our PPE appropriately. This is a good example of the unavoidable time lag in communication with Dispatch, between what the 911 call taker gets on the phone, types into the shared info screen, what pops into the dispatcher's queues and screens, what they type for our computers, then what they say over the air. We might already be at or inside the door when pertinent info gets through this chain. Once we are off the rig, we cannot see any computer updates.

The first weeks, these announcements from Dispatch have an urgent, grave tone. There is a tension of the mysterious and sinister unknown added to such calls. Over months, then the entire year, and then into the tedious beyond, Dispatch will continue to follow these prompts and duly warn us of "potential ILI symptoms" or "positive CVD screen," requiring us to affirm that we "copy the notice," even though the prearrival screening is overly broad—to the point of being useless. "Do you have a cough?" "Do you feel sick?" "Have you possibly been exposed to someone with Covid?" Anyone who says yes to one of the questions trips the "Possible-ILI" flag, and we get warned. So, as with our "possible heart" calls, the net of "caution" sweeps up excessive flotsam and jetsam that are not cardiac and not Covid.

My first call once Covid was declared loose on the streets of Minneapolis, I walked up to a house for a report of a child not feeling well. Nothing in the prearrival info gave any reason to think Covid or respiratory illness. Nowhere had we seen info about CVD and children. It was a "'regular' kid feeling sick" call.

And then I got to the door. The panicked mother ran up to me, thrust the baby into my arms, and she and another adult surrounded me, urgently telling me in Spanish how sick the child was. I was translating in my head as they spoke frantically. While the infant was unlikely to have Covid, the other adults in the house might—two looked ill, flushed, sweaty, *sick*. I stood on the porch, holding the baby as the worried family surrounded me. There was neither time nor space to back out and upgrade my PPE.

This was why I wore an N95 mask on all calls from the outset. I wear safety glasses all the time already (I have been sprayed by blood and spit, and bloody spit, multiple times, so, I'm a believer in glasses).

This is also why I am skeptical of the administrators' plans: they operate in the conceptual. Reality, especially in emergency medicine, does not play fair. There is an inherent tension to these positions. The lag time between one protocol to the next *might* be the space through which fatal infection gets us.

Honestly, I am more concerned by asymptomatic transmission, the Trojan horse patients. But that is too abstract: our command staff is trying to assess how much quarantine we will be facing, how many exposures, how many sick, or dying, coworkers. So, they have emphasized what they can: obvious presenting symptoms. Which doesn't change the fact that research is clear that asymptomatic transmission is a real threat. (And, again, why my crew and I—and other nerds across the city—are wearing N95s on all calls.)

Here is where Minnesota—the Midwest—is different from those epicenters of the virus: we have few active cases (for now). It is a pandemic that is remote (for now). Our concerns and precautions are essentially conceptual (for now). Which makes it harder for many people to buy into the social distancing, the need for discipline and stoicism, to appreciate the very real threat. Minneapolis is not Manhattan. We lack the crowded residential areas, close quarters on streets and sidewalks and buildings, the vertically stacked spaces with elevators as necessary conveyances. It's all close quarters there, and the pandemic is rampant. I have friends in NYC, some who work in medicine and others who are residents. They have all lost an increasing number of friends, family, coworkers. For them, this is very real. They are seeing the damage and casualties caused, and it is indelible. We are fortunate, here, that we have the opportunity to dodge this bullet.

Conversely, being cautious about a seemingly remote global pandemic strikes many of us as silly. This delusion has been sustainable here because the Twin Cities have not been hard-hit the way other cities have. For now.

//

1300. On our daily rounds, we take the pulse of the Southside. Few other city workers are wearing masks. They give us mild grief for ours, macho jibes. At the grocery store, it's a mixed bag. Some people are masked, some are not, still others are using odd items for improvised masks (bras, plastic bags, socks, a T-shirt). There's both politeness and tension in the aisles, camaraderie battling paranoia. We each shop for our next several meals, hurrying in and out.

We see people congregating too closely. We wear our masks on the rig to provide some mutual protection, but, as important, to offer the public a visual cue and reminder: *Mask up, folks!* None of us is too important, too tough, too cool. Protect yourself, protect your family, protect my family.

We go to a gas leak, often a daily experience with the wildcat crews digging up every street in the city while updating the fiber-optic network. The gas vents into the air. There is no explosive hazard. We stand around, a mostly symbolic gesture toward "safety" until the gas company (the skilled ones) arrive to fix the leak. The rookie's first potential explosion! I offer Jenn some practical guidance about hazmat calls, everyday emergencies, protocols, and the difference between a routine call and an actual emergency. Our masks are an added encumbrance between our Nomex fire hoods, our helmets, the tall collars of our turnout coats. *Nevertheless, we persisted* . . . to the rank and smirking derision of the same dudes who keep striking gas lines while digging for fiber-optic cables. The rain has returned, but frozen. We stand there, squinting in a pelting sleet. We keep our distance from the street crew (and not just because they tend to smoke around venting gas leaks). These are strange times.

//

1715. All day and through the evening, we listen to radio traffic across the city. The quarantine has tamped things somewhat. It is slower out, but then any SOB or respiratory call feels ominous. Dispatch diligently warns if any caller reports something remotely ILI, and the responding crew must acknowledge directly. It's helpful, even if the reporting is often inaccurate or misunderstood. Only a few potential CVD calls are run, none confirmed or official.

Wednesday, April 8, 2020: Day Two of Our 48-Hour Shift

Our second day is generally low-tone; we are tired and conserve energy to ride out the shift. With the nebulous Covid protocols, we use a metric shit-ton of bleach when we mop and wash down the station. We make our meals separately and sit apart, scarfing our food before masking up again. I scour medical websites: CDC, IAFF, MN State, our own departmental emails. Changing information comes from CDC directly, and then hours (or days) later, echoes from our HQ: the delays complicate our understanding of the ever-growing pandemic.

The city feels spookily empty. The 911 calls drop off, for the most part. Citizens with health concerns are scared or worried or panicked. How to convince someone who has no symptoms that they are fine, when their fears are untethered from any signs or symptoms? This becomes a common event: ghost fears and insufficient factual responses.

//

The Night. In between the phantom-smoke and no-fire fire-alarm calls, we respond to a nursing home for a resident with respiratory issues. Prearrival info states: no fever, no coughing, no ILI symptoms. I garb up in my Chernobyl party wear, leave the crew outside the lobby, and head up. It's an older man. He looks, frankly, like death. The nurse wears a simple mask, nothing more. She states the patient has advanced dementia, which has slackened and contorted his gaunt features. His SpO_2 SATs (oxygen saturation levels) are very low, significantly below healthy. He feels warm to me, hot even; *not* not-febrile. The nurse has put him on O_2, but he absently paws the mask off, over and over. The medics arrive. They too wear simple masks, no goggles. I help them lift and shift the patient onto their stretcher. We grab and lean against his bedding. He tugs the mask down again. We are all in his air space. If his exhalations were contrast dyed, the plume would cover half the room, definitely spraying all three of us.

I help them get him set up in the ambulance. Even with high-flow oxygen, his SATs remain dangerously low. The medics declare him to be a presumptive Covid-19 patient. They drive off. I do not expect the man to live much longer, whether coronavirus or flu or plain old (deadly) pneumonia. I am glad I put on a plastic gown, though it looks ridiculous. I decon myself outside our rig, spray down my shoes, then change clothes at the station.

My crew seems reserved: *Well? How sick was he?*

What they're wondering: *Could you tell he had Covid? What is it like? Is it as bad as they say?* We aren't supposed to be afraid, and, even for emotionally grounded firefighters, it is difficult to place these new conceptual threats within the context of our standard tragedies and messy horrors.

Because it *is* a mystery, still so abstract and unclear. For a profession that deals with all forms of hazards and unknowns and weirdness, the virus feels a bit like a hazmat call: something invisible and untraceable that damn sure might kill you.

There's paperwork now, a lot of paperwork. Just in case. I make notes of location, call number, patient's name, then crawl back into bed—only after I scrub myself down one more time.

Thursday, April 9, 2020

0643. Another non-emergency call killed sleep at 0615. We groggily responded. I geared up and went inside a small apartment. Someone didn't feel great, but their issues were worry, not illness. (And even these calls now feel loaded or ominous.) The underprotected medics arrived, clearing me directly. Jenn stood on the front steps, eyes big with expectation and uncertainty. She was half-asleep on her feet, worn down after forty-eight hours of constant nervous energy and random adrenaline surges. I can't imagine being new to all this—amid *all this*. The wind has teeth. We shiver and hustle back to the rig. I spray my shoes, pants, arms, hands, and face (!) with germ killer, and we return to the station in sleepy silence. The inside of the rig has the tang of alcohol from our aggressive use of the disinfectant spray. It is a constant odor now, jarring and dissonant. The night drains away to the west. We make coffee and stand awkwardly apart, semiconscious and semistupefied.

This is our work life, foggy within the blurred, burning edges of sleep dep, relying on adrenaline surges to pop us awake on calls. Over the next hour, the oncoming shift arrives. We update them on what's new and noteworthy. I type up my reports then decon the computer, the keyboard, the desk, the chair. I change clothes, putting my uniform into a plastic bag to stew until I wash it next shift. It is twenty degrees colder, and a biting wind, for my return commute. I pedal slowly, tired on many levels. The bike paths are empty. I pull my buff up over my lower face, regardless. Eyes are covered by glasses; nose and mouth (and ears) hidden—and protected, I hope—by the double-folded buff.

It begins to spit snow from the iron-gray sky, the wind aggressive. April in Minnesota is a weird month. Now it feels ominous. I pedal home to my family.

Twenty-Eight Days Later . . . Semi-Brave New World

Our EMS deputy, Chief Amber Lage, worked furiously to come up with official language and designations around our Covid calls. I was of the opinion that we were wading through a sea of illness, that the external attempt to fathom it via Dispatch was unworkable and risky. We were on our own. This is our job, our duty, and it is on us (me) to figure out best habits. As the lady said, *The life you save may be your own . . .*

Soon, I would assume I was walking into Covid on every call. There was no reason *not* to view it this way. It was easier than hoping otherwise or worrying we *might* get ambushed by it. Though I went in alone initially on all calls, my stalwart crew wore N95s when they joined me. A good number of my coworkers did this, too, but—disconcertingly— many more did not. On all calls, I put on two pairs of gloves, my goggles (which immediately fogged over), an N95 mask. Six weeks in, we were given the much appreciated but unwieldy face shields, which added a semilayer of protection but also fogged up (these personal sneeze guards were a good bonus layer, to complement masks, yet a stunning number of people wore them in lieu of a mask, which, given the drafty open end, seemed a poor choice). If there was a "positive pre-arrival screening," I donned the hazmat suit—one-size fits none. I looked ridiculous, sweated profusely, and had no way to hold my radio or gear.

We sprayed down *everything* with industrial-strength sanitizer: gear, clothes, shoes, goggles, skin. I stripped down outside the rig and my crew sprayed me with vodka-smelling germ killer. We did this for weeks, a few months, even. Until time passed without everyone becoming Covid zombies. Then, only some icky calls necessitated a thorough douching. If it didn't *seem* like an infectious call, I beckoned Jenn to join me. This brief four-month period was the only concentrated training our rookies got (not because it's a good system, but because it is how our system dys/functions). I was trying to give her a chance to learn how to read people and scenes, to get familiar with our tools and tasks, to get comfortable amid hazards and panics. Covid, isolation at the station, restricted contact with patients, MFD leadership vacuum, the killing of George Floyd, and the riots: *Welcome to your career, kid.*

Middle-of-the-night calls, we'd straggle from bed, grab our masks, and get on the rig. It was harrowing, humbling, and awesomely gross how much funky bad breath the simple masks trapped. Our masked barriers pulled double duty: germ killers, of course, but they spared the unsuspecting and undeserving patients our raggedy night mouths. Our crew lived on beans, thanks to FMO Tracy Terbell's membership in the Rancho Gordo Bean Club. Beans, jalapeños, and garlic staved off vampires and Covid. We broke ass with aplomb: we were duty bound to ensure none of us had lost our sense of smell. It's not juvenile—it's science! (While I am being facetious, a good example of firehouse and generic hetero chauvinism is the disparate responses to farting. Men fart constantly. At work, we fart avocationally and competitively. Some pranksters enjoy farting on people's heads. Ah, the Brotherhood. But the first time a woman rips one to match the boys: *That's unseemly. That's inappropriate. If you don't have a medical problem, you need to stop that.* Not so for E17, #southsidemagic.)

//

It was all new and unfamiliar to us, and we—like most everyone in the world—were learning in real time. Dispatch would ask a caller, "Have you been coughing or running a fever today?" as the prearrival screening.

The time lag from exposure to seroconversion to infectious upended any clear *Yes or No* parameters, but this is the framework that Dispatch had to follow. It took but one word to trip a "positive screening" designation, which necessitated garbing up fully, which spiked my adrenaline and worry. Equally, answering *No* inaccurately could cause a false comfort. And our department leaders refused to acknowledge the existence of asymptomatic transmission (more accurately, *presymptomatic*). What I wanted to know: "*Will* you be coughing or feverish in the next several days?"

I had to shape an understanding *and* keep irrational worries and comprehensive fears at bay. Thus, I focused less on *conceptual* unknowns than the actual, deadly unknowns. We were *not* hiding away, *not* isolating, *not* shutting down. Though, unlike the brave and at-risk doctors, nurses, and techs in the EDs, we weren't being smothered on all sides at all times by sick people. We entered their homes, moved through their ill exhalations, their contaminated surfaces and family members, did what we could—including physically carrying the sick and weak—then deconned in the fresh, cold air.

Once I gained a functional baseline about risks, exposure paths, and PPE, I tuned out the rest. As with much of our cultural conversation, the twenty-four-hour news cycle fuels itself on hype, empty rhetorical questions, and endless speculative pull quotes.

The department could not follow the same quarantine protocols that regular citizens did. If each time one crew was *possibly* in direct contact (exposed, small *e*) with someone *suspected* of having Covid-19, and that crew had to quarantine for seven to twelve days, we would run out of personnel before the first test results came back.

//

There was no "New Normal," just ever-changing frenzy and fear. Covid was everywhere, on everything, in everything, invisible and invincible.

Or was it?

The learning curve was occurring while we were going on runs, interacting with the public—and not just the public, generally, but the very ill, specifically. People were told to stay home, or they were too scared to seek medical help, and they would find themselves direly ill— from a range of non-Covid issues. We would respond when they were very sick. For varying reasons, some had waited too long.

We started seeing Covid-sick people in their homes. Most of these resembled bad flu or pneumonia cases, neither of which are to be trifled with. What was *scary*, though, were the people whose first impressions indicated no issue, but their SpO_2 numbers were dropping to levels previously considered near death. Many were, in fact, approaching respiratory failure—they just didn't know it. The inconsistency of Covid's signs and symptoms was fascinating to consider abstractly. It was unnerving and scary to consider practically. There were no true signposts. Or, those we had were not exclusive: patients could be very sick and not suffering loss of taste or smell, not struggling to breathe (yet).

People were terrified they *might* have the virus, or, if they had tested positive, that they were going to die. Some folks were scared and wanted reassurance, calling 911 to be re-transported. Some patients' families were worried, and they called us back, wanting us to *Do something* for their sick relatives—or to guarantee they would be okay.

I would gear up, breathe deeply to calm myself, and walk in, fearing the germs that were everywhere. I would find someone very ill in bed. Some had been diagnosed already, but there was nothing the hospital could do yet, so they were sent home to treat the virus as a (very contagious) flu: rest, fluids, aspirin. The obviously sick patients resembled bad flu patients—except Covid is far more virulent and does more damage than the flu. Too, not everyone presented as sick, which made everything feel dodgy. We truly couldn't tell just from appearances. And I would look at family members, in varying levels of masks themselves, and count future patients and collateral victims. It was a shitty deal. We would encourage people to mask up and take it seriously. (This was before the Confederacy of Anti-Antifa turned it all stupidly "political.")

It was difficult to speak across race and culture and nationality, with language barriers, to try conveying that *yes, this person was sick, but, no, we were discouraging them from going back to the hospital.* Multicultural catch-22 for the sick, explained in pidgin and pantomime. I felt their panic, their fear, and their mistrust. *Were we lying to them?* The medics and I tried to help the scared, but we had no firm facts for those first months. And we really had no good news to share: *Stay home—until you are VERY sick. (And then hope it's not too late.)*

I was disconcerted by the people who seemed fine when we arrived, and then were critical a few hours later. Some were dead before dawn. It was hard to follow up on patients. FMO Tracy wasn't coming in on most calls, so I seldom had info other than whatever generalities I could remember (the driver serves as scribe on EMS runs, collecting patient information for the medics and for the supervisor's report later). In my Devo outfit, I had no place for pen or paper, so no means to obtain patient info. Without my driver's help, I often had no name to attach to a patient or call. Beyond that, the hospitals were spread so thin, as was our EMS staff, that requests for patient updates were futile. I would have been worried about tracking transmission and documenting infectious patients—except we were covered by presumptive language. Essentially, to encourage us to keep coming to work, we were protected. Unlike with most other infectious connections (MRSA, HIV, hepatitis, etc.), I wouldn't have to chase down names, dates, addresses; we wouldn't have to fight to prove we got sick while doing our jobs.

Mind you, this presumptive language did nothing to prevent me from contracting Covid—or spreading it to my family. It protected my job if I got sick and ensured my family would receive death benefits if I died. If I got sick, I'd be covered. So, there's that.

As captain, I worried about my crew, two of whom had young children. My biggest concern remained our bringing germs and the virus home to our families. I tried to put myself between the virus and my crew whenever possible. I wrestled with the weight of that risk, though. The pressure of absorbing our worst Covid calls alone, of trying to protect my crew: it was constant, with no clear answers. My crew didn't need me to protect them. They are professionals, and adults. But I was responsible. Many of my fellow captains felt that weight.

The first months, I would wash up before I biked home, then wash again. I worried about infecting my family. I worried about my younger daughter's health, and my own. The virus appeared to be exploiting undiagnosed, latent health issues. What if I had some unknown lung issue that acted as death's Trojan horse? That would suck. I swallowed the fear, took my precautions, did my job, and tried to allay my family's fears. Over and over. Until it became habit, unconscious—but the worry never left.

//

The early stages of the pandemic did feel like Chernobyl, except without a Geiger counter or fatal radiation. We suspected Covid was everywhere. Because no one could tell us with certainty, there was a scary, doom-laden aura on all calls. An invisible, untrackable, potentially fatal mist: how to avoid that? Protect against that? How to function normally? How to live? People were sick. We couldn't see it or know where it was and was not. Would it get us through our shoes? Our belts? Our sleeves? I tried to stifle the uncertainty and worry.

Think of how claustrophobic and sick-humid a bedroom is when you've got the flu or a bad cold. Now, imagine entering, feeling the illness and wheezing and fever dripping off the walls, radiating off the patient's body, flicking off the sodden bedsheets. Tell yourself your mask works.

I didn't disbelieve in Covid. I trusted my gear *and* I carried massive worry and weight within myself.

This was how it went for me: Trying to remain present with these people who needed help. Touching them, carrying them, which violated the protocols and guidelines, because the six-foot rule doesn't work with dying people. I was covered with patients' sputum. I felt their hot, sick breath on my face as I guided them—slowly, because they couldn't breathe and were weak and wheezing—from wherever I found them (generally a hot, close bedroom) out to fresh air and the waiting ambulance.

I was tremendously scared in the early stages. I had to steel myself and go into those death-smelling rooms, touch, hold, carry the direly ill. Unlike with COPD or GI failures, where I have treated people as they died, have watched them die, compassionately, but without worry that I, too, would catch it and die. I have been splashed—doused even—with HIV+ blood. I am fairly comfortable with risks and realities. With Covid, we didn't know. And I didn't have any promise or guarantee, or even indicators, whether I'd contracted it on any of these calls.

I'd fill out notification paperwork, and a week to a month later, I'd receive a cursory "Not an Exposure" official response. By which time, I might have died—*had* I contracted it. I'd sigh and stick the useless paperwork in my cubby. It felt like an exercise in absurd, futile bureaucracy. Being "exposed"—in the lag time between the physical interaction and the official decree of "Not Exposed"—brought no quarantine or break. I kept waiting to be infected, kept hoping my gear held, kept touching and hoisting and holding the very sick.

A word on CPR, the forceful compressions and especially the oxygenated blasts of air we deliver. When I worked for Rita Juran on Engine 14 in 2006–7, we went to a fellow one night who had been shot in the head. He wasn't dead yet, still had a pulse, so we worked him. I was on the ventilations, and each time I squeezed our BVM, a misty geyser of blood would spray up from his eye sockets. Every six seconds, as the air went into his nose and mouth, it would force aerosolized blood (which was pooling where it shouldn't, thanks to the bullet in his brain) out of his eyes. We created a monochromatic Pollock painting on the carpet, on his head and chest, and on our arms from that spume.

When we did CPR or provided ventilations on unresponsive people during the pandemic (whether caused by Covid or drugs or regular old biological demise), all I could think about was that night with Rita. Except now it wasn't merely a bloody mist, it was Covid, aerosolized and filling the air all around me, getting on my skin, my clothes, in my ears. *Would it get through my goggles? Was my mask on tight? What are we doing?*

Systemic Dyspeptic

Our station had the department's Patient Zero, a firefighter on another shift. Admin's response: ordering him *not to tell his crew!* Orders came from the top to downplay his illness, to keep the info from spreading. But we work together, we look out for each other. We knew immediately that he was positive *and* that they'd ordered him to hide his status from his coworkers.

And you wonder why there's both a bunker mentality in the stations and such fertile ground for preposterous rumors starting: the truth is often dumber and more absurd than lies.

A revealing point, one that reinforces my argument throughout this book, is that the only suggestion the top staff came up with to address the risks for our personnel on EMS calls was to cease responding to medicals. "Save our people for the fires!" was the idea.

If we don't count the aftermath of the riots, which took place May 26–31, there were scant working fires in the city of Minneapolis during the first months of Covid. Our job as emergency responders is to serve, help, and protect the public. A mentality that continues to privilege a sliver of our actual duties serves no one well. Further, I argue that the bosses did not take the pandemic's implications seriously, did not see how we fit into public health and service, and offered poor leadership from that blind vantage. And that set the stage for the later petty rebelliousness about masking, as well as the incredible number of lost-time cases due to avoidable, nonresponse exposures.

After the first months, when we continued not to get sick and gained a larger understanding that infection came via droplets and respiration (transmission via the eyes was a concern in the early weeks, but I'm not sure how true a threat that was), many of us developed a grounded sense of our risks. But only after a lot of stress and uncertainty and unknown worry.

Masks work (worn properly and not made of fishnet). If I have been infected and am now off-gassing cooties, my mask keeps the germs in my mouth or tamps down their spray, protecting you. If you are infected and unmasked, then my mask protects me from your germs. If you are infected and wearing a mask, and I'm wearing a mask, I can be more present with you, less worried about getting your illness on me. Simple. So simple I went a bit crazy listening to all the complicated alternatives and magical thinking.

No matter how icky a call, as long as I said I'd been wearing a mask, gloves, and glasses, I was deemed "exposure free." I made the distinction, semantic and categorical, of capital *E* Exposure versus regular exposure. Because it was a bit crazy making, trying to figure out what qualified: "I carried a man from his bed through his attic apartment, down the stairs, through the narrow halls, and out to the ambulance. He was SAT-ing at around 84 percent, coughing constantly, sweating, looked like warmed-over death. I carried him. He coughed into my face the entire time."

"You had on proper PPE?"

"I did, yes. But—"

"Then you should be fine. No exposure."

"But—he was wheezing visible mist into my face . . . ?"

"Make a note of it in your report. Doesn't sound like an exposure."

Sigh. This wasn't out of cruelty. Our EMS boss worked herself to the bone, with very little institutional support and only one assistant. My locker remains filled with such notes: scraps of call slips with date, address, name (if we got one), run number, and whatever salient details might jog my mind down the road.

Not an Exposure, I'd report back to the crew. We would laugh incredulously and grimly, and continue our shift. That became the hobgoblin for me, and, later, the balm: we walked and worked among the sick, dying, and dead; the infectious and infected; and while I assiduously wore a mask and gloves and goggles, I understood how easily mistakes occurred, that in lifting and loading someone, my mask gets bumped. And yet, but still: no infections. My mind was boggled.

Because I continued not to get infected, it was hard to sustain the constant fear-vigilance. If CPR in a small space didn't give me Covid cooties, I felt my odds were pretty good passing you outdoors with a five-to-ten-foot berth. *Yea, though I walk through the valley of the shadow of Covid, I fear no Exposure, because the N95 is my shepherd (and HQ sez it's not an exposure).*

After two months, the department was moving in fits and starts:

taking EMS response more seriously, but struggling with the immediate notions of community prevention—where *we* were the community. Most crews continued to sit together, unmasked, watching TV, eating together, riding in the rig unmasked. Too many crews around the city were stuck on "But we *always* eat together! We're a crew—that's what makes us firefighters!" and "It's just *us* in the rig. We don't need masks. That's dumb."

As if the circle of trust in each station would protect everyone from our collective poor decisions and actions (i.e., the individuals running blithely unmasked among us). It became a widespread version of what I address in chapter 8, "Ante Up," our delusion that the free doughnuts and earnest tributes from the grateful public translate to our invincibility or excuse us from the need to honor that same public. And, connected to that: our red line of silence. We cover up for our worst behavior because, frankly, we implicitly understand how much crap we get away with. The prospect of actual accountability is a heavy threat to the man-boy army. Reality versus Theory for firefighters has been exposed on many levels during the pandemic. Frankly, many of us have been found lacking—in terms of our professionalism, our own health, our duty to the public welfare, our concern for ourselves and others.

After someone tested positive and potentially exposed the entire station, causing mass quarantines and overtime replacement staff for ten-plus days each time, the excuse given was "There was a brief moment when we were eating dinner that we didn't all have our masks on." The administration, to save face, accepted that illogic (or overlooked its cumbersome transparency). It's who we are, unfortunately. *Gee, Mom, I don't know how I got pregnant. We were just holding hands, honest.*

Just as Hope is not an action plan, Luck should not be one, either.

The root of what wormed its way deep into my psyche is this: the admin, adhering to CDC rules, put entire stations on quarantine over (allegedly) brief unmasked exposures. Simultaneously, all of us who were slow dancing with the walking dead were presumed unexposed. How could one be true and the other false? The only difference was— holy shit! Masks work!

If I wasn't getting infected through the truly sick people at work, I was comfortable out in the world, whether on the streets or in the empty aisles at Target. The emptied parking lots, the emptied shelves, the silence, the wary eyeballing of others: they did evoke some postapocalyptic movies. *Who* was a threat? How to be a good human *and* be safe? How to show you are friendly solely with your eyes?

//

And then what happened?

Oh, right: The police killed an unarmed Black man again, and the city erupted—briefly. The riots lasted four nights; the damages will echo for years. Most of us have never experienced the spasms of violence and destruction, the blocks of buildings immolated, the rage and sadness blending into a furious force. *If* we can learn from this, we might spare ourselves—and our children—having to experience it again.

The racial justice marches and protests were *not* superspreader events. The Black community took care of itself. In Minneapolis, at least. At the marches and protests I saw widespread and self-conscious masking on the part of the white participants. The weight of guilt and demonstrations of care were apparent. *(Yes, the police just killed another Black man. I will do my part by putting this sign on my lawn and wearing a mask to the protest march.)* During the riots, with the tear gas and video surveillance, people were incentivized to mask up. Regardless of motivation, we did not see a spike in infections in the weeks after the uprising.

Here's the thing: wearing a mask gave me confidence to engage with the public, to be in proximity—at a time when people were keeping distance. Masked, I worried less about my health or spreading the virus to the public (on the chance I had been infected). I felt comfortable in large crowds, interacting with people during the protests and at what became George Floyd Square, standing close, listening to what people were saying. These are all real parts of our job, I believe, and my comfort level in a mask improved my comfort level among the citizens, building better relationships, overcoming mutual wariness. I did a lot of expressive eye movement, communicating with my squinty-smize eyes that I was *not* there to fuck with people, that I recognized their suffering and humanity, that I appreciated the history that lay all about and upon us, no matter the simple interaction. Many people were doing the same: effusive, manic nodding and gesturing, trying to express both concrete and existential support. That is a lot of weight for our eyes to carry . . .

regardless, masked up, I felt comfortable in proximity to everyone we encountered, anywhere we met.

I have never felt my "liberties" or "freedoms" were infringed upon or sacrificed by wearing a mask. I am confounded by those who claim to believe this. Masking is my duty to myself, my family, my coworkers, and the general public.

I worked on my birthday in January 2021, and, because it was work, I forgot I had my simple mask on when I went to blow out the candles on my carrot cake.

Guess what?

I couldn't. I put my face next to and above the candles and could not force air through—the flame did not even wiggle. I tried thrice before remembering my mask.

"Pretty cool," I said to my giggling crew. *Science.*

//

Events of the summer of 2020 soured me—on the optimistic notions that we can fix our health and racial issues, that we even wanted a better, healthier, racially just America. We had lost the path (we = white folks). Too, all of us emergency responders faced a juxtaposition between what we saw at work and how the rest of the world dealt with the pandemic (those of us who didn't leap aboard the Deniers' Armada). I spent so much time wading into sick air, trusting (hoping) my gear would protect me, that when I encountered half- or unmasked people who couldn't be bothered, or who spouted regurgitated illogical rationales about the virus, I had fury. I wanted to *show* them the truth: those who suffocated in their own fluids and died horribly, the grieving families, the exhausted health care workers.

But that isn't how this goes, ever. It gets harder to maintain that balance, from what I know and experience at work to what I see in the madness of everyday life. The accumulated stress came out sideways at random people. I was a sharp-tongued grouch at the hygiene theater, whether done out of well-meant but misguided worry, or as performative business model. And for the nervous folks who clung to "an abundance of caution," I tried—and badgered, likely—to get them to trust that they could safely walk outside without dying.

At the tail end of 2020, coming on either side of the election and the uncivil MAGA rebellion, we started catching the post-Covid deaths. People who had spent weeks and months in the hospital, made it home, but then their systemic damage, their comorbidities, caught up with them. We went to a lot of DOAs in the fall and early winter of 2020–21. Family members and friends would report that these people had been very sick with the virus, early on, and were trying to get their lives back, and then—well, there we were, standing over another dead person.

These were sudden, and fatal, respiratory collapses: systemic failures and bloody ruptures from Covid-damaged organs. Most of these people had significant health issues before they got the virus. The survivors we saw (those still alive) by and large reported being as sick and miserable as they had ever been. From what we encountered, I believed them.

The constant weakness, the ongoing effects, the fear: the long-haul patients were in rough shape. It must have been a strange limbo, having survived but not healed, not free of it. And then, to die suddenly, horribly. The dire forms of suffering and death we saw added gravity and brutal reality to my view of the pandemic.

Pandemic at the Firehouse Disco

In these next paragraphs I commit apostasy, or sedition, against Ye Olde Brotherhood of Fireville. I have tried to be honest and fair about the types and stereotypes of my work cohort. There are so many good, noble men and women who dig deep for their fellow humans, some despite conservative, even racially problematic, beliefs about the people we serve.

As a specific demographic, firefighters aggressively pushed the limits of denial and resistance to commonsense masking and the vaccine. More firefighters and police officers died from Covid in 2021 than in 2020, when we didn't understand its transmission and didn't have solid protocols for PPE, let alone vaccines. The overwhelming majority of these deaths were not work related. These were *not* noble, risky sacrifices providing care to the sick and needy. These were men (overwhelmingly men) dying *because* they refused to mask up. Dying because they thought they were too tough to get a vaccine or wear a mask, defiantly flouting guidelines and rules, going about unprotected. Then they caught Covid. Then they died. We should know better. We should do better. It is a preposterous tragedy of entitlement and delusion.

The initial Covid reports brought alarmist cries that we were all going to die, that "the city doesn't give a crap about us," even as policies were forwarded to protect us and cover our potential sacrifices in the name of the public good.

Then came the blustering, the macho posturing and denial, for no scientifically valid reasons. *We're not going to let some "alleged" virus scare us!* Then, when there was funding to protect us against the expected widespread infection rate among responders, and when there was presumptive sick-leave protection and money for OT to keep rigs filled, we saw it as free money and free time-off. So firefighters continued to be slack about masking and distancing. Many firefighters wouldn't wear masks on the rigs. They wouldn't wear masks around the stations. They pooh-poohed the available health information.

Impossible to ignore here: many shape or derive their worldview from Fox News and conservative talk radio. These are the same members who support conservative politicians whose "tough talk" they identify with, even though they are voting against pensions, city funding, public health policies. This disconnect became a significant issue over the following year-plus. And with an abject failure by the upper leadership to genuinely take the pandemic—and our roles—seriously, the drifting ship remained rudderless.

I received some blowback for a mild comment that made it into a *Star Tribune* article (published April 24, 2020): "Some of my coworkers have differing interpretations of *mandatory*" [when it comes to masking]. I was criticized for putting our business out in the street, but the true issue was that we were doing our jobs poorly and selfishly. Firefighters typically want to keep our foibles and felonies on the down-low. Which is another example of our enabling, self-sabotaging "brotherhood."

The Minneapolis Fire Department spent more than a million dollars on overtime to cover repeated station-wide quarantines that occurred *not* due to work-related exposures. These monies were intended to protect those who caught cooties in the line of duty, not in the line at Buffalo Wild Wings. Our genuine line-of-duty infections were negligible. No, American Heroes didn't wear masks at home and came to work, where they also didn't wear masks, and then as a precaution *everyone* had to be sent home for two weeks when one dude came up sick.

The city of Minneapolis literally spent a million-plus dollars for utterly avoidable personnel shortages.

(Ironically, our former chief refused to fill the rigs fully, let alone staff up spare rigs, to address the five nights of widespread arson and comprehensive destruction—in a vainglorious attempt to save his job by upholding our budget. Looking at the smoldering, cratered wreckage of the city, a reasonable leader would recognize that the city's budget had burned the first night. Doing more to protect the city, and support his overwhelmed firefighters, *should* have been his priority. The two opportunities for a veteran emergency response chief to show leadership were brutal, comprehensive failures, revealing an all-too-naked emperor of a paper kingdom.)

Significantly, the virus exploited underlying health issues, and firefighters were certainly not immune. Too many responders (men) have creeping health issues that we refuse to examine: we are overweight, inactive, diabetic, smokers, have sky-high cholesterol, have chronic heart failure (CHF) or sleep apnea. We refuse to have these addressed, because that would mean acknowledging we are not as powerful as we wish we were. Covid exploited the hell out of our compulsory machismo. Denial and impunity are hellacious twins.

I return to this: At the end of 2021, the approximate death count for American firefighters due to Covid-19, according to the National Fallen Firefighters Foundation, was 230. This is only for those deaths that were *reported* as due to Covid or as complications from Covid (others may well have been listed as pneumonia or cardiac or pulmonary embolisms, or their families did/would not admit to Covid). However, and here comes the bold print: In 2020, when we didn't know *anything* about the virus, when we handled sick people without clear PPE guidelines, when there was no vaccine, 86 firefighters died nationally. In 2021, with vaccines offered to us ahead of the public, with solid masking info, guidelines, and protocols, 144 firefighters died. Nearly twice as many died *after* we had information and protection against the virus. From the reports I read (via Chief Billy Goldfeder's essential FirefighterCloseCalls.com), nearly *all* those deaths were from nonwork exposures. And the vast majority were men.

Each man died not "doing the job he loved" but due to the Trojan horse of "the lifestyle he clung to." That is unconscionable, and a profound, wasteful tragedy. Overweight, health-compromised firefighters died from Covid's nefarious exploitation of systemic weaknesses just like everyone else. Our mustaches and helmets don't actually save us, sadly.

Winter-Spring 2021: The Needle and the Damage Undone, Vaccination Nation!

The vaccines broke the clot of stress that had pressed on my psyche since the onset of the pandemic. Everyone I knew in health care found immense existential *and* practical relief with the vaccinations. The actual protection and notional barrier against the ever-present threat of the virus, of breakdowns in PPE, in accidental failures to protect ourselves: they mattered. The vaccines don't solve everything, but they certainly cut a massive chunk out of the threats against our well-being during work (and in regular life).

Until late 2021, when breakthrough infections became a real threat, the fact that few vaccinated people were severely sickened or died provided respite from the stress and worry. For that brief, bright span, the truth was that a clutch of vaccinated people sitting together could not spontaneously manifest the virus. Our comfort level, especially having waded through so much actual sickness, was solid.

And that was it. We beat Covid!

Syke!

As Shirley Li wrote in an article in *The Atlantic*, "Early 2020 felt dire; late 2021 feels dissonant."

When the delta variant of the resurgent virus hit Minneapolis in the autumn of 2021, those who were sick were very, very sick. We were still sifting through that when omicron arrived and when studies showed a predictable decline in vaccine efficacy. I didn't know how to distinguish or differentiate the strains. Could I tell the difference between alpha, delta, omicron? Did it matter? For a while, we'd seen fewer CVD-sick patients at the home and street level, and then we saw more and more. I'd ask friends at other stations and get the same response, *Yeah, lots of really sick people.* Patients had SpO_2 levels at the lowest I'd ever seen, under 50 percent (which signifies imminent fatal respiratory collapse). *Deeply* sick folks. Some, I presumed, would die in hours or days. Others, I didn't know, and I wasn't going to add more work for the overextended nursing crews by requesting follow-up info.

Here's the part that we as a nation seem incapable of accepting: in 2021, the majority of our unvaccinated neighbors, relatives, spouses, children, and coworkers who died after contracting Covid *would not have died had they been vaccinated*. Yes, Bob had cancer, and Susan's diabetes was a problem, and Doug had that CHF, and Pat hadn't been the same since his pneumonia. Sure. But: they probably *would not have died* when Covid mixed with their ongoing health compromises if they had been vaccinated. *Covid exploited their health issues.* We were told it was doing so, which was why isolation, masking, and vaccination were so important.

We have lost hundreds of thousands of citizens unnecessarily. For those who simply could not accept the reality of Covid, what more did we need to say to convince them? But those who looked at the world around them and chose denial, chose "rebellion" or "defiance"? I don't know what to say. Those who flaunted their noncompliance, their childish refusal to look life in the eye and act like adults: they continued to get very sick and clog the EDs and ICUs and exhaust the beaten-down staffs, forcing non-Covid issues ("minor" stuff like cancer treatments and hip replacements) to be delayed or canceled. For those who were already unhealthy, their paths continued to the ICU, to intubation, to ventilators—if available. Many simply died.

I recognize there are some who were unvaccinated for legit reasons. But very few. There is no solid "religious" objection. The hysterical mistrust of vaccines is born of wrongheaded impulse and impunity. At this point, to be a holdout is to put oneself, and those with compromised immune systems, at risk. To be a denier is unconscionable.

The nurse who gave me my booster also worked at a hospital not far from the Twin Cities. Outstate Minnesota, like most of the United States, tilts significantly conservative, reactionary, white, and both Trumpian/ MAGA and anti-mask/vax. The weight of the sick, dying, and dead was compounded by the widespread deniers. The nurse said, "I see nothing but unvaccinated people in our ICU. Folks who are in denial *even as they die.* Most who come in have secondary issues: smokers, diabetics, CHF, the usual stuff. Except: Covid gets into their lungs and hearts. If they get intubated, most are dead within a couple of days. The very few who survive, they aren't going home, they aren't getting back to regular life. Their functional lives are over. They're patients in care facilities, wasting away. And their family members are still—*still*—asking if I think Covid is real or if they should get vaccinated. It's killing me."

Frankly, it becomes tedious to lifeguard people bent on swimming in the sewer. I'm not victim blaming. It is a requiem for common sense and civic engagement, nuance and reason. My back hurts, my head hurts, my heart hurts.

//

We cannot talk about Covid without discussing race, class, and social-societal-systemic dysfunctions. While a great many citizens were heroic and caring in their efforts and sacrifices for the common good, and, for those of us in health care, our proximity to and helpless witnessing of the victims of Covid caused us a great deal of emotional and psychological turmoil, the pandemic revealed the decay of our national ethos. Sadly, the sports team fervor of political identification caused obscene deaths. Tellingly, America's economic and racial inequalities were factors in health care outcomes and vaccine delivery across the country.

Writing in *The Atlantic,* journalists Katherine Wu, Ed Yong, and Sarah Zhang stated it clearly: "Working-class Americans are vulnerable too. In the pandemic's first year, they were five times as likely to die of COVID-19 as college-educated people. Working-age people of color were hit even harder: 89 percent fewer would have lost their lives if they'd had the same COVID death rates as white college graduates. These galling disparities will likely recur, because the U.S. has done little to address their root causes."

I don't know when we will gain clarity and perspective to adequately dissect the multiple facets of the Covid-19 pandemic in American life. I don't know if we will. Can we muster the courage, clarity, patience, and objectivity to accurately and honestly examine what happened, *why* things went how they did, and what *could* and *should* have been done differently? This travesty has occurred within a specific cultural moment, shaped by the prevailing winds of our current decline.

I imagine, wistfully, how it would have been had this pandemic struck us before the rampant metastasizing of ignorance, the proliferation of shallow hot takes, and the death of nuance.

Oh, sweet Jesus: what if it had arrived in 2002? The Republican majority would have been putting the vaccine in our freedom fries. Instead of screaming nonsense about horse dewormer, denying the facts of the virus's existence, and creating hysterical false-libertarian proclamations, we would be fascinated by and engaged over this ever-morphing, silent and tricky disease. We also would not have botched the opportunities to starve it out initially via lockdowns, isolation, and masking, so it might only have lasted those first months. Imagine that.

Language and science were made partisan issues. These cultural battles caused untold damage, death, and grief. I'm dejected at how batshit crazy this nation has become. Glibly and with the wild-eyed, reckless verve of an amphetamine binge, too many of us have collectively jettisoned compassion, reason, fair play, civics, and spelling.

I would like to bring charges against all the cable personalities and politicians who've given weight to the lies—while themselves safely vaccinated, with primo health care and priority treatment.

As I wrote about those early April 2020 days, when none of the other city workers (street, water, sanitation, maintenance departments) wore masks, these blue-collar, mostly white men remained largely resistant, and later hostile, to the ideas of community efforts and collective good. Many of them were (are) Trump supporters, if not aggressive MAGAists. They scoffed at the notion of wearing masks as a gesture to the common good, as well as to protect against an invisible threat.

This class and racial balkanizing had been in process for years, but it became a systemic cancer over the summer of 2020. Men who needed to feel *like men*, to "reclaim" their freedoms, their streets, their country: the indulgence of contrived victimhood put them on the warpath over imagined and contrived slights. The literal attack on the Capitol was the apex of this psychosis.

Gender dysfunction was a horrific culprit. What does it say about our culture that so many men were so insecure that the fear of being tagged as "weak" for wearing a mask allowed them to jeopardize their health and that of their families—with predictable, tediously tragic results? A stunning number of these deaths were wholly and easily preventable. But we couldn't, we wouldn't take good care. And so even more died.

The pandemic revealed the limits of our system, the too-human flaws in the machine, and the Trojan horse of our lost attention to fact, detail, and nuance. A steady diet of nothing left us weakened, primed for exploitation. If "beliefs" need no connection to objective reality, then the subjective surreality becomes a legit playing field. Which is what has happened in this country.

The problematic and undermining role of the evangelical churches—combining with their nihilistic embrace of the most godless man to hold office—caused untold avoidable deaths. Jesus wasn't going to protect the unmasked, I have to remind folks. Beyond all the evangelical preachers who tried to snake-handle Covid and died, look at their flocks who took poor guidance from the pulpits, suffered, and died. Same with right-wing talk radio dudes: taunting their imperviousness to Covid, owning the libtards and sheeple, and ending up quite dead.

WWJD? He would wear a mask for the sick, weak, needy.

There is a grimness to the finality, to the objective waste and avoidability. And yet it is the human parade. Something similar struck me with the pandemic: seeing the searing number of deniers who died long after there were info and options for avoiding infections, seeing the people who sought out the virus—then died. We don't need to prove gravity (though people still do). The childish, churlish performative gestures that turned fatal. What a waste. What squandering of human potential. *There is no pleasure but meanness,* as Flannery O'Connor wrote.

//

I want to contrast the preceding comments with a very different, very American parallel: the generations-deep mistrust and ingrained suspicion between communities of color and the historically problematic, and often actively racist, medical establishment. Reports proliferated from across the country of the disproportionate ill effects of Covid on nonwhite communities. The stark imbalance of Covid per capita, as well as disproportionate deaths along racial lines, did *not* occur in a vacuum. In the early days, as the pandemic claimed lives wantonly, those with significant health issues were victimized, although the role their co-morbidities played was not clear until months later—not until enough deaths gave scientists a sense of the virus' path. As several writers have noted, it splits a corpse's hair to quibble about dying *from* the virus versus dying *with* the virus: the person remains dead. The sociology of health and health care, however, shaped who was *more* susceptible to Covid's threat. The checklist of cultural issues that ordinarily beset communities is direly represented in the Covid reports: lack of primary and regular health care, inability to access medical facilities, crowded living conditions, poor employment options and work conditions, multiple ongoing and underlying health issues, quality of education and information access. These citizens were concurrently the least healthy and least able to stay abreast of the changing health information—with the most limited opportunities to alter their circumstances to isolate and avoid exposures. (I encourage readers to check out the articles included in the reading list at the end of this book. The writers for *The Atlantic* were incredible, thorough, nuanced, and steely, especially Ed Yong.)

When I'd read articles about the disproportionate effects of the virus on Black communities, my reference points were the people I saw in Minneapolis, some ardent in their individual and collective efforts to protect themselves and each other from harm, others engaged (as I inferred) in a communal rhetoric that reinforced mistrust of (white) information as a form of racial solidarity. When options are limited, and history has proved the dominant culture to be actively hostile toward one's race, group, community, there is a dangerous vulnerability a virus can exploit.

Our crew responded to homes where ten or more immediate family members had contracted Covid, some dead, some dying from it, some not yet dead (but I saw where it was heading even if the family remained unaware), others beset by ongoing complications. Too many individuals could not see the connections between their in/actions and their health reactions and consequences. Too, Covid's tendrils exploited the many comorbidities that are also documented by-products of existing as Black in America: diabetes, heart issues, stress, depression, kidney and liver issues.

My experiences in Minneapolis largely saw the Black community wearing masks out in public. At the post office one day, two older women got on the clerk for eschewing hers. "You know," one of the elders said. "You got to stay healthy. White folks don't care if we catch this mess and die."

"But it just bothers my nose," the clerk said, pouting. The elders were adamant. She relented. They looked at me and one said, "Nothing personal." I nodded and replied, "Nope." After they left, I told the clerk I had seen a lot of people sick with Covid and the two women were right. She repeated that it bothered her nose. As I walked out the door, I caught her tugging her mask down.

There are significant, historically poignant differences between the reasons white and Black citizens resisted the vaccine, initially at the end of 2020 and through the initial surplus/scarcity issues and prioritizing in early 2021. Again, access, health care, and information all shaped people's ability to get the vaccine—separate from beliefs or worries about the jab. Many people of color had no easy access to clinics, could not take time off, did not have idle hours to put in trying to even register for a shot. My sister and I both spent focused time getting our parents registered in D.C.'s vaccine lottery. All the slots in their wealthy, primarily white section of the city were filled immediately (powerful people find ways to the head of the line). Consequently, the only available slots were in poorer, nonwhite areas, where the demands were not as high.

Another white conspiracy. I struggled with the entrenched African American wariness, denial, and refusal: not because they "should" listen to me, but because of how clearly deadly the virus was, how much carnage it caused. How could I chide Black people to protect themselves better, given how treacherous our nation has been? (For a detailed and personal view on this, please read Elaine Batchlor's article in *The Atlantic,* "I'm a Black Doctor. My Mom Still Won't Get Vaccinated.")

I am a white man who works for the system—within and representing the system. I cannot presume any "simple truth" in addressing generations-deep issues. *And* I see that people continue to die unnecessarily owing to generations-deep issues. I am not the one to lecture Black people about vaccines, or diabetes, or smoking, but I am also aware these things are killing people who have survived centuries of my people's attempts to break and crush them. How to convince folks that *this* time we mean no harm? I do not blame them: look at the reactionary white ugliness that surged openly and aggressively into our daily lives in the aftermath of President Obama's terms. How can we find true common ground? How can we save ourselves?

//

My understanding of race and America has been heavily influenced by James Baldwin's work. In "An Open Letter to Sister Angela Davis," he wrote, "The will of the people, in America, has always been at the mercy of an ignorance not merely phenomenal, but sacred, and sacredly cultivated: the better to be used by a carnivorous economy which democratically slaughters and victimizes whites and blacks alike. But most white Americans do not dare to admit this (though they suspect it), and this fact contains mortal danger for the blacks and tragedy for the nation."

Refusing despair, I challenge myself to hold steady, and I steel myself with this other bit of Baldwin, from *Just Above My Head*: "Not everything is lost. Responsibility cannot be lost, it can only be abdicated. If one refuses abdication, one begins again."

These lines are stamped in my psyche. They echo, inspire, and haunt me: here, in this writing, and there, out in the streets.

At the fire department, we had white objectors and faux libertarians, and we had Black religious and Black secular objectors. Different sides of different unvaccinated coins. When cities and agencies instituted vaccine mandates, many white heroes threw tantrums and threatened Kraken-releasing furies. Lots of "Don't Tread on Me" memes flourished. Most of these folks got vaccinated eventually, but some actually left their jobs. The number of firefighter Covid deaths has slowed, and not one I've seen published in the past year-plus was vaccinated. Not one.

There is a cultural and sociological distinction between being a white man working as a paid emergency responder who ignores the science of his health issues and being Black in America.

Here is the woeful truth of American culture: the historical record that shapes Black wariness is a very real thing—no matter how much actual history the defensive MAGAists strive to strike from the records. And the white hysteria is based on—*What?*

They are not equal or equivalent. This is the fundamental disconnect—disassociation, really—tainting American identity.

Thousands of unvaccinated Americans died to prove something— something they didn't remotely understand. The "sympathy for the vaccine refusers and Covid deniers" cant is tired, because it's another version of the "sympathy for the self-sabotaging white Trump voter." I *had* hoped that J. D. Vance's mercenary tilt at a cash windfall as the prodigal hillbilly would be just an elegy, rather than the beginning of a nefarious political career. So it goes. And, while I can shrug and say *So it goes* about so many people's fatal, futile illogic, the collateral damages are what I see as the sin and the shame.

Turning anti-information into a blood sport cost lives and damaged our nation's spirit. I looked at the voting map after the 2020 election: cities with any statistical diversity voted pro-democracy. These places—and Minneapolis is certainly one—are far from truly diverse, but the truth is that living and working with heterogeneous others opens people's minds, hearts, and understanding of human complexity. That has certainly been true with teaching and the fire department.

//

For twenty months, there was seldom a five-day span when I was not in proximity to or contact with someone who *might* be infectious. I work forty-eight hours, am home for ninety-six, and return (plus traded and overtime shifts). I was never not *potentially* incubating. A test today would tell me only what I did or did not catch several days ago. It had no bearing on what I might have caught at work yesterday. I remained asymptomatic and continued to go to work and respond.

But don't you want the peace of mind? Take a test and know that you're negative?

I explained to family, relatives, friends, again, the constant math in my head. Whatever security or clarity the test offered, by the time I took it and received the results, I would already have been exposed again—the test's accuracy would expire before I got the results. I would either need to test every day, or not at all—unless I became symptomatic (at which point, the test would be redundant).

I truly cannot fathom some folks' distance from the disease's realities, and they who were spared my immersion and proximity, they cannot fathom my experience. This is a solid through line for this entire book: what we see and accept as normal can prove challenging for a regular citizen. I am reporting to you the various ways that functioning within this job's toils warps a person (i.e., me).

Be that as it may, someone needs to answer the bell, show up for the sick, scared, and dying. It's our job and honor to be the ones who do.

In his memoir *Every Minute Is a Day,* Robert Meyer wrote about the weighty tensions that many of us in the emergency medical fields experienced with Covid: "I feel embarrassed when anyone calls me a hero. Not with all those bodies. I'm not a hero. I'm a doctor. A scared doctor—scared, just like everyone else . . . Doctors are well intentioned. *But good intentions aren't always enough,* and during Covid when we didn't know what we were dealing with, we couldn't help everyone" (emphasis mine).

During the pandemic, I did not learn a new language, did not make bread, did not craft a funky Zoom background or knit a new personality for myself. I went to work. Our crews showed up and held steady. Sure, it involved a bunch of extra scrubbing, and oodles of bleach and antiseptic spray, and, yeah, masks. But this, oddly, kept me quite sane while so many people lost their bearings.

We weren't ER docs and nurses, witnessing ceaseless and cruelly unstoppable deaths. We saw the sick, the scared, the dying in their homes and on the streets. We helped as we could. We carried or escorted them to the ambulances: it was a strange, intense version of our normal. Once I wrestled an understanding of the virus and our risks and precautions, I enjoyed going to work. I kept a routine, had a purpose. I felt fucking great.

And when I write "I felt fucking great," I mean that, despite and within the pervasive, constant crushing worry, I had a furious clarity. A mission. As with the best parts of this job, my duty to serve provided guidance and purpose. As with the other by-products of this job, I could not shake my insights into the risks of people's self-defeating behaviors. The gnashing, constant anger at those who chose to stick the loaded gun of biology/virology in their mouths and pull the trigger: no wonder I'm a bit batty.

//

I give mad props to my crew: firefighters Jenn Hall, Steve Mudek, Dan Bellis; FMO Tracy Terbell; Battalion Chief J. R. Klepp; and, as ever, Deputy Chief Kath Mullen (now retired), who provided better leadership than the upper admin combined. We were among the few crews who fastidiously followed the proper masking and distancing rules throughout. Deputy Amber Lage and Captain Steve Pleasants did heroic duty navigating uncharted currents, in the face of regular hardheaded firefighter questions and behaviors, plus the extreme idiocy, threats of lawsuits and bodily harm by those they were trying to help. I am so grateful for their dedication. We avoided the virus, all of us on our crew, until after the vaccinations and boosters reduced the threats. One by one, most of us got caught at some point: bad colds, deep coughs, weakness, one case of pernicious long Covid. And one of us danced in the rain and somehow didn't get wet.

(Special thanks to Steve Belber and Flannery Enneking-Norton for their feedback and suggestions on the early drafts of this essay. It is 88 percent less vituperative, thanks to you.)

12
KETAMINE OR KILL A MAN?

> *I learned . . . that to be a Negro meant, precisely, that one was*
> *never looked at but was simply at the mercy of the reflexes the*
> *color of one's skin caused in other people.*
>
> —James Baldwin, *The Price of the Ticket*

I WAS SITTING IN MY FIRE STATION IN SOUTH MINNEAPOLIS ONE MORNING in early January 2023 when I learned of the death of Keenan Anderson after an encounter with the Los Angeles Police Department. I was sitting in the same chair the night of May 25, 2020, when the Minneapolis Police used overwhelming physical force on a forgery suspect, a man who stated from the beginning of their interaction that he was anxious, claustrophobic, and hyperventilating. That man, George Floyd, died on the street six blocks from where I sat. He was not fighting the police: he was fighting to breathe.

My crew and I responded and assisted paramedics in the futile attempt to restore Mr. Floyd's life. In the days and weeks afterward, we responded to the spasms of anguish and fury on the streets. In the years afterward, we have worked with the residents, the activists, and the protesters to find a better way forward. Our connections have been at the interpersonal, not systemic or structural, levels: meeting person to person, as human beings, not types. Wherever I have traveled in this country since 2020 (Boston, Oakland, D.C., New York, and small towns along the way), I have seen Mr. Floyd's likeness painted on walls, in store windows, on posters, packaged as merchandise, his name invoked as synecdoche and cri de coeur. Mr. Floyd and his death were not a symbol or construct for my crew. It is strange and haunting to have

194

been involved, literally and physically, in something so profound, so complicated.

I testified in the state and the federal trials of the officers who killed Mr. Floyd. The defense lawyers, parsing legal technicalities, almost obscured the basic fact that the officers crushed the man's life out of him. What changes has Minneapolis made? Or any city in America? How have we learned nothing—not since the Minneapolis police killed Mr. Floyd, but long before: how many unarmed Black men have been killed by police, witnessed and recorded, with no substantive intervention or correction from the governing bodies, the courts, the police themselves?

You might reasonably believe that there have been significant changes and reforms to how emergency responders, police especially, engage the public. That Minneapolis's "strong" mayor and diverse city council demanded investigations and significant change in the police department (regarding how the police engage civilians, especially those displaying crisis or incoherence). That the spark from Thirty-eighth and Chicago in south Minneapolis ignited a national awareness and improvement.

You would be wrong.

In the raw beginning of 2023, police in cities across this country killed multiple young Black men who were not attacking them. Again. Yet again. On camera. Three separate young men, including Keenan Anderson, in one week in Los Angeles. In February, two St. Paul officers shot Yia Xiong, a sixty-five-year-old Hmong man in a crisis; one officer was African American, the other Hmong American. Tyre Nichols in Memphis—fatally beaten by Black officers (these last two support arguments that the uniform trumps the skin color of officers, and that the system and culture are irredeemable). In mid-March we learned of the death of Irvo Otieno in a Virginia psychiatric hospital, a man whose family called 911 explicitly for help with a mental health emergency. He was treated as a threat, physically restrained and beaten by police officers and hospital employees over several hours and locations, resulting in fatal asphyxiation. They knew he was in crisis and still defaulted to physical domination. The videos are horrible. The deaths absolutely preventable. The systemic failures comprehensive.

I cannot muster surprise. I cannot say, "I *thought* things had changed." I still work on the same streets where Mr. Floyd was killed. I know better.

In my twenty-two years as a firefighter/EMT, I have been on many scenes with agitated civilians. I have seen many incoherent people unreachable through words and force due to a range of conditions. I have seen far too many interactions go south explicitly because of responders' aggressive, blind demands for immediate acquiescence and submission—generally the police, but at times EMS, too.

Adjust the dial forward two years or back twenty, and there seems little genuine movement by the cities, the courts, or the departments themselves to address and prevent police killings of unarmed Black people. Minneapolis had an opportunity to prevent further deadly incidents, to examine how all authorities engage with citizens on the streets. Specifically, we could revise our understanding of "normal" behaviors, "coherent" subjects, "reasonable" orders. If we reframed "normal" and adjusted our expectations—and reactions—appropriately, we would provide far better care, and cause far less harm, to our public.

That has not happened. More civilians nationally were killed by police in 2022 than in the two previous years. The cities failed. The states failed. The nation failed. We—the structural, systemic, and individual we—absolutely failed to begin again.

//

Several interrelated and underexamined issues form this essay. My primary point is that too many non-white men have been killed by authorities who mistook or ignored what should have been clear signs of emotional or mental distress, perceiving instead aggression or deliberate resistance. Moreover, little distinction has been made between officers overreacting and forcing violence on someone in crisis and the narrative that the officers were defending themselves against violence and aggression. Our society has tolerated hundreds of such deaths, accepting that the only plausible explanation is that the individuals were threatening and dangerous, or they were perilously unhealthy. They died from their actions—not because of the adrenalized, excessive aggression of badged responders.

There are connections here that I have not seen articulated in medical, police, or legal discussions, and this strikes me as part of the problem: the holistic connections have seldom been recognized. Doctors focus on medical facts, often in postmortems: they look only at the result and do not question *how* or *why* a person came to harm. Lawyers operate on precedents and narrow, technical definitions: their complex machinations do not address the *how* or the *why.* Police seldom question their actions, particularly not their behavioral choices; all roads lead to *justified* actions. And the system has rarely interrogated itself: the city leaders, the mayors, the legislatures all defer to police self-reporting. The connections are causal, yet even we, the players, remain wholly unaware of them.

I want to identify and distinguish the multiple links in the chain that begins with a 911 call to Dispatch. From how the dispatchers code (label) an incident, to the official response by MFD, police, and paramedics, to physical interactions, to possibly fatal consequences, to the vexing injustice of the aftermath. Because by the time the citizen is dead, it is too late. There is seldom substantive reflection or review.

Here are the composite ideas/topics that will be covered, largely in order:

1. 911 callers and citizens in the wild
2. Dispatchers' inferences and limitations
3. Fixed mindset mentality of responders
4. Plan B? Taking personally an incoherent response (mistaking altered mentation for resistance)
5. Overwhelming and deadly force
6. Sedation
7. Whitewashing; systemic avoidance and evasion
8. Systemic failures to reform

We continue to kill unarmed, nonthreatening nonwhite men. Afterward, we (the white "we") continue to profess confusion about how it all happened, but we don't actually investigate, and we certainly don't make substantive reforms. Why must it take a riot to get us to pay attention? What will it cost us before we make actual changes?

//

Let us begin.

There is a man on the ground. The man lies prone (facedown) with his wrists handcuffed behind his back. Around him are several police officers, possibly two paramedics, maybe a few firefighters.

How did he get here? What led to this situation?

He isn't responding to commands.

Is he sleeping? Ignoring the officers? Playing possum?

Wait—someone should check that he is breathing. Is he?

Is he?

Does he have a pulse?

You *think* so?

Is unresponsive the same as unconscious?

What led to this man's current condition?

He was resisting? Wait—he still isn't moving. Are we *sure* he's breathing?

He's not? Hmm.

So, what—he's *dead?*

Weird. He wasn't a few minutes ago.

The man up and died on us. Must have been drugs. Or an underlying medical condition.

These things happen. Well, now what?

Who is going to investigate this unfortunate occurrence?

Will there even be an investigation?

The police said *he was fighting them; he was resisting them.* They were *afraid for their lives.*

If bystanders record and share images of the encounter that led to the man's nonalive condition, will that measure against the officers' version? *He resisted. He fought. They were afraid.* The video shows something very different. But who knows more than the police? They are the experts.

The officers' reports will say they encountered a man who resisted, who refused their commands, who became violent. There will be a terse uniformity to their reports, almost as if they discussed what to say. Or were given guidance.

So, they shot him.

No—this time, they Tased him.

No, wait: This next time, no guns! They just held him down.

Until?

Until he stopped resisting.

But now he is dead.

If only he hadn't resisted.

He shouldn't have resisted.

What did he resist?

The police were investigating a call about a strange man on the sidewalk. Someone looked out their window, saw a man they didn't recognize, and dialed it in. The officers were seeking a *suspicious male.*

This man, Black and wearing clothes and breathing; sitting or walking or standing: he fit the description.

What made him suspicious? Did the man have a gun? Was he hurting anyone?

Did *he* know he was suspicious? Did anyone explain to him what was happening?

The official reports state: *He resisted lawful orders.* The Public Information Officer will say the same thing: *A man resisted the officers; there was a struggle. The man suffered a fatal bout of death. It was tragic, and unavoidable, possibly due to a medical condition.*

Their reports will not state what the officers did to escalate the situation, or if they created the man's agitation or upset—only that *he resisted their commands and orders.*

What orders? To explain his existence?

The 911 Caller and the Systemic Response

When the 911 system sends me and mine into the streets, we possess the official sanction and the responsibility to enter strangers' lives. Most people, having called for help, are relatively happy or relieved to see us. Not everyone. Some are paranoid, or hostile to authorities, or addled by drugs or alcohol, or medically psychotic, or just brimming with oppositional defiance.

Also: the person we are dispatched to is often not the person who called.

The concerned citizen who calls 911 about the person splayed in the bus stop has no inkling that the "patient" might be combative or schizophrenic or paranoid or a fugitive or high AF, or just chilling out. Too many people merely call with a general concern, then drive off.

This is deeper and far more complicated than you might think.

White people call the police on Black and brown citizens for nothing, zero: walking down the street, standing too long in front of a store, sitting in a car . . . ad nauseum. White people, whether maliciously *or* unintentionally, will use language that brings police response: *suspicious, acting odd, possibly armed, might be on drugs.* The police respond with their default mindset—and their biases.

Consider the room for error. Dispatch is taking unchecked information in real time, quickly processing it within a strict algorithm, then sending us out. "I see a man on the bench. I can't see him breathing. I'm afraid to get close to him. He might be dead," is a not-uncommon call to 911. Dispatch plugs in the info and gets "One unconscious, possibly unresponsive. Possible heart attack." EMS crews come sailing in, lights and sirens a-spinning. We are there to *save* the person in distress.

We show up and check to see if the person is alive, conscious, breathing. We presume they need help. *Hey, bud! How you doing? What's going on? You all right?*

The person might just be sleeping, and not happy to be roughly awakened, certainly not grateful that we've dragged him to his feet. He might be drunk or high or incoherent or disassociating. Many times, they are dozing on a bench, in no distress. They crack an eyelid and shrug at us. Some cuss and grumble. Some pop up, insist they are *fine, fine, fine,* and stumble or sprint away.

They may be distressed—and threatened—by a bunch of people in uniform surrounding them, barking pointed and personal questions. Some people demand to know: *What gives you the right to enter my personal space? I don't have to talk to you: I am a sovereign citizen!*

We do not interrupt our dinner to go pester someone. We were summoned by the 911 system. In our minds, we are legit. We are cogs in the system, lawfully fulfilling a nominally valid request to investigate an unknown situation. Those of us with badges are charged with making, and legally obligated to make, Official Inquiries. We operate under the aegis of the Good Samaritan policy. We do not want to be arguing with a grouchy stranger when we could be back at the station, arguing with each other.

From a responder's perspective, we cannot leave without investigation: that would be abandoning a patient, gross negligence, dereliction of duty. Anything impeding our investigation is a problem. Resistance is perceived by many responders as a threat. It generally is not a threat. This is the crucial departure point in our interactions: *Responders take something personally and react aggressively.*

Is it a threat to be contrary and refuse to cooperate with us? No.

Are we all experiencing the same realities in this situation? No.

Are we even speaking the same language (literally and figuratively)? No.

No.

EMS and police respond because someone has reported something. We show up and are in job mode: our context seems self-evident and obvious (Dispatch tells us "one unconscious"; "SOB, possible drug issue"; "one acting dangerously"; "one self-harming," based on whatever the caller says and how the algorithm interprets). Truly, we should start by checking the veracity of the call, but too many of us take literally or implicitly whatever pops up on our screens.

If someone will not or cannot answer our investigative questions, we get testy or directive. We demand cooperation and compliance. The person must answer our official questions. Yet, even here, at this early juncture, there can be a significant distinction between *cannot* and *will not* answer questions. Mistaking one thing for another can lead to poor public service, bad treatment, fatal conflicts.

I repeat: responders take umbrage at a response from someone they know nothing about, who might not even know what is happening. We make it personal and then we react aggressively. This point does not receive enough focus or significance, not in our training, not in incident reviews, not in investigations of deadly force.

We must (but often do not) look closely at the person and the situation. I ask myself, *What is the actual issue? Is this a misunderstanding? A communication error?* I stress to myself and my crews: *Is this an emergency or a mistaken call?* Too many responders fail to perceive what and who they are actually seeing. We act automatically, and things go south.

//

If the 911 caller utters, "He might be on drugs" or "He seems aggressive," then the Potential Threat/Risk box gets checked and Dispatch ups the safety cues, adds police, and stalls EMS until police "control the scene." That is a lot of power behind "might be" or "seems." Many police officers take a vague verb as affirmative, and they approach with bristling force. They *must* control the scene.

There is a short trip from "Hello, sir, how are you tonight?" to "I *order* you to stand up! Quit *refusing* my commands!" to a chokehold, baton, Taser, bullets. It happens far too often.

Why?

Again, responders often arrive with a fixed mindset—either taking Dispatch's description literally or presuming a straightforward interaction in which the person gladly accepts our offer of assistance and complies readily. Or interpreting a thirdhand description to imply that an upset and voluble person intends violence. We must investigate and adjust our perceptions.

Makes sense, no?

But that presumes a whole lot that should *not* be presumed.

Our presumptions get people killed.

For most "possible" threat calls, EMS crews stage until police arrive and declare it safe (Code 4). The ambulance and the fire rig wait outside the scene: staging up the street, around the corner, or several blocks away. The idea is that the scene is violent, chaotic, or unstable enough that we need police to restore order before we can enter. *Our safety is the highest priority.* Sure. But: My point throughout this is that the well-intended caution by Dispatch too often triggers the "Stage for Code 4" command for scenes that are not remotely dangerous, unstable, or violent. This means we delay treating someone who is having an actual medical crisis due to systemic or structural default—without any factual information determining an actual threat.

I have staged helplessly, uselessly, a block away from scenes for five, ten, twenty, up to forty-five minutes, waiting for police to arrive. Prohibited by protocol from investigating, from using my common sense. People have died on the street while EMS staged. They *might* not have survived, but we certainly did not give them a better chance. That is a systemic and structural failure.

//

The conflation of civil roles gets messy as well: depending on what the person calling 911 says, the call might be entered as a medical emergency, a safety threat, a self-harming danger. The police respond for reasons of public safety (to control unruly or potentially threatening citizens) and to investigate a possible health crisis (they are the ones who write psychiatric holds). Those are two significantly different constructs. The line between public safety functionaries and armed-force agents blurs quickly when it is the same mind doing the investigating. Many hats, one gun. (Well, two: the Taser. But that in itself can be deadly, and officers have mistaken one for the other, with fatal results. RIP, Daunte Wright.)

The police are intended—and expect—to bring order, to simmer people down. They have the vested authority to detain someone. "Intended." In reality, their arrival freaks many people out, and their first actions (demanding personal information, ordering people around, physical intimidation: anything necessary for control) can exacerbate tensions, leading to physical restraint and violence. A disagreement about whether someone sits down is not the same as that person threatening our lives. But the refusal to "comply" can lead to physical engagement by officers, which can turn deadly.

What constitutes a threatening suspect? A random caller's unvetted words to 911: *suspicious, weird, drugs, danger, gun.* The police are told there is a threat and they respond accordingly—without much interpretation, not until the "threat" is neutralized. It's (white) America's Pavlovian response. Strict literalism is a systemic problem for emergency responders.

The *I'm not racist, just concerned* type who says, "I see a suspicious man standing on the corner. He's Black and wearing a hoodie. I'm *worried* he might rob somebody—I think he *might* have a gun," guarantees there will be a pointed police response.

And if it is just your Black neighbor about to go running, headphones on, holding his phone? The police swarm him: this suspicious man, possibly armed, "refusing" to answer commands he cannot hear. *Just doing our job. Safety is key.*

This issue is ripe for systemic and individual evaluation and retraining. An uncritical response is a problematic, dangerous response (for everyone present). And when police officers have to play multiple roles without clear guidance, training, or emphasis, they are very humanly inclined—and trained—to go with their most natural option: force.

Obeh Mah Authoriteh—or Else

Let us consider the patients themselves. They may be wholly unaware an "emergency" has been generated on their behalf. Here are several categories of people we might encounter:

Someone unconscious or unresponsive

Someone uncomprehending, oppositional, or incoherent

Someone with altered mental status from drugs or alcohol, or both

An emotionally/behaviorally disturbed person (EBD), someone in crisis

A non–English-speaking person (in crisis or not)

Someone with a seizure disorder

An Alzheimer's patient (in crisis or not)

An autistic person (in crisis or not)

Someone mentally compromised or emotionally traumatized

Someone experiencing a schizophrenic or psychotic crisis

A person who is deaf or has a speech disability (in crisis or not)

Someone walking with headphones on, wearing a hoodie and cap

Look over that list of possible conditions or situations. Consider the reactions and responses these individuals might offer, before there is stress or challenge involved. There are vast differences between these people's conditions, issues, and needs; their abilities to communicate and receive information. There are examples across the country of people in each of these categories being manhandled, falsely detained and charged, or killed. These folks deserve close attention and thoughtful engagement before we simply grab them. How can we help if we don't even know what and whom we are addressing?

Incoherent people do not play by straight-world rules. Literally. By definition, the drunk, the agitated, the unstable, the high: they are not thinking clearly. Someone experiencing a mental or emotional crisis is not going to react well to being accosted. Someone who cannot fathom what is being said to them—calmly stated lawful orders or shrieked, panicked, aggressive commands—is not going to respond "appropriately." Putting hands on someone without permission seldom calms them down. They get more upset and struggle harder. And so we escalate, holding them, forcing them to stay put, yelling "Stop!" And that doesn't produce calm. They fight more. We restrain harder. Until what?

We used to shake people awake and roughly "help'" them to their feet, "rousting a drunk" in old-school parlance. But I no longer do. Why? Because I have no option, once I wake someone, but to control them—in case they lurch onto the train tracks or into traffic or faceplant on the street or assault a passerby. I have started and complicated the interaction. Moments before, this person was peacefully passed out or nodding off or sleeping, then I jostled him awake. Note: If someone is on their side, breathing adequately, whether asleep, high, or drunk, I let them be until police or medics arrive—they have a means of transport. If the person is in distress, we begin treatment directly. The two are not equivalent: we must evaluate the person's actual condition.

To protect ourselves (both in terms of liability and physically) and our patient—who, remember, did not ask for help—we need to stop them from fleeing. We must contain them. And someone who does not want to be contained? Well, there we are: at loggerheads without Plan B.

It can quickly become a tense physical battle—often with someone who doesn't comprehend *why* they are being bodied, someone in manic panic, someone who has adrenalized, scared, angry, or drug-fueled strength. These are volatile scenes, very dangerous for everyone involved. A physical wrestling match, whether in an apartment hallway, in a bathroom or bedroom, in a car or on the street, is scary, unpredictable, and dangerous. Flailing hands and feet can be weapons (unintentionally, and purposefully); headbutts break noses and teeth; teeth rip into flesh. Almost anything in a kitchen can be used as a weapon.

There is a connection between physical restraint and exacerbated reaction. The escalation of emotional and physical tensions—unsurprisingly—frequently provokes an agitated, feral, response. It is primal. So, let's pause. Give ourselves a moment. Take a look at what we are doing, what we are creating, what the person actually needs.

When the police presume that everyone *might* be a threat and act to subdue anyone who doesn't comply promptly, ordinary citizens who are not threats take umbrage at being bodied. Being grabbed and restrained causes fight-or-flight reactions and defensive anger. It is human nature, hardwired. And then the officers have what they claim they saw initially: resistance or perceived aggression, which means they must up the battle (which *they* started and escalated) with more force, harder blows, chokeholds, weapons.

Consider the essence of tactical engagement: the police are taught to inflict pain (joint control, pressure points, wrist locks, knees to bone) in order to force someone to yield and comply. The idea is that the sharp physical discomfort will break through a stubborn person's resistance. Once they stop "resisting," the police will (should) release their holds.

But that presumes the person is coherent, lucid, sober, in control. It presumes the person can overcome their pain and their panicked reactions. I've seen enough situations on calls, and certainly enough body-cam and civilian videos, where the police do their trick and it not only fails to achieve the desired effect but makes things worse.

And then what?

Additional officers jump in. They see a struggle and rush to protect their brethren, adding more force, more pain, more bodies. It happens over and again: the brute pile-on, the adrenalized physical attacks, the multiple shouted commands. The police escalate a situation, provoking or causing the individual's reaction. If the person even touches the officer, that is felony battery, or resisting (even if no arrest has been made).

The officers are ascribing willful resistance and noncompliance to a *physiological* response (which they are causing). They are seeing challenge where someone is incoherently *reacting* to their actions.

My understanding is that, to the police, the potential threat of a violent person trumps any possible imposition or rough treatment. *Safety* as paramount. Fair enough. None of us wants or needs to die on the street. Except, of course, look how many dead citizens—predominantly people of color—we have in interactions that were *not* violent. The police have killed someone who was not attacking them, was not violent, was not committing a violent crime. Peace officers, over and again, killing people. And nothing significant is done about it.

Why am I writing about all this? I am a firefighter/EMT, not a doctor or lawyer. How dare I? Because we keep getting called in the aftermath to revive the person who would not be dead had the police not done what they did. And I have been on the scenes as they played out. I have witnessed enough of these to understand how they occur. Too, the systems: the lawyers, city leaders, courts, police departments, medical examiners continue to treat these as routine and anomalies both. The system has not investigated itself.

Here's a simple reason why I am doing this: the killing of George Floyd by Minneapolis police officers was not my first death-by-police. None of the deaths—unarmed Black men—have merited substantial structural reform. Status quo or same old, same old. From the very start of the interaction, Mr. Floyd stated he was panicked, needed to catch his breath, was claustrophobic. The officers forced him into a small space, causing a panicked reaction. The senior officer, Derek Chauvin, arrived and jumped in without asking for information, background, or context. He saw a "struggle" and showed his rookie officers how to be tough.

They killed the man with their bodyweight. The city and nation erupted. A lot of tears and blood spilled on the streets. And yet: What has the city of Minneapolis done to address any of the above? What investigation or reform of the police department has the "strong" mayor or the city council accomplished? They've done fuck all.

//

I include here several instances from calls I've had, situations that exist in the murky gray areas I've described. The patients' conditions, our responses as emergency workers, the close quarters and in-the-moment intensity, our few options: there is much to consider. My experiences and what I learned from them were pointed rejoinders to the simplistic *The person refused our orders.*

This is the key point, where we lose focus and bodies pile up. No one has evaluated the *causal* connection between joint locks or pressure point aggravation and panicked physical response. Rather than truly evaluating the person and the situation, responders plow forward, see or declare noncompliance, and then escalate. We have started with second-hand descriptions with no guarantees of accuracy. We are investigating the hypothetical or inferred or implied.

Add several officers crushing down on the person's body, and the literal suffocation adds more desperate panic. All of this falls under *We were attempting to subdue the suspect, who was resisting.* There is deliberate semantic dissembling at work here. If you twist my arm, I will squirm and jump. Is that "resisting"? Is that "fighting"?

If the person cannot comprehend or respond to the officers' shouted commands, if the person is not responding coherently or cogently, what next? What is your Plan B? Because that is what the majority of the deaths of unarmed people at the hands of police have shown: there was an incoherent gray area into which the police inserted lethal force.

There are many possible reasons for someone not answering or not responding "appropriately" (consider the list earlier in this chapter). The very act of not following orders—whether clearly given or shouted by many, even conflicting orders given one upon the next—can indicate that the person is not coherent or lucid. The individuals who are defiant in their resistance are explicit: *Fuck you. I'm not doing that. Try to make me!*

How can we justify maximum force on someone who has shown no inclination or intention to be violent or threatening? Preemptive force—and for what? A taillight, a cigarette, a parking violation, a bogus twenty?

The number of nonwhite citizens who have ended up dead in encounters with police where the officers were not there to stop a violent crime or person—these are staggering in their frequency and their routineness. Once the officers begin physical altercations, there is the distinct chance that they will "feel" (fear) the person is "reaching for" their gun—which will justify a fatal shooting. Or they will continue to "control" someone by using painful physical stimuli or respiration-compromising restraints until the person yields, collapses, or dies.

I repeat this: There are dozens (historically hundreds) of fatal interactions caused by power struggles: a nonthreatening, unarmed Black or brown man is killed by police officers sent to *investigate* something, not stop a violent crime in progress or protect the innocent from deadly threat. Ask questions. Check things out. How and why do so many investigations escalate without provocation into fatal violence? And why have we the people allowed these avoidable killings to be normalized and accepted?

I do not ascribe deliberate malice to the officers who have hurt and killed nonthreatening, unarmed civilians. There are profound cultural and racial dynamics involved, unchecked suppositions, reflexive impulses, ingrained biases. But: the essence of how police officers are trained is with an emphasis on control. *Overwhelming force* is the term used. Control is a zero-sum game, a most deadly game.

Videos show officers choking or crushing or shooting Black and brown men who had not been acting aggressively prior to the officers' use of physical force. Is there any credible reason to believe that Eric Garner was going to attack the officers (selling cigarettes)? That Philando Castile was doing anything other than what he said, namely, offering to show Officer Yanez his paperwork (dubious traffic stop)? That Jamar Clark intended to attack and overpower Officers Ringgenberg and Schwarze (reported domestic assault)? That George Floyd was going to lay siege to the Third Precinct with his allegedly ill-gotten snacks (forgery and intoxication)?

The galling insult to these deaths is that grand juries, police review boards, city investigators continually find no wrongdoing by the officers involved. Their actions are always deemed appropriate or justifiable. But how? Why? Based on what?

//

Here is an example of a close call I was on years ago, with someone whose incoherence could have led to a fatal outcome. We had scant training and even less public understanding of the perils of bodily restraint at the time.

A guy had driven his car badly while acutely high, smashing into multiple parked cars along Penn Avenue North, then careening across an empty lot and crushing a wall. Bystanders pulled the man out, as his now-totaled car was smoking (from spilled radiator fluids; it was not "about to blow up," contrary to the cries of the crowd. This is also common for us). We followed the swath of spectacular damage, arriving at a demolished SUV against a toppled brick wall. The driver was floundering on the ground.

He was sweaty, flailing arms and legs, babbling; his body was misfiring. His eyes were unfocused. Something caused him to hit all the cars before he hit the wall (meaning: he passed out or lost control and couldn't steer or brake, or didn't notice he was ramming other vehicles). Likely causes: diabetic issue; seizure disorder; stroke; drugs. Because of the impact, he was considered a risk for possible head or internal issues, so we had to transport him to the hospital. He could not speak to us, could not answer our questions. He was very large and quite agitated. He appeared to be a threat—to himself and others, not from deliberate violence but incoherent lumbering.

So: how to convince a large, agitated man that he needs help, that we are helping him, that he must stay still, that he has fucked up his car (and several other cars, whose owners might respond violently), and that he must go to the ER for evaluation?

We tried to calm him, to talk to him. We tried to check his vitals. We tried to passively contain him, blocking his movements with our bodies. We tried to actively restrain him, putting hands and legs on his limbs to stop him. We achieved nothing. He was very large and strong. He was blindly thrashing and grabbing. Not *attack*-attacking us, but . . . It took three firefighters, two medics, and three transit cops to get him on the stretcher, then secure him with the safety belts, then wheel him to the ambulance. He bucked and writhed wildly. He caught my hand at one point. I thought, *Great. I can control at least one limb.* Except he was far stronger than I was. He dug his fingernails deeply into my hand, drawing blood.

There were moments he would go still, the wild energy subsiding, not quite unconscious, but close. We kept trying to reassure and calm him. Nothing penetrated wherever he was. We couldn't get his BP for all the flailing. His pulse was racing, well over 130. His respirations were fast and shallow, gasping and panting, well over 35/minute—until he'd suddenly subside, and drop to under 10. He'd be still, briefly, and then with no apparent cause, he'd start again, bucking, thrashing, fighting us and the restraints. An ambulance, I remind you, is close quarters, without space to maneuver. We were less than a mile from North Memorial, but it was a fraught, tense, chaotic trip.

We arrived at the hospital and four burly guards immediately piled on top of the man, crushing him against the stretcher. Literally, they rushed up and jumped on top of the man as we wheeled him in. My captain tried to intercede, telling them futilely that he was not aggressive but out of his head. But they saw a large Black man "fighting" the medics: they interpreted their duty was to subdue him. *For safety.*

My captain raised her voice, as did I, trying to stop them from hog-piling the man. They could not hear us. Nothing in their tunnel vision and adrenalized aggression could open their eyes to what was actually happening. The guards thought they were doing their job. The patient finally let go of my hand, so we were able to leave. I did not want to be there if he went into cardiac or respiratory arrest. (This was in 2006 or '07, when much less was understood about all of this, even as it was happening all around us: PCP, racial bias, hogpiling, acidosis and positional asphyxia.)

We learned later that he had significant amounts of PCP in his system. The stories about PCP mania are true. It is real *and* it demands conscious engagement from responders, not brute force and violent submission. The man was tripping balls, incoherent, out of control. The medical examiner's report would certainly contain his toxicology screening ("A man was on drugs and suffered a fatal medical event") and, given his size, likely coronary artery disease or high blood pressure ("Underlying health issues"). From the police reports and the strain to his system, the ME would likely add "excited delirium" as potential contributing factor. Not everyone who smokes PCP freaks out like this, and not everyone freaking out incoherently is on PCP. But when someone is that tweaked, there is no simple way to communicate with them, *and* we must stop them from being a threat to themselves or the public. But: the only place "excited delirium" would enter the discussion would be in a postmortem, had the man suffered a fatal consequence of our physical restraint. We didn't look at him thrashing in the snow and say, "That's guy's got a clear case of the ol' *excited delirium!*" We realized quickly he was high and incoherent. Our physical engagement with him—which was necessary—provoked his physical reaction.

So, what then?

None of us were trying to hurt him. Maybe the hospital bulls felt inclined to assert their dominance, but our fire crew and the paramedics were simply trying to stop the man from hurting himself. He easily could have suffered a fatal respiratory or cardiac event. Easily. Many men in similar situations have died. No charges were filed in those cases. The coroners' reports mention drugs, health issues, "excited delirium." The actions of the officers and medics are not considered factors. All we were trying to do was get him help—and not get hurt ourselves. We had no gauge for what was a dangerous amount of stress. Had he died on us, I am confident we would not have been charged, and I'm confident we would have had no clue that *we killed him.* And, I will add, his race played a role in the aggressive reaction of the white guards. They saw an "aggressive Black man" and went with full-on power and physical force.

The Subject "Experienced" a Medical Emergency

In the aftermath of a fatal event, the police public information officer (PIO) offers the neutral (neutered) statement, "While being investigated by officers, the subject became aggressive, and while being restrained, he suffered a fatal medical emergency." Or, alternative version: "The officers feared for their lives and took action to stop an imminent threat" of an unarmed man they had thrown to the ground.

This is standard procedure, relying on the default playbook: "The officers stated they were afraid for their lives." "They felt threatened." "He refused to comply." "The suspect was resisting arrest." Not arrest: detainment. Many aren't even under arrest when they're killed. This is the confluence, if not collusion, of structural, systemic, and individual bias. These statements have been sufficient to protect officers from accountability, but they have (more significantly, I believe) allowed the systemic disorder to persist unchallenged and unchanged.

The profound tragedy of these deaths increases with both their frequency and habituality. A single fatal confrontation with an unarmed citizen ought to be enough for public safety officers across the country to immediately reevaluate their tactics and approaches, and for city leaders to mandate and enforce changes. Instead, it is nauseatingly commonplace.

In my research, I have been struck by the disconnect, by the absence of holistic understanding of these pile-ons, the multiple sources of pain inflicted, the citizen's increased panic and frightened writhing, and, frequently, fatal medical complications. I have found no substantive connections made in medical, legal, or police articles. This isn't a conspiracy but a reflection of the limited perspective of each entity. The medical investigations only address the aftereffects, the corpses. They seldom investigate *how* the person came to be crushed, strangled, Tasered, or shot. The legal system runs on precedent, and, until very recently, no officers had ever been found guilty of killing an unarmed Black man. The police? Well, they seldom investigate their own officers internally, let alone allow outsiders to weigh in. That Blue Wall is real.

The system, if you will, does not question if the force was appropriate—only repeating that "the suspect struggled with the officers and suffered a medical emergency." The "investigations" focus on avoiding responsibility and justifying the force—never examining what happened or what could be done differently to ensure no more gratuitous deaths. For the very rare instances in which officers are investigated for their fatal actions, the departments strenuously defend their training and protocols, in the process either exonerating the officers or scapegoating them. What sort of organizational structure and culture fails its members so horrifically?

These deaths have been written off by the police, by the courts, by our larger society. This isn't a matter of "a few bad apples." Nor does it simply reflect racist animus. It is a conflation of systemic patterns and attitudes, fundamentally problematic and unsound training, *and* individual biases. The presumption is always that the officers made objective, necessary decisions, or that they had to assess "credible threats" to themselves in a flash. And no one can say they didn't, because the officers are the sole arbiters of each scene's danger. The legal system affirms and upholds this.

If the officers presume that anyone (anyone not white, I mean) might be potentially violent, why can they not also presume that same person might instead be high, drunk, troubled, in crisis—needing help not submission? All we (they) have to do is *not* start a potentially fatal physical altercation with someone who might be "weird" or "acting strange" or even "suspicious" but is not aggressive, violent, or truly threatening.

When firefighters lead with presumption on medicals, we can misjudge or overlook someone's condition, but the paramedics are the next level of investigation. When the medics low-ball someone, we should advocate for the patient. If we get sucked into a physical altercation with someone incoherent, we can cause harm. When firefighters go into buildings blindly, we can get killed. When police respond blindly, civilians get killed.

//

The police maximum-restraint reflex reached its hideous apogee with the killing of George Floyd. I write in greater detail about the death of

Mr. Floyd in chapter 15, but I will share some context now, as it pertains to this discussion. It is an infamous tragedy, recognized by many. I use it to deepen the reader's understanding of the systemic issues at play. Rather than the usual "split-second judgment"—that is, adrenalized or panicked reaction and shooting—the officers slowly crushed him. They were not intending to kill him. But they did not examine the likely and eventual consequences of their actions. In the prolonged, gruesome span while he begged for his life, his literal breath, and while the horrified witnesses cried out for the police to look at what they were doing to Mr. Floyd, to hear his cries, to check his condition, the officers stolidly persisted. Nothing could penetrate their tunnel vision. It was the same reckless disregard as with previous chokings and shootings and asphyxiations—except it was captured in slow motion.

The officer who started his investigation of Mr. Floyd had no problem presuming threat and violent criminality when he approached Mr. Floyd. Officer Lane pulled his gun in seconds. What was the threat? Over and again, police preemptively increase the power, control, and physical domination of nonwhite citizens. The original call, and the info to squads from Dispatch, stated: "Possibly counterfeit $20 bill. Suspect is very intoxicated."

How was this information used in that call? *Was* it used?

Watch the bodycam footage from Officer Lane: Mr. Floyd was sitting in the car with his companions, apparently under the influence, eating takeout, when Officer Lane approached to investigate a possible phony twenty-dollar bill. Why did Lane pull his gun on Mr. Floyd? Literally, what made him think there was a need to point his gun at the man eating food in a car? (Spoiler alert: well, you know. Black man loose in the American mind.)

From this point of the interaction, Mr. Floyd's behavior is consistent with someone panicked, high, incoherent, distressed. When the gun is put in his face, he babbles that he is scared, that he has been shot before, that he is claustrophobic. He never fights or actively refuses to comply. He is unsteady on his feet, slurring his speech. Over and over he states that he is scared, cannot catch his breath, needs a minute to compose himself. *Never* does he threaten or try to flee. Mr. Floyd was a textbook example of someone drunk or high, and panicked. His last words before he began begging for his life were, "Okay, I'm going down.

I'm not resisting. I need to breathe. I can't breathe. Please, Mr. Officer—I can't breathe!"

Was he *fighting* the officers? Was he *resisting*? Resisting what, how? Again, he had not been arrested: he was being detained for investigation. He might have—no, he was never given the option; a white dude like me, though—simply pulled another twenty from his pocket, paid the store, and gone about his day. He said he was panicked. He behaved like a panicked person.

Officers Lane and Kueng did a decent job adjusting at first—largely due to Mr. Floyd's size—and they had him sitting, calming down and gathering himself, first against the side of the building, then in the open door of the squad. This is an improvised Plan B, a wholly reasonable approach. They were deescalating and allowing the process to move forward. Mr. Floyd was cuffed and not trying to fight or flee. Only when Officer Chauvin (their training officer and the senior man) approached did Officer Kueng start physically shoving Mr. Floyd, becoming "decisive" and escalating for control. And from there, things fell apart. Within seconds, the fatal tussle began; within a minute, Mr. Floyd was facedown on the ground; within ten minutes, he was dead.

This was *not* a fight. He went down, cuffed, begging for help. The officers piled on and their weight on his body caused him to struggle in pain *and* for breath. He yelled and he squirmed. Over and over, he said he could not breathe. But the police response was the same: More force. More weight. When officers pin someone down—someone who is freaking out, whether from panic, incoherent distress, or drug reaction; someone who is incapable of following clear commands—they are trying *not* to shoot the person. But is that enough?

There was no need to force the issue. They had their man in custody, they were treating him fairly, they were being patient—there was no hurry or crisis. But their training officer arrived. The rookies had to prove they were tough and weren't letting some "street thug" push them around, so they escalated—despite everything Mr. Floyd had said and demonstrated.

Again (from Officer Lane's bodycam footage), when the officers grabbed Mr. Floyd, he said he was going down. The three officers piled on him; he cried out, "I can't breathe." Over and over. He cried out, "Help me. Help me. Help me." Their knees and bodyweight and elbows on Mr. Floyd's joints and soft tissue caused—as intended—acute pain. Their crushing weight on his chest impeded his respirations: he literally could not get a breath.

Truly, what did it gain them? Five more minutes while the man calmed down was too much? And now, they had killed a man—over what?

They failed to see what—and whom—they were responding to: they did not see the human being before them. Chauvin arrived ten minutes into the interaction and did not inquire before jumping in physically. He *thought* he knew what he seeing. He saw what he presumed, and he responded with physicality, not investigation. They were "restraining" a "resisting" suspect. They did not use their guns. No chokeholds—except Chauvin, first with his arm, then his knee. No Tasers. They did not kick or punch Mr. Floyd in the head. They knelt on him, waiting. They had not been trained to anticipate consequences, to understand their actions. They did not consider what they were doing to him. They *had* been trained to ignore the suspect's cries. They killed the man slowly.

Even in testifying against Officer Chauvin, Police Chief Medaria Arradondo stated that Chauvin failed to put Mr. Floyd on his side when he was unresponsive, as per police protocol. That ignores the fact that putting someone into unconsciousness might already be fatal (and wholly excessive and unnecessary): this part isn't questioned.

Excited Delirium: The Con That Keeps on Exonerating

The pressure-point locks and the crushing bodyweight of multiple officers are intended to subdue a person. But someone who is incoherent for any reason cannot think clearly—especially not while being pinned down, crushed, hurt. They thrash and flail, becoming more upset, agitated, panicked. Their frenzy brings more officers, more force and weight on top of them. This is a fundamentally illogical approach, an incoherent plan, yet it is standard procedure.

When agitated and incoherent people are restrained, pinned down, crushed under the weight of multiple officers, they often suffer acute medical distress, leading to fatal cardiac and respiratory collapse. They thrash and buck and strain—until their hearts and lungs fail—and they die.

Because the officers will not relent until there is *total* submission, the pressures exerted do not let up until the person stops—meaning, goes unconscious or unresponsive. By then, the person's body has been severely taxed and attacked, and they are often in grave danger of respiratory or cardiac collapse. Until recently, no one has suggested that everything the officers have done actually precipitated exactly these fatal outcomes.

If fatal, the medical examiners and coroners have continually failed to put the blame—or the responsibility—on the officers. "Excited delirium" gets listed as a contributing factor in the death report. "Excited delirium" is declared the "cause" rather than a contributing factor. The PIO and city investigators will say, "A tragic medical situation. Unavoidable. Underlying health issues." (Not "will say." They *do* say, have said, frequently.) This is a disingenuous angle but an effective one.

Because this is America, the implication is that Black men have a disproportionate susceptibility to excited delirium, an innate physiological weakness. Not that police respond more violently and excessively to Black and brown men, and give white guys a pass. Over and over, in official investigations, court cases, defense accounts, the system points to the phrase "excited delirium" and that's that: *Underlying medical condition. Nothing we could have done.*

Excited delirium does *not* kill a person. People higher than high-as-fuck do not suddenly succumb to "excited delirium" while spinning in circles. It is a useful blanket phrase; without specific or quantifiable components, its mention implies that nothing could have been done, responders were powerless, and the individual's fate was out of their hands. (See the section "Policing and Systemic Violence" in the reading list at the end of this book for references to the medical establishment's struggle to agree whether it is an actual condition.)

When emergency responders attempt to subdue and control someone who is incoherent and agitated, the act of forcefully restraining them can cause a fatal systemic reaction. Too many bodies pressing on a person restrained and held facedown on the ground begins a fatal process. Prone restraint, with its attendant compressed lungs, acidosis in the blood, and positional asphyxia, kills people. It isn't that Black men are more likely to suffer from "fatal excited delirium," which, I repeat, is a misleading (racist) canard. They *are* more likely to have three to seven officers pinning them down, crushing their chests, causing positional asphyxia. "Excited delirium" does not exist independently—only after the fact, in the coroner's report.

In police (and some EMS) trainings, the "naked and sweaty guy" has been taught as the indicator of excited delirium, with the warnings *These people are very dangerous and must be restrained immediately. They will not respond to regular commands and have superhuman strength.* The officers aren't taught to consider what might be causing the incoherence—just "drugs or a mental issue." Which is shoddy oversimplification and reduction. The officers have been taught to respond with force—and fear. Add to that racial bias or insecurity, and the potential for fatal aggression is massive. The results are tragic and predictable, yet no cause for change.

Locally, there has been no systemic investigation into the connection between MPD engagement and the mental/emotional condition of the citizens involved. There are after-the-fact lawsuits when responding officers have killed citizens experiencing mental crises; there might be payouts but little official acknowledgment of wrongdoing, and no substantive reform.

In 2010, David Smith, a man experiencing a mental health crisis on the downtown YMCA basketball court, died after being restrained in prone position with two officers on his upper back and lower legs. He was acting incoherently, aggressively, and was out of control. He reacted physically to the officers' attempts to detain and remove him. They "fought" and brought him to the ground, then knelt on his prone body until he stopped fighting. He stopped fighting: he stopped breathing. Part of the eventual settlement by the city (in 2013) was to have department-wide training on the risks of positional asphyxia and prone restraint. Spoiler alert: the city did not uphold its end. (I include a thorough and depressing article from the *Washington Post* in the reading list. It is tellingly titled "How Minneapolis Police Handled the In-Custody Death of a Black Man 10 Years Before George Floyd" [August 25, 2020]. Some might prefer the shorter but accurate alternative title: "Same Old, Same Old.")

This essay, and a deep vein of this book, reflects the horrible fact that I have responded to several avoidable, unnecessary civilian deaths caused by the Minneapolis police. Not merely that, but there have been scant changes to the police operations. More so, the city and the department actively avoid addressing a rogue culture: mentality, training, behavior, structural defenses. I am not anti-police. I am anti-murder, anti–abuse of power, anti–craven dishonesty.

In twenty-two years, I have *never* responded to a patient suffering from so-called excited delirium. I have been on many calls with people experiencing and exhibiting some form of altered mentation. I have seen autistic men in crisis, uncontrollable. I have seen many people in deep, drugged frenzies. I have encountered folks experiencing psychotic breaks, diabetics in severe crisis, and people in the throes of some combination of these. None of those was ever diagnosed as "excited delirium" *unless* the police caused significant medical crises that resulted in death. And only in the postmortem would the phrase arise.

When we tried to restrain the person—for safety or control—their feral response, their physical reaction was still connected to whatever the triggering issue was. Once they were restrained, they became more incoherently agitated, became hypoxic (were not getting enough oxygen to their brains), and hyperventilated (took fast, shallow breaths that did not deliver enough air to their systems), which increased their hypoxia. They were often positioned prone to protect us from their spit and teeth, which further compressed their chests. They fought against their restraints, causing buildup of acid in their bloodstream. We had to hold them down, restricting their lungs' functioning. Panicked, hypoxic, smothered: they were berserk, fighting to breathe. Their frantic frenzy taxed their system further, exacerbating the panic, hypoxia, and stress to the system. It is a cascading collapse.

None of that is independent of our engagement with them. *Our attempts to help them were putting them at risk of death.* Again, I stress that when responders look past the details and treat everyone as if they are coherent and deliberately resisting, we have launched a very dangerous rocket.

Fortunately—finally—as of early 2022, many medical experts have recognized the flaws in the "diagnosis" of excited delirium. They are contesting the concept, no longer teaching it, and declaring it (or its semantic equivalence—extreme agitation) *medically unsound.* Unfortunately, there are so many dead men—Black and brown men—whose death certificates list "excited delirium" as a contributing factor, one that allowed no investigation of or changes to how responders engaged with these people.

And even still, the medical side of the system does not know how to direct the police or even emergency response side. As of late 2022, the new Hennepin Health (formerly HCMC) emergency doctors are providing information sessions to urge us to no longer use the term *excited delirium*. What they are not providing is guidance for *how* to respond to and engage people in multiple forms of altered mentation. "If you encounter someone in crisis, be careful and notify EMS," was the bottom line of a recent police training video. *But we are EMS. What do we do?* No answer. "Awareness" is great, but being aware without tangible, practical skills leaves us in a poor predicament (still).

I reference the police killing of Mr. Floyd because it is the most widely seen example: the officers contended they were actively trying to control a man "fighting" them. They were crushing him to death. The flailing was his desperate attempt to breathe while being asphyxiated. The initial medical report listed excited delirium as a secondary, contributing factor to his death: an unavoidable medical issue. The term *whitewash* has fitting connotations.

//

Several years ago, we were called with police and paramedics to an apartment building for someone who was acting aggressively and incoherently. En route comments indicated this was the building's caretaker, and the caller thought he was having a medical issue. We arrived just ahead of police and medics, and located our patient rolling on the ground in the alley behind the building. He was a white man in his thirties, tall and lean, sweaty in disheveled clothes. Sinewy muscles flared and rolled in his forearms and neck as he communed with the dirty alley. He spun and writhed, making feral groans and grunts. His eyes were dilated and vacant, wild: *no one home.*

The caller—a resident of the building—told us she'd encountered our patient looking confused in the hallway, standing amid tools for a repair job. She went into her apartment, thinking little of it, until she heard a disturbance minutes later. When she peeked into the hall, she saw the man banging his head against the wall and flailing his arms and legs. She'd retreated into her apartment and locked the door. Another resident said he'd heard the noise and tried to speak with the man. As he approached, our patient had pushed past him and run down to the first floor, where he crashed against the door repeatedly and threw whatever he could grab. Someone walking in from the alley had opened the door, and the caretaker had knocked him over and wambled outside. Someone had called 911 at this point. He'd been wandering in circles and throwing himself against the parked cars as we arrived, when he staggered into the alley proper and fell to the ground.

"Hello, sir. We're paramedics and firefighters. We're here to help you, sir. Can you tell us what's going on today?"

No response.

"Sir, can you tell us your name? Do you know where you are? Are you okay?"

No response.

"Sir, I need you to stop grinding against the asphalt. You're hurting yourself."

We put our hands on him to restrain him from hurting himself. Sometimes, a gentle touch will calm a person. This (and, frankly, most) time was not such a case. The man was feverish with incoherent frenzy—dirty, sweaty, bleeding from multiple scrapes. He thrashed at our touch, lashing out with arms and legs. More of us joined in, one per limb, to control and steady him.

"Easy, buddy. Easy. It's okay. You're safe. We're trying to help you. You're all right."

We struggled with him. He'd whip and twist and free a leg or arm and start firing blindly at us. He reared his head up and tried to bite the medic next to his shoulder.

Then he started spitting.

Dear reader, please consider the intimate vulnerability of this scene: to protect him from himself, we are holding him down. He tries to bite us; he spits at us. He has bitten or cut his lip, so it is bloody spit. He has multiple open wounds now. He is sweaty and violent. We are getting dirty and kicked, and his blood is splattering us.

The man was having some sort of psychotic episode. Maybe a mental break, or drug reaction, or possible diabetic crisis—although he was too aggressive for most sugar-related issues. From bystander reports, this was a sharp and violent deviation from his normal behavior. He was incoherent, unreasonable, uncomprehending. He was a threat to himself, to us, and to the public. There was no reasoning with him, hearing him out, no passively containing him.

The police arrived. He did not respect their authority, either. He fought furiously against us. It took six of us to get him onto the stretcher and strap him down. Any slack in the restraints allowed him to worm himself free and lash at us more. We had to use two spit hoods to protect us from his bloody sputum—and his teeth. We were stressed as we labored, but no one was taking it personally.

And that is the peril: the acids build up in his blood with the stress and effort; and, restrained, his blood cannot circulate. All that blind effort against the cement and the gurney and us: it puts dangerous strain on the heart and lungs.

The medics gave him a shot of ketamine, finally, and he went under. We were able to secure him, assess him, check his vitals, and transport him.

Did we violate his agency or "freedom"? There is implied consent for treatment when someone is in need and unable to answer cogently. Had we left him alone, he would have continued to assault himself, the other residents, random bystanders, us, and the property. Had we continued to restrain him and force him down, he would have continued to put lethal strain on his system. He did not need to die, and we did not need to be wounded. He was transported to the hospital and received help. He lived.

Cartman jokes aside, the police did not feel sufficiently threatened to choke, Tase, or shoot this violent white man. Had he been Black, their perceived threat would have been existential. One reasonable explanation is generations of projecting fear and insecurity onto Black bodies, and policing and controlling them to assuage those projections—and, I suggest, the ingrained socialization to see white men as equal, human, of the law.

I emphasize this: a white man spat on us, repeatedly. He tried to bite us. He fought us and we struggled to control him. He got sedated, not shot. Our human frustration likely added forcefulness to the wrestling match, but there was no racial multiplier. I've seen young Black men dropped on their heads for demanding the officers explain why they've been stopped. Had it been a Black man freaking out, spitting and trying to bite? Hell no: the *perceived threat* very likely would have required fatal resolution. That is the place our unconscious biases spring into violent, deadly reactions.

Ketamine, the Drug of a Nation

When someone is unconscious, they give *implied consent* for treatment. Otherwise, they will be stone-cold and rotting while we await their explicit yes. When someone is drunk or high, they are considered incapacitated, incapable of clear reasoning, legally unable to make rational decisions. They have essentially forfeited their right to make (further) bad decisions for themselves. Or better: were they lucid, we infer they would not be making self-harming decisions. As such, we intervene, despite their slurred protests. This is predicated on the idea that we will solely provide appropriate care.

There is a lot of room for errors of judgment in that paragraph. There was a tragic incident in which Washington, D.C., Fire/EMS misjudged a man they found down on the sidewalk. He was disheveled and incoherent. The crew presumed he was "just a drunk." He was the victim of an assault who was presenting with altered mentation due to head trauma. They did not investigate well; they did not provide immediate, advanced care; they did not take him directly to the closest trauma hospital. He died, in part from their delayed treatment. He also was a well-known reporter, and white. His family had the clout to push against the system, seeking answers and accountability. (There was bad press against DCFD, and the city settled a lawsuit with provisions for improved training, but from accounts I have read—just as with similar agreements Minneapolis police have made—the actual follow-through has been spotty if not shoddy. Again: the city doesn't truly police itself.)

Again and again, when we act without investigating, without thinking, we put people at risk.

Back to our incoherent or high or dissociative patient on the street. If we cannot reason with someone, what then? If someone is incapable of answering us or following reasonable directions, what then? If someone is an active threat to self or others, what then? If we put hands to stop the incoherent person, what then? If we stand by while someone harms themselves or others (or us), we are failing the public. Physical restraint can lead to panicked physical and emotional reaction, acidotic overload, positional asphyxiation, and cardiac or respiratory failures.

I insist both that we (emergency responders) can exacerbate situations and that there are people who are dangers to themselves and others. To restrain these people—for their own good and our safety—might put them at risk of death.

So, what then?

Sedation is a valid and necessary option. Sedating someone who is incoherent, out of control, and a threat to self and others is a way to prevent further harm to everyone involved. Sedation is an alternative to the hogpile. But: we must control the person long enough to get the shot in. The medics don't carry blowguns.

In some cases, sedatives are used late in the event, either because the medics arrive after the police have struggled with someone, or they themselves have been involved in the bodily interaction and are stressed and frustrated (and mad or scared). Why does that matter? Because, if the physical engagement has caused the person to be pinned and restrained in prone position, there is a good chance of an imminent cardiac or respiratory crisis. Adding a hastily injected sedative can exacerbate the problems—even leading to death (which then gets labeled "fatal excited delirium"). Essentially, medics can misjudge a person's true condition, and crisis, within the chaos of the scene's surface appearance.

Ketamine is a sedative commonly used by medics in prehospital settings (a.k.a., the streets, the wild). A number of other sedatives are available, but many hospitals have used ketamine for its virtues: fast, efficient, effective, short duration. Ketamine was more known as a party drug in the 1990s, and it has lately proved successful in treating several emotional/psychological issues. But, for our purposes, it will sedate someone quickly and does not last long. Hennepin County Medical Center medics began using it in 2008. Their medical leadership conducted a study on the effectiveness of ketamine as a prehospital sedative.

In 2018, local investigative journalists looked into the study. The HCMC medical team did not handle the inquiry honestly or forthrightly, and they were caught dissembling. The resulting story and follow-up caused a roiling controversy. The gist was that medics were shooting up people without their consent, the sedation was causing dire medical conditions, and police were telling the medics to sedate inconvenient people.

The optics were horrible. Clarifying context and facts were missed, and the HCMC brass botched any chance of gaining public trust. Once the administrators got caught in evasive misstatements, no one was interested in parsing details. Citizens are fed up with being lied to or ignored by the system.

The implication that police and medics were in cahoots to "snow" innocent citizens did massive damage to the ketamine study and the public's understanding of what actually occurs on these calls. The *Star Tribune* article is marred by some sloppy edits and several inaccurate statements: Claiming "ketamine caused heart or breathing failure, requiring them to be medically revived," implies someone died and remained inertly dead under the medics' indifference until miraculously revived at HCMC. More accurately, the person was sedated and regained consciousness (appropriately) when the sedative wore off. Otherwise, it would be akin to saying I went "unresponsive" when anesthetized for surgery and was "revived" later in post-op. As with surgery patients, someone who's been sedated in the field requires intubation and ventilation, and constant monitoring. Those are all standard actions.

The docs in the ED do not have to handle cases on the street, in close quarters, and without support or backup. Some are martially minded and see "safety" for responders as the be all and end all (again, the study's lead doctors moonlighted as suburban deputies). A cultural mindset can have deep roots, no matter that the spokespeople for the hospital and city declare they know nothing about anything. I feel a lot of doctors are only directed to (or feel comfortable examining) the consequences of restraint or sedation. Meaning, they believe the tactical aspects of these calls to be outside their purview: *That is police business.* But a medical framework to help *start* the interactions would benefit everyone involved.

Medics should not arrive on scene and randomly poke someone with a needle at the cops' request. I would say *do not,* but some medics enter a chaotic scene, see a person flailing beneath the officers, and take the police at their word: the seemingly berserk person must be sedated immediately. Insert here *He's on PCP! It's excited delirium! Must be meth and crack!* This is how police and medics in Aurora, Colorado, combined to kill Elijah McClain in August 2019. It was very bad service by the paramedics; it was criminal negligence, likely homicide. The sloppy mistreatment of civilians is the true cause, while lawyers and various "experts" will bat about the responsibility: police choking and restraining Mr. McClain or the paramedics overdosing him with ketamine. Likely, it was a combination of both. He was in severe crisis *before* the fatal dosage was injected. The police bullied and brutalized a five-foot-six human being, put him in respiratory distress, and the medics did not assess him well, shooting him up with an excessive dose of sedative.

Beyond the very real issues of racial bias and presumption that can blind medics' perspectives, the interagency cooperation has no formal structure. We show up and try to get along with the police. It's awkward to challenge them, especially in the middle of a scene. We are wildly different creatures, with radically different purposes, goals, and outlooks. Some medics (frankly, too many for my comfort) also bring an "us or them" mindset to calls, buying into the police narrative that we are waging war in the jungle, that everyone (i.e., Black and brown people) could very easily be suspect, hostile, violent. These medics are quick to escalate, quick to (over)react, quick to make things physical. Based on what? "Safety" precautions. They mistake their duty as unconditionally supporting police actions, no matter what. I have been called a rat and a traitor for stating what I've witnessed on scenes: the implicit notion is that it must always be us versus them. Any breaking of the code is traitorous.

If EMS stages until a Code 4 is given, we will not witness the struggle. We will not see the person's actual condition, nor what has happened to him before we arrive. In many cases, the person is so hypoxic and distressed after being restrained by the police that they are on brink of collapse: frothing, hysterical, incoherent. This is the essence of the disconnect in the killing of Mr. Floyd: paramedics arrived for a reported mouth injury and were handed a dead man; the firefighters were dispatched belatedly and arrived with no better information. The medics had no inkling—and could not have fathomed how egregious the mistreatment had been—what had transpired in the fifteen minutes before they arrived.

As a consequence of the uproar over ketamine, the paramedics were reluctant to use sedatives on incoherent patients. Which left us with what? Bodily restraining them. This is how people get killed, which is why sedatives are a very useful tool.

I was on some of the calls that appeared in the ill-fated HCMC ketamine study. If those weren't the precise calls, all the truer to the point: there have been many calls very similar to the ones in the study. My experiences with someone too agitated and incapable of heeding directions, whether from unknown substances like meth or PCP, or psychotic reactions, or combative diabetics, have shown that when someone is a risk to self and others—right there, right now—and there are no coherent connections with words, we must use meds. Because the physical is dangerous for everyone.

Does that mean ketamine is the only option? No. We need a fast-acting, injectable sedative. There are many available. The bad publicity and poor handling of the issue by HCMC leaders, the optics and public backlash: these made ketamine a bogeyman, and the medics became hesitant to use any sedative, given how little institutional support they had.

But no one has addressed the realities of volatile calls with the public. In some corners, police-minded doctors continue to emphasize the implied dangers of incoherent people and the need for bodily control—skipping over an actual assessment of the person, the situation, the options. Nor have solid alternatives been offered to the medics, or to us. Which means, in the absence of a ready and approved sedative—and with heavy awareness of the public scrutiny and likely backlash—paramedics are hesitant to use meds. They will allow (force) the police (and firefighters) to physically restrain someone who is violently incoherent. So: we are all fucked.

//

The call was for "one on drugs, cutting himself with a knife," and the caller was the father of the patient's girlfriend. It was happening inside his apartment. Those are enough details to get a general sense of the scene, even if the caller is panicked, or angry, or scared. The details, the reality: that's the grist for the mill. Sometimes we find an amateur abattoir, blood everywhere. More often, it's a moody teenager sulking and throwing big words at the world, or it's a nail file making slight scratches in a distraught person's skin. This was not one of those times.

We entered on the heels of the police, four officers in a row. The door was ajar, and we saw an older white man (*ahem*, my age) wrestling with a younger white man, who was screaming and thrashing about. There was blood. Blood all over the younger man's arms and clothes. Blood on the clothes and hands, splattering the face of the older man as he tried to contain the younger one. Blood on the floor and walls, splattered as they wrestled. There was a hysterical teenage girl adding to the cacophony.

The older man said, with considerable calm, "I need a hand. He's trying to get that knife." He gestured with his chin toward a large bloody kitchen knife on the floor. One officer secured the knife and two others moved to help restrain the younger man. I grabbed his legs as he fell. The father stepped away, wiping the patient's blood from his hands to his pants. The girl continued to scream. Our guy flopped and rolled and squirmed and kicked. Sweat and blood made him difficult to control, and his loose clothing did us no favors.

The father looked grim and focused, calm with the furious resignation of a parent whose kid makes profoundly bad choices. "That's her boyfriend," he said. "He's on meth. A lot of meth. She called me home from work because he was freaking out, again, and scaring her, again. She's worried about the baby, too."

The baby? In the corner, in a tilting playpen, was a small kid, also screaming.

"Dude, come on."

"Knock it off—we're trying to help you. Stop it, man. You're scaring the baby. This isn't going anywhere. Let us help you!"

"*Stop* flailing, man!"

Five of us were on the young guy, holding his limbs and torso, trying to stop the spray of blood. He was facedown, screaming and groaning and bashing his head against the floor. The girlfriend screamed at him to stop. The father, exhausted, snapped at her to shut up. The baby kept crying. The sprawling mass of us were blocking the path between the mother and the baby.

We struggled for several more minutes. He was restrained and no longer able to cut himself, yet he fought against us, grinding and thrashing and flailing. He was feral. One officer put a towel under his head to prevent him from braining himself on the wood floor. Still, there was nearly a thousand pounds pressing down on him. I asked my rookie, the former paramedic, if we should be concerned for his heart. He nodded. *Yes, very.*

The rookie encouraged the senior medic to consider the risks and the urgency for subduing the man's fury. The cops agreed: *Do something to stop this crap!* The medics conferred then shot the man with ketamine. He calmed quickly and we gained several minutes to carry him down to the stretcher, secure his airway and provide oxygen, address his wounds, stop the bleeding, and get to the ER. Two officers accompanied the medics to the hospital. We gathered the wreckage of our gear in the aftermath, the furniture tossed, rugs askew, blood streaks along the walls, counters, ceiling, and pooled on the floor where we restrained him. The baby cried in its mother's arms; she cried into its neck. The dad looked tired, deeply tired.

Had we not intervened, this incoherent man would have gutted himself (or the family). Had we not sedated him, he would have strained against us until he suffered a possibly fatal medical event. This really is how it can go.

Incurious "Good Intentions" Cause Fatal Consequences

How can we continue to hurt and kill people we are summoned to help? If we don't properly examine the context, the actual facts of the scene, and instead rotely perform human transport, we can provoke a significant reaction when we grab a person (consider that list of possible conditions or personality types or situations). We *think* we are doing our job and the person "suddenly freaks out" or "attacks us without provocation." Overlooking or not truly investigating what we are seeing; leading with presumption: these can have fatal consequences too. When police officers jump in blindly to help their brethren, putting full force on the "resisting" person, when the medics take the agitated scene and the police officers' hectic shorthand at face value: these all demand evaluation, investigation, reform. It is disingenuous, or delusional, to ignore the role played by racial and sociological blind spots and bias. These could be the starting points for structural reform: acting without evaluating the scene, without considering the consequences, misperceiving a person's logical reaction as violent aggression, mistaking incoherence for resistance or threat.

Reframing our concept of threats and resistance will go a long way toward saving lives.

My thesis holds water: too many of these calls go sideways because the responders apply a reductive presumption to everyone. We are making instantaneous snap assessments, utilizing what we've seen before and what we've been taught. Many, many patients present consistent signs and symptoms. But not all. I quoted Frank Huyler in chapter 3: "When the eye is too cold . . . everything seems the same. This life, or the next. This man, or another. . . . But everything is not the same, and you have to see that, too." Perhaps it makes more sense to the reader now.

Given the human truths of this career, most of us have a Rolodex of "This, then" references or memories from previous calls that helps us form action plans in the first moments on scene. Call them the real-world application of the signs-and-symptoms mnemonics from training, or experiential learning. They can also cloud our ability to see what is actually before us. Call it an EMS version of Wordsworth's "film of familiarity." Not only are things not always the thing they resemble, they often are not what we tell ourselves we are seeing. White Americans' racial myopia has proved deadly.

Gender's role is also relevant here. Too many medics (white and male) regard women's anguish as an irritation to quell rather than an expression of a deeper root cause. This is cultural, not solely the medics' blindness. Add to it women of color, and we double down on the condescension and dismissiveness. Men's fear of male violence keeps us at bay—until we smother with overwhelming force. Women seldom present the same threat, and, physiologically (absent a weapon) they generally are seen as easier to "handle." Except: women's emotional upheaval, which is every bit as real as men's (if better and more frequently voiced), is too often regarded as noise pollution and psychic irritation. We downplay their anguish *because* we aren't as scared of them. WTF is that?

Conversely, though, our fear of men, especially Black and brown men, makes us respond with fearful force. In neither version do we stop and investigate, reflect and analyze, what might actually be happening.

Look Me in the Eyes . . .

Why haven't there been more reforms, more investigations, more change? The lack of systemic review is, frankly, nearly criminal (and literally criminal in some cases). Remember: we write our own reports and there is scant genuine oversight. Not for us, nor the medics, nor the police. We carry the subconscious concern that (a) things go sideways quickly, and once the mess starts it's tough to find a clear path out of it; (b) it might very well be one of us next time it goes sideways, so we protect one another; (c) no one wants to be a rat.

No one explicitly tells us to overlook and protect bad behavior. They do tell us, though, that the only thing between you and death/injury is your partner. It's the cultural mentality of "us versus them," and it's deeply ingrained, toxic rubbish.

This code is implicit and self-enforcing. The few of us who have reported aggression or patient mistreatment have received serious backlash from our cohort—even when we have reported the behavior of well-known rogue or abusive coworkers. And the investigations are paltry, so you risk your career, safety, and reputation for a system uninterested in truly examining and addressing its flaws.

Firefighter/EMTs are generally folks who joined the MFD to fight fires. I am among the minority who understood (and embraced) the fact that the job entailed medical work. Most people from top admin down to rookies remain stuck thinking our job is *solely* fighting fires. The police are trained to emphasize controlling scenes, and their system and mindset reinforce a zero-sum domination. Neither of these two frameworks lend themselves to parsing nuanced social, societal, sociological issues. We get little hard-fact teaching on the soft-skill tactics required for a great many of our citizens. Many police, firefighters, and medics are incredible at relating to folks, at de-escalating situations, at staying cool and not ramping up the tensions. Seriously, many of us have seen enough that little can leave us nonplussed. *We are the plussed . . .* But many of us respond reactively, whether out of fear, uncertainty, insecurity, blind resentment, or bias.

As of late 2021, Minneapolis has begun a pilot program that sends trained nonpolice responders (the BCR, Behavioral Crisis Response service) to investigate and provide help for nonviolent EBD folks on the street. It is a great start, albeit a small step, with limited support and minimal buy-in from most agencies. Significantly, this program does not address the originating issues: how people and situations are described to the 911 operators.

Even with nonpolice, nonintrusive, peaceful approaches, some calls require and demand physical interventions: calls that start with, or spiral into, violence solely due to the person's actions; calls with people—whether consciously or unintentionally—hurting themselves or those around them. But not all of them are.

This is not always *that.*

I was in New York City right after Mayor Eric Adams made headlines with an announcement that, to combat the perceived increase of violent acts by mentally unstable people, the police would be given the authority to detain and remove people from the streets and subways—even if they had not been violent. It was a bullish plan with very few details and little likelihood of addressing the profound financing and structural changes required to house and treat so many people (people who were adrift largely because of decades of policy and insurance decisions). I was riding the subway with friends while we were discussing the "plan," and there was a woman in our car who seemed mentally off, likely unhoused, muttering gibberish, smelly. I told my friends to consider her. "If anyone complains to the subway police about her," I said, "they will engage her. She is clearly off: talking to herself, making little sense, not acting 'appropriately.' The officers will order her off the car—to prevent delays, they will likely try to remove her from the car directly at that stop. How will they do that? Does she look like she is going to go willingly? So, then what? They will physically drag her off the subway. Will that make her compliant? What next? They will have a very upset person acting out on the platform—a person in crisis. Was she in crisis before they put hands on her? She was not. *Now,* however, they can deem her a threat. They can fight her through the tunnel and up the stairs, or they can call for EMS to sedate her—or they might pin her down until she stops resisting and fighting. How many people like her are in the city? Hell, are on this train? This is a very sketchy plan."

//

Frequently, by the time we are called the person is acting out and there is no calming them—in fact, that's often the reason we are called. Can we deploy passive restraint? Can we wait someone out? Sure, we can try. But it requires really perceiving, interpreting, and understanding a situation—one that is in process, with no clear narrative or context provided.

From a 911 caller's initial descriptions to our first impressions and second actions, there is abundant room for error—and to course-correct. We have a slight margin to recognize that someone is not lucid and adapt our approach. Or else we start down a perilous path.

The 911 system has been the primary response and stopgap for a legion of unhoused, poorly treated, mentally ill citizens since the 1980s. We know this: We must show we *understand* it, we must *act* on it. If firefighters, medics, police officers cannot and will not discern the range of individuals we encounter with little notice or context—and cannot recognize the limits of direct communication—we put ourselves *and* our citizens in peril. If we initiate or escalate a physical situation due to un/conscious biases or presumptions, we are far afield from our duty and purpose. If we "must" restrain someone who cannot be calmed, we need to be clear that it will likely go badly. If we cannot use sedatives, we are left with forced physical restraint, which can be fatal.

The efforts to bring trained nonpolice responders (mental health or community engagement specialists) to these scenes are good. But substantive reform of the 911 algorithms would improve the spectrum of non-emergent responses. Why not train firefighters, medics, and police to recognize and have skills with people who are not "acting normally"? I would love to partner with the BCR to better understand and develop more skills to approach any of the range of people we encounter.

There can be solutions, real means to solve this mess. But we need engagement and understanding, clarity and review, at the structural and systemic levels. We need to recognize what happens "invisibly." Change the structure and system; improve the administrators who shape the policies and training; then hold the individuals accountable. We can certainly effect reforms at the individual level, but, without upper-level support and actual change, reforms are empty. And the system continues *not* to act, waiting for some better time to effect change, hoping to avoid any future bad calls. Until the next dead body shows we are eternally too late.

//

Our man in the street at the beginning? Well, how did he get there? Was he a crazed and dangerous threat to society? Or was he:

Someone experiencing a psychotic break?

An agitated autistic person?

A deaf person in crisis?

Someone tripping balls, methed to the gills, cracked out?

A non-English speaker in crisis?

An EDP (emotionally disturbed person) or PIC (person in crisis)?

A person having a diabetic reaction?

Who decided what this person's issue was? Based on what evaluation or facts? Did anyone step in to offer second opinions, or break the spell of power games? Did the responders consider what their actions were causing?

Are they still kneeling on a dead man?

13
ARBITERS OF EXISTENCE

I AM PAID TO RESPOND TO ANYONE AND EVERYONE WHO DIALS 911. I'M HAPPY to do it. But the ceaseless non-emergency runs steal my sleep, my focus, my patience. Just as endless false fire alarms don't merely frustrate us—through the surging adrenaline and nervous energy that builds for the purpose of dealing with hazardous emergencies—but also train us to anticipate *nothing* rather than *something,* so too do nuisance EMS calls lull us into being complacent, jaded, and resentful. The hard calls, the real emergencies, demand something of us, and this makes me more protective of myself on nonsense calls.

As I've shown, we get what we get, when we get it. That may sound simplistic and clichéd, but there is no preparation for the emotional toll of our calls. We walk through a door and whatever is there, that's ours to carry forward. Having a sense of purpose provides clarity, direction, and distraction when faced with horrific things. It should, at least. Our duty to serve and perform essentially removes the choice from a hard thing; that obligation provides armor against what is often a stark human tragedy. Except: even protected by purpose, we still absorb the sights and sounds, however gruesome or jarring. That dissonance can cause our detachment from humanity, or it can haunt us.

//

The call came near midnight. "SOB," updated en route to "*one uncon-scious.*" We arrived at a triplex and headed upstairs to the top floor. It was a small unit. A teenager slouched in a chair in the tiny living room, enthralled by the computer screen, Facebook's telltale white-and-blue glow reflected on his face. I'd *just* been scrolling down a parallel street in that cyber neighborhood. The boy didn't glance at us. A woman stood in the narrow hallway. I could hear her on the phone with Dispatch: "They just arrived. They're here now."

She waved us toward her, then pointed into a doorway. "I just dozed off. When I didn't hear his usual heavy breathing, I woke up. He sleeps loudly."

I stepped past her into a small bedroom. There was a large man faceup on a queen-sized bed that consumed all but a narrow strip of the space. He was shirtless, his belly protuberant even while horizontal. I touched his arm. The skin was cold. "Sir? Sir!" I rubbed his chest then checked his carotid pulse. "He's cold," I said while searching for, hoping for, a pulse.

"The fan," his wife said. "We had the fan on."

I checked his wrist. There was nothing. His neck was crimped forward atop a thick pillow. A bad angle: a good way to cut off air to the brain, especially someone his size. A trickle of drool spilled from his mouth down his cheek to his shoulder. I put my hand under his back then beneath his neck. There was some warmth between the skin and the mattress. I opened his eyes. They were gauzy, pupils unreactive. *Fuck,* I thought. I lifted his head and removed the pillow, adjusting his neck, tilting it back and upward to open the airway—in case that was the problem and one big, unobstructed breath would solve it.

I glanced over my shoulder, but the woman had left the room. I turned to my crew, still waiting at the door—there was not enough space to fit beside me. "I can't find a pulse. Fuck—he's fucking cold." I stepped back, motioning to the durgan. "Check, will you? I can't find anything."

While she checked for a pulse, I felt up and down his body. The surface was cool. There was warmth only where the skin connected to the mattress. Sandy shook her head: *No pulse.*

He was dead.

In most circumstances, we would work him. Do the whole deal with no expectation of recovery, largely to give the family something to grasp on to while the reality sank in. Was it possible we could get him breathing again, restart his heart? *Possible* is a tricky, expansive word. We work people whenever we can, as long as we can claim we were reaching for *possible.* It's palliative and placebo, both: once we start the process, the medics continue it, and we all work hard for someone who is and will remain dead. I looked around the room. *Fuck me.*

Cardiac failure, respiratory failure, brain bleed, traumatic compromise, volemic compromise. Dead is dead usually, no matter everyone's best intentions. In the safety and sterility of the ER, it's easy to be rigid. The docs aren't standing in the cluttered room with the family surrounding them, demanding and praying and imploring and threatening us to *Save him!* The academics of biology are less concrete when humanity is factored in.

But still: Good faith efforts. Good Samaritan gestures. Why *not* try to help the family feel less lost? It's not scientific, but it is compassionate.

When possible.

I looked at my crew, and him, then around us again. The crew was looking at me, awaiting an order. *Fuck.* There was no space. If we pulled him off the bed, there'd be nowhere to squat beside him—let alone five of us, once the medics arrived—to do compressions and all the high-intensity, close-quarter ministrations. Not the hallway, also too narrow. The living room was too tight, with nowhere to dump the furniture. The landing outside the apartment door? Nope. He was a sizeable man, easily three hundred pounds. It would be awkward and dangerous for us to drag him from the bed through the small room and narrow hallways, around the tight corners, down three flights to the front lawn. I checked him for pulses again and scanned the room fruitlessly. *Fuck.* We had no space to work. He was large and he was cold.

I had to weigh what I was seeing and feeling against the word of his wife. She'd said she'd just dozed off, but "just" can mean a minute or fifteen to twenty, or more. Healthy, sleeping people are not cold to the touch. Brain damage occurs about 10 percent per minute. I sighed, touched his body one more time, and shook my head to my crew. We would not be working this man.

I walked down the hall to the main room, where the teen still idled on Facebook. The woman came out of the kitchen, looking at me expectantly. "Well?" she asked. I stared at her a moment, nonplussed. Our perspectives are so different. Her normal is that her husband is alive. My normal is people call us when someone is dying or dead. "Is he okay?"

"I'm very sorry. He's dead."

That phrase. I am decreeing something existential, literally removing her husband from the living. It's heavy on my heart and mind, being the arbiter of existence.

The other hard part is what follows.

"Noooooooo," she screamed. Her world dropped away, leaving me standing before her, the emissary of death. "No! No! No!" She moved as if to hit me. "No! No! No! Do something. *You do something!*"

"I'm so sorry, ma'am. He's gone."

"*No!* Do something. *You do something!*"

For the next several minutes, we repeated this exchange. She screamed, yelled, wailed, implored. I stood in front of her, receiving her grief, repeating my paltry condolences and firm assertion that her husband was dead. The medics arrived, having not received the information of the DOA from Dispatch. They poked their heads into the apartment, took in the situation, looked at me for confirmation, then left. I sent my crew out to drop the equipment. My durgan came back up, standing behind me in the hallway. At some point, the teenager removed his headphones and realized what was going on. He began crying, too. The mother was still yelling at me, but it was tapering, replaced by inconsolable wailing.

The mom shoved her phone at her son, telling him to call family. She wailed and implored the ceiling, the air, me. Every coherent word she spoke cut deeper:

Although her husband looked fifty-five, he was thirty-five.

She was pregnant. "Our baby—we have a baby coming! His baby!"

The son was barely a teen. "Your daddy's dead, baby! Daddy's gone!"

"*Noooooooooooooooo!*"

I stepped away to give them privacy. The only place to go was back to the bedroom. For chain of evidence, firefighters or medics must remain until the police arrive, even in "routine" deaths. Thus, we are present for these first unbearable minutes of grief. We then embody and symbolize the reality of death, of loss. Over and over and over. That is what I get paid for. If we cannot save someone or if we are notified too late to help, we bear witness. We receive their rage, fear, panic, sadness so that they can get it out of their system and move on to the details, to whatever comes next in their decimated lives.

This is not in our job description, but it is the essence of my job. I cannot do justice to the grief. *Grief*: it is too short, too light a word for what it describes. There should be something heavier, a harsh, multiple-syllable word, for this, maybe something German. Writing is both an attempt to capture and a necessary failure to detail the depths of this emotional obliteration, over and over and over. For each family, a rare and violent savaging of normal life. For us, part of our workday.

I checked the man, again. He *was* dead. I had made the right call, and I felt awful about it.

The police arrived. I briefed the officers on what we found, how we'd found him, and her, and that we hadn't noticed anything out of the ordinary (other than the dead man in the bed). I offered another useless condolence to the now merely sobbing mother and son, and we left.

The ride back to the station was somber. We discussed whether we should have worked him. *Should* have, *could* have. A thirty-five-year-old, at his size, likely suffered sudden and comprehensive heart failure. That didn't make any of us feel better about it.

I was up for a while after this call, wrestling with uncertainty. There's always room for doubt, to examine my choices and actions. Too many of us refuse to do this. *The call is over and done. Why dwell? Move forward.* It's a default defense of insecurity, the Achilles' heel of can-do machismo. It serves us poorly, though. Being comfortable with self-evaluation and self-criticism allows us to learn faster and become better at separating objective lessons from defensive avoidance. This one was needling me. Our job is to save people, at its essence. I remind myself that we cannot save those who are already lost. Fact. But it was my call not to work the man, if only for the wife's and son's comfort. It weighed heavily on me. The helplessness I felt in the face of the woman's abject grief, our futility standing over the dead man: that was unfamiliar and destabilizing.

I think we can handle so much of the gruesome and hard things we encounter simply by having a purpose and agency. That *doingness* might be a shield, a protection against all that is so truly horrific in our work. The gray area of this call stripped both the cold certainty and the noble clarity of purpose. Had we been able to work him, the result would have been the same: a dead man. But the woman and her son would have had something to cling to, if only for a few more minutes. And I would have felt better about myself, essentially, for offering her something, for trying. It is not my job to provide a placebo of hope solely to forestall grief—not for the bereft and not to protect my own feelings. The man was dead, and nothing could bring him back. This one landed hard.

//

A few hours later, we caught an "Assist the police" call, which can be anything from using our keys to get into a building to forcing a door open or throwing a ladder to get to a roof. Or it's a Tasered suspect having cardiac failure. Or it's George Floyd, dead beneath officers' bodyweight.

We rolled out, getting no further information on our computer screen. A block away Dispatch updated that the scene was safe and they needed EMS Code 3 (immediately). We pulled onto the street and were confronted by a riot of squad cars, lights flashing. There were officers roving about but no guns drawn and no frantic edge to their movement. My driver slowed, looking for a place to stick the rig. I jumped out and hustled down the street. I passed a dozen officers, but no one was upset or barking orders. Whatever it was, the thing had happened: this was the investigation now.

Reaching the address, I saw five young people sitting against the chain link fence, wrists manacled behind their backs. Several officers stood over and around them, but I couldn't tell from the cops' expressions whether these were suspects or hostile witnesses. I hate the ubiquity of that tableau: young Black men handcuffed and arranged on the ground as white police stand over them, the red-and-blue flashing lights strobing off the cops' badges. It is so common that we (*white* we) do not question its validity or necessity. We accept it blindly. An officer held the front door for me and pointed up the stairs, which I climbed, the AED banging against my leg.

I didn't hear screaming, yelling, or wailing. At the landing, there was another officer putting tiny evidence cones over a scattering of bullet casings. He looked up, I nodded at both apartment doors, and he indicated the one on my right. "In there," he said, cautioning me to watch my step as I crossed his work area. I opened the door and found several more cops by the entry. At their feet was a man, arms and legs splayed, mouth ajar. I looked at him a moment as I took in the room. "The fuck?" I blurted. "This guy's *dead.*"

There'd been no info from Dispatch about a shooting or a person who'd caught the bullets. Nor about his condition. I didn't mean to say it aloud, especially before checking him, but that was what came out. I stepped closer, knelt, and checked for pulses. His eyes were open, staring at the ceiling. "Hey, man," I said. "Can you hear me?"

I wasn't getting a pulse. He was warm. There was no pool of blood. I put my hand on his chest and rubbed it. "Hey, hey! Sir! Can you hear me?" I looked him up and down. There were blood droplets on his pants but not much, and no entrance or exit wounds. Suddenly, I felt a convulsion in his chest and neck. I jumped back. His jaw twitched and he took a breath. Not dead?

I watched him a moment, still feeling for a pulse. No further movement. I rubbed his chest again. It felt rock solid. I looked more closely at his shirt. Below and beside where I was rubbing his chest there were three or four small holes in his shirt. Hmm . . . Center mass, close-range entrance wounds. He was done. Then his torso and neck stiffened and quivered again, and his jaws gaped further open a moment.

The medics reached the front door at this point. I moved to the other side of the man so they could see. I said I had no pulse but there'd been a couple agonal breaths. The younger of the two knelt beside me, checked for a pulse, and exclaimed, "Let's get him down to the bus!" He dropped their canvas stretcher along the man's left side and motioned me to grab his upper body, positioning himself by the legs. The second medic looked around and down at us. "Did he arrest?" he asked, meaning cardiac arrest, a heart attack.

"Shooting," I said, gesturing at the bullet casings.

"Not an arrest?" He looked closely, noting the blood pooling in his chest. "GSW, to the chest? Is he breathing at all? Do you have a pulse?"

"Negative," I said.

His partner started saying it was a load-and-go. They could work him in the ambulance.

The senior medic squared up, surveyed the room, then shook his head. "He's done. Just leave him. This is a crime scene." To his partner: "Jesus. Stop touching everything! Leave it!"

The young partner was still hoisting the guy's legs like he was moving a wheelbarrow, sidestepping to the canvas litter. He looked perplexed. I understood. With penetrating trauma, dead *really* is dead—especially from a close-range cluster to the chest. The agonal respirations implied some form of residual activity within the potted body, but nothing workable or savable. I glanced from medic to medic. Yep. Dead.

We laid his legs and torso back on the floor and stepped away. This was the police's scene. I helped the medics get their bags and the canvas together and we left. My crew was wending their way through the police officers. They'd had to move the rig twice for more squads and to let the ambulance squeeze in. I shook my head and nodded toward the rig. "Let's go."

"Nothing call? Whiner? Not even hurt?"

"Definitely hurt. Definitely dead." We walked past more cops, most of them milling about inside the perimeter being established by several officers with scene tape. I spied the two from the earlier call and approached them. "Sorry I left you with that DOA. Shitty call. She was devastated. Rolled over and her old man was dead."

The officer shrugged. "She calmed down. It wasn't too bad. Sad deal, but she started to think clearly again."

It sounds cruel, but sometimes we can only judge these things by how much they affect us. We're just bystanders at a shallow grave. I said goodbye and we got back on the rig.

Our driver asked, "So, the guy up there, DOA?"

"Yep."

"What's up with all the cops, then? Homicide?"

"Police shot him."

"Thus all the squads. Shot badly? A dirty call, you think?"

"Who knows what happened," I said. "There were shells at the top of the stairs, none in the room." I relayed how the younger medic mistook the agonal gasps for actual breathing. "He was arguably *less dead* than that guy we had earlier—but, *dead*. It's metaphysical, I guess. Blood flow, brain activity, 'energy.' The first guy's heart stopped; his system crashed: he was dead as fuck. The other had his system terminated prematurely. Otherwise, he'd be living still. He charged them, they shot him. Took a bunch point-blank in the chest.'"

"Yikes."

"Yep. Hell of a way to go."

//

We found out the next morning that the man had been threatening his lady, and a neighbor called 911. The woman and kids and whoever else was in the apartment locked themselves in the bathroom. They called for help too. The police arrived and he met them at the door with a knife in hand. They fired. He had several felony arrests for assault, abuse, battery. It's hard not to say *Fuck him*. I feel boundless sorrow and sympathy for our first DOA, and his wife and her son and the unborn child. I have less remorse for an abusive jerk who was threatening people with a knife.

I genuinely feel for the family members of the abusive man, though. Because they are victimized by the abuser, then by the violence of his passing, the stigma, and the complicated tension between police and community. It can feel like, or be seen as, betrayal. Three years later, Sean (the driver) and I were interviewed for the investigation of the police-shooting call. A lawyer found the deceased's family—one always does—and the family got the woman and her kin to alter their statements, so it was now a wrongful-death case.

The police were accused of murdering the man. The new version was that the family had been hanging out, laughing and chilling, and the police showed up and shot the man, then planted a knife near him. An opportunistic lawyer capitalizing on tragedy, playing the odds the city will pay rather than face bad publicity.

Fortunately, the original 911 call was from the downstairs neighbor, who objected to the cussing and screaming, the threats of "I'm gonna kill you, bitch!" from the man who was shot. The neighbor called the police to protect the screaming women and children. And all the inhabitants of the apartment who made the subsequent 911 calls, screaming that the guy was threatening them with a knife. The case went nowhere, but it's a bummer of a footnote on a bummer of a call. It's a shame the man is dead. It's more of a shame he bullied his supposed loved ones, that he challenged the police, that in his death the splintered survivors felt no better options than to stand with a scumbag lawyer and seek money from the city on baseless grounds.

These are complicated calls, fraught for everyone.

If the first dead guy had been in the second apartment, we would have had space to work him. We would have worked him hard—and the outcome would have been the same. And if the second man had been even slightly less dead, we would have worked like hell to keep *him* alive too. As Faulkner wrote, "Any live man is better than any dead man but no live or dead man is very much better than any other live or dead man." It doesn't matter how you got shot, or if you are a bully—we will work to keep you alive. Unless you're already beyond return. For those, there's nothing we can do: not hope, not prayer, not CPR, not anything. Dead is dead.

14
THINNEST OF MARGINS

*To be an American writer today means mounting an unend-
ing attack on all that Americans believe themselves to hold
sacred. It means fighting an astute and agile guerrilla warfare
with that American complacency which so inadequately
masks the American panic.*

—James Baldwin

I HAVE BEEN ON SEVERAL OFFICER-INVOLVED FATALITIES OVER MY CAREER.
While reflecting on them, I was struck by the white-boy realization
that our lives hang in the balance by the thinnest of threads. Not "our"
lives. *Black* lives. Largely, but not exclusively, Black men's lives. Police
disproportionately kill Black men. The deadly, immoral consequence of
aggressive policing: hundreds of unarmed and not actively threatening
people of color are killed by police officers, and their killings are dismissed as *The officer feared for his life and thus deadly force was justified.*
It is erroneous to say cops are racist. It would be accurate to say *Black
skin (race) is frequently the determinant in fatal police interactions and
the inequality of legal and extralegal interactions.*

Look at the actual testimonies, legal wranglings, official reports in
the myriad unprosecuted, unarmed-civilians-killed-by-police-officer
cases. That wording, over and again: "The officer feared for his life,
and shot [three, twelve, forty-one times] to stop an *imminent threat* to
his life." An unarmed man, whether sitting in his car with his hands

---

This essay was written in late 2017. I have largely left it in its context from that
time—the tragic prescience capturing the brutal, enduring nature of the systemic
problems.

in sight or running away from the armed officer, is deemed threatening enough for summary execution. We must not question the officer's perspective.

When EMS crews arrive at most officer-involved fatalities, the scenes are chaotic with layers of police investigation, with procedural actions happening on multiple levels. Sometimes we work the bodies, trying unsuccessfully to pull them back to the living. Other times, the corpse is evidence already. There have been distraught family members present on at least two incidents I attended, and their anguished objections added to the chaos. There are almost always bystanders: traumatized witnesses whose pain or shock merits little to no consideration in the official process. The initial officers involved have been taken from the scene to be interviewed (to get their stories straight, frankly), and all the subsequently arriving officers are speculating or passing hearsay among themselves. The recurrent lines are the same: *There was a struggle; the officers were defending themselves; the person* [dead or dying on the ground in front of us] *resisted or threatened the officers; the victim was on drugs.* Every time: *He was on something. He was fighting. He reached for the officer's gun.*

At no point does anyone with power suggest this scenario defies logic, or that its logic reveals profound, problematic racial bias.

The police are called to help someone who's reporting, say, a domestic assault. The officers respond quickly, adrenalized, ready to protect and save—but also amped up to face unknown threats and hazards. These aren't random encounters. A call has been made to 911 by a frantic, scared, agitated woman (or child) who states a man is threatening violence and causing trouble. The dispatcher tries to calm the woman, taking whatever details she can give while listening to the chaos in the background and the terror in the caller's voice. (My respect and awe for dispatchers is boundless. They absorb so much terror, pain, and trauma over the phone. Bless them.) The dispatcher is typing while on the phone, sending the call to the nearest squad. The mobile computer will give the nature and assignment, "Assault in Progress" (Asslt Prgrs), with an address. On their squad computer, additional details might appear, updating as Dispatch gains further info. The responding officers may get a clear idea of who they're looking for, or how many people are in the apartment, or what the nature and severity of the situation is. Or they may not. Or the caller is too agitated to give clear information in those brief, frantic seconds.

The police arrive with the intention of preventing further wrongdoing from being perpetrated. In their mindset, order must be restored and upheld. It may well be dangerous and chaotic, always potentially threatening to them. *Potentially.*

Here is where my epiphany took flight: In a very short span—in seconds—the police must determine who is or *might be* a threat. Anyone who does not instantly comply is resisting. Anyone resisting is a threat. An officer fearing a threat to his life is justified using deadly force. The officers open the door and are confronted by an agitated man holding a knife. He is within ten feet of them. In swift succession: they order him to drop the knife, he doesn't drop it instantly. They open fire. He collapses. He dies.

By law, they have done nothing wrong. A man has been killed. The weight of that on the officers—to say nothing of the damage to his family—is not erased by legal wrangling.

Here, though: How quickly did they presume the man posed a threat and open fire? Did they even finish giving their orders? If it had been me on the other side of the door holding the knife, would my whiteness have bought me an extra second? In the moment the officers recognize a white face above the knife, then pause to assess what actual threat I pose, the bullets remain in their guns. I remain alive. My whiteness literally buys me the split-second reprieve of their fingers not pulling the trigger. That single moment's hesitation grows, expands, stretches, and in it, I stay alive. They could order me, again, to drop the knife. They could keep me at bay while talking me down. As long as they do not shoot me, my opportunities to survive the encounter remain.

If they shoot as soon as they see someone who resembles the threat in their minds, there will be no time for humanity, no space to look, think, evaluate. To say, "Well, their lives depend on it" (as myriad defenders of police killings *do* insist) is to say they are given freedom to shoot anyone who troubles their fraught minds. Is that racism? Racialized conditioning? Racial myopia? *Yes.* If they can manage not to shoot me and all the (armed) white men they encounter, the streets remain tellingly littered with Black and brown bodies *only.* Further, this disproportion of corpses reinforces the spurious claim that the killings are due to nonwhite men's inherent criminality, rather than officers' inherent and trained biases.

Not only do I believe this from my own experiences witnessing police officers escalate in the name of "controlling the scene," but dozens of videos show officers executing unarmed or nonthreatening men of color, while dozens more videos show officers chatting, stalling, even retreating from white men who are waving guns and knives at them, even *threatening to kill them.* The recordings of officers appealing to gun-wielding white men's "common sense" or "decency" (essentially a shared humanity) stand in stark contrast to the immediate aggressive engagement officers deploy for Black men and boys. The ability to not shoot a white guy brandishing a gun on the street, shouting "I'm going to kill all you cops," stands in brutal contrast to shooting twelve-year-old Tamir Rice within seconds, before the squad car had even stopped. The gun- or knife-wielding white guy gets patience and protracted negotiation. Meanwhile, a Black man shopping is gunned down on sight for carrying the pellet gun he'd come to the store to buy. The white man is given endless opportunities to stand down, surrender, or relax, and the very concept of a Black threat necessitates immediate lethal force. And the refrain afterward, on repeat: *I was afraid for my life. I felt threatened.*

But we cannot as a nation (as a white supremacist culture) acknowledge that these facts only point to blind bias, hysterical overreaction, or cold malice. We *will* not. We must create tortured illogic to explain away these dead Black bodies, the damning videos that contradict the officers' statements.

The legal protection for the officers is that they are entitled to use deadly force when they "reasonably feel their lives are threatened." A "reasonable threat" burns the throat, and soul. A twelve-year-old boy holding a toy gun is a reasonable threat? A man trying to show you his paperwork is a reasonable threat? As is a man running away on a misdemeanor stop? *That* is the cloak and ax of white supremacy: that we accept these completely unconscionable killings because, to us (the white general public), the Black person is so profoundly threatening that any situation could be deadly (to our diseased, trembling minds).

That is a shame.

To acknowledge that there is a filter of racial perception might begin the process of addressing it. Too many lives are lost and ruined, over and over again, for something so noxious—and preventable. In the aftermath of shootings, it is too late to recognize the roots of their fear. In that "split second of terror," the officers have legal standing to fire away. And this is the grave hundreds of unarmed, nonaggressive Black men have been buried in, along with any substantive investigation into the actions of police. *I feared for my life. I felt an imminent threat.*

What about when it is not a hair-trigger impulse but minutes and minutes of kneeling on a powerless, restrained man? How can those gold-standard defenses succeed?

Police defenders are quick to state, "You weren't there. You have no idea what it was like, what dangers they had to deal with." Again and again, the cornerstone to their defense—why cities don't charge the officers, grand juries exonerate them—is both the unique dangers faced by and the skilled perception of these guardians. We cannot criticize because we weren't there, we don't know what the officers faced. They are trained. They wouldn't take such drastic, fatal actions without good reason. Right?

What about when one *is* right there? When one *does* watch it unfold? There are abundant videos now that show how these incidents go south. Yet the system is caught on the old script, saying the same lines, despite the fact that we can see how threadbare and false they are. Despite the fact that we can see ourselves how wrong the officers have been.

Jamar Clark, RIP

I came to this understanding during the weeks of unrest and tumult stemming from the police killing of Jamar Clark in 2015. From the first reports I heard, it seemed a problematic situation. Unlike many of my (civilian) friends, who heard that another Black man had been "executed" by the police, that a young man—unarmed and peaceful—was murdered by racist cops, I learned of the case the following morning through one of the paramedics who was on the call. His angry, defensive, frustrated social media post, along with a link to the radio traffic from the call, dropped a rock of anxiety in my gut.

It was clear that this had been one of those calls no one ever wants to catch. As one who wears my heart on my sleeve, my empathy for the medics who caught this shit call in 2015 was genuine, not a "better you than me" relief. I was not tithing against some future bad call we might catch. We get what we get.

The information I found was that the medics responded to a young woman who said her boyfriend had hurt her. Further comments indicated there had been a call to this address earlier in the evening for a fight during a birthday party. Now the woman was reporting a minor injury to her ankle. While the medics were assessing and treating her inside the ambulance, a young man appeared outside the ambulance, and the patient identified him to the medics as her boyfriend. The medics requested a squad to respond to investigate the assault report, stating that the woman had identified the man as her assailant. The next transmission was more agitated, saying they needed squads immediately. An emergency call went out for squads to help medics with someone who was interfering with their treating a patient. The comments also indicated the man was the reported assailant in a domestic abuse case.

I wasn't there. I did not know how agitated the woman, or Clark, was. I didn't know what was said, whether threats were made, or if Clark physically interfered with the medics. I have been on calls where the volume of name-calling, threatening posturing, and emotionally charged screaming has seemed concerning. But words are not actions. Yet if we say, "Well, some folks just yell like that," and then someone gets shot while under our care, we have failed. If we expect Black people to "act like white people," angry people to act like rational people, poor people to act like middle-class people, altered-consciousness people to act sober, we are missing crucial distinctions: differences of race, class, culture, language. I know it is disconcerting to be amid a crowd of screaming, angry, verbally abusive people—and I also know that *uncomfortable* is not synonymous with *dangerous*.

For more than a year, my inference was that Clark was outside the ambulance, banging on the doors, yelling, harassing both the medics and the patient. Maybe making threats or taunts. Maybe getting others from the party to besiege the ambulance. Maybe trying to force his way inside the bus. That seems like a clear-cut need for assistance. I have been on similar calls that went south, where we retreat from a hostile space to the ambulance in order to treat our patient, and then find ourselves trapped by an aggressive or agitated crowd. When we (Fire or medics) call over the radio, "Firefighters/medics need assistance," that is an SOS call. Any police squads in the vicinity will come hard and fast to protect us. They come in forcefully, with a clear-the-deck intensity. There is seldom time or emotional clarity to distinguish between "Hey, I've got someone being a jerk and no free hands to deal with him," or "Help! This fool has a gun in my face!"

The ambulance dash videos that were released after the case don't provide any audio, but they obliterated all my inferences and suppositions.

I was wrong. Absolutely, completely wrong.

The videos broke my heart. Rolling toward their tragic, foreknown end, these silent, harshly black-and-white hunks of data nauseated me. I felt ill watching, waiting for the thing—not his killing as much as the triggering event. Whatever precipitated the police bum-rush and the fighting and *then* the fatal shooting. My anticipation and dread mounted with each slow minute of the tapes, where nothing happened. Nothing. Jamar Clark did nothing while standing outside the ambulance.

Nothing.

Clark is not aggressive, not actively interfering. He remains outside the ambulance while the medics are within, treating the woman. He does not enter the ambulance, yell (or even speak), or agitate the scene. What is said inside is not captured. Whether his presence serves to intimidate or upset the young woman is not clear either. A paramedic supervisor arrives, and the video shows him talking peacefully with Clark a few steps away from the ambulance. Again, no violence or threat is seen. He is not aggressive or agitated, not gesturing or making fast movements. The supervisor and Clark stand and talk, idly. The squad arrives. The EMS supervisor steps away. My sense is that the supervisor was there for the Help call, then, seeing it wasn't actively violent, stalled until MPD could arrive to investigate the domestic assault issue. The officers approach Clark, words are exchanged, and within seconds one officer attempts to take Clark down. They struggle. They fall out of the camera's view.

The struggle is brief. It ends with the young man's being fatally shot.

Why the need to aggressively take him down? Once the physical struggle begins, it is going nowhere good. Any flailing hand is depicted as "going for the officer's gun." Was Jamar Clark attacking or threatening the officers? Was he threatening the paramedics? Was he actively violent? No, no, and no. A brief exchange of words, one officer jumps on him, and down they go.

For a full year, I argued in defense of the medics and police, saying that I had been on volatile scenes, I had been on calls where the crowd became aggressive. Domestic abuse calls are terrifyingly unstable. I presumed this call was like the other calls. I bought the line that Jamar Clark was violent and aggressive. I was wrong.

The video obliterated that deceit. For twelve to fifteen minutes, the young man had stood calmly outside the ambulance. The police arrive and within two minutes, he is shot in the head. Those who said it was a bad killing, an unnecessary killing, an injustice: they were correct. Yet a grand jury did not see fit to charge the officers. Clark's presumed guilt, his apparent spontaneous impulse to take on two police officers, wrest their guns from them, and go on a killing spree was more plausible than the images of the police escalating a struggle with the young man, feeling threatened they were losing the wrestling match, and shooting him.

Would I have received the same treatment? Would they have put hands on me so fast? Would they have pulled the trigger of a gun (not a Taser) to stop the threat I embodied? Or would we have talked outside the ambulance, or back in the house, or by the squad car, discussing it like (white) men?

A great many white people persist with the immodest proposal that "he shouldn't have resisted. If he had done what they said, it would not have happened." Yet the video shows the officers aggressing on the man. This default response protects white people from accountability, from acknowledging the weight and history of police bias and violence, the very essence of which originated before the Civil War to patrol and control Black bodies. Black people are seldom afforded the right to object or throw a tantrum over systemic intrusion. White people have rioted over mask requirements in shopping malls. Our abounding comfort and privilege permit this arrogant delusion. Tim Wise puts it better in his essay "Denial Is a River Longer Than the Charles":

> If we are to dismantle systems of racial inequality, the way in which folks of color experience white-dominated institutions will have to be understood. This means respecting that incidents can be experienced as racist even if racist intent is lacking. . . . *Between the*

actor and acted upon, there is a vast territory known as history. And
within that territory lay the memories of a thousand terrors, fears,
and insecurities. (emphasis mine)

My first MPD-involved killing was in 2002, on a domestic disturbance response. The police ordered the man to sit down. He refused,
saying he wouldn't be bullied in front of his family, under his own roof.
The cops insisted that he sit, making that the issue: a power struggle to
establish dominance and control. They engaged the upset man physically. He struggled against their attempts to force him off his feet. They
claimed he was going for their guns, and they choked him out. They
snapped his windpipe and he died. They called us, and we worked him
in front of his traumatized family—who had called 911 for help because
he was agitated.

He was making no aggressive actions or threatening them. In his
mind, it was his house, and two white cops weren't going to boss him
around. Ego? Pride? Petty defiance? Certainly. But the context of an
upset working-class Black man confronted by two white police officers
carries with it America's racist legacy. To the police, he was a (potentially) violent Black man. His refusal to comply with their command to
kneel, essentially, conflicted their need for utter subjugation. His refusal
to show deference signified a threat to their construct. I feel the phrase
"reckless eyeballing" still carries weight, subconsciously, for many peace
officers.

This is the failure of American policing. We can see video after
video of officers escalating a verbal interaction immediately, without
provocation. Their attempts to physically restrain, dominate, control
African American men raise the stakes; too many cops will not—are unable to—back off or find another path. The line between standing one's
ground and fighting to breathe gets blurred. The encounters go south
fast and result in dire consequences within seconds.

"Control the scene" is the be-all and end-all, but the how and why
of it needs examining. Black people have been mistreated since the police were slave catchers. That is a very real history, living still in the literal and figurative embodiments of police treating Black people—men,
especially—as criminals, suspects, afterthoughts.

The MPD officers shot Clark within sixty-one seconds of arrival.

Compare that with the dozen-plus minutes officers circle and plead with the armed white guy in the street.

Sixty-one seconds.

The squad came in hard and fast, because a cry for help from other professional service members generates more alacrity than a regular call. They charge in as if our lives depend on it. Fortunately, most of the time, our lives are not in jeopardy. But adrenaline and uncertainty spike, and the cops come wired. It's a horrible dilemma: preparing for deadly conflict, then having to swiftly de-escalate while also engaging unknown, potentially abrasive or aggressive individuals. This was a reported perpetrator of domestic assault, so there was the belief that they were rushing to apprehend an actual criminal engaged in violence. When further reports indicated Clark was agitating the patient and interfering with their ability to treat her, it's understandable that the officers were amped up.

But that doesn't mean amped to kill. Once on scene, they experienced no threat, no belligerence, no violence.

Be very clear: this young man was killed after police put hands on him and wrestled him to the ground. They instigated a physical conflict rather than talk to him. It was an *investigation* of a minor assault. The need for dominance is the root of both policing and its failure to serve the public. Elected officials who have done far worse are allowed to remain in office. We have white mass murderers who are accorded more sympathetic treatment. What is there besides hysterical malice, profoundly internalized fear, and racial bias to explain how, again and again, police officers abuse and kill unarmed Black men? No one in power saw fit to charge the officers. There was no crime in this killing. The system churns on.

The official statements declared that Mr. Clark died while attacking the officers. He was shot because he was reaching for the officer's gun. White citizens maybe frowned, tsked, sighed, but largely accepted the official narrative. There was anguish and anger in the Black community afterward. There were protests, marches, public gatherings. Citizens encamped along the street where Clark died, two blocks from the MPD's Fourth Precinct, which was also targeted by protesters. The people took over the street, shutting it down.

Protests, a familiar part of these cyclical killings, were expected.

Black grief and fury, as well. The same public demonstrations occur over and again. But the inconvenience of Plymouth Avenue, a major artery, being blocked was too much for Whiteworld. The audacity of Black people taking over the public space, making demands, forcing their grief and anger into white lives: that soured many "moderate" whites toward the cause, the protest. *Well, he shouldn't have fought the officers. He should have done what he was told. I mean, it's sad, but this blocking the street—it's too much!*

Bad Cop/Worse Cop

August 2017. I'd finally convinced my crew to run stairs with me at Powderhorn Park, about a mile from our station. We were midway through, melting in the swampy humidity, when we got called to a drive-by shooting outside Cup Foods. The comments from Dispatch stated the victim had been crossing the street when someone opened fire from a moving car. We were close, and fell in behind a caravan of MPD squads balling down Thirty-eighth Street to the corner of Chicago Avenue. It was extremely unlikely that the shooter would drive around the block, slalom through the pack of squad cars, run into the store, and open fire again.

So we went in.

What follows is an examination of what occurred in the next few minutes. It happened fast. The scene was chaotic. It was a chilling glimpse of how scenes escalate until officers "need" to use deadly force. The blind, adrenalized actions of the officers revealed the level of tunnel vision—blindness, really—that causes extralegal killings. The cascading effect was also a stark example of the differences between police protocols and on-scene behaviors and the fire department's protocols and hierarchies.

//

We made our way past the first several officers toward the cashier's cubicle at the rear of the store. Several men were at the counter, one with a bottle of soda in his hand. Several officers surrounded this group. All of the police were white. All of the other men were Black. One officer was trying to talk to the man at the counter, who insisted he wanted to pay for his drink. The officer demanded the man stop what he was doing, and the man rebuffed him, repeating that he was buying a damn drink.

Right as we reached the group, two officers grabbed the man's arms, forced them behind his back, then cuffed him. This triggered immediate chaos. The man objected to being grabbed, squirmed against their wristlocks, their knees against his legs, their shoulders pressing him against the counter. He got mad and loud, crying out in pain. The man's friends started shouting at the cops that the man was shot and needed medical attention, and why were they cuffing him?

No one answered, so the man in cuffs and his friends got more agitated, which brought more of the cops into the small area. I tried to get the lead officer's attention, asking if this was our patient and, if so, could he let us examine him. The officers bulled past me, dragging the man who was now screaming that his leg hurt and why were they arresting him and he needed a doctor and let him go. I tried again, waving my gloved hand in front of the officers' faces: "Fire/ EMS. He's hurt. Just stop so we can examine him." They kept moving. I was invisible.

More officers poured into the store's narrow aisles. Everyone was shouting. The wounded man's friends were irate, screaming and trying to stop the cops from dragging him on a wounded leg. The other cops swarmed and blocked the victim's friends, grabbing and pushing them. They got angrier, more upset. I was stunned, regretting my thought that the scene was controlled. I stayed to the side of the lead officers as they struggled to force the injured man up the aisle.

I repeatedly asked the cops to stop dragging him, to at least sit him on a pallet of twelve packs by the door so we could evaluate him. I raised my voice and waved my hands again to get their attention. I stood in their path. Nothing: they looked through me and continued dragging the now-screaming man. The main officer had dilated pupils, a frozen, vacant gaze. He pushed me aside. The other men continued shouting, angry and upset, indignant, tangling with the thickening wall of uniformed police, who were shouting back. More officers rushed into the store, hands now on their guns. Each successive officer responded with more aggressive behavior toward the men who were victim and witnesses, not assailants.

I saw that the police had no plan, that they were piling in and blindly joining the melee. In slow-motion clarity within this surreal scene, I realized that *this is how it happens.* The man's friends were irate:

they'd been shot at; their pal had been shot; the cops were treating them like suspects or a problem to control. Their emotions were honest and appropriate. The police only saw Black and loud.

No one knows what is actually going on, I saw with terrifying clarity. The scene was reaching a tipping point. I turned to the first officers, who were still dragging the wounded man on one leg. "*Stop* dragging him!" I hissed. "At least sit him there so we can help him." No response.

They heaved our patient outside and, adding absurd insult to unnecessary secondary injury, one officer attempted (and twice failed) a "combative" leg sweep to get the patient to the ground. "Dude," I barked. "What the fuck? He's hurt. Stop that shit."

The third time, the officer managed to force the patient's uninjured leg to buckle, and he laid him out on the sidewalk. Our patient was apoplectic. Two officers leaned over him, shouting at him. *Stop resisting!* My crew was attempting to take the patient from the cops, but more of them kept rushing over and—shouting and looming and pushing against the wounded man, who was spraying invective, anguished indignation, and pained complaint. Finally, I got one officer's attention. "What are you doing? We need to treat him."

"We're making sure everything is safe."

"He's the damn victim!"

"He is?" He paused. "Him? You sure?"

"Yes. He is the fucking *victim.* He's been shot!"

"Well, we need to secure the scene."

"Can you uncuff him, please?"

"It's for everyone's safety."

"It's not helping. He is our fucking patient. He should *not* be cuffed."

The officer looked at the patient. "Will you be good if I uncuff you?"

I answered for him, since he was volcanic in his cussing. "He's fine. We're fine. This is just making everything worse."

The officer uncuffed the patient, hovering over us as if anticipating some sudden aggression from our man. I nodded and my crew set to assessing and treating him. Several officers came over, peppering him with questions. *Who shot you? Why were they shooting? Did you see what type of car they were driving? Are you in a gang? Do you have beefs with anyone? Can you describe the car or the shooter? Do you know who might want to shoot you?*

My patient responded the same way approximately ninety times. To every question or statement from the police, he said, "I'm Black." Over and over again.

One officer interjected, "C'mon, man. We're trying to help you."

We all looked at the cop: *Seriously?*

Our patient: "Ha! I'm Black."

Fair point.

One of my crew members is of mixed race, and he was able to connect with our patient. This is another good reason for diversity, even if skin color and gender don't guarantee like-mindedness; a splash of color in the sea of white male uniforms is helpful. We slowly were able to get the patient to calm his breathing, feel less attacked.

Another officer came over. He was higher ranked, judging by his stolid demeanor. "Sir, I'm told you were shot. Can you provide any information that would help us catch whoever did this to you? Do you have any beefs with anyone? Any reason someone would want to shoot you? Drug deals? Girl problems?"

Our patient stared at the officer for seconds, then almost chuckled. "I'm Black."

I tried not to laugh. It was a bit late for the second half of the bad-cop/good-cop routine. I explained to the officer that our patient had been mishandled and likely didn't feel much trust with the MPD. The officer stressed that safety was the primary concern on shooting scenes.

We had our patient calmer, allowing us to take his vitals, check his wounds. He didn't want his pants cut apart—either because he valued them or the symbolic sense of being stripped in the street. Fair enough. It was a small wound and we were sliding his pants down when the medics arrived (they had staged until police gave the Code 4, which was likely delayed as we were already there, and the batshit bedlam the police created on scene). One medic came rushing in, waving the trauma scissors like a dagger. He practically slid to a stop at the patient's side and grabbed a hunk of trouser to cut. "We're good," I said. He ignored me. "Hey, stop," I repeated. He kept going. I put my hand on his arm: "Yo, *stop!* We're good. It's a small caliber shot to the haunch. Just chill."

It was a young, newer medic. His eyes were big and in his flushed expression I saw *GSW protocols: Patch wounds! Start IVs! Intubate and bag him! Code 3 to STAB room!* He gaped and stared, sputtering. His adrenaline was high, he was so amped he could barely hear. That, too, was instructive: good intentions gone south due to adrenalized, half-panicked blind actions.

The senior medic and I have a good relationship, and he heard me, took in the scene. He gave direction to his partner, and we all worked smoothly to get the patient loaded and off to the STAB room. An officer accompanied us, as protocol. The patient gave him nothing. His anger subsided, as did his adrenalized bravado (*I got shot, but I'm gonna grab this damn Fanta!*). The wound *did* hurt. He *was* scared. The initial injury had been lost in the wholly unnecessary interaction with the police. Now, the pain and uncertainty surged through him. We reassured him and talked about normal shit.

Afterward, I felt tingly and agitated for several hours. I'd witnessed firsthand the type of scenario that leads to Black men being shot by white cops. Anyone saying "They should have done what the officers ordered" misses the point. There were *no* orders given, just shouted, incoherent demands.

I repeat: the officers escalated and agitated, without clarity of plan or action. Everything is a nail if all you are is a hammer.

Each successive officer arriving added to the chaos. They don't have set communication protocols on such scenes, not the way firefighters do, no flow of operations other than "gain control." The officers were trying to do just that, even if they were utterly failing at their stated and sworn goal. Not just failing: actively making everything worse, more chaotic, less safe.

I was upset. We were far too close to another police shooting— and why, over what? I wanted to report the incident. I wanted measures taken to prevent such poor and risky police work from occurring again. But whom could I tell? The police don't police themselves. They do not welcome outsiders telling them they are wrong. Politicians don't want to open a legal-liability investigation that will expose the city to lawsuits and take heat from the Police Federation. Everyone has to be *tough on crime.* I carried my frustration silently.

I'm very glad no one else got shot, because the officers would have genuinely had no idea how or why the scene went bad, only that it did and they "were forced to defend themselves for fear of their lives." And I would have been faced with the tension of testifying against the officers on a bad killing, calling them on their disregard for human lives. *And* I would have felt the eternal guilty weight of not doing more to intervene, of failing to protect that man. Except in 2017, America was not yet at the place where it could see Black men as victims deserving the state's protection, nor police as fallible, even flawed, actors.

Past is prologue . . . my lord.

> *Black Lives Matter, the movement founded by the activists Alicia Garza, Patrisse Cullors, and Opal Tometi, began with the premise that the incommensurable experience of systemic racism creates an unequal playing field. The American imagination has never been able to fully recover from its white-supremacist beginnings. Consequently, our laws and attitudes have been straining against the devaluation of the black body. . . . The American tendency to normalize situations by centralizing whiteness was consciously or unconsciously demonstrated again when certain whites . . . sought to alter the language of "Black Lives Matter" to "All Lives Matter." What on its surface was intended to be interpreted as a humanist move . . . didn't take into account a system inured to black corpses in our public spaces.*
>
> —Claudia Rankine, "The Condition of Black Life Is One of Mourning," in *The Fire This Time*

In 2015 or so, with the resurgence of social protest and activism, the citizens who formed Black Lives Matter to bring attention to the galling disproportion of Black people killed by police officers in nonviolent interactions were predictably reviled in the white world for their "radical" disruptions of the status quo. The essence of the movement's name: that Black citizens deserve better than summary extralegal killings—when their white counterparts avoid the horrifically varied forms of state-involved murders—and that, after these tragic, unnecessary deaths, no one is held responsible. Because, in our society, Black lives, Black pain, Black fear are not worthy of interrogating the system or its agents. What does it say about the United States that this statement of the obvious reveals the obverse: that we aggressively do *not* value Black lives?

Never letting facts interfere with America's racist blind spots, Fox "News'" pitched hysterical fear of a Black planet and spread snively disinformation. Black moderates were forced to renounce the movement not for its message, content, or intent but for the aspersions heaped on it by outsiders who could identify none of those things—insisting only "It's a racist hate group."

Because the police are the ones who shoot unarmed Black men and women (and get away with it: *qualified immunity* remains deeply problematic), they merit scrutiny for the unquestioned social and legal structures that allow these tragedies to happen so frequently. A justice system that has failed to *ever* convict officers of wrongful deaths is not a fair system. This is not a radical argument. This is the historical record. BLM wanted the acknowledgment that killing young Black men on sight is not legal or just. That these killings by panicked police were emblematic of either incompetent officers or a racist system (or both). That Black people deserved the half a second it took to not shoot on arrival.

The cops got defensive, and the response became about how dangerous their jobs are, and how they're "targeted" every day, and how not shooting immediately would mean they'd all be dead.

Except the reality is that officers are killing *unarmed* citizens, many of whom are shown on film doing nothing aggressive.

Except the number of attacks on and shootings of police officers has dropped steadily for forty years, to the lowest point in decades.

Except the overwhelming majority of police shooters are white men. So, the police are shooting unarmed Black folks out of fear for their lives when the reality is that they are literally shooting the wrong people—and, even more problematically, not shooting myriad white men waving guns at them.

Yet all these facts are irrelevant to the emotional ballyhoo.

A group that wants public attention to the endless stream of Black lives being terminated for no reason or misdemeanors (playing in the park? walking through a store? traffic stop? sitting in a car? walking down the street?) is not saying *police don't matter* or *kill whitey* or *kill cops* or any of the nonsense white society has attributed to it. But that's not how white America functions. The hysterical revulsion to Black peaceful social protest was loaded with overt racism, lazy misattribution, and wildly inaccurate claims. There was no discussion of the facts, only ad hominem attacks and spurious claims of "reverse racism."

Soon there were police "ally" stickers: Blue Lives Matter. Several of my coworkers have such stickers. Other coworkers wholly embrace this illogical mentality. There is no equivalence: no one has shot an officer and not been charged. Deaths of police officers are treated as tragedies and crimes, with investigations and solemn memorial ceremonies. No one is dismissing the shooting of police as *Well, that's part of the job. They knew that when they signed up.* Except when Trump instigated an insurrection and his mob attacked the U.S. Capitol, injuring multiple police officers. Then the All Blue Lives Matter crowd caught mighty laryngitis.

Look at the killings of Black and brown men by police, men killed while showing no aggression: white America might frown and say "What a shame," but there seems no palatable way to address the police and judicial morass that doesn't cause white discomfort. And the citizen juries keep deciding that, no matter the details, no matter how excessive the aggression, these Black men (and children) were *fundamentally* threatening, causing or embodying existential dread, so summary killing was justified.

This isn't new. Video showed four Los Angeles police officers beating Rodney King like a human piñata; the jury of *their* peers found their actions legally valid in 1992. Over and over, videos capture inhumane murders, and white society goes about its living, while Black people are traumatized and terrorized. It almost seems like that might be the point: know your place.

//

Right after the 2016 Super Bowl and Beyoncé's halftime "Formation" dustup, I started this essay by writing the following:

"Black Lives Matter": not racist.

Beyoncé: not racist.

Beyoncé's song/video "Formation": not racist.

Colin Kaepernick: not racist; *not* kneeling to insult living and dead soldiers. He's kneeling to peacefully point out that the anthem does not speak to all Americans. He's pilloried as "racist against white people," a traitor, a radical; someone who hates this country, the military, the dead soldiers. He is none of these.

"Blue Lives Matter": racially problematic, reactionary, and missing the point. A job, a uniform, is not a racial determinant. I am struck by how thin-skinned white culture is, that the response to the cries of Black citizens against extralegal killings is hysterical, racist reactionary fits. To petition to be seen as human is perceived by the majority as a threat. That says all we need to hear about America's fatal flaw.

In December 2017, Beyoncé Knowles-Carter spoke at the *Sports Illustrated* award ceremony at which Colin Kaepernick was honored for his activism with the Muhammad Ali Legacy Award. In her remarks, Beyoncé commented, "It's been said that racism is so American that when we protest racism, some assume we're protesting America. So let's be very clear, his message is solely focused on social injustice for historically disenfranchised people. Let's not get that mistaken."

That should be a basic, self-evident statement. And yet . . .

I'm reflecting on this line from Baldwin's *The Price of the Ticket*: "One was expected to be 'patriotic' and pledge allegiance to a flag which had pledged no allegiance to you: it risked becoming your shroud if you didn't know how to keep your distance and stay in your 'place.'"

What seemed an obscure Jeremy argument in 2016 seems far more resonant now: Kaep remains blackballed by the NFL, which has used Jay-Z as cover for its endless racial imbalance and money-threatening images issues. The hysterically overwrought objections to Beyoncé, Kaepernick, "Formation," and Black Lives Matter were rendered trite in the summer of 2020, but the towering hypocrisy of the racist animus remains vivid.

//

If I had been the knife-wielding domestic abuser in chapter 13, "Arbiters of Existence," my whiteness would have bought me a second, a minute, enough time for the cops to de-escalate the situation and disarm me. Had I been Black like him, I, too, would have been plugged on sight. If I had been outside that ambulance instead of Jamar Clark, they would not have put hands on me, nor attempted to subdue me, nor felt threatened enough to summarily fire their gun. My whiteness would shape the officers' conditioned response—a nonlethal response. I would benefit from the privileged shield of white impunity. They would pause enough to study the situation. Pause enough to make the reasonable decision not to shoot me. Pause long enough for me to remain alive.

Because what is on the other side of these dead Black men? Jamar

Clark, just standing there. Christopher Burns, arguing about pride. DelShawn Crawford, a jerk holding a knife—*not* attacking. Philando Castile, sitting in his car, trying to give the officer the paperwork he had demanded from Castile. On and on and on. If we remove the police's fatal aggression, what, actually, is happening? Black men being human. Fact.

I have knelt in the blood of Black men, blood spilled by white police, and seen that none of it was necessary. There were no threats that the police themselves did not instigate.

Some of my coworkers struggle with similar biases and blind spots. It poisons their perceptions of citizens, obscures the humans before them, denies them the ability to examine our biases and privileges and unintended consequences. Then we're stuck with *a Black guy took my buddy's job . . . I was afraid for my life . . . He fit the description.*

For George Floyd, Jamar Clark, Philando Castile, David Smith, Christopher Burns, and all those before them—and, sadly, all who have followed and will follow them into premature, unjust graves.

Rest in Power. May something righteous finally arise from the fires this time.

15

THE ASSASSINATION OF GEORGE FLOYD BY THE COWARD DEREK CHAUVIN

Forgive them, Lord, they know not what they do.
Curse, judge them, Lord, they care not what they've done.

—Me, channeling Dylan Thomas, riffing on Jesus

TRUE HORROR STORY: IF DEREK CHAUVIN HAD "MERELY" SHOT GEORGE Floyd, none of this would have happened. None of the subsequent up-heaval, not the fumbling gestures at racial justice, no flailing attempts at change and inclusion. The four police officers involved likely would still be employed. Had Chauvin shot Mr. Floyd, it would have been over too fast for witnesses to record it. The usual process would have played out, providing the officers legal cover. The judicial system affords the police extreme discretion and defers to their "expert" perspective. *Afraid for my life* has been the standard defense in multiple extralegal killings by police. Even in this case, despite the officers' own footage of a crowd calling out for them to help the man in distress beneath their knees, their defense continued to throw that canard at the jury. For hundreds of dead citizens, the actions of the police have been sanctioned as lawful and correct within the system. No matter what the officers do, the cover-all remains: "It was a split-second decision in a chaotic and dangerous

---

I recognize this chapter might be what drew the reader to the book, but I suggest reading chapter 12, "Ketamine or Kill a Man," and chapter 14, "Thinnest of Margins," first, for a larger, more thorough context.

situation, where the officer had to make profound choices while under duress and fear for his life."

Over and over: *The officer was afraid for his life. So he shot the unarmed man in the back. So he shot the man running away from him. So he shot the handcuffed man. So he shot the child. There was a threat, in his expert opinion. So he shot what scared him.*

Had Chauvin, or one of the two rookie officers, pulled his gun during the scuffle and fired, claiming afterward that Mr. Floyd was "reaching for my gun," there might have been protests, but the incident would have transpired so quickly, the standard rhetoric would have sufficed: *a split-second decision in a heated struggle.* The world would not have seen the murder play out minute by agonizing, immoral minute. The police department's version would have followed the usual narrative: the officers' bodycams would show a brief, hectic struggle punctuated with fatal gunshots—had they even released the footage. And that would be it. The notion that Mr. Floyd was senselessly murdered by the police would not have gained traction in mainstream (meaning white) America.

Black people would know, of course.

In the immediate days after Mr. Floyd was killed, then up to and through the trial, Chauvin's defenders and defense deployed those standard tropes. However, with bodyweight rather than bullet, and slow death rather than immediate, and the videos seen widely, the "split second" decision protected by their underqualified immunity fell apart. Impunity fits better than immunity. Mind you, it only fell apart *after* the city erupted in flames and mayhem. We (the white *we*) felt impelled to action only when our comfort was threatened, when our social ramparts were breached. *Then* we woke up. Briefly.

No matter how egregious the footage in previous cases, that same set of phrases has exonerated umpteen police officers—*if* the cases even made it past the investigation stage. White America is conditioned to accept that script and shrug. *He shouldn't have resisted.*

Let us be clear: The police killed a man, slowly, in front of a crowd of witnesses who did all they could to stop the officers from doing what they were doing—while never physically interfering with them.

The crowd was small, very contained. They beseeched the officers to get off Mr. Floyd, to listen to his cries, to *look* at him beneath their knees. Neither Officer Chauvin, the senior man, nor Officer Thao, another veteran officer who was nominally maintaining crowd "control," checked what the bystanders were yelling about. They did not allow any facts to inform their behavior. The fatal process continued without purpose or reason. The officers' defense suggested that the noise of the crowd caused the officers to lose focus. Blaming the people, who became vocal only *after* the officers were ignoring Mr. Floyd's distress and cries for help, is pretty damn DARVO (deny, attack, reverse victim and offender) of them.

During Chauvin's state trial, the defense tried to get Firefighter Genevieve Hansen to say that having a loud crowd at a fire scene would impede her ability to do her job. She fell into his trap, insisting that she would ignore all and any distraction, that she would tune out the crowd to do her job. It was a trap either way: blame the crowd for distracting the officers, or back up the officers who ignored the crowd in executing their suspect.

The defense did not ask me this question, unfortunately. Because after twenty-plus years, with fifteen as a supervisor, I could have clarified several points for the defense (well, for the jury).

One: We multitask. It is our job to handle multiple things at once. As captain, I am constantly sifting through information to find what matters in the moment. I walked through the small crowd of people shouting about "the police killing that man" and entered Cup Foods. I was looking for a patient; I *heard* what they were shouting; I did not *see* a victim. The police officers I encountered on scene said *nothing* about an unresponsive man. Only once I entered the ambulance, when I saw the gravity of Mr. Floyd's condition, did I have a context for the crowd's cries.

Two: People yelling is not in and of itself either distracting or threatening to me. I have been on many chaotic scenes; I have worked in agitated crowds; I have been yelled at.

Three: If I am "spraying water on a house" as the defense suggested to Firefighter Hansen, and a group of people start yelling at me, I can listen to them *and* spray water. But, if people are shouting that I am spraying the wrong house, that the fire is *next* door, and I do not consider or check their claims, I am doing my job poorly—and failing to serve the public. *That* analogy works better here.

Four: What evidence did the police have that trumped what the bystanders were saying? Did they know better than the witnesses that Mr. Floyd was not in peril? How? They did not even check his condition.

That tragic handful of young people became justifiably agitated. It was a grotesque, slow-motion nightmare. The bystanders were traumatized by what they witnessed. They watched the police murder a man slowly. They were further traumatized afterward by the insidious notion that they allowed it to happen. And then they were blamed by the defense and cop defenders for *causing* the police to become so distracted they clean forgot about the man dying beneath them.

The police officers did not have any clear plan, no stated goal. It really is as simple as this: the officers ignored Mr. Floyd's cries and pleas; they held him down in a dangerous fashion, waiting for an ambulance to arrive. The junior officers followed Chauvin's lead. They did not respond to Mr. Floyd's cries of distress. They did not follow their own protocols about positioning a person to avoid the fatal dynamic of prone restraint and positional asphyxia. They did not indicate to Dispatch why they requested EMS. They did not address his deteriorating condition (which was *caused* by their actions).

It is obscenely, maddeningly simple. They knelt on a man until he died.

Past Is Prologue

If the crowd had succeeded in getting the officers to listen to them and to stop killing Mr. Floyd, there would also be no investigation of the police officers' actions, no discussion of all the things they did prior to Mr. Floyd's death. Nor would a global focus on racial in/justice and policing have been ignited. Had I been walking by off duty and jumped in, the result would have been the same: Mr. Floyd would likely be alive. I would have been arrested and faced departmental discipline for "interfering with police business" and "assaulting an officer."

But nothing whatsoever would have been done about the police doing what the police do. Stop: I cannot even write this. They killed the man, the city burned, and *what*? To this day, there is no apparent review or investigation of the police actions that led to Mr. Floyd's killing, no apparent training to distinguish between someone "resisting" and someone panicking. No review of the excessive force they deployed rather than patience. Nothing has changed.

Had Ms. Frazier's video not gone public, the official line on the killing of Mr. Floyd would still be that "a man experienced a medical emergency while being detained. Police called for EMS. The man died at an area hospital."

I stress this: there would have been no investigation, no arrests, no trial. Another dead Black man. This is the standard procedure. Without the video and the ensuing uproar, the usual plot points would have been struck: neutered and victim-blaming statement by the police, solemn *This was a tragic, unavoidable situation* by the mayor, little pressure on the police to investigate themselves, no outside pressure. Everyone played their role: *Back the badge; Blue Lives Matter; You don't know what they were facing,* all that rot.

As I revised this chapter in February 2022, while waiting to testify in the federal trial of these officers, the MPD killed another Black man, Amir Locke, while serving a warrant for St. Paul Police, one that was not requested to be a no-knock operation but which MPD insisted on. The first, second, and third official statements by the police chief and mayor were riddled with misleading, dissembling inaccuracies.

//

How often have we been assured that *the video doesn't tell the whole story*? That *you cannot know what was actually happening* when seeing footage of police killing civilians? And how often does the footage make it clear to reasonable people that it *was* an avoidable killing? That the police escalated and increased the violence at a scene? The apologists and relativists tried that with Mr. Floyd's killing: *The police bodycam videos will show you what that kid's phone missed.*

Without Ms. Frazier's video, Genevieve Hansen, the off-duty firefighter, would have been harassed by the police for being intrusive, whiny, not-knowing-to-keep-her-mouth-shut, a troublemaker. Many firefighters would have taken the same approach toward her, out of a reflexive or deliberate fidelity to the police. I know this because, in the first few days, that *was* their attitude, toward Firefighter Hansen, and toward me, for speaking out. Except, we did know. We were there. *We saw.*

No one in power initially felt any reason to call this a crime. Not the police chief, not the city leaders. Not until the streets filled. Not until the furies erupted, smoke burning eyes and throats. Only after the standard ploys failed and the crowds got loud, angry, and destructive, did the city take action. Should people have politely stayed home and waited for justice? Yeah, right.

Their own body cameras, the multiple security cameras, the city's street footage, and FFR Hansen's phone video all confirmed what Ms. Frazier's video captured: the unthinkable, slow killing of a man crying for help. There was no mystery here, only our societal inability to *believe* these things happen, and to call them what they are—despite their occurring again and again. Without the uproar and tumult that arose in response to Ms. Frazier's documentation of the killing, the other hardcopy videos would have remained unexamined—or hidden from the public. The witnesses on the street, hell, even the paramedics—and me: no one in authority, with the power to do anything, would have asked for our testimony. (This was the dilemma I alluded to in chapter 14, "Thinnest of Margins": who exactly could I go to with my complaint about police malfeasance? All I would do is put a target on my back.)

//

I ask you, what should the next crowd do, witnessing the next imminent police killing of a Black man? Trust that the officers learned a lesson from Mr. Floyd's death? That they know what they're doing? Wait for them to de-escalate? Write a letter to the editor? If everyone goes to jail but the next George Floyd lives to see another day, isn't that a fair exchange? What would you have the citizens do?

Even now, the MPD has made negligible—if any—changes to their policies, protocols, and culture. This last is the most dangerous and damning. There was a similar situation (see the section "Policing and Systemic Violence" in this book's reading list) in early May 2020 when a Chauvin-led crew of officers, including both Thomas Lane and J. Alexander Kueng, responded to a domestic disturbance call and assaulted a man. He wasn't involved in a crime, wasn't suspicious, wasn't connected to the 911 call. He walked out of the building and the officers "detained" and "subdued" him. He was simply a resident of the building. And he was understandably upset at being manhandled by officers with neither warning nor explanation. He objected, his family and bystanders objected: the police responded by escalating their "control measures." The man responded to pain and confusion and anger—fight *and* flight. They used more painful tactics to subdue and control someone "resisting." The police then detained the man and arrested his brother, for "interfering with the legal process."

Resisting what? What is a lawful order in this context? The man was literally guilty of being Black—*he fit the description.* Is there any more brutally telling example of the ubiquity of racist blindness in America?

Hours later, both men were released and the charges dropped. The kicker was, none of it merited any follow-up by the police: not that the officers simply grabbed the first Black man they saw, then failed to sufficiently investigate the issue they'd originally been summoned for ("The crowd was hostile and non-cooperative. We left" seems a shady, self-exonerating evaluation of the scene). The MPD also did not apologize or address the issue with the wronged citizens—not the individual officers and not the department. Most important, there was nothing in the official police log about this abysmal failure to correctly be peace officers.

Had the MPD taken that botched call seriously, there might have been corrective action or a glimmer of self-reflection by training officer Chauvin in the next few weeks. Someone in the police chain of command might have instructed all officers (or perhaps just those under Chauvin's watch) that bodily swarming random, nonaggressive citizens is not good policing. And that might have had ripple effects in how officers deal with the public, how they accost people, how they pay attention, on subsequent interactions. Including the "possible forgery" call for an "intoxicated individual" on May 25, 2020.

But maybe not. The issue—systemic and structural—is that they do *not* have to consider what they do.

The prior bad-policing incident I had at Cup Foods, which I write about in the preceding chapter, "Thinnest of Margins," falls into the same void: I witnessed an egregious miscarriage of police work, public safety, and community service, where people were nearly shot by multiple police officers blindly reacting to chaos that they themselves were solely creating and exacerbating. Nowhere was there a single line written by the police to investigate how that shitshow occurred—let alone what could be done to prevent future miscarriages.

In late 2021, I finally located the official police reports from that 2017 call. They are antiseptic in the underplaying of the details, specifically the role officers played in shaping the precarious uproar. Not one officer mentioned the mistreatment of the victim. The officers' narratives sound incredibly similar to what they wrote on the early May domestic call. All of their reports state: "Victim was uncooperative." "Witnesses were hostile toward police."

That was at best a partial truth—and I was there. I watched it play out. The officers' blind aggression twisted an investigation of a shooting into the abuse of a victim (which they did not report, because they do not police themselves). They nearly caused a melee with the victim and witnesses of a drive-by and it's not worth a moment's reflection? Not an iota of evaluation of their protocols or communication after assaulting and harassing the victims they are putatively there to help? Do I need to insert race here? Black male victim and companions; white police officers. I will believe race does not matter when I see Black men treated like white men—and vice versa.

This is where the system, the culture of the Police Department, is dangerous for everyone. Because the police suffer, too. Unintentionally killing the people you are supposed to help is profoundly damaging. Whether because of defensive hubris or merely jaded indifference, no officer on scene thought they did anything wrong, despite manhandling, insulting, humiliating, and aggravating the pain of a shooting victim. Can Black people *ever* be victims? Presumed criminality is what I witnessed that day. Three years later, rookie Officer Thomas Lane started an investigation of a bogus twenty-dollar bill by sticking his gun in Mr. Floyd's face.

//

It is strange, to say the least, to have landed in a worldwide incident. Even afterward—after the upheaval, protests, the riots and *burn-that-shit-down* furies—many of my coworkers remained oblivious to the connection between the call and our crew at 17s. We are a myopic lot. There are so many such frequent, shitty calls that people lose track. Too, though, it has been interesting to witness the aftershocks and cultural shifts across the country and globe, to have responded to Mr. Floyd—and to have continued to respond to regular calls afterward.

Civilians who learn of my connection ask about it as if the world had ripped apart from the moment it happened. As if there were riots already when Engine 17 arrived. Or that everyone recognized how horrendous the killing was—and took to the streets immediately.

I want you to keep in mind that none of us (the responders: the medics and my crew) knew what was happening as it happened. The scene was surreal, at the time and on reflection. The odd thing for me was how unlike this scene was from the previous police killings I'd been on. There wasn't a swarm of additional officers, no backup squads blocking the area, no scene tape up, none of the hectic rapid movements of *securing*—everything: evidence, the perimeter, witnesses, suspects. Not the pressing arrival of each successive level of supervisor and brass. None of that.

Just the mystery of where our patient was.

The police were nonchalant; their actions seemed almost mundane. The two officers standing at one corner seemed confused about our arrival, definitely not concerned. The first officer (Tou Thao) can be heard on the body cameras saying, "Someone call for Fire?" And when I got off the rig, he asked, "What are *you* guys here for?"

I retorted, "They said they needed EMS Code 3 for something," as I moved past him, toward the store.

"Just EMS, though. Just needed to transport someone high," he said, without clarifying, giving no sense of gravity. Another officer was nearby. He did not display urgency either. Neither officer told us the ambulance had *already* left, with an unresponsive patient in critical condition. From watching the bodycam videos, it did not seem to register to them. The crowd was sparse, pacing the sidewalk, upset, on their phones and yelling at the officers: "Y'all are punks." "You killed that man." "Fuck the cops. Y'all are killers."

But I had nothing to go on: no patient, no information from police. I radioed Dispatch for an update. I still didn't know the medics had come and gone. Genevieve Hansen popped up as I was scanning the inside of Cup Foods. She was beside herself. *Is he all right? I couldn't see a pulse. I tried to help. The cops wouldn't let me. I think he's dead. I think they killed him!*

I had no idea what she was talking about, only that she was distraught. Nothing made sense. I was confused and failing to build an understanding from the scene. Again, I had no patient. I didn't know the ambulance had been called ten minutes before us. Farther into the store, I encountered an MPD officer (J. A. Kueng) speaking to the employees. He told me the ambulance had relocated because of the crowd but gave no indication of the patient's grave condition. Nothing at all. As he spoke to me, his radio and mine reported from our separate Dispatches that the medics needed us Code 3 at Thirty-sixth and Park Avenue.

We left the store, climbed on the rig, and drove to where the medics had pulled over. Only at that point, from our rig computer, did we glean it was a full arrest. But no other info was given.

Two minutes later, my junior partner and I entered the ambulance, and I gasped. *Holy fuck.*

Nothing had prepared me for an unresponsive man, intubated, with the LUCAS compression device already in use, the two medics working furiously to get the first IV line established, the stunned officer (Lane) trying to ventilate the patient. *This man is fucking dead,* I thought as I took over ventilation and attached the O_2 valve. I realized the crowd I had walked through had been yelling, *accurately,* about a man dying in police custody—or being killed. Their anguish and anger, Genevieve's disconsolate fury: it clicked.

I've been on contentious scenes before. Just because people say someone isn't breathing doesn't make it true. In this case, the "untrained" citizen bystanders had the truth, the accurate description—but I hadn't known that yet. Without a patient, or a victim, we had nothing to go on. The police did not offer us anything. Rewatching the bodycam footage, I am struck by how oblivious all of the officers were to Mr. Floyd's actual condition (dead). Even Officer Lane in the ambulance, who was new and likely unclear about the absence of magic in reviving the dead. None of them appeared to recognize that they had *killed* a man.

As we assisted the paramedics trying to revive Mr. Floyd, the implications of the call surged through me. I radioed back to our rig for my other two crew members, Firefighter Steve Mudek and FMO Tracy Terbell, to return to check on and protect FFR Hansen at the scene. She had been sputtering with anguish and anger, near hysterical, when we spoke inside Cup Foods. I'd had nothing to contextualize what she was saying—same with that small crowd of bystanders I walked through at the outset. They were unified in their distress, their clarity that the police had killed a man before their eyes. Until I saw Mr. Floyd, I had no idea. Even once I saw him, the entire time we worked him, I had no clue what had actually happened.

My concern for FFR Hansen was utterly unrelated to the crowd. Contrary to the police narrative, it was not a dangerous or threatening scene. I *was* worried that she would be harassed and bullied by the police. I wanted my crew to give her support, to shelter and protect her: if only by their presence, they might deter rogue police intimidation. The lockdown or clampdown or sweep: whatever to call it when police swarm a bad scene of their making. Her distress, now that I had some context, was striking. I wanted familiar faces to be there for her and to witness what might happen next.

Firefighter Hall and I left the STAB room stunned. She was so new and it was all unfamiliar; with Covid protocols, we had transported very few unresponsive patients together. But I was clear that we'd been on a bad police killing. The glaring contrast between previous death-by-police calls and the eerie nonchalance of the officers on scene when we arrived at Cup Foods has haunted me. They had knelt on Mr. Floyd's lifeless, unresponsive body until the medics lifted him into the ambulance, and none of the officers appeared to recognize anything was amiss. The crowd was anguished. The officers were oblivious. It was like no police scene I'd ever encountered.

The rig picked us up, and we had a quick debriefing. Tracy and Steve had learned nothing from the scene. They had spoken to Genevieve Hansen and encouraged her to come directly to the station, if only for support. None of us, and none of the medics, knew the truth yet. Not what really happened.

I informed the deputy of the death-in-custody as well as that FFR Hansen was an off-duty witness. I stated I was worried for Genevieve: the horror she'd witnessed and the potential threat from bullying officers. We returned to our station, and I wrote an official notification through our chain of command to inform the fire chief. I wrote my incident report, choosing my words as deliberately and accurately as I could. I wanted to put words to paper officially, to protect all the witnesses, to prevent another cruel whitewashing. People at work tease me for my verbosity and my vocabulary, but I wrote that report with fierce clarity: I wanted to capture contemporaneous details, accurately convey what I saw and heard—without editorializing—and ensure there was a counter-narrative to the likely police statements about an unruly and aggressive crowd. I did not expect to see my report linked on the *New York Times* site a few days later (I'm glad I used proper punctuation) and I stand by every word of it. I emailed the paramedics' supervisors to share my experience working with them, commending them for their hard, good efforts.

I'm trying to express to readers who think they know what happened that in those first hours none of us knew clearly what had happened nor what was about to explode. I anticipated the city's likely response, how the wheels would turn. I still did not know the actual details. I had heard the scattered cries and shouting of the bystanders and witnesses as we searched for our patient. I had seen the dead man, whom we had worked zealously but futilely. I had a nagging irritation at the dismissive disconnect between the police officers on scene, the bystanders' anguish, and Mr. Floyd, but I had no idea how egregious the killing had been. How could I?

Did I anticipate the upheaval that was brewing? Did it direct my actions in that first hour or so? No. I was genuinely trying to prevent the usual dishonest game. No one had seen any of the videos from the scene yet. I had no idea who George Floyd was, but I knew he deserved better than what he got, and if no one spoke out, his death would be another "accident."

Firefighter Hansen came to our station soon afterward and told us what she'd witnessed, how she had tried to intervene to help or get the officers to stop. She was so upset it was heartbreaking. She had several minutes of her own cell phone video. It shows her perspective on the curb and in the street, blocked and challenged by Officer Thao as she cries out for the officers to check Floyd's condition. The video captures several other witnesses calling for the police to release Mr. Floyd, to let him go, to get him help. George Floyd is partly visible; he is not moving, certainly not fighting. The footage did not show the beginning or the duration of the incident, but it was surreal all the same. The disconnect between the crowd's perspective, their cries and pleading, and the officers' silent, stolid, passive restraint. Even with all this, the actual details, the eight minutes and forty-six seconds of three men crushing down on a restrained, begging man: that was not inferable.

And then we saw Darnella Frazier's video.

Remember: everyone on the authorities' side started out in default mode: police press release, official statements, utter inaction and implicit condoning by police administration. I wish I had contacted the mayor directly, to caution him to caution the police chief that their standard (disinformation) press release would bite them in the ass. (It did. And they would not have taken me seriously.)

The machine functions the way it is intended—until a sizable disruption either tears the veil from our collective eyes or jams a monkey wrench in the gears. Ms. Frazier's cell phone video, uploaded and shared, was that monkey wrench.

//

I've said this wasn't my first death-by-police call, and it was less disturbing—initially—than the others had been. That first night it was just (another) "unfortunate occurrence," in the city's defensive parlance. Because a death by police is too, too customary in America. The script played out in its normal, formulaic manner: the police spokesman spun his li(n)es; there was public outcry in some quarters, silence in many others. People gathered to grieve, to protest a lost life, to voice their fears and furies.

I hope I have sufficiently conveyed how seldom anyone has challenged the police version, how few responders have tried or been able to contradict the official narrative. Darnella Frazier's video achieved that. So, the actions I took that first evening were gestures against futility. Genuine attempts to protect others, yes—but with no hope there would be actual consequences for the officers. I thought of Genevieve, and Derek and Seth, the paramedics, as well as that small group of people I saw on the street: they all deserved whatever I could do to keep them from getting thrown under the bus. I stuck out my neck because it was the right thing to do.

Ms. Frazier's uploaded video spread across the city, the country, the world. Blame the quarantine, or Trump's incessant racist animus, or just admit that too many innocent Black and brown citizens have been killed by the system. The gruesome spectacle of Mr. Floyd's killing provided the frisson to set it off. *Nevertheless, they combusted.*

Mainstream society (a.k.a. white folks) got scared to waking—

briefly, barely, slightly. Spasms of genuine concern but coming from profound depths of unawareness and unawakeness: It was destined to be too little, too late. As Gil Scott-Heron tells us, "The revolution will be no re-run, brothers. The revolution will be live."

Moreover, it was but a small portion of white Americans who took to heart this racial injustice. The yawning mob of whiteness remains aggressively indifferent, inured, oblivious to the implications of our slanted system. And, when challenged and the gates are rattled, many white Americans (starting with the president) responded with petulant, indignant fury. After the Los Angeles riots in 1992, I pondered: Turn that rage at its rightful cause, you'll scare them (us) into listening—*and* into a violent counterreaction, for power doesn't yield willingly.

It is a frail hope, given this country and our policing of nonwhite citizens, that we might prevent another event by better understanding the last event. There were multiple police killings of young Black men here *during* the trials. Hope seems a paltry delusion.

Look at the hysterical and explicit overreaction to the second wave of racial justice protests later in the summer of 2020, the militarized overkill in response. They (the system) were not going to cede the streets or the cities, the concept of "order" to a mob—stop: a Black mob. Not twice. Concurrently and subsequently, white mobs actively threatening violence and seeking to interfere with the legal process were given free passage into state houses, malls, streets, and public areas with their aggressive, armed show of anti-mask, anti-justice force: a precursor to the violence of January 6, 2021.

//

I keep challenging the false notion that when the paramedics arrived on scene, they knew what they had. The claims that, by the time Engine 17 rolled in, we knew what was going on. Everyone has seen the video now. Everyone "knows" what happened. We should have known. *Why didn't I go right to the ambulance? Why did I go into the store? Why were the medics just sitting there?* It was obvious. Right?

No. We knew nothing. We were given nothing. I cannot express how haunting that is.

I stepped into the ambulance and saw Mr. Floyd's unresponsive body beneath all the resuscitation equipment: that was my first connection to what the witnesses on the street had been saying, what Firefighter Hansen had told us and why she was so upset. The medics had a ten-minute head start on us, which itself is anomalous. We are dispatched together for any serious call. I didn't understand how they'd accomplished so much if we had been dispatched only a few minutes before.

"What the fuck happened?" I asked the medics, who shook their heads. We discussed it as we worked on Mr. Floyd. The only "information" from the police was "drugs" and "not really fighting much." Our deduced options were possible heart attack, fatal asthma attack, drug overdose, worked himself into a frenzy and choked? Nothing made sense. If we'd known the police restrained him facedown, arms manacled behind his back, with several officers pressing down and preventing his chest from expanding for air: that would have helped us.

Does that change—would it have altered—the medics' treatment plan?

Not really. Airway, breathing, circulation: the fundamentals remain. The clock, though: the police handed us a dead man, one whose heart and lungs had stopped several minutes before the ambulance arrived, with police maintaining their deadly weight upon him until the very last. He had been agitated and in a frenzy for ten minutes before hitting the ground, then his panic increased as his ability to breathe or catch a breath was crushed. Eight-plus minutes with their weight upon him, restricting his chest and lungs as he fought to breathe, as he suffocated. Then several more minutes after he stopped breathing: no actions to revive him, no oxygen, no compressions, no release of his crushed lungs.

Mr. Floyd was unsavable. He was dead.

Nothing about the officers on scene at Cup Foods, their dispositions, the info they gave—none of it provided us any clue. It was unimaginable, then, that Mr. Floyd had died how he did. How could the police slowly crush a man to death while he begs for help, while the witnesses beg them to let him breathe? In what world does that happen?

//

How many marches have we seen, for how many decades? Have any of them provoked actual change to society's default obtuseness? No. The claims (by white authorities and citizens) that the horror of Mr. Floyd's killing shocked them into consciousness and action is, frankly, bullshit.

There have been televised killings since Emmett Till's mother held an open casket funeral to show the world what white people had done to her son. This was not new; it was barely news (at first).

"March all you want, folks," the system says. "Antiwar? Anti-Bush? Antiabortion or anti-antiabortion? Pro-peace? Pro-women? Anti-homophobia? Pro-Black? Anti-Black murders? Sure. March away. Clever signs you got there, kids. Ha-ha, nice *pussy hat.* We see you out there. We'll put you on the news, after sports. We absorb and subsume you. See you next time."

That is how it's been. How it's gone. "What's past is prologue," for sure. But maybe it would be better to quote James Baldwin and Langston Hughes than Shakespeare when addressing this poisoned American mind. Because, as has been promised, foretold, warned, pleaded against: the fires next time *will* explode.

And that's what happened.

The city, the powers that be, the authority machine (white people power structure) made an error born of centuries of comfort and convenience predicated on Black endurance, graciousness, self-restraint: the presumption that, because there were not riots after Jamar Clark's killing by police, there would be no riots this time. The precise fact that there were no riots last time—and there were no changes in policy, policing, politics, perception—almost guaranteed there would be something larger, angrier, anguished this time. JFK riffed on MLK when he said, "Those who make peaceful revolution impossible will make violent revolution inevitable."

Only when white property and lives are challenged does society at large take notice of issues that we have conveniently ignored for generations. Police killings of unarmed, nonthreatening Black men are tragically and typically far too common.

Slow killing played out on video, to a homebound pandemic-agitated nation? Something new.

Ahmaud Arbery and Breonna Taylor were fresh on the public radar. It was—it is—clear that the killing of Black citizens would continue unabated, with no intervention or correction or justice. If video and public pressure had not occurred, neither of those cases would have received coverage. Had Ms. Frazier not shared her video of George Floyd's horrific final minutes, Mr. Floyd would have been a statistic, another rendition of *A suspect experienced a medical emergency while in police custody. EMS was called. He was pronounced dead at a local hospital.*

The prevailing logic of (white) America put all Black deaths in the line of acceptable, whether "justified" or "unfortunate tragic accidents that couldn't be avoided."

We reached the tipping point, the end date of the festering deferred dream.

Our legal system is problematic, unwieldy, and archaic. Even its staunchest defenders say it's an imperfect process, which is a wildly Caucasian understatement. A system that originated in 1215 with Britain's Magna Carta seems poorly structured to handle body camera footage. In most courtrooms, only the judge and the lawyers for the two sides are actually speaking the same language, with clear understanding of the game afoot. The witnesses, the jury, the accused? We are less than pawns. The game of what can be included—and thus referenced—in the evidence escapes most citizens. Juries after their trials are often shocked to learn there was ample material for the viewing, but it had not been entered into evidence—or it had been excluded.

In the trials of the four officers, letting their body camera footage be viewed fully would have clarified whether Mr. Floyd was "resisting" or the crowd was "threatening" the officers. The police, their defense teams, and their defenders leaned heavily on the "threatening crowd distracted the officers" angle. I repeat that the small crowd became vocal only in the course of Mr. Floyd's slow, anguished death. Someone viewing the bodycam recordings of the officers could see the glaring discrepancy between Mr. Floyd's consistent, agitated, breathless condition, and how they treated him. How consistent he was in asking for help. How completely they ignored him. I have watched them all, multiple times. They are ghastly. They are unequivocal.

The officers' lawyers also pushed Mr. Floyd's drug use, and they lofted "excited delirium" as a "cause" of his death. His agitation, his incoherence and panic, his claustrophobia, his hyperventilation: he was clearly showing some form of altered mentation from the very beginning of Officer Lane's engagement with him. Their aggression and domineering were against a man telling them he could not breathe, that he was claustrophobic, that he was not resisting. Officer Lane tentatively mentioned it while they were crushing him, but did nothing to protect

Mr. Floyd's respiratory system. Nowhere in the time since May 25, 2020, has the Minneapolis Police Department or the city of Minneapolis acknowledged or addressed this fundamental issue. Chapter 12, "Ketamine or Kill a Man," addresses the deadly failures of responders to recognize and treat those with altered mentation, and the systemic failure to investigate and legislate change.

So, the defense pushed the "threatening high man" and the "aggressive crowd" narratives.

I remind you it's a perverse double insult to blame the bystanders for distracting the police *and* to blame them for not doing more to save Mr. Floyd from the police.

Please remember, there are so many cases in which bystanders are arrested and hurt because the police take their efforts to intervene as threatening. It is the success of our violent, white supremacist system that all Black citizens know as their toxic birthright the perils with which they cross the vast blue line of the police.

//

Even with the ample video evidence and the rare presence of so much eyewitness detail, the medical experts could not agree on a clear cause of Mr. Floyd's death. He had existing health issues; he'd had Covid; he was under the influence—but none of those were in the same realm as having been crushed under three men while gasping to breathe. Derek Chauvin's overt and symbolic racism became the easy answer. His knee became synecdochical for America's policing of Black men.

That knee, however, keeps the pressure and focus on the single rogue officer, not the entire system. Officers Thao and Chauvin both had years of excessive force complaints against them—most of which were round-filed rather than investigated or processed. These were not aberrant rogues but established senior officers.

Chauvin's knee embodying racist policing is a fitting metaphor. It serves as a ghastly, apt embodiment of American police mistreatment of Black citizens, but I don't think it is scientifically correct that Chauvin killed George Floyd by himself. I quibble because the lone "killer knee" puts the blame on an individual rather than the group of officers, rather than on the system and culture of policing itself.

Mr. Floyd's plaintive calls for help, mercy, his mother came through an unfractured windpipe. (I have been on a call for a man whose windpipe was crushed by the police. The result is the same: death. The physical and physiological damages are different. I apologize for making such grim distinctions, but they are real.) The weight of the officers on his chest—from neck to haunches—pinning him down and preventing his chest and lungs from rising to move air (causing positional asphyxia) seems more fatal than Chauvin's knee.

Both/and.

Chauvin is guilty. He is responsible for Mr. Floyd's death, but his knee seems less the cause than a significant contributing factor. His ill leadership of the officers killed a man whose only fight was to breathe.

The system, the other officers, the Minneapolis Police Department, the city of Minneapolis must not escape their accountability. All four officers failed to protect a man in their custody. All four officers ignored both their duty and a man's cries for help. Saying "Derek Chauvin killed George Floyd" rather than "Derek Chauvin was in charge and all of them ignored a dying man's cries for help" allows the others to skate from full legal consequences, and allows the department—its culture, especially—to avoid accountability; if established rules are routinely ignored, that indicts the culture, the system, and the department. (I wrote this chapter before the federal trial of the officers and the state trial of Officers Thao and Kueng. If two to four years feels like a victory for killing a man under the color of law, this was a "victory" for justice. But a symbolic one.)

Note how Chief Arredondo and multiple other administrators were adamant that the *individual* officers failed, not the system. Painting Chauvin as an anomalous bad apple makes him a scapegoat for the department and the city.

If we are prohibited from attributing systemic or cultural roots to these (not actually rare) incidents, we must find some individual cause, which is pretty ludicrous. The hairsplitting legalisms demand we find some "reason" the officer chose to ignore and violate department policy, common sense, human decency, and do something horrible. *That isn't who we are,* people insist after someone does something that is definitely a reflection of their culture and values. Plausible denial has entrenched legal and political currency.

So Officer Chauvin was a lone, rogue agent that day, and the MPD had nothing to do with it?

But wait: There are multiple previous complaints of brutality against him? Has Officer Chauvin been disciplined for any of these previous complaints? Oh, none were substantiated. Actually, most weren't even investigated? They don't exist on any official record? There we are.

I have no love for Derek Chauvin, whose many transgressions over his career failed to earn any departmental sanction. I am not saying he was framed or railroaded or unjustly scapegoated. But he was not a lone wolf. He is a bad cop and an embodiment. The department will not police itself, and the city will not force it to.

I have even less love for the department and the city that allowed this to be so. The culture of the Minneapolis Police Department was disallowed as a legal entity for the prosecution: you cannot prosecute an ethos for a crime. This entire tragic fuckery is explicitly a *product* of the MPD culture. It is a damning indictment of the culture of policing. Yet it remained hidden in plain sight, untouchable, while these men were judged as derelict, rogue individuals for their crimes.

The striking number of abusive officers and recorded violations of policy should make this ploy a laughable failure, but this is the system. Meanwhile, the victim remains dead, killed gratuitously. He will be slandered in the press and courts—standard procedure, to muddy the picture and give the police irrational justification. (They did not know the man's history when they killed him: how can his previous arrests be relevant?) The witnesses remain traumatized, and, worse, undermined, dismissed, blamed. It is crazy making.

I feel for Officers Kueng and Lane. Truly. They should have been poster boys for a new generation of police. They should have known and done better. They *are* guilty. They followed the lead of the senior officers, abided by department culture and custom. They were unprepared—no, badly prepared—for this scene, this dynamic. They defaulted to what they were taught: follow the senior guys' lead, use overwhelming force.

I have written throughout about the noxious prevalence of cultural machismo and systemic obtuseness—yes, in the fire service, but in life, in sports, in family. Men taught to be the wrong sort of men. New guys who get cowed into following the herd, doing what the others do, even if they know it's wrong: the pressure of social conformity. Or guys so desperate to fit in, acting tough, playing the hard case, that they never learn what they're supposed to do. Young firefighters who recognize the disconnect between our cultural narrative and the objective facts of science and sociology face this challenge: how to speak up when they have scant practical experience, and the leaders they dare contradict are their bosses, who evaluate them and are supposed to keep them safe and alive? Conversely, macho firefighters who talk shit about every other crew but who tremble with flop sweat when they're the ones in the smoke and heat: they plunge blindly into bad situations because they cannot admit they are both inexperienced and uncomfortable.

The actions that day of Officers Lane and Kueng can be examined through this duality. Lane knew the right thing to do. He recognized Mr. Floyd's distress. But he wasn't empowered to speak up, he'd been trained to defer to the senior man, he was afraid for his position in the pecking order. This might sound simplistic, but it is more plausible than the notion that he was a homicidal maniac. His lack of temerity proved fatal. Officer Kueng represents the other side: he saw and heard the senior man approaching, and he *had* to show Chauvin that he was tough enough, that he wasn't a punk. So he upped the physicality, the macho shoving match. He acted blindly and rashly, which started the fatal cascade.

//

Many people state that George Floyd was lynched. That he was assassinated. That he was executed. My initial reaction to those claims was to quibble with the figurative meanings, to assert the denotations of *lynch, assassinate, execute.* What bloody Caucacity. What utter privilege. For me to insist on clear, accurate language—All Words Matter—while ignoring the legacy of unprosecuted murders of Black civilians, is white blindness. (I laughed at myself: parsing semantics at the expense of Black lives. Someone ought to make a slogan and a movement to remind us that Black lives do, in fact, matter. Oh, wait.)

Mr. Floyd was not a king, a prince, a saint. He did not need to be any of those for his life to matter and for his death to be a crime. I wholly understand the need to assert and reclaim a dead man's value, to make space for him in a society that is so deliberately, comfortably numb. This society, this system, this country has done murderous injustice to nonwhite citizens since its bloody inception. I fiercely recommend

Robert Samuels and Toluse Olorunnipa's Pulitzer Prize–winning *His Name Is George Floyd,* a biography and sociological study of the man in the context of the dismal American system.

Mr. Floyd was a human being who committed a nonviolent transgression worthy of a misdemeanor charge, an apology with proper payment—at worst, being 86'ed from Cup Foods: the issue easily resolved. He was high, possibly drunk, not making clear decisions. Whatever he was on, plus his history with the police, rendered him anxious, claustrophobic, emotionally fragile. But he was not attacking the police and he *deserved* humane treatment.

Mr. Floyd never fought the officers, never attempted to flee. He begged for his life, over and over. He was trying to comply.

The image of Chauvin kneeling on Mr. Floyd's neck while staring into the void contrasted with Colin Kaepernick kneeling to protest the failed promise of the national anthem offers a ripe juxtaposition about America's cultural and racial dynamics. But the figurative, the metaphoric: these are not the truth of the image. Does that matter? Am I splitting hairs from my comfort as a white man? Yes. And no. Impact over intention holds weight here. I argue that Chauvin's criminal indifference to Mr. Floyd's humanity is the truth.

Derek Chauvin did not take glee in killing Mr. Floyd. Chauvin did not kill him intentionally. There was the brutal malice of absolute control, the callous and cruel indifference to the humanity of Mr. Floyd. Chauvin likely thought he was doing a better job than using a Taser or baton. He might have thought he was showing the new guys how to do the job right. They had their man subdued; they were waiting for EMS to check him out before putting him in the cruiser. All standard protocols. What a damning failure.

I will quote Laurence Gonzales in *Deep Survival* again:

> A faulty mental model is part of the explanation. . . . You see what you expect to see. You see what makes sense, and what makes sense is what matches the mental model. . . . The word "experienced" often refers to someone who's gotten away with doing the wrong thing more frequently than you have.

Please hear me: three police officers, with a fourth keeping watch, knelt on a man for nearly ten minutes as he cried for help, begged for his life, pleaded that he could not breathe. The phrase "I can't breathe" became emblematic for the cruel killing, for police violence, for the knee to the neck of Black America. But Mr. Floyd said "I can't breathe" almost twenty times before the officers knelt on him. I say this not to undermine the devastating impact and implications of the phrase, nor to diminish its power as emblem, as signifier. I say it to emphasize that the police had all the information they needed from the outset: the first caller stated the man appeared significantly under the influence. They were dealing with someone in crisis, someone who needed treatment, not manhandling and smothering. He cried out in panic. They piled on. He cried out steadily, horribly. The officers ignored it all. His last minutes were spent gasping, begging, pleading. They did not assess his condition, did not provide treatment. He went unconscious and unresponsive, finally, and they did not relent. They killed him by their passive stolidity, ignoring a desperate group of people who saw what the officers would not. It is as horrifically simple as that. They crushed him to death without intending to kill him.

He was not an actual human being beneath them: that seems the only answer.

//

As the world focused on Thirty-eighth and Chicago in south Minneapolis, and the scene my crew had entered belatedly became infamous and inescapable, I could not shake the question: Would I have been able to do more, had we arrived sooner? Once we saw the videos, and I spoke with Firefighter Hansen, who tried and failed to break through the robotic trance of the police, I could not avoid wondering. *Would I have been able to get Chauvin's attention? Could I have made Thao turn to actually see what he was ignoring? Could I have interrupted their fatal in/action? Could I have saved George Floyd?* I don't think the answer is firmly yes. I have been on similar police scenes before. They do not see anything outside their target. *But maybe I could have . . .*

Off duty or on duty, does it make a difference? Maybe. As a civilian, as a middle-aged, gravel-voiced white man, I would have been given more credence than the half-dozen Black citizens or the young white female off-duty firefighter—no matter that we were saying the same things. That is how this country functions. But could I have *stopped* them? Had I put hands on their shoulders, identified myself, asked them to flip Mr. Floyd over—would they have listened? It ate at me.

Could I have saved him?

Not likely. I would have been tackled, roughed up, arrested by the police for challenging them, for disrupting a scene. They would say *I* was the problem—not them, their mindset, their system, their knees. And then I would have suffered the Back the Blue backlash.

But I wasn't there while it was happening. I didn't randomly wander into the scene. That is fantasy, a spasm of my own traumatic reaction.

On duty, it is a different story. The officers called for EMS as a protocol, not because they actually recognized Mr. Floyd was in grave distress. Once they radioed for medics, neither of the two senior officers (Chauvin and Thao) actually checked Mr. Floyd's condition, or listened to his cries of distress (until he spoke no more), or heeded the insistent and consistent pleading from the crowd. Had any of the officers told their Dispatch that they needed EMS for "one having trouble breathing," we would have been summoned promptly. That is how our system works.

I harp on this throughout this book: Dispatch is not clairvoyant. They cannot infer from a terse, perfunctory request that there is a man's life in the balance. If any of the officers had said "breathing issues; respiratory distress; SOB"—anything—we would have been added to the call directly *and* we would have arrived in under three minutes. So rewind that video and look at all the opportunities the officers had to ask for help.

That ten-minute window, from when the officers said "EMS Code 2" and then upped it without explaining why to Code 3, until Engine 17 was dispatched, is the difference between Mr. Floyd's being alive and his death. If we had been dispatched at the same time as the paramedics, this would have ended differently. Our station is six blocks directly west of Cup Foods. If we had arrived sooner, could we have reversed the respiratory distress? Saved his heart? I don't know how much damage he had suffered at that point.

More important, could we have stopped the condition that was contributing to his decline (their bodyweight on his cuffed, prone torso)?

Yes.

Yes, we could have. Yes, we would have.

If Fire dispatch had been notified at the same time police dispatchers notified EMS dispatchers, they would have sent us and we would have arrived at 8:23, not 8:33.

George Floyd went unresponsive at 8:25.

We would have arrived in time to stop them from killing him, in time to keep him breathing. This is not fantasy. Nor is it self-aggrandizing. It is fact. Brutal fact.

I will carry that for the rest of my life. We could have intervened had we been dispatched sooner—had the officers given Dispatch any reason for upgrading the call. But they did not. They crushed the life out of George Floyd while we sat in our station six blocks and under three minutes away.

By the time we arrived, nothing could have revived him. The cumulative effects of what killed Mr. Floyd in the custody of those officers were irreversible. The paramedics arrived with scant information, found a wildly unexpected and incoherent scene, and had to put a medical response together on the fly. They did their best, worked hard and fast, but it was futile. Mr. Floyd was dead when they arrived.

For those who are unclear, let me clarify and explain something that has come up multiple times. The paramedics arrived to find an unresponsive man still pinned down by police, with bystanders crying out at the officers' callous failure to help Mr. Floyd. The medics conferred briefly with Chauvin and decided to move away from the scene, to work without distraction.

But why didn't they just drive directly to the hospital? Why did they waste time on the street? Why did they pull over and just sit there, waiting for your crew?

Remember, for prehospital emergency medicine, paramedics essentially have three types of patient conditions: stay-and-play, load-and-go, and, well, dead. In traumatic events such as stabbings, shootings, car wrecks, and falls, there will be severe, life-threatening internal injuries. Other than stopping the bleeding and starting an IV to boost fluids and blood pressure, there is little to be done in the field: these patients need emergency surgery, load-and-go. For cardiac and respiratory issues and arrests, paramedics can do far more interventions to save the patient, right there, right then. Medications and ventilation and IV lines: work that can save someone's life. Stay-and-play.

The paramedics pulled around the corner as we were heading out of the station, and we missed seeing them by seconds, although we also had no information, and we would not have blindly followed a random ambulance. We do not have rig-to-rig radio communication. The medics were not idling on the curb waiting for us to show up. They were doing multiple crucial things in an attempt to bring Mr. Floyd back to life. Intubation, ventilation, compressions, IV lines, medications.

We arrived at Thirty-eighth and Chicago with no more info than the medics had received: "one with a mouth bleed." While Firefighter Hall and I walked past several police officers (none of whom gave us any useful information) and through the small crowd, then into Cup Foods, the two medics, with Officer Lane attempting to help, had already started resuscitation efforts on Mr. Floyd. After our initial goose chase, Hall and I joined them, clearing Lane, and took over ventilations and accessory tasks for the medics. Together we worked hard and efficiently.

For hundreds of calls over the past two decades, this has been the case. A fatal cardiac event, a fatally traumatic incident, too much time without breathing, someone down too long: we arrive as fast as we can after we are notified, and we find a body. And people—family, friends, coworkers, strangers—are screaming for us to do something to fix the person. Who is dead.

But you don't know for sure unless you try.

Both of these are true: George Floyd was dead. We worked him furiously.

The result was the same. Dead is dead. It was futile. It was the right thing to do. We can't go on. We must go on.

//

Some rhetorical questions for those still unclear on actions and responsibilities, for those who take at face value the police claim that this was not a murder.

Officer Chauvin arrived, thought he saw a struggle, a suspect challenging his rookie officers. He barked commands, then physically engaged the suspect, roughly forcing him down and kneeling on his neck. He did not ask Officers Kueng or Lane for any detail until several minutes in. Why not? Was he responding to a picture in his head? A presumption? His default mental model?

Did Officer Chauvin ever check Mr. Floyd's condition?

Did Chauvin have any information or knowledge that caused him to ignore the plaintive cries from the bystanders—who were correctly and accurately stating the man was in distress and the officers, especially Chauvin, were causing his deteriorating condition?

What was Officer Chauvin's reason for ignoring the tentative suggestions by Officer Lane about Mr. Floyd's condition? Why did they not reposition him, or check his level of consciousness?

Even though two officers radioed their Dispatch for EMS, why did neither do anything to investigate the subject's condition or treat him?

Why did Officer Thao ignore the crowd's pleas, as well as Firefighter Hansen's observations that Mr. Floyd was in distress?

Did the officers make a plan, discuss what they were doing, have any regard for what the person in their custody needed? Or did they blindly follow their leader?

Can we acknowledge the force and weight that cultural customs play in this scenario? The citizens did not attack the officers to liberate Mr. Floyd; the junior officers did not force Officer Chauvin to pay attention, follow protocol, check their suspect. At the end of this chain of events, erasing the role of systemic behaviors allows it to continue.

If I am drowning you, it is great that I call 911, but I should also take my foot off your neck and let you come up for air. That seems obvious. But it has not been raised or addressed in the trials or discussions. The officers radioed for EMS but did *nothing* to address the man's condition. More to the point, they were the ones creating the dire situation. Where is the review on that?

When does a scene shift from police control to EMS? There is no clear line. The police were still treating Mr. Floyd like a suspect to be restrained while the paramedics were recognizing horrifically that the man beneath the officers was not breathing, was unresponsive, was dead. The police have Authority with a capital A; they have the guns. We yield to them, for better and worse. Not only do they have scant medical training, they do not consider injuries relevant to their actions. This is another example of systemic failure.

How do you reform something that is invisible and ubiquitous? How do you reform a system that reflexively erases, denies, buries the very things you are looking to address?

//

I want to acknowledge what the state and the federal government, represented by the judges in the two cases, seemed to consider moot: the horrendous guilt, shame, anger, and sorrow borne by the witnesses of this killing. The small, fervent, but unthreatening crowd witnessed the officers' killing of Mr. Floyd. They watched a man die, slowly. They did not force the issue. Because it was surreal and, of course, they knew the risks of stepping into an agitated police scene. That is their birthright as Black citizens. Firefighter Genevieve Hansen, to her credit, stepped off the curb and into the edge of the fray, about the best use of white privilege we have seen in years. Bless her for that.

As the world absorbed the horror afterward and the video and images became iconic, the witnesses carry the weight of their memories and powerless guilt, and are subject to the idiot online amplifications and distortions. It was an unwinnable situation. They must continue their lives with those images—and the sounds of Mr. Floyd's desperate, dying cries—burned into their psyches. Judge Cahill denied the legal validity of the traumatic effects on the youngest witnesses. Was that rooted in legal theory or shaped by a habituated indifference to Black suffering?

I want to recognize the following people:

Mr. Charles McMillian, who tried throughout the early
    stages to "talk sense" to Mr. Floyd (we hear Mr. McMillian's
    voice from the outset, when Mr. Floyd is saying he cannot
    breathe in the back of the squad car).
Christopher Belfrey, who began recording from his car
    when he saw Officer Lane point his gun at Mr. Floyd.
Christopher Martin, the Cup Foods employee who received
    the bogus twenty-dollar bill and called the police. He stated
    from the jump that Mr. Floyd seemed high or drunk but
    was not threatening.
Donald Williams II, who was most articulate and direct in
    asking, telling, pleading, calling out to the officers as they
    knelt on the distressed Mr. Floyd.
Alisha Oiler, witness and video taker.
Darnella Frazier, video taker, and three minors, witnesses.

Jena Scurry, a 911 Dispatch operator who witnessed the
scene play out via the public-safety camera pointing down
from the northwest corner of Thirty-eighth and Chicago.
Genevieve Hansen, witness, off-duty firefighter/EMT with
a duty to provide aid, who was rebuffed repeatedly by the
police.
Paramedics Seth Bravinder and Derek Smith, who arrived
to "one with a mouth injury" and found three officers still
pinning down the prone, restrained, unresponsive, pulseless
man; who were given no good information from the police;
and who attempted to orchestrate resuscitation despite
being well behind the curve and shorthanded.
Firefighter Jennifer Hall, who entered this scene after the
fact with just two months of experience, who worked with
me in the ambulance to support the paramedics' resuscitation efforts.
Firefighter Steve Mudek and FMO Tracy Terbell, who were
on scene but outside the ambulance, unaware what was
happening, carrying the weight of it afterward.

My heart breaks most for Mr. McMillian, Mr. Williams, Ms. Scurry, and
then for Paramedics Bravinder and Smith as well as Firefighter Hansen.
Mr. McMillian has lived his life as a Black man in a racist society. He
was playing the role we have shaped, at point of death, telling Mr. Floyd
to relent, to yield, to let the cops do their thing. He was being "sensible,"
realistic about the odds and the police. And Mr. Floyd still died. Mr.
Williams, younger, trained, and fit, could have fought the officers to save
Mr. Floyd, but he made the wise choice not to. He is alive today. He even
called 911 to report the police. I cannot fathom that weight. Ms. Scurry
watched stunned from the Dispatch center, unbelieving what she saw
on the closed-circuit monitor. Frozen by cognitive dissonance, she now
carries the weight of what played out.

The paramedics entered late, worked hard and well, yet still are
vilified, still are easy targets for the blame machine. And my scrappy
young coworker, Genevieve Hansen, must fight the weight of blaming
herself for not doing enough, as she continues to respond to our range
of EMS calls. She has been tormented by anonymous cowards via email

and USPS, and faced recrimination from some police and firefighters. And then there's the comments section of the videos . . .

These good people are haunted. There is no good path through grief, or guilt, or blame, or any of it. This event has affected each of us in different ways. But those folks on the curb, that motley "crowd" that the police and its defenders smear as the "cause" of the officers' distraction: how much must they carry, knowing they did all they could, knowing it was never enough?

Timeline

Here I provide some context or clarification for readers who have not watched the multiple body camera footages and reconstructed the timeline. I use time stamps from our aggregate dispatch software as well as from the body cameras of former Officers Lane, Kueng, and Thao. I watched the footage from all three multiple times as trial prep and while writing this essay. I do not recommend that any person of color watch it. I do encourage white folks to see it: watch and listen, focus on words and actions. *It is horrific.*

Times are in military format, consistent with our framework: 2002 = 8:02 p.m.

2002: Call comes in for MPD to investigate a possible forged bill; caller states the suspect appears intoxicated.

2011: Officer Lane makes contact with George Floyd, who sits in an SUV with two friends.

2012–2016: Officers Lane and Kueng engage Floyd, struggle to get "control" of him as he panics. They sit him against the wall of Dragon Wok, and he calms down a bit. The two officers walk him across Thirty-eighth Street to their squad, sitting him against the wall of Cup Foods. They try to get him into the squad car and his panic soars. He states he is claustrophobic and needs a minute to catch his breath, multiple times. He sits halfway into the squad. He says he is and appears terrified of being shut in.

2017: When Chauvin arrives, Kueng escalates physically. Chauvin barks "Get in the car!" as he approaches; a struggle inside the squad car ensues as the officers force Floyd into the squad.

2018: Floyd says, "I'm going down," as he falls to ground. Officers kneel on him.

2019: Floyd says, "I can't breathe."

2020: Lane requests EMS Code 2, for a mouth injury.

2021: Chauvin has Thao up it to Code 3. Neither gives Dispatch any further info, nor do they assess or address Floyd's condition.

2022: Floyd is listing everything that hurts, saying he cannot breathe and begging for help. Chauvin tells him, "You're breathing fine." Floyd is yelling, pleading, begging. The effort to speak while the officers pin him down, plus his emotional exertion, is notable. Crowd is objecting to Chauvin's knee on Floyd's neck.

2023: Officer Thao tells the crowd, "This is why you don't do drugs." He responds to their cries that Floyd cannot breathe with "He's talking." Floyd's energy wanes. He is losing consciousness. His breathing is a raspy wheeze. He stops moving, stops speaking.

2024: Lane says, "I'm worried about that excited delirium, you know." Chauvin replies, "That's why we have EMS coming."

2024: The crowd entreats the officers to get off Floyd, to put him in the car, that he is not struggling. Floyd goes limp and is silent.

2025: Floyd appears not to be breathing. Lane suggests they roll him over. The three officers remain on top of the still man. Firefighter Genevieve Hansen attempts to intervene, identifying herself as a Minneapolis firefighter and EMT. She is rebuffed and ordered to the curb by Thao.

2026: The crowd becomes more agitated and vocal when they see Floyd go unresponsive. They are screaming at the officers to help the man.

2027: Ambulance arrives, not having seen or been advised of any of this. Paramedic Smith has to make Chauvin move in order to check Floyd's pulse. His partner, Paramedic

Bravinder, gets the stretcher. Smith uses his own keys to free Floyd's hands from the handcuffs. Chauvin still tries to recuff GF to the rails of the ambulance.

2028: Smith converses briefly with Chauvin, who nods that they should leave the scene—due to the crowd's noise. Bravinder radios to their Dispatch that they need Fire Code 3. (It takes almost five minutes to get through the two Dispatch centers to us. None of the dispatchers has been given clear information.)

2030: CPR starts inside the ambulance. Lane does compressions while Smith gets advanced airway.

2032: The ambulance relocates four blocks away, facing downtown on Park Avenue at Thirty-sixth Street, and Bravinder joins Smith to work on Floyd. They establish an airway, set up the LUCAS compression device. Lane switches to ventilations. He does not attach the oxygen to the BVM, which I do when I take over for him.

Meanwhile:

2030: E17 is dispatched for a Code 2 "assist the police" for "one with a mouth bleed." This seems an echo of the call the medics got ten minutes earlier, at 2020. As we pull on to Thirty-eighth Street, heading east, Dispatch updates it to Code 3. We hit our lights and sirens and speed toward Thirty-eighth and Chicago, receiving no further information.

2032: E17 arrives at the intersection. There are several squad cars, both MPD and Park Police, a few officers standing about the street, a handful of people on the sidewalk. No patient. No ambulance. No one waving for us or directing us. The rookie, Jenn Hall, and I get off the rig, get nothing of use or substance from the first officer we encounter (Thao). We walk into the store, passing through the half dozen or so young people who were the "crowd." No one threatens us, attacks us, impedes us. They are upset, yelling at and about the police. I hear "They killed him!" "The police killed that man!" but I do not see any patient or victim, not on the street or sidewalk. No one says the medics have come and gone, that the man in question is with them in the ambulance. We speak with Hansen as we enter and look for a victim in the store. I speak with another MPD officer (Kueng) at the back of the store, where he is talking to the staff. He tells me the medics relocated—a few blocks south, he says, mistakenly. He does not say anything about the patient's condition, or what happened. Just that the crowd was why the medics moved.

2034: Both MPD and Fire Dispatch are announcing that medics need Fire Code 3 at Thirty-sixth and Park. We leave the store and get back on the rig, driving to find the medics.

2036: Hall and I get in the ambulance, clearing Lane, taking over ventilations, assisting medics with IV setup and whatever else they request.

2048: We leave Thirty-sixth and Park Avenue for HCMC.

16

A HASHTAG BRINGS NO ONE BACK

We need to gather ourselves, for we are in the eye of the storm. We must find the courage to make the bold choices necessary for these after times. And we cannot shrink from our rage; it is the fire that lights the kiln. We have to look back and tell a different story, without the crutch of our myths and legends, about how we have arrived at this moment of moral reckoning in the country's history.

—Eddie Glaude Jr., *Begin Again*

Smoke Gets in Your Eyes b/w Blood on the Tracks

Early June 2020, Minneapolis

In the week following George Floyd's death and the ensuing upheaval, our crew responded to two different but significantly affecting calls, incidents that stung me at the time and haunted me afterward—even within the fraught context of the uprising, the riot damage, the tragedy of Mr. Floyd's killing. The calls involved young Black women who were both emotionally overwhelmed by the choking indecency of white-ruled America. Young women my daughters' ages who were suffering breakdowns as a result of fatigue and sorrow and anger. One was having a near-psychotic break. The other attempted self-harm. Both were out on the streets. They were exhausted to the depths of their souls, emotionally drained, at the breaking point. They needed help, rest, safety—something. Someone called 911 for them. We responded. These were mental health emergencies. Public safety and welfare demanded our involvement.

Both of these distraught young women looked up and there we were, a wall of white faces in uniforms. Our presence did not calm them, did not ease their pain, did not help in any way.

We are there to help, to support, to treat, to listen. But we embody, are the representatives in form and function of, the brutal racist system. There is nothing I can say to make up for the generations of abuse we have perpetrated on BIPOC. There is nothing I can do to guarantee it will not happen again. Most of my coworkers try to do right by people, but still. Everyone is tense. The streets are still roiling. Wrecked buildings still smolder. Charred wood, broken glass, jagged and gaping walls of concrete. It is a surreal landscape. We are wary of what's lurking in the shadows. Personally, I'm afraid of the opportunistic white supremacists running down the alleys with guns and gasoline. The trauma of another police killing of another Black man is a festering wound for Black people. *This* is where we meet.

In each case, the young woman became more agitated the more we attempted to help her. We, who have been summoned by well-meaning bystanders, are obligated to engage. It is negligence to abandon someone. We cannot step away and let someone else come help them. There is no one else coming.

And even though I have been avoiding involving the police in any call I can justify handling alone, in Minneapolis the police write the official hold for self-harming individuals, so they must come. Not because they want to lock her up, or because it gives them any pleasure, but because it is their job.

How the police behave when they arrive, of course, will vary by officer. But when the person we've all been called to help is screaming at us to *fuck off!*, shrieking that the sight of us is *fucking killing her!,* that she just wants to be *left alone!,* for all of us *white people to disappear and let her die!,* we quickly are at loggerheads.

What can I say to reassure someone whose world has been so toxically whitewashed that before she is twenty she is disassociating or suicidal? What can I do—in the moment, right away—to cross the chasm between these women's pain and our legal obligations?

I cannot imagine what it would be like to have lived these women's young lives with endless Black bodies piling up, nary a substantive discussion, reform, or any court conviction. At every turn this system, this society, has failed them, and failed without pausing or feeling it-self at fault. Both young women are the age of my older daughter, who has never felt one iota of the existential, structural, paradigmatic weight of a racist society's perversely obsessive homicidal impulse. I cannot imagine.

A hashtag brings no one back.

On both of these calls, there were other white men (paramedics, police, firefighters) who took umbrage at the women's anger, who ob-jected to being yelled at and blanketed with "you all are fucking racist fuckers!" Irony abounds. #notallhonkies? These men saw neither forest nor trees (context or causation). They could not perceive these women's anguish, could not recognize our role in the systemic injustice. Instead, they shouted at these wounded humans, escalated the scenes. They per-sonalized something that was as deep and old as America's foundational blood sin.

There were better-skilled white men and women present, too, but we were doing triple damage control at that point. Both incidents ended with tension, anger, frustration. They were hard, futile calls. The jagged weight of those women's anguish hung over us. Our profound useless-ness was striking, a slap in the face, a punch in the heart.

No matter how hard it is to feel that deep pain and fury and hurt, and be powerless to address it, I know it is *nothing* compared to what has caused it all in the first place, for so very long.

What a horrific reality that, when a young person cannot stand the weight and breaks down, the person who responds to help is indistin-guishable from the agent of death. That is not a flaw in her vision: it is the inescapable by-product of this system and our culture.

August 2020, Minneapolis, America: White Fungibility

If one has been reading much on social media, there have been abun-dant discussions about how to fix things. White America suddenly had an accurate test to detect racism. *This is a new beginning. In these unprec-edented times. We hear you, we see you, we honor you.* Many directives have sallied forth, and then been virally reposted, retweeted, reshared. However, barely a month into the next Great Awakening from denial and delusion to basic recognition, some white people were already com-plaining that they were "confused," "frustrated," "put off" by the range of reactions, suggestions, corrections from BIPOC. I heard the swiftly mounting fatigue in many putatively liberal white people: *The rules keep changing—I don't know what to do! Whatever I do is wrong! I can't say anything without getting attacked. I supported all the BLM stuff until they started rioting. Violence is never the answer!*

It *is* a lot to undo our ingrained, reflexive, unthinking constructs. I remind myself that for more than four centuries, whites have played the okey doke on everyone else. Eddie Glaude Jr., in *Begin Again*, his meditation on James Baldwin's writing and thinking reexamined in our current context, writes, "Grief and trauma joined with disappointment as Baldwin watched white Americans turn away from the difficulties of genuine change, often embracing a nostalgic appeal for simpler days, when black people knew their place and weren't in the streets protesting, in order to justify their refusal to give up the lie." It is fair to ask whether anything has truly changed, whether we whites have actually looked at the world we have wrought.

How many shootings, killings, extrajudicial abuses have we swallowed with our weekday dinners, never considering how constant and profound the injustice is? Have we given any genuine thought to all the ways we hoodwink our Black citizens? *Act like this and we will accept you as human. Dress like this and you won't be profiled. Talk like this and you will be hired on merit. Do (or do not do) this and you will not be arrested for fitting a vague description, will not be killed for throwing such a scary shadow across the armed officer's psyche that he must shoot you enough times to stop the fear from consuming him.*

The fatally flawed but enduring moral suasion argument. Despite four hundred years to the contrary, we still use that over anything else. Because the alternative is too terrifying to consider for white people (Toussaint Louverture, Nat Turner, Chris Dorner). And the specter of Black citizens taking back their lives is precisely what fueled President Trump's seething, racist rants, his calling for the military and state violence against peaceful protesters, as well as the aggressive white reaction in every city of the country. White America is afraid of facing its sordid legacy. We are quick to use violence to suppress and repress when the laws and history and regular police fail.

Is this where I insert the blanching contrast to a few months prior, late April and early May 2020? Armed and screaming hordes of white folks taking to the streets over barbershop closings and moronic, insip-idly lazy "conspiracies" about a pandemic that is killing the fuck out of humanity? (And can we truly be surprised by what happened on Janu-ary 6, 2021, given this indulgent, myopic frenzy?)

//

Was it how slowly George Floyd was killed that struck such a chord? I think so. He was no better or worse a man to be martyred: what un-armed person who has been killed by the police *deserved* that fate? We (white people, white culture) have let the world spin on, time and again. Only when the windows were broken, the fires raged, the anger stripped away our buffering denial, only then did we wake up to it. Our fear trig-gered our awakening.

Not justice or love or hope. *Fear.* We have failed a reverse moral suasion test: can we genuinely care about Black and brown people when our interests are *not* threatened?

We still are barely at the beginning of unpacking four hundred years of sanctioned injustice. Again, what eats at me is not what most white folks are talking about—and I am unlikely to explain it without ruining their day. The dysfunctional leaders of the Minneapolis Fire De-partment did little to structurally address either Covid or the June upris-ing. We operate in a void, largely, so I must make my own best-intention decisions and hope for the best.

Hope is not an action plan. That might be my epitaph.

Whenever I get fed up with the earnest white guilt and shame and apologies and declarations, which quickly merge into performative ges-tures of "wokeness" (whatsoever that is or is not), I think of the two young women—their pain, anguish, sadness, rage seared into my mind and heart, representative of and embodying the mass suffering of Black citizens of the United States—whose feelings, hurt, and struggle were *not* conceptual. These are whom I worry about, whom I wish to help—in the moment, on scenes, as well as in the big picture. I want to fight the obdurate indifference and denial of all of us white folks, to break open a sliver of understanding, in hopes that those two young women, and the multitudes experiencing similar social terrorism, can experience a better society.

Thus, I strangle my complaints, keeping my eyes and ears open. The battle is long and not easy.

September 2020, Minneapolis: Reflections of the Fires This Time

George Floyd's killing at the hands and knees of the Minneapolis Police Department unleashed a long-brewing social upheaval, sparking a chaotic flurry of protests, direct actions, and destruction—here and in cities across the United States. Locally, the images of the pained and angry citizens in the streets were eclipsed by the nighttime riots, the battle-garbed police facing off against T-shirted youth, sweaty skin glowing in the flares, klieg lights, and arson fires. The widespread destruction was stunning: not since the civil rights battles of the 1960s had so much of the city burned. In the aftermath, many people reached out to see how I was doing. Some did so because they knew I lived in Minneapolis. Some knew I was a city firefighter, and the vivid images of south Minneapolis burning put me in their minds and hearts. Only my family and closest friends knew (at that point) that I had responded to Mr. Floyd's killing, that my rookie and I jumped in the ambulance and assisted the paramedics working hard to save his life.

Many out-of-towners seemed to think the city was still on fire, still in pandemonium. "How are you doing?" they asked, even into late summer 2020. "I can't imagine—how *are* you?" Pause. "I mean, are you scared out there? It must be so crazy and dangerous and scary."

"I'm fine," I would reply. "It's fine. I'm all right."

"But, seriously, it seems terrifying. Are you okay?"

"I am."

"But, really. How *are* you?"

I found myself getting irritated, prickly. "I am fine."

And this is where people think, *Lo, but thou art not fine! I know when people say "Fine" they are avoiding their pain. "FINE" = fucked up, insecure, nervous, emotional (or feelings inside not expressed).*

And that is where I think, *Yeah, I saw that meme, too.*

Because I *was* getting irritated trying to explain to people, especially those not in Minneapolis, that what they were seeing on their screens was not what we were living. The riots, the fires, the looting: that was a five-night deal. Things had quieted down before the National Guard even arrived—their escort was awkward overkill, an armed phalanx protecting us from shadows on the desolate streets. Yet folks inquired weeks, even months, later, as if we were still under siege: "You good?" *Sigh.* I'd say, "We're *fine.*"

I wasn't in denial.

What was scary to me was not what they assumed.

My stress was white people. My people. We. *Us.*

For real.

From the overzealous, brick-throwing, mad-at-dad white boy rioters to the unhinged cosplay race warriors to all the nice white folks shocked to realize that voting for Obama twice didn't solve either racism or our own fundamental role in the racial inequality that shapes and propels this racist country: white people. And all the *He should have done what he was told! Back the Blue! Blood and Soil!* white men: those fuckers definitely had me twisted.

In the weeks after the riots scared (some) white people to attention, it was stunning to consider the speed at which we (white mainstream America) gained painful awareness of racial inequalities, historical and structural racism, unconscious bias, the Confederacy's generations of bastard offspring. It's as if we might not have been paying much attention.

Colin Kaepernick taking a knee suddenly became far less "offensive" compared to the people taking out the police precinct.

From the first hours after Mr. Floyd's killing, as the outrage and upheaval spread over the next days, my crew—all my coworkers, but particularly the three crews here at Station 17, six blocks from where George Floyd was murdered—responded to the consequences of the killing: the protests, the fires, the violence, the fears. Possible bombs discovered, attempted arson, panic attacks, shootings.

In the fervent first days of June, my crew on Engine 17 visited the murder/memorial site at George Floyd Square to pay our respects as citizens and as reps of the city. We made connections with the loose leadership inside the makeshift blockades, particularly the medical teams. We had face contact and familiarity, then, when we showed up in the agitated crowds for ODs, heat exhaustion, shootings. The leadership around GFS was, strikingly, a matrilineal endeavor: Black women leading and shaping the community that sprang from the literal ashes of the burned-out, contested street. Their vision for the site, meaning the memorial *and* the community, was something radically inventive and positive. For the people, by the people.

But, whether by intention or unexamined reflex, any medical call to the amorphous, randomly expanding "vicinity" of Thirty-eighth and Chicago came with a default warning from Dispatch that "the scene is not secure, not Code 4. All EMS units stage for police." Essentially, every 911 medical call for blocks in every direction was labeled "potentially violent." By whom? I do not know. The umbrella term, the default rationalization, is always *safety.* Vague, amorphous, abstract—"safety" is the trump card of officialdom. Many paramedics refused to enter without a police escort. They wanted no part of the reported "mob scene" of "angry Black people": a safety issue. Their leadership issued firm restrictions: for their "safety." Some of my coworkers took the same approach: *We won't risk our lives. Procedure prohibits us from entering an uncontrolled scene.*

That there were no riots after the second day of June was irrelevant. That there were no menacing, violent crowds was irrelevant. Too: there were no attacks or assaults on any police officers after the four nights of tumult at the Third Precinct. No attacks. None. That it was simply regular citizens needing help was smothered in the default "safety" net. There were several shootings in the rough vicinity of Thirty-eighth and Chicago, violence that had nothing to do with racial justice. One was a horrible domestic assault, another was an argument settled with a fatal bullet. In both cases (and two other traumatic calls), EMS crews were told to stage "outside the area" until the police arrived. And the police did not come fast. The result was that multiple bystanders and local residents suffered trying helplessly to address a fatally wounded person's injuries. There was no reason for EMS to stage endlessly, but that is how it played out. My crew caught a shooting, the victim of a drive-by. He'd been struck in the upper torso while riding his bike several blocks away. He'd biked directly down Chicago Avenue to the medical tent at GFS. I read the comments from Dispatch, and we entered the scene (again, a shooting from a moving car several blocks away is not an ongoing gun battle). We arrived; the site's medical team was already addressing the young man's wounds. We took over and worked together. The medics, we learned, were staging for police. At this point (first days of June 2020), the citizens were demanding the police not enter the area. There was a standoff. I looked up and saw a lot of tense police with long guns facing off with citizens, some of whom were also armed. Finally, the medics arrived. Everyone was a thousand times too amped up. The poor kid, a random victim of gun violence, got poor care—due to "safety" concerns.

I tried to explain (to my supervisors, the paramedics, nervous co-workers) that there *had* been riots, but that did not mean the chaos was endless and ongoing. The issue was perspective: we would be entering a voluble, majority-Black environment, something many of us were un-accustomed to. We were interlopers, our uniforms initially marking us as suspicious. Some people talked smack; some vented at us; some were welcoming; some were quite funny. But *no one* prevented us from doing our job. Most people were appreciative. Absolutely no one physically threatened us. Yet the blanket "safety" decrees lumped the entire crowd (and entire race, frankly) into a troubling category: a possibly dangerous scene caused by an implicitly dangerous people.

There are significant differences between a potentially volatile scene, an actually violent scene, one that is merely chaotic, and one in which people have been injured and bystanders are upset. If we won't approach to assess the situation (before we even reach the injured), we are failing the public. No one in Dispatch was explicitly saying "No-Go Zone": they were operating within a framework of heightened aware-ness and vigilance. It is frustrating and complicated, running face-first into procedural and administrative blanket objections. Again, "safety" as default rationalization, as structural intransigence, code, retaliation.

"*Possibly* unsafe scene" as default = "you people."

I have been stressed every shift, putting myself and my crew in the balance, trusting that most people distinguish between cops and Fire. More important, it is our job to help the public, even and especially when they are upset. And most important, not to lose sight of the truth that the great majority of people had zero interest in messing with any-one: not the police (who were unwelcomed and perceived as menacing intruders but not attacked), not paramedics, and certainly not us, the MFD crews. White as I am, no one threatened to hurt me. So many good people were at George Floyd Square: grieving, bonding, sharing, healing. There was amazing community work done. It was not a lawless gangland, not an open-air drug or weapons market. But that was not how the press covered it, not how officialdom depicted it. White fears colored Black grief and hurt as threats—threats to what, our comfort?

Our discomfort—and fear—is figurative, hypothetical, anxiety driven. Black anguish is real, and generations deep. White discomfort is conceptual and indulgent: born of foundational (constitutional, even) protection and unquestioned access to privilege and priority. These are not the same. Yet, in true American style, we continue to value white comfort over actual Black lives.

On medical calls following the upheaval, we wandered into the crowds, moving calmly but with purpose, scanning for victims, for helpers, for antagonists. I would report the scene was safe, call for medics, and try to keep things calm and stable before the police entered. We assessed and treated people, knowing that until the stretcher or ambulance arrived, we were simply holding steady (and for many of the noncritical calls, that was enough). We waited a *long* time for the medics on many calls. That was a helpless, crappy feeling. In the first weeks, the crowds were agitated, and many individuals were upset. Rumors and counter-rumors about police actions kept tensions high. In the night, our fire truck's lights and sirens were indistinguishable from a convoy of police or military vehicles arriving to bust up the memorial. Moving purposefully through the crowd those first weeks, I'd catch some guff, a few hotheads yelling indiscriminately: "Y'all ain't doing shit!" "Racists! You don't care!" "Look at them: they're *walking!* They don't care if we die!" "You're all cops! Fuck the police!"

Not only is there no point arguing with upset people; trying to explain just wasted time and would get us nowhere—because what was upsetting them was something far bigger than whatever the incident was. I've caught this same guff working in crowds Northside over the years. This is all part of the larger system, wheels upon wheels. Yes, we were not the enemy. And yes, we represented the system that felt oppressive. And yes, I reassured my crew we were safe and there was no reason to stage out of abstract "safety" concerns.

But there definitely was tension. I believed it was not threatening, just uncomfortable. And that was true. But I couldn't claim there was no risk.

Because it only takes one asshole with a gun or a brick to ruin everyone's day.

If someone popped off and attacked us, I would be accountable. I would have failed my crew. I am fortunate to work with good-hearted, engaged people. But that weight was real, and on the calls where random people jumped in our faces and berated us, I felt that tension deeply.

//

So, my response to "How *are* you? It must be so scary" derives from a far different context than what the person imagines. My experiences and perspective do not readily translate. That is part of this job, the weight I carry with me.

I am not scared of Black people—but I know we are not immune to random bullets falling from the sky. I am not worried about BLM "militants" attacking us as we fight a fire: those are the hobgoblins of fragile white minds. I am far more worried about white racist violence than any Black attackers. BLM did not start riots. BLM is not racist against whites (still not a real thing). BLM is not burning down the cities. BLM has not killed cops.

Throughout the month of June, as we were confronted with the grotesque wreckage of south Minneapolis's commercial scaffolding, the specter of dirty bombs, brick-and-bottle-tossing punks, targeted arsons, even snipers, was more weight and worry for us while focusing on our regular emergency calls.

Because people continued to fall down, get sick and hurt, be old, get depressed, commit suicide, drink too much, OD, struggle in myriad ways with mental illnesses (treated and untreated). And Covid was still out there, unseen, and (depending on who was speaking) either pervasive or a myth—much like racism.

We had been battling Covid and its deniers since March. And once the riots and fires subsided in early June, we still had Covid and its deniers, plus the upheaval of long-entrenched racial patterns and inequalities. (In chapter 11, I identify the audacious hypocrisy of the white anti-mask protesters, who took up arms and menacingly—and without fear of being shot—flaunted their weapons at state houses and governors' homes: the performative protest of whites angry about sports bars being closed co-opting the righteous language of racial justice marches. It was All Lives Matter: appropriating a deep issue and undermining it with petty glibness.)

We come to work to help sick and hurt and scared people, do the right thing for the citizens, figure out what the right thing even is. We reassure our families we are safe, we are taking precautions, that the people on the street tell us, "We've got no beef with y'all. There's no song called 'Fuck the Fire Department'!"

Human denial and our obscenely mucked-up social systems mean I spend my career running face-first into abject tragedy and suffering. I show up and often I am helpless to do anything but witness and put my hands to the sick, suffering, dying, and dead. With America's racial sickness, I worry about our failures of communication, of rational thought, of imagination, of humanity. I have nothing but my worries.

Interregnum? Rebirth? Nope: Same Old Shit

> *The after times characterize what was before and what is coming into view. On one level, it is the interregnum surrounded by the ghosts of the dying moment, and on another, the moment that is desperately trying to be born with the lie wrapped around its neck.*
>
> —Eddie Glaude Jr., *Begin Again*

May 2021, Minneapolis: Justice?

The trial of Derek Chauvin for killing George Floyd revealed the disconnect between legal maneuvers and real life. The verdict was never a sure thing. For once, the Black person did not get thrown beneath the wheels of the state's machinations. At least the jury did not overlook the video evidence. At least they managed to hold an officer accountable for an extralegal killing. At least the city did not burn down.

But: Justice?

Just us, *still here.*

Meanwhile, the city of Minneapolis was turned into a military fortress for the trial: battened down, cleared out, heavily surveilled. Who, it might be fair to wonder, did the authorities think was coming? What rough-hewn beast was slouching down the Hennepin Avenue of our collective mind?

Fear of a Black Planet remains the top-tier hysteria of white America. I humored myself that, possibly, there were upper-echelon intel officers who knew the realities of the earlier uprising, after the police killed Mr. Floyd: that far more damage was caused by white agitators, by white supremacists looking to undermine the movement, that this trial was a good opportunity for those people clamoring for a race war to strike the match.

Did we hear any of that in the discussions? Nope. It's as if the authorities presumed Chauvin would get off and the city would erupt in righteous fury—that he was guilty but untouchable, because our system had yet to hold an officer accountable for killing a nonwhite person. The authorities could only envision out-of-control, violent, destructive Black people—despite four-hundred-plus years of forbearance and patience (and ruthlessly violent socialization). Despite the significant role of white agitators on left and right. There was no Plan B, neither for a guilty verdict nor for the potential of white supremacist interlopers.

The aftermath of the guilty verdict was stunned and anticlimactic around the Government Center in downtown Minneapolis: an eerie absence of protest. Across the city, there was rejoicing and celebration, but no riot, no arson, no mayhem. The state packed up its Jersey barriers, the spools of barbed wire, the battalions of soldiers, and *poof!* All gone.

July 2021, St. Paul: The Waiting Room

> *Panic ensues when crises reveal the truth, because we are snatched from our fantasies and forced to confront who we really are.*
> *We evade historical wounds, the individual pain, and the lasting effects of it all.*
> —Eddie Glaude Jr., *Begin Again*

I'm writing in the dense, humid wildfire-smoke mists of July 2021. The sky looks apocalyptic, orange-hued and clotted with toxic particulates, yet it is midmorning in St. Paul. The West is burning. It is difficult to have faith in much of our secular system. I carry the stress as I work, trying to maintain the stolid and steady, while my mind wanders, worries, and waits. I try to partition the stress while I edit this book, which, given the material, is a losing game. I am trapped in a holding pattern, waiting.

Waiting for the next wave or waves or inundations of Covid infections.

Yes, it happened. Delta. Omicron. Ad infinitum.

Waiting for the next extralegal police killing of an unarmed Black citizen.

Yes, it happened. Several times.

Waiting for the politicians and powers that be to goat-fuck their every opportunity to make substantive and systemic change.

Yes, they continued to goat-fuck everything.

Waiting for my crew, or my coworkers, to get caught in crossfire by idiots who shoot at random.

Not yet, fortunately.

Waiting for us to respond, yet again, to the aftermath of another stolen car joyride gone tragic. Another child shot by an errant bullet from the gun of a wayward youth. Another protest against a system that does not see how structurally screwed it is—and cares for little but the bottom line and good optics. Another spasmodic riotous arson binge.

All of which, sadly, exhaustingly, predictably, happened.

Waiting for some added personal tragedy to underscore any of our usual traumatic calls.

Waiting, as a family, to see how, when, *if* my daughter's autoimmune disease will be considered stable—or if there will be a near-deadly reversal that will tell her *This is how it is, and will be.*

I tell myself, *Don't worry about what you cannot control. About what isn't here. It will come, if and when it comes. Breathe.* As my D.C. idols Fugazi sing, "I am a patient boy. / I wait, I wait, I wait, I wait. / My time, water down a drain. // Everybody's moving / Everybody's moving . . . / Please don't leave me to remain."

I feel a constant mass of stress, not heavy as much as turbulent and smothering, wrecking my insides (inner peace, inner space, intestines, soul, brain, heart). I am aware that my waking hours are spent with this gurgling tension active inside me.

Breathe.

I wait, I wait, I wait, I wait.

The weight of the wait is straight crushing me.

I recognized (finally) that what I've been carrying for over a year is not the usual weight of life. It is all of these things, of course: issues of family, of work, of middle age, of declining parents. These aren't unmanageable even as they are heavy at times.

And it was not strictly the worries about Covid that any of us who aren't deniers wrestle with, nor was it the abstract concern about America's tawdry racial legacy.

I recognized (again: *finally*) that I am worried sick we *will* catch the next killing of an unarmed Black person by police, that we *will* have to work amid the anguished and angry people yet again, our uniforms signaling connection if not allegiance to the brutalizing cops. And, because I have responded to previous police killings before Mr. Floyd, I am not being figurative. It is not subjunctive but future tense: *will*, not *might*.

I am terrified our crew will respond to a call that kicks off the next, angrier explosion.

That is what I'm carrying, what I am struggling with: witnessing America refuse to change, watching it continue to ignore its demented essential machinery, and then responding to the avoidable tragedies when, yet again, the predictable horrors are committed.

I know well-meaning people, optimists (white folks, clearly), want to declare that things improved in the aftermath of Mr. Floyd's killing and the riots. That the guilty verdict signified a new era, a better system. I feel worse for their naïveté, frankly. "Sure," I say. "Isn't it pretty to think so?" I mutter to myself. *Signifying nothing.*

What have we learned in a year? Just outside the city limits, Daunte Wright was "accidentally" killed by a police officer during a traffic stop in April 2021. Just two months later, Winston Smith was shot to death by U.S. marshals serving a warrant in the Uptown area of Minneapolis. In February 2022, an MPD SWAT team member shot and killed Amir Locke while serving a warrant that was not for Locke's arrest. The mayor and police chief misspoke (lied) about the circumstances. Our city has not forced any substantive review or changes on the police department; the MPD won't police itself. The mayor, who ran for reelection on a "strong Mayor to control the PD" claim, looks stunned and hapless at each press conference. The American cycle of same old, same old.

I need to get this published before the list of next-killed Black men spills off the page.

//

If the police have not reformed themselves, and the city has not enforced any substantive changes, I worry the true lesson will be that, next time, the crowd must do *whatever* necessary to stop the police from killing an unarmed man. How long will the people remain on the sidewalk while police violate the peace in front of them? The final word—the last option—of Langston Hughes's "Dream Deferred" poem is *explode*. It's a logical eventuality, since being polite, asking and begging, even yelling, did nothing to prevent the police from killing Mr. Floyd. That sickening powerlessness haunts me.

I have also worried a police officer would be shot by some jerk in a crowd, undermining all the efforts of the peaceful and engaged activists (no matter how endlessly futile these peaceful efforts have been, falling on indifferent or mendacious or stony-hearted authorities). I worried then about the blowback and subsequent counterviolence. About the hysterical and the furious self-righteousness of all the white people whose resentment and racial animus had been suspended from public expression in the overwhelming violence and injustice of Mr. Floyd's killing. We've seen small-scale versions of this already, the *I feel bad about that man, but looting and burning? No. That is unacceptable!*

Since early June 2020, I have spent each shift anticipating, or trying not to worry about, a call that would cause the city to erupt: the next extralegal police killing, the next white supremacist shooting into a crowd, the next fatal misunderstanding. I was waiting for the levee to break, the storm clouds to open, the rotten sun-broiled raisin to explode.

Because I could still feel the panic in the crowds, and the anguish and anger and fear, from the year before. This is visceral for me, for us. It is lived experience. My crew members, my coworkers: we are hurting. When we discuss the "trauma" of this work, the sight of a dead body is low on the scale of upsetting things.

The breaking point has felt endlessly imminent. Which call will send everyone into the streets? And there we'd be: staged a block away while someone bled out on the ground, while police stepped over a body in the performance of their investigative duties, exacerbating both tensions and damage. "Engine 17, stage for Code 4 by police" puts us on ice, and *we wait, we wait, we wait.* Outside the rig, on the street, lifeblood drips away and the bystanders are traumatized doubly. And when we, finally, respond to the corpse who was not long before a person, we are useless, we are an insult to the public welfare, we are emblematic of a racially unjust system. And then, someone in that crowd of anguished witnesses might (finally) take aim at us.

That was the specter choking my subconsciousness.

I carry the tension of willing peace to hold; of putting myself between the authorities and the people on the streets; of using us, my crew—myself—as ante in the pot for human connection. People are angry, scared, reactive, shortsighted. I try to explain, to translate. Who am *I* to dare? This tension weighs heavily on me. Only recently have I been able to recognize it for what it is, was, has been. When I wrote the beginning of this essay in the summer of 2020, I couldn't fathom how little would change, and how much stress that would cause.

//

What has been learned or changed? On the MPD level, the Fire Department level, the city council or mayor's office, the judicial system? Have we done or examined anything to concretely prevent the next fires?

I am haunted by Mr. Floyd's death. I am more haunted by the system that killed him. I know, because our history proves it ad nauseam, that this would have been just another by-product of American policing had the video not surfaced. We haven't even acknowledged the existence of the system that crushed him: not the "lone rogue cop" but the entire machine, carceral and police state and legal in/justice.

Had there been no riots, the process would have played out along familiar lines, and according to precedent.

The death of nuance serves us poorly. It is hard to walk amid the smothering heat, the blistering smoke haze, see the evaporating Mississippi River and the drying-up ponds, watch the news, witness my fellow humans act like shitheads, and not despair. Again: it is something out of Beckett.

Are we really so incapable of seeing the truth despite our conditioned flaws? *Sits down and watches one hundred hours of YouTube footage of police officers not shooting armed and threatening white men, while blowing away dozens of unarmed, nonthreatening Black men—and remaining unprosecuted. Sighs. Throws himself off a building.* A hashtag brings no one back.

17
ORPHANS

I WAS ON SHIFT ON SEPTEMBER 11, 2001. THE FALLING TOWERS DID NOT REACH south Minneapolis, and I spent the day transfixed like much of the world, staring at the television. I was with two crews of guys who had never been to New York City, who had no idea the scope of what had happened. I worried about friends of mine in the city. It was a heavy, shocking day. I got off shift and went home, looking to hold Annie (whose birthday, September 12, had a definite pall cast over it) and snuggle baby Flann. As I got out of my car, I said hello to the neighbor across the street. He was walking from his car to his house, as well. We weren't close, but, you know, America had just been attacked. Human contact was at a premium. "How're you doing?" I asked. He stopped and looked at me, blank and lost. Before I even finished the thought that he was taking it harder than I was—and I'd spent the day with fireguys who both second-guessed FDNY's actions with the sublimely stupid confidence of people who have never seen a one-hundred-story building, while also fighting furiously to suppress the raw terror of what those New York guys had experienced—he gestured vaguely. Not toward the eerily blue sky, as I expected, but at the car, then their house. *She's gone. She's—she died. Yesterday.*

His wife had been sick with cancer. We were not close. I had no idea how ill she was. *I'm sorry. I'm so sorry.* He stared some more then walked inside. I didn't remember his name. The poor guy's wife died on 9/11. His grief was enormous, and specific. It wasn't the flash of the planes striking the towers, or the jet fuel immolating the damaged floors, or the surreal collapse. No. His wife died of cancer, died in a hospital bed with him by her side. He likely watched the television coverage as she slipped away. Every TV in every room, every channel, every doctor, nurse,

315

orderly, every family: everyone focused on the same unthinkable monstrosity. It was inescapable. He now faced the aftermath of the attacks and her death, alone: walking alone out of the hospital, driving home alone, walking up the steps alone, entering the empty house, alone. Her death eclipsed by the myopic national panic and grief of the terrorist attacks. What room would there be for his sorrow?

The world spins on. It always does. Your heart is broken, and someone is mad about a lunch order. Your wife dies, and your boss still needs the report by Monday. People got sick and died unrelated to the racial justice unrest. People died from things other than Covid. We went to work and responded to the panorama of human experience, as is our charge, as we do.

//

Shortly after shift change one morning—I don't remember when specifically, but early winter; before Covid, since we had no masks, but after 2017, since I was back at 17s; the years blur—we were called to "one unresponsive" a couple of blocks east of the station. We arrived within two minutes, entered the house, and directly encountered the patient. It was an overnight cardiac, a dead man hunched between the recliner and coffee table. He was a young Black man in a T-shirt and shorts. No blood, no mess, no drug gear or pills, no signs of a fight. His skin did not yet show pooling or lividity, but it was cool to the touch, and his limbs were tight with encroaching rigor mortis. Directly to the left, about seven feet away, was an infant bouncing and laughing in a baby-jumper hung between the dining and living rooms. As we confirmed the man was pulseless, without respirations, cold, and stiff (dead and unworkable), a little boy zipped across the room, jumped onto the chair's thick arm. We all flinched, reflexively tried to stop him, then froze as he threw his arms around his dad's bare shoulders. The kid was too fast.

He hugged the dead man and then jumped down and looked at all of us. "Who are you?" he asked.

The man's wife was standing in the middle of the room. She looked at her husband, looked away, looked back, shook her head, searching frantically—for nothing and everything, seeking something safe, solid, real. Not this. She was tall, with striking green eyes clouded with pain and panic. There was no answer on the couch and nowhere to turn.

We all felt the horrific imperative of her two young children. She kept saying, "No, no, no, no," her voice rising and croaking in a strangled cry. She didn't want to upset the kids. Yet it was inescapable—to me, and my crew—the crushing truth that her two young children were fatherless. Their dad's corpse, halfway off the easy chair, was undeniable. Thanksgiving was a week away. This family's holidays, their future, were marred. Infinitely, indefinitely. This was the start of their new life, the death of the husband-father.

I told the crew to take our gear back to the rig and then return. We would be staying on scene a while.

These situations offer a strange limbo, an awkward foreknowledge. We *know* what we are seeing, what it means. We are waiting for the survivors to grasp this new truth. It sucks. I touched the woman's arm and asked if she needed to call anyone. She stared at me, then shook her head, then nodded. She was clutching her phone still, the 911 dispatcher still giving prearrival instructions, muffled in her palm. I took the phone from her, told Dispatch we were there, and hung up. I grasped her shoulder calmly. I peered up into her face, forcing eye contact. "I'm so very sorry. I am sorry this has happened to you all." I put the phone back into her hand. "Several things will occur in the next hour or so, and I will explain what they are. First, is there anyone you can call? Anyone you want to tell? Family? Someone to help with the kids?"

She started at the word, glanced around for them, pulled the boy to her. He twisted and squirmed out of her embrace, hurtled over the table, and knelt beside the jumpy seat, bouncing his little brother. The boys looked like replicas of each other, one five and the other about a year, but stamped from the same mold. The woman's face contorted, desperation interwoven with grief.

"Is there anywhere we can go right now, to talk?" I asked, guiding her away from the couch. It was a tiny house; the small galley kitchen opened onto the living and dining rooms. Not there. Two small bedrooms beside the lone bathroom just off the kitchen. No real space for privacy. "Let's go in here, yes?" I asked. She whispered the boy's name and as he rushed to her, grabbing her hip, they went into his bedroom.

I stood by the door to the room, shielding their view of the corpse, the dead man, their husband-father. The woman stared at her phone, shaking. "Ma'am?" She looked up emptily. "My name is Jeremy. What's your name?"

She stared at me, mouth forming letters.

"It's all right," I said.

"Amina."

(A reminder that everything depicted has happened, and none of it being recounted here violates the private experiences of any living or dead person. There is no "Amina." There have been many sudden widows.)

"I'm so sorry to meet you like this, Amina. Let's take some breaths. In, nice and slow. Hold it. Out slow and easy. Good, good. Again." She stiffly complied. Her son climbed into her lap, trying to wipe away her tears. I guided her through some breathing exercises. The boy thought it was funny and mimicked her.

"Good job, Amina. Keep breathing. It will help you think." I had no solutions. Nothing for the short or the long term. There are none, just live through it. There was also no real hurry, sadly. She could call whomever, or she could sit with her son in her lap and cry. Either way, her husband was dead. She had eternity now, without him. Our end of things, the official process, was in motion.

I leaned back to check on the infant, who continued to bounce and gurgle. The medics arrived and I briefed them. The woman started speaking into her phone, gasping bursts of sorrow. It was family, I could tell. These calls sound alike. The gutted staccato spurts: "It's [husband]. . . . He's gone. Yes, dead. . . . He died last night! . . . Come here. . . . Yes. Right now. No. Yes. Yes! They're here now. No. They said he's gone. He's gone! Come now."

Even though the medics were cleared, they stayed too. The tragic contrast of the little tyke bouncing happily in front of his dead dad struck us all. One medic went into the room to talk to the mother; the other medic and I gave the deceased a more thorough examination. My first check had shown no signs of struggle, violence, or self-harm. But I'd also been processing the kids and the shocked wife. Whether an OD, suicide, or natural causes, it was essentially irrelevant. But, still, we have to check, and I didn't want anything sharp sticking out to cut anyone, if that were the case.

The police squad arrived. The medics left and my crew remained.

The officers needed official information and tried to speak with the mom while she managed a flurry of incoming calls. The boy stared up at them, half hiding in his mom's loose nightshirt. The room was cramped. It was early winter and fairly cold. They couldn't step outside to interview her. We didn't want the boy to see his dad—let alone climb on him—and it was too far below freezing to distract him by playing in the yard or exploring our rig. The baby started fussing a little, and the woman went to him, followed by the officers.

My durgan and I remained in the room with the boy. About the best option we could manage was to act as the world's most awkward babysitters while the police spoke with the mom in the small dining room and little brother bounced, bounced, bounced suspended in the doorway. Behind them, the man remained dead between two pieces of furniture.

The boy sat shyly on his bed, looking down. He started snuffling, not quite crying. We bent down and comforted him. He was in shock. Or, no, I realized: not even shock. This was beyond his comprehension. The word *dead* is an abstraction to a kindergartener. His dad was still at home, he just wasn't moving. We stayed with the boy. He sat back against the wall and stared at us. I asked if he was all right. He shrugged. *Poor little dude,* I kept thinking.

We stood, or knelt, beside him, struggling to make small talk. Everything seemed irrelevant or too loaded. The voices in the next room flowed to us, the woman's bursts of weeping or crying out, the officers' steady responses. The boy started each time his mother wailed for her husband. My durgan tried asking questions about the posters on the walls, the constellations painted on the ceiling. The boy would answer vaguely then trail off. They had a sweet house, nice personal touches, good artistic flourishes. This was a warm home, the love and purpose apparent everywhere. I couldn't tell if this comforted or disturbed me, considering the desolate places we generally find ourselves. We kept trying: to engage, distract, block out the pain from the front room.

The boy was silent, pulling on his fingers. I knelt beside him and said, "I lost my mom when I was a little kid. I was even younger than you. My sister, she was a baby just like your brother. Our mom died. It's really hard. But, you know, I guess the clichés aren't wrong. Life goes on. Here I am. You'll be all right. You will."

My crew member gaped, peering with horror at me over the kid's head: *What the fuck?!* I shrugged. This kid is caught on profound currents, things he knows nothing about. His dad is stiff in the living room. What will he remember later, or tomorrow, or next month, or forever? Worrying about whether my abstract analogies would confuse him was as useless as giving him my turnouts to wear. *You're the man of the house now, son.* Ugh.

I asked the boy how he felt. He also shrugged, his eyes searching the room. He suddenly sprung forward and grabbed something from a pile on the floor. "Look!" he said, triumphantly holding an action figure aloft.

"Cool," we said, loudly and with maniac enthusiasm—anything to stop talking, and not talking, about his dead dad. "Spider Man is rad," I gushed.

The boy and my durgan both said, "No, it's the Black Panther! T'challa," as if I were the most oblivious person in the world. *How could you not know that?!* "Sorry," I said. "I've got daughters—and they're older."

The boy looked at me oddly, pondering the notion that I was an actual person, with kids even, not just a stranger in a uniform. He hoisted his action figure and launched into that excited nonstop blast of narration, explanation, imaginative thinking. "Wait," he interrupted himself, then rushed past us into the main room. My durgan looked at me again. *What the fuck?* was a sufficient encapsulation of the scene. The boy sped back into the room and triumphantly presented me with two action figures. One, Black Panther; the other, Iron Man. "Cool!" I said again. "But, really, I wasn't totally wrong. I mean, they're all in the same franchise."

The boy looked at the heroes in his hands. My crew member stared at me. "Really?" he asked. "You're splitting hairs, arguing with the kid? Now, here? Really?"

"It's not like I called him Batman, right?"

We both laughed, then talked superheroes with the boy. He wanted to show us something else and rushed again back to the room where his dead father, grieving mother, and bouncing brother were. "Do we, like, stop him, or something?" my durgan asked, rhetorically more than practically.

I shrugged. "It's his house. Putting hands on him might freak him out—stranger danger and whatnot. He's doing all right. We can only do so much to distract him." We looked into the living room, where the boy searched around the table, nearly ignoring his dad's body, then rushed between the police to his mom and pulled her down to loud-whisper into her ear. He wanted to bring his baby brother into the room to show us how they play Black Panther. The mother smiled a broken grin and told him to wait a few minutes. My heart kicked me in the throat.

We heard car doors slamming in the street, feet rushing on the walk, and then three or four people burst into the room, crying out at the sight of the dead man, enveloping the woman in loving hugs, sweeping the boy into their circle. With family present, we were redundant and conspicuous. "I'm so very sorry" always feels a woefully insufficient leave-taking.

//

Back at the station, we discussed the bummer of it all. I wondered how the woman would remember the immediate minutes after finding her husband. What would her memories be of objective and practical details? What sticks amid, or despite, the shock and grief? I thought of that small, sad family the following week, on Thanksgiving, and then leading up to and through Christmas. The boy, his mom, the baby, their fractured lives.

Neither of my crew members that day had children. They had no real sense of how kids process, what they grasp, what filters in or out. What would the boy remember later? His sibling would bounce and laugh, cry and eat, nap and soil his diapers, in the simple yet essential routine of infancy. He would never *know* his father; he would hear a name, see a few photos, some video of him not-yet-born, a bump inside his mother perhaps. Their memory lane ended that morning, with the baby too young to walk yet. But my little buddy: what would he remember? He was a bit older than I was when my mom died. Time in illness and death is quite relative. The man died suddenly overnight. My mom's cancer "journey" lasted under four weeks from diagnosis to death. Annie's dad's journey was the time it took to put the shotgun to his head and pull the trigger. We all lost a parent. The big-picture hairsplitting about death matters very little to the orphaned kids.

I have no solid memories of my mom's sickness, of seeing her die, of her funeral, of the aftermath, though I was there for all of it. I've been told I ran up to every woman who entered our house over the next two years (whether babysitter or date for my dad) and demanded, "Are you my new mom?" My sister was five months old when our mother died. She has no memories at all. The sparse few I retain are largely tales I've told myself, animations of photos I've found squirreled away. The 1969 professional advice our father got: *Move on, don't dwell. Kids are resilient. They won't remember her.* He took it quite literally. I was eighteen when he first asked if I had any questions about her.

I was and am absolutely empathetic for the bereft mother, for the implications of her loss. And I'm aware, having stood before dozens (hundreds, likely) of suddenly widowed humans, that the world had cracked open and swallowed her. In her grief, she was shell-shocked, literally, incoherent and uncomprehending. That she was unaware of her son climbing on her dead husband, not cognizant that she was still in her nightshirt and holding her toothbrush. She kept muttering that they had argued last night, and he had gone to sleep in his recliner. Now she will blame herself, forever. *I killed him. If we hadn't fought, he wouldn't have died.* It is not true, but truth holds no power over feelings like that.

In this short, shocked period, she was oblivious—she needed some guidance and direction to function in the fog of loss. I stood with the bereaved woman, allowed her to be lost, provided help where I could, and I also thought of their future. Hers was a scramble, a chasm of heartbreak and brutal logistical hell. The weight a now-widowed parent must pull: micro details and existential riddles simultaneously. This isn't a cold that one hunkers down and recovers from: this is a life sentence. Brutal, jagged, heart-rent life.

The boys, though.

I wrote at the outset that my bumpy childhood likely shaped my worldview. This job has reinforced and broadened it. I see myself in every orphaned kid we encounter. I scrutinize their unknowing, their lostness; I extrapolate my own path. The days, the months, the years; the unlived lives, the unfulfilled promises. The absence, the haunting absence. We swear our village will look after each orphan, but life gets in the way. I want to fight for the kids, offer them what too many adults failed to give my sister and me. We grew up knowing nothing of our mom. Her friends did not talk about her around us for fear it would *upset* us (or, not us as much as the tenuous equilibrium of a family reconfigured, the self-evident absence of the dead mother). Their collective silence was not malicious, but, because of good intentions and social niceties, they failed to help us in ways only they could.

Mary Oliver describes it strikingly in her essay "Staying Alive":

> Adults can change their circumstances; children cannot. Children are powerless, and in difficult situations they are the victims of every sorrow and mischance and rage around them, for children feel all of these things but without any of the ability that adults have to change them. Whatever can take a child beyond such circumstances, therefore, is an alleviation and a blessing.

I concur. I also, at this point, have witnessed enough of these heartbreaking situations that I see the uselessness of tactful reserve—it seems something that comforts the awkward witness, not the grieving person. I have almost no filter and am shit with small talk. So, I try to puncture that crushing quiet in the few minutes we spend together, asking questions, allowing the bereaved to open up. Talking about the deceased person won't make them any more dead, and "sparing the feelings" of the grief-stricken survivor is just selfish comfort.

The primary reason I remained in Chattanooga after my first year teaching was because my dear friends Paco and Ann Watkins had a baby. I was there through the pregnancy, the birth (not literally: I took care of their dog while Ann did the work), baby Patton's earliest weeks, months, then his first three years. I wanted to see—needed to fathom— what he saw as he approached the age I was when my mother died. I looked at the world through his eyes, watched how and what he perceived and clung to. I understand now, of course, that all those hours of playtime, of reading, of imbibing the world around him, might be scant slices of recollection for him—at best. I am nothing but a name his parents might fondly mention, part of a tale he was present for but has no memory of. But it shaped his life and papered his growing mind. Judy died when I was pushing three, the height of mother–child (son) attachment, the cusp of the Oedipal journey (for those who believe). By all accounts, Judy was smitten with me. I was a much-loved, swell baby. In some ways, my preposterous sense of self was forged then. And then she died.

Mary Gordon writes in *The Company of Women*: "A fatherless girl thinks all things are possible, and nothing is safe." I'd argue that works across gender and parent. Losing my mother warped my sense of a safe world. If we consider Piaget's developmental stages, losing my mom at stage six of Object Permanence was a profound mind (and heart) fuck. Is it any wonder I expect that everyone will die, that no one will come back? My default worry is that the worst *will* happen. Yet this job has provided profound context: life is a path of loss, sadness, doubt. These aren't exceptions, nor unfair attacks. All of these punctuate and emphasize our love, laughter, lightness.

Factor in systemic and generational issues, health and welfare challenges, and some families lose far more than their "fair" share. Our crews respond to such folks, for whom the single traumatizing death might be stacked in a heap of losses. They lose one family member, then another, and another. We might walk into someone grieving their fourth dead immediate relative or distraught over what seems like a routine cold. It isn't an abstract worry but the brutal truth, their reality. And when we respond to folks having "dysfunctional" or "hysterical" reactions to seemingly small events, if we can't fathom what might be behind their worries, we dismiss and misserve them.

//

My sister and I lost our mom before we knew her. That marked us, shaped our paths and our narratives. My aunt Linds lost her big sister, the rock of their family, when she was twenty. A year later, she lost her mother. And then she lost her brother a couple of years after that. A grandmother and an uncle I never got to know, in addition to my mom. These are entirely different scales of loss. Of heartbreak. Concrete loss of family is different from being orphaned, left bereft of the person and the symbol. We lost our future, Linds lost her frames of reference: the connections to past, to self, to memory, to blood. It isn't a competition, who has lost more. And it's good to remember that many people suffer profoundly and keep on living heartily.

Linds told me some years back, "You know, it's too bad Judy died—well, for a bunch of reasons . . . *Obviously*." (We both chuckled mordantly.)

"But," she continued, "I'm thinking specifically that it would have been interesting to see how she turned out. She loved you, loved being your mom, but I don't know that she would have been satisfied as a full-time mother. And then what? That's what is so sad. The paradox was that she was fierce and independent, yet held horribly regressive—or, typically traditional, for the sixties—views about women staying out of the workplace. She might have become someone radically progressive or she might have curdled into a D.C. Junior League Stepford Wife. And we'll never know. It remains a mystery."

And that was interesting, because for the decades I had not known my mom as anything but a mythic absence, a saintly ghost. I presumed that she was all-good, all-loving, grounded, centered, clear-eyed, virtuous—*perfect*. I had one small photo of her that I hoarded and hid away growing up: we were forever a two-by-two-inch faded color snapshot. Our brief lives together reduced to that one moment (one I had no real memory of). The notion of her actual human flaws was inconsistent with the hagiographic fantasy I'd constructed, having nothing else to go on.

Also, the specter of a non-awesome mother was startling. *Of course, she would have been perfect. It was nothing but a tragedy that we had been deprived of her boundless embrace and wonderful cookies.* But: I have no idea if she could bake or even liked children. To consider she might have been crazy, or a bully, or some phony society matron—not out of the realm of the possible, given her upbringing and proclivities—was jarring.

Wait, I thought. *I don't have anything to go on, so let me at least pretend she was perfect. Give me that.* Which is unfair to her siblings, of course. They knew and experienced her temper, whims, flaws. And my dad, too. Maybe they were an unhappy couple, or he felt bossed around by her, or they hated each other's taste in music? But, with her long dead at such a young age, we will never know. And that is its own shame.

Annie's dad was a suicide. He was a sorcerer: compelling and seductive, and also darkly manipulative and abusive. The suicide of a father, the deliberate abandonment by a parent: that eclipses anything else—for years if not lifetimes. As long as I've known her, she's grasped at his shadow—*If only I'd been more—if I'd been less—if if if, he wouldn't have killed himself. He was everything to me (and he was abusive).* The hole in the heart and mind cannot be filled. Reason cannot touch this void.

I'm not suggesting that anyone would be better off with their parent dead. I'm saying that with these deaths, we never get to see anyone grow older, fix their wrongs, or simply fail to be better. We (they) are spared disappointment but deprived of redemption.

But we are also deprived the other universes of Schrödinger's cat box. Yes, it's a god-awful tragedy that Billy and Susie never knew their parents. And we tell ourselves that everything would have been great. But, looking at the rest of us flailing through our own not-dead lives, we *must* consider that, maybe, John would have flaked out on you, or cheated, or abused someone. Maybe Jenny resented the trappings and trap of domesticity and would have cut out, or become a drunk, or a shopaholic. "Regular" relationships curdle and fail; domestic resentment and misery abound. We will never know how things might have turned out. And that, of course, is the crime, the shame, the tragedy. We never get to see our beloveds, our parents, our kin have the opportunities to grow, fail, recover, live.

I think of that when I see orphaned kids in the aftermath of a parent's death: how brutally their lives are being altered, but also the fact that it might be years before anyone suggests or considers that the dead parent had feet of clay. Too, the surviving parent must shoulder the weight, the worry, the guilt—all of it—for the absent parent. The ghost expands to fill the hearts, minds, and lives of the bereft. The orphans always seek that dead mom or dad, while the surviving parent keeps plugging along, often sacrificing their own grief and hurt, anger and loneliness, to protect the kids. That is the essence of parenting. No matter what, the survivor will fail the one thing the kid demands: to bring the dead parent back to life.

When people now imprint their memories and the images of their deceased in the amber of social media, it provides a far better, more concrete repository of memory and tactile connection, a virtual footprint. Kids can google their dead parents, for better *and* worse. And our society recognizes that utter silence about the dead doesn't help the kids. Advances in psychology have shown that *Get over it. Move forward!* is not an effective grieving tool.

My affinity and allegiance are with the young kids, of course. But the ways their lives are marked will be revealed over time. *Tomorrow and tomorrow and tomorrow.* There will be time for such a word (provided someone has the guts to speak it). But those who are widowed: thrown naked and shivering into a harsh, hostile landscape, hearts ravaged, futures obliterated, children to be fed and consoled. In these moments, this immediate chaos, what actually matters? What can any of us do for them? I pragmatically considered that devastated mother and my interactions with her. I'd be curious what *her* perspective was on our time together. I expect I am nothing but a blur, if even that. But maybe my manner or tone was too brusque? Or she mistook my help for egregious condescension? Maybe we did her a kindness, distracting the boy and stalling as she began to wrap her head around the fractured family. Or maybe I was simply another anonymous official peering into her cavern of grief. I certainly embodied the official death of her husband: I wouldn't blame her. My feelings are irrelevant, but I will stand before a new widow again. If I can learn better ways to be of use, to help someone when they most need it, I want to know that.

Propriety is often useless in emergency situations. But respect and compassion are essential. We see the naked and the dead where they lie, and if we are squeamish or cowed by propriety, we fail to help when someone needs it. My mom's dying before I could ride a bike savaged my fealty to *proper*. I have little filter, and less use for demure social niceties. But my heart is capacious, and I will look you in the eye and honor your pain and fear and messy humanity. We don't get taught about these esoteric human skills. We trust our guts, or instincts, or previous experiences. Families don't fill out surveys afterward. It may sound awkward, and gloomy, and blunt, but someone else *will* die while I am working, and we will rush into their home and find what we find. With the dead beyond help, we turn to the living.

As Nora McInerny says, "Every single person we know and love will die someday." The challenge for each of us is to learn to be present with the grief and the grieving. Honor the dead and the bereft, be patient and kind, and cut people slack, but don't rewrite history. Allow the dead their full humanity; allow the survivors their measures of grief and gall. As we say at work, *Do right. Be kind.*

For JCR and Linds; for Liza; for Cheri, Annie, Drea, and Aimee; for Nora and Ralph; for Mimi; for all the widows and orphans.

18

TRAUMA SPONGES

The Things We Carry

Even that is typical firefighter exaggeration. I *almost* caught one. As always, the mother and gravity had done all the work, delivering the child moments ahead of our arrival. So, I've yet to *actually* receive a living newborn's descent into this world. This kid was barely minutes old, and the scene was unexpected and wonderful.

What resonated afterward was how happy I felt, jubilant even, for much of the rest of the shift. It was a rare, truly happy call. The mom and dad were present and functional, the baby was healthy and wanted, there were no complications, the medics had been cool and supportive. All went well.

None of this is routine for our OB calls, never remotely a given. This was a bliss fest. Even the presence of six strangers in their birthing room wasn't intrusive. Gratitude and glory all around. Of course, the mom had been up for fifty hours laboring and her postnatal hormones were flooding the Southside . . . But still.

My voice memo from two days later: *Okay, so after eighteen years, I finally caught a baby.* [mumble, chortle] *Ha—I didn't even catch it, just walked into the aftermath. Thing is, it was awesome! So positive and wonderful. So rare for us. It was a healthy baby, full term, wanted by the couple, who were both present. Midwife was on point. Medics arrived, and they weren't dicks. It was a unicorn of a call. It was great. I got newborn-mama-uterus blood all over my sweatshirt and pants, and that's all right. I think I was grinning more than the dad was. Because, well, it's not my kid and I get to leave.*

As I mused on how nice it was, we went about our shift, running the usual spate of calls. We responded to one of our frequent flyers, then, soon after, another one. I was happy to see them both, feeling fondly toward all my fellow humans. As we left the second call, a man whose legs don't work and who drinks a lot—we respond to heft him from wherever he's fallen in their house and carry him back to his wheelchair. His sister is also confined to a wheelchair, and they spend their days watching separate TVs while they drink, arguing or ignoring each other—I felt jovial still. The man had been sober, just low blood sugar, and they were preparing for Thanksgiving with family.

The truth is, with most of our frequent flyers, when we get a respite from seeing them, it's seldom because their health has improved. They've either moved (been moved) to another rental property, where they become a different crew's new frequent flyer, or else their health has declined further until they're institutionalized—or they've died.

There are very few happy endings in this work, even fewer for our chronic 911 users. Our default outlook, shaped by repetition and experience, is that almost every sick person gets worse, and everyone dies. We show up and attempt to resolve people's emergencies, whether chronic or acute, but we aren't solving much. Bandages. Duct tape. Spit and dirt. *Hope is not an action plan.* The futility of responding to help people who cannot or will not help themselves can undermine one's sense of purpose. This creates a tough dynamic: Don't blame a person whose minor complaint brings you out at 2:45 a.m. Someone who keeps eating bad food and complaining of "heart attack" symptoms that continue to be indigestion does not intend to be a waste of time. It's unfair to compare a smoker's shortness of breath with the fatal asthmatic arrest of a twenty-one-year-old you just finished working the call previous. But that is what happens, and we have to address it all, to find (or fake) patience amid the waste and gross negligence.

The standard advice to rookies when I started was "Buck up, kid. Gotta get tough or it'll eat you alive. *They* will eat you alive. All this bad shit, that's on *them*. They ruin their own lives. We pick up the pieces. Job security, baby." The fire service remains a peer-based social environment. I witnessed the cultural values demonstrated and inculcated: posturing and crass indifference, inappropriate and caustic humor, obliviousness to the suffering or feelings of those around us. Vulnerability and sensitivity were coarsely policed by the guys sitting around the table. There is utility in learning to shield ourselves from the rough edges of our work, but there are enough layers to the sociological mix that we ignore, deny, or oversimplify at our peril.

The detachment that allows us not to take things personally also puts thick calluses and blinders on us, until we stop seeing the person in front of us. We become so desensitized we border on indifferent. Refusing to locate the humanity of the people we serve, losing our empathy. It does none of us any good.

Someone reading an early draft of this book wanted to know, "But what did you think about that call? What was *your* response to it?"

What do I think? Sometimes nothing at all. I'm blank to the biological or human carnage before me. It just *is*. Life happens, as does death. The first time you encounter a corpse, it's creepy or fascinating or haunting. When you've seen dozens, then hundreds, it's mostly just work. The fact of the body. The details that stick are either horrific or else grossly inappropriate for general citizenry. I see the natural where most civilians see the unfathomable or tragic. Too, so many people live in denial that their surprise event is often predictable and consistent with their conditions. Biological facts are what they are. *That man died hours ago; he had been dying for several weeks. That woman is drowning in her own fluids; she will keep smoking. You broke your leg: it hurts and it ruined your plans, but it is not fatal—unless you catch an infection at the hospital, but that's not on us. Yes, that driver ran a light and totaled your car. Shitty, but you are alive. Your grandfather was ninety-four; he ran out of breaths, of beats, of time—it is not a tragedy. Honor his long life with love, not denial.* With deaths and family members, I remind myself that it is often someone's first loss. It is often just a corpse to me, nothing more. And yet sometimes I am reliving two decades of similar suffering all at once, a roomful of bloody, howling ghosts—not simply the dead but those who survive.

It's hard to explain pithily. Life is too, too much upon us.

I've tried to express the cumulative and holistic realities of this work. There are many small tragedies, many brutal cases, many horrors. Many are senseless, if predictable or unsurprising. We try not to judge the people we treat, but we also recognize the weight and cost of human foibles and ignorance and malice.

Because if we take personally those who misuse and abuse the 911 system, robbing us of sleep, health, interfering with real emergency work, we become caustic and ugly. If we detach and refuse to involve ourselves, we slide into indifference and disinterest. Damned either way. Scylla and Charybdis for the EMS set. The empathy exams are not graded on a curve: we must be present and ready on every call, or we risk failing when it matters.

//

I have spent a lot of space in this book arguing for more compassion, for emergency workers to use the generative imagination of empathy to see the humans we encounter as not merely problems but the result of complex, generational, systemic sociological dynamics. And I deeply believe that. The reality, however, is that the crews who work in the poorest and most unstable neighborhoods can drown in the suffering of others.

When I worked on Engine 14 on the Northside, we were *busy*. All day and night responding to people for the consequences of accumulated bad health conditions or poor habits, routine and non-emergency calls, long-delayed minor but worsening complaints. People who used the 911 system as personal transport to the ED for non-emergent issues. So many folks with preventable yet ignored health issues. The cycles and the grind. But in between all these calls, which ruined sleep and stole the joy from our minds, we caught the hammer fist of the Northside: violence in more forms than one could count. So much tragic gang violence, with obscene collateral victims, innocents young and old struck down in errant crossfire. And these were kids, scarcely young men, shooting at each other. Dead or jailed before they knew any better. Look at the map of shootings in Minneapolis: Station 14 is right there. These crews catch most of the injuries and deaths. Young and old, gang squabble or random citizen: shot, hurt, dead. Blood and anguish. And then, even more: brutal calls that eclipse the "normal" mayhem everywhere else. Fires caused by negligence, ignorance, malice, or just the usual bad cooking or faulty wiring or lazy smoking. High-speed car wrecks, either from joyrides in stolen vehicles or flights from the police. Abused and neglected children. Abused and savaged dogs. Poverty and despair.

I would return from shift exhausted, burnt, worn down. I would try to convey to Annie what I'd experienced, to illustrate the realities of my work and their lives. Most of the tales were grim, bleak, and sordid. I would forget that what was quotidian to me was foreign and disturbing to civilians, even my wife. One morning, as I was recounting a series of shitty calls, she stopped me. "Hey, you sound kinda racist. Are you aware of that?"

I looked at her as I considered what she said. "How so?"

"You keep telling these horrible stories, and you're making it sound like this is how things are. You sound racist."

I got defensive, I'm sure, my feelings hurt. I responded, "Look, we went to *two* separate homes yesterday for *two* different women who couldn't spell their own adult kids' names. Twice! Names these former teen mothers gave their own sons. Two forty-year-old grandmothers. I've seen nothing but neglected children, homes with big-ass TVs and no light bulbs, never a functional smoke detector—because the damn beeping *bothers* people who keep burning greasy food on their dirty stoves or they needed the nine-volt for the remote for their big-ass TV. They leave a cigarette smoldering on the couch, but instead of the detectors catching it right away, the couch burns, the apartment burns, they lose everything. For what? A whole generation of babies having babies who have babies, and no one has had the time or opportunity to learn a damn thing about life skills—and everyone keeps fucking smoking around their kids, so we keep going to 'asthma' calls for kids who just need a bit less nicotine in their tiny lungs. And then teen boys go out and shoot each other over some perceived slight, and no one will say anything because of a T-shirt slogan about snitching!"

I was nearly shouting. Gritty with sleep dep from every shift for months, my nerves were raw, my tone coarse, my temper short. I saw her point. But I was too raw for white guilt and liberal platitudes. I was responding to the endlessness of these cycles, our futility. Hate the sin, not the sinner; hate the game, not the player: shit like that. Racism was real, and so was neglect. She didn't spend time where I did. It was wholly foreign to her, inconceivable even.

I slowed myself, caught my breath. "It just keeps coming. It is generations deep, and no one can find workable solutions—definitely not at our level. All we do is tend to the aftermath. I am *not* saying, 'This is what all Black people are like.' I don't think, '*This* is Black people.' There are so many very functional Black folks Northside—the majority of the residents. They are way more distressed than I am about their neighbors. But it's not just one or two bad dudes. Hundreds of messed-up people threaten everyone else's well-being. And that's my workspace. That's what we do. This *is* the reality of their lives and my work. Poverty is a motherfucker."

Over time, I've understood what I was trying to do then, and still do now, is share with Annie, and our kids as well, a context, whether the rough outline or some selective details, of my work life. Sharing the tales frees them from my head and heart. It lets them in on where I'm at, or what's eating me. There is so very much I have spared them, years of horrors and disturbing facts and images I reflexively edit and omit. But this context, this tension: I was unconsciously trying to explain to her the frustrating, overwhelming, incessant challenges of working in a rough, poor area.

This was venting, not problem-solving. We were powerless. It was a literal cycle of futility, problems generations in the making. A battered Ferris wheel of misery. Very few of the people we responded to ever had good options. Too few people had steady jobs, health care, stable homes, functional family legacies. Many, many people struggled nobly but they were fucked for fair, too much stacked against them from long before they were born. These were the consequences of our racist, unequal, broken society. We were interlopers, but the depths of the struggles and the hopelessness for resolving the macro or micro level issues could break a person.

Purging this stress, even if I sounded ugly to an outsider, was a healthy way of preventing soul rot and a protective rigidity from creeping in. But it takes constant vigilance to be a margin walker. Many of the old-time Northside crews were calloused, if not outright callous. They came to work with no hope or expectation for anyone's life to improve. Some made no attempts to empathize or understand, to put themselves in anyone else's shoes. They picked their rigs because north Minneapolis is where the fires are, where the action is.

Certainly, many white firefighters did not have racially problematic attitudes, but some did. This slice of the population was their sole exposure to the African American community, and thus, from their experiences at work, they only saw the dysfunctional, the hopeless, and the ruined. Empirically, I could argue about all the good people living in all the homes we did *not* get called to, but that wasn't convincing to many guys. These firefighters' defensive walls were up, they could not—would not—be convinced to empathize with the community outside our station. They did not see the population as fellow humans; there was only *Them.*

This means those race-blinded fireguys missed all the expressions of and opportunities to join in Black joy: the community events, the church BBQs, the block parties, the joyous annual National Night Out. The random backyard parties we stumbled into because someone fell over, we showed up, and we were feted with platters of good food and neighborly interactions. All the people making real efforts, as they have for decades, to create, support, bolster their own community, to help each other. Our job duties expose us overwhelmingly to the hard places and sorrows. If we remain open, we can partake of the joy and humor and resolute spirit of the citizens.

Many more of my coworkers choose to work Northside *because* it is a hard space, *because* people there need us. They are proud to serve the community, to do right by folks who seldom get good breaks. It is an honor to be of use, to contribute, to help people who need it. The adrenaline surges and crazy calls keep everyone amped. In much the way I feel connected to and responsible for the people living in 17's box, especially during the pandemic and after the killing of George Floyd, my coworkers dedicate themselves to the Northside. This focus and dedication enrich the work, provide meaning or resonance. But, for all of us, our noble intentions and genuine efforts to put ourselves into the bad calls and hard scenes do not save us, do not protect us.

The ceaseless overnight runs, the bleak futility of so many calls, the unresolvable poverty, the abject and tragic violence: it crushes your heart. I try to protect some core of myself so that I have heart and mind and spirit for my family, for my crew, for myself—and for the next patients. I would go home and purge the frustrations, the horrific absurdities, and heartbreaks, and I would return the next shift with that small portion of my heart reopened for the kicking.

//

The worst dead-children calls have occurred Northside. We are the ones who carry the limp, lifeless kids from the fires or shootings or wrecks, who try to stop their tiny bodies from bleeding out, who forgo policy and breathe mouth-to-mouth into their charred little lungs—because it's a gesture against the obscenity of wasteful death, even if futile. Their families' cries, the neighbors' screams, their surviving siblings' wailing: we are drowning in anguish and grief as we try to revive children who had no chance. Theirs were preventable deaths, caused by human errors of desperation, poverty, ignorance, horrendous judgment.

We are the last to touch the children before they are officially deceased. We fight for them while the parents stand behind us screaming at the heavens. We carry the frail bodies in our arms and lean over them, working them, trying and hoping and pleading, even as we look down on their tiny dead faces and know they will not return. Their burned flesh, their blood, their smells: we get this on our clothes, in our noses and flesh. We carry them deep within.

And we go back to the barn, restock our equipment, clean the human off our gear, and wait for the next call. Soon, we'll stand in another living room where people are using the oven to heat their house, are locking the door from the outside while they run "real quick" down to the corner bar, are escaping into drugs and drink while their kids are ignored. We cannot shake these next parents, cannot show them the faces of those dead children or the horribly human parents who now carry the weight of their dead kids on top of all their other regrets and failures.

We say nothing. We take their blood pressure, give them oxygen, turn off the oven, open a window, walk them down to the ambulance, and we say nothing.

I know. I *know* that what we should blame is the ignorance, not the ignorant; the desperation, not the desperate; the dysfunction, not the dysfunctional. But we stand face-to-face with the person who, for whatever reasons, made the decisions that brought us all to this spot. It becomes hard to clock the larger sociological framework—even though it is very real and ever-present. Its totality renders it nearly invisible. And then we're kneeling beside someone, looking judgmentally (or not at all) at the culmination of decades, if not centuries, of complex systemic injustice. I'd say *systemic failure,* but I'm not sure this isn't how the system was designed to function.

When we talk about PTSD, traumatic response, psychological

distress, this is what gets us, far more than one single "bad" call: being keel-hauled night after night in depths of brutal suffering, powerless witnessing. It is crushing. And the alarms keep sounding and *someone* needs to respond to the next one.

The greatest trick the devil played . . .

//

We need far less *us versus them*. We fail to serve the public when we see only indistinguishable types or clichés. We perpetuate racial and class biases when we won't examine the real systems and circumstances that put the space between us. The fear, too, of letting compassion and sympathy become overwhelming drives many to actively keep these walls high. Because if we think too much about what—and who—we're seeing, what roles we play in the systemic inequalities, we might crack.

Gallows humor helps cut the dread and tension from these shitty situations, but it's not enough. We laugh about stuff that is as horrible as it is absurdly funny, because the alternative would break us. We share morbid observations with each other after messy calls. We rant about the inane complaints, the wasteful dummies, the squalor and poverty and desperation—because we were there together, and we understand.

And then, the calls for which there are no quips or wry jokes.

Few of us get through unscathed. More so, I believe—and we're seeing it borne out across the fire service now—that those who are least compassionate, most aloof, those who refuse reflection or introspection, are unprepared when this caustic immersion takes its toll on them.

Some of the most macho of my coworkers, some of those quickest to mock the *sensitive new-age soft-boys,* have found themselves humbled if not buckled by the weight of accumulated denial or repressed emotional reactions. The trauma spills out of whatever hidden chamber they've stuck everything for years. Their inner world suffers or those around them suffer. Others have struggled to contain all they've encountered, becoming overwhelmed by a career of hard calls. We are so very male, so dedicatedly macho, that asking for help or acknowledging feelings remains anathema. The "manly man" culture left us unprepared when we hit our own murky emotional currents.

Current studies show that many emergency responders are developing PTSD from delayed, accumulated stress. The traditional thought was that there's the *one bad call*—the dead baby, the smoking corpse, the dying eyes locked on yours—that sticks a knife into your heart. Now, researchers are finding it's a cumulative effect. Essentially, years of ignoring the witnessed and experienced trauma, suppressing healthy emotional reactions, desperately building walls around feelings: it all comes at a price. *Death by a thousand small cuts* . . . Except these aren't paper cuts. It's a career immersed in the suffering and trauma of others. Hundreds of objectively disturbing calls. What is that?

This crisis of traumatic stress, depression, and suicide among emergency responders gets covered by the umbrella term PTSD. We need something better: accumulated-stress trauma, traumatic-immersion response. I've seen it aptly described as complex trauma response. If those vetting the fifth edition of the *Diagnostic and Statistical Manual of Mental Disorders* cannot even agree on the forms and variations of "basic" PTSD, we might be out here awhile, treading water in roiling seas of sadness and hurt. Bergen Evans wrote, "We may be through with the past, but the past is not through with us," which feels like a riff on Faulkner's "The past is never dead. It's not even past." Yet even as we convene panels and focus groups to study this and seek solutions, many of us continue the tough-guy charade. Because: as long as it hasn't happened to me, I can look askance at my coworker's crackup. *He was weak. I am not.* That's all there is to it—until I find myself looking up from the bottom of a lake of sorrow.

//

I've been a longtime supporter of critical incident stress management (CISM), which has falteringly gained support by increments in the emergency services. That old approach—*Suck it up, buttercup*—never solved much. Showing emotions was the same as showing weakness, and that was verboten, seen as "unmanly." The fortress of machismo was built with poor habits, bad rationalizations, horrible coping skills, and broken relationships.

Boozy bravado isn't a great healing plan.

I am always grateful I stopped drinking young. Beyond responding to innumerable alcohol-related travesties and tragedies at work, I've witnessed too many friends and coworkers entangled in the predictable traps of alcohol abuse and self-sabotage. Yet it's still a cultural presumption: Miller Time, shower beer, wine o'clock, mommies and mimosas, a shot of liquid courage . . . Turning from a bad call to a bottle of booze, then burning the candle at all ends to avoid facing the demons inside: that is a familiar path to wreckage.

I repeat now something from earlier: far too many of us truly do not even understand what we are signing up for when we start. *Firemen!* Except: you are more likely to get carpal tunnel lifting your turnouts onto the rig for hundreds of EMS calls than you will dance with the Red Devil. You cannot save what is already lost, whether a human or a house. And yet we blame ourselves for "failing" to rescue the dead. Car wreck, CPR, suicide, house fire: victims dead before we were dispatched. Or we compare ourselves to some ludicrous mythic firedude who would have extinguished the fire single-handedly and rescued a dozen people without buttoning his coat.

I have tried to monitor how I feel, how I process, how I react and recover. I write about work. I talk about it. I am clear-eyed about the Heroes' Fallacy (*If only I'd gotten there sooner, I could have saved them all!*) and recognize what is and is not possible. If we screw up on a call, that rankles me, but many calls go south despite our good efforts and best intentions—that's the essence of the game. This entire book is my response to, my gesture against, the weight of emotional and mental trauma.

I mentioned earlier in the book the gratitude I felt for Roger Huder, a retired firefighter/medic whose *Gutter Medicine* was one of the first to address the scope and damage of a career in emergency response:

> [I] do know that when you work with people who desperately need your help, it's a real struggle to not judge your success or failures through their living or dying. . . . You end up with a long string of intrusive images slamming their way into your off-duty life. . . . The only satisfaction I could find was the knowledge that I did try, and that I had enough of whatever it takes to climb back onto the truck, week after week, month after month, and year after year. . . . *If there is courage in the job, it is the knowledge that you will face more smoking babies and still keep showing up to work.* (emphasis mine)

A couple of years back, I found myself wrestling with an unfamiliar morass of heavy, gloomy feelings. I had worked my regular forty-eight, taken a day off, then worked seventy-two hours, taken two days off, worked twenty-four, traveled for five days on the West Coast (never settling into one time zone), then returned and gone directly to work for forty-eight. I was *beat*. Two weeks of work and poor sleep, travel and poor sleep, and more work with poor sleep: a steep accumulation of sleep dep. I fried my reserves. I felt raw, irritable, sluggish, vulnerable.

Driving home from my next shifts, my eyes blurred with fatigue. I walked into the house and some small undone task grated my nerves like a marital infidelity played live for a crowd. The dogs were literally assaulting me with their needy cold noses and whining with joy at seeing me after two days away. It was Thanksgiving. I had a lot to be very thankful for, yet I felt churlish and grouchy about the obligations ahead. I mopily drove to my in-laws' for the holiday meal, gnashing my teeth about the futility of human connection, the inanity of enforced pleasantries, the bland cooking.

I know the holidays drive many people deep (deeper) into despair. A suicide on August 24 is a tragedy. A suicide on November 24 means the holiday is marred eternally for the survivors. And those who exit on December 24, well, *Ho, ho, ho, horror.*

I am fortunate to have caring in-laws and a family and a place to celebrate holidays about which I'm ambivalent. I get that. And still I was withdrawn, disconnected. None of this was particularly revelatory to me. I could feel it but not solve it.

What was striking was how quickly I nosedived into brooding moroseness, how fragile my equilibrium was, how easily the world's rawness slipped past my guard. And then I felt overcome with weighty emotions, about nothing specific—just emo kid at fifty-one.

Wow, it was as if being severely overtired left me unable to cope.

A few weeks before, I'd participated in a panel discussion about PTSD and stress in the fire service. The effects of sleep dep were widely discussed, even if the specific connections were not yet drawn. After reading Huder's *Gutter Medicine*, I was more cognizant of the roots of the "epidemic" of PTSD and traumatic breakdown in the fire service, the way things build cumulatively. I hear a lot of my peers say, "Well, I've never had that one bad-bad call that haunts me. So, I guess I'm all right." It finally struck me: *Maybe it's not one "bad" call. But I have had nearly two decades of deeply disturbing calls, a litany of suffering and tragedy.*

I'm not sure I could even recognize a bad call anymore. That's probably not healthy either?

I was exhausted and beat down. I laughed at my obliviousness. I apologized to the family, cut out from the holiday gathering, went home, grabbed the dogs, and went for a run in the woods. And then I got some fucking sleep.

Guess what? I felt better the next day. Sleep helps us process and heal. Sleep is the bomb. But empathy fatigue, physical exhaustion, emotional deadening or overload: those are also bombs, and they're always primed, waiting for a match to strike.

//

My crew at 17s was on a bummer streak as winter descended not long ago. We'd caught a bunch of ugly deaths too many shifts in a row. Our next shift started with a SOB call right after 8:00 a.m. The comments from Dispatch stated, "One who has fallen. Caller says her husband isn't answering her or moving. He is between the bed and the wall. His leg feels cold." This last bit shifted the anticipation from picking up an invalid to likely finding someone unconscious or dead. We arrived and entered a spotless, cheery house. The caller was upstairs, yelling for us. "Up here. Up here. Please hurry."

We hustled up the stairs and encountered a stout woman in a festive holiday cardigan. She held the phone in one hand and pointed toward a bedroom with the other. We passed her and entered the room. The body was not trapped in a crevice between the far wall and the bed frame, as I'd expected. He lay against the mattress at an awkward angle, one arm crossing beneath his torso, fingers splayed and pointed upward. We went to him, put our hands on his wrists, his throat, his cheeks, checking for responsiveness. He was cool to the touch, with stiffness already spreading. The fact of the body, yet again. My durgan and I looked at each other. DOA. No signs of a struggle, no blood, no apparent injuries. It appeared he had collapsed and landed in that awkward position sometime in the night. Dead where he fell.

We stood slowly and left the room. I radioed Dispatch to cancel the medics and start a squad. My partner took the AED from me and descended with our gear. The woman was standing in the hallway, watching us with panic and fear. "No—no—no. So soon?! No, no, no, no! You can't leave! Help him! Can't you help him? Please! Please help."

I inhaled slowly, letting her finish. She grabbed my arm and we looked at each other. "He's gone? Oh, please don't tell me that."

"I'm very sorry, ma'am. He's dead. He died overnight, hours ago. There is nothing we can do. I'm really sorry."

She crumpled, erupting in the violent broken fury of sudden loss. I stood by, giving her space but maintaining my presence. She grabbed her phone and started calling her kids. She was incoherent. I got concerned. It was an icy, slick morning and the mother's anguished garbled wailing into the phone would propel them pell-mell onto the highway, rushing to her, hurrying as if there was something yet to be done for their father. (My mind multitasks. My mind defends itself. I experience the world via allusions, quotes, references. My thoughts at that moment were fear for her agitated children. Then I thought of Ron Burgundy's glass case of emotion. And then, once again, of Robert Frost: "And they, since they / were not the one dead, turned to their affairs.") At the second call, I moved beside the woman and gently took the phone from her, introducing myself to the voice on the other end, clarifying what his mother had said. I expressed condolences and stressed that he should drive carefully. We repeated this for the other children.

Those calls, the first horrible duties, completed, the woman sank to the couch. She sobbed hard, then shrieked, "What am I going to do? I can't be alone! He was my everything! The kids! My poor kids! They will be broken."

She told me she had been baking holiday cookies and was surprised he hadn't come down already. The house was a warm, lovely place, modest and pleasant, with comfy furniture, artwork, lots of photos of the couple and their kids over decades. We were wrapped in the cozy odor of the fresh cookies. I asked how long they'd been married, whether they'd raised all their kids in this house, where her kids lived. I listened as she loosed a roiling flood of disparate details and memories. I nodded at the outlines of a good life together. She worked herself through the sudden shock, the first deluge of grief, the grasping at this hard new reality. She grew calmer. I encouraged her to call each of the kids back to let them hear that she was all right, and to remind them to drive safely.

She grabbed the arm of the sofa and shook it, then said, "I knew he would die, eventually, but not so soon. Not *now*. It's too soon. We're not ready. My kids aren't ready. What will become of us?!"

Contrasting her plaintive "I can't believe this happened to him!" while she listed all her husband's medical issues, as well as his advanced age, I considered the recent deaths we'd had, the range of "unexpected" or "unfair" deaths. It is not a competition, but still. I could not ignore the contrast, the gallery of our recent dead. The young man who died of an aneurysm. The old gal who slipped on her back steps at night and was found frozen, blue, with a halo of dark blood surrounding her, the trash bag in the snow, one slipper orphaned on the stairs. The worst: a girl my daughter's age who OD'd while doing homeschool. Her dad got home from work and found her slumped in her beanbag. I walked in to see him doing compressions on his stiff, curved, dead child.

It had been a bad stretch for us. Inside my head, all I could think was the facts: *You've had fifty-six years together. Your kids are my age! He was old. He had cancer! And high blood pressure! And diabetes! Jesus fuck, let the man go.* But I said none of that. Sure, feelings are valid. But the world is big and mean and hard, too. And I *cannot* erase the scenes I experience. They are too vivid, the details too stark, to pretend otherwise.

"I knew he would die. I mean, he'd been in poor health. I just didn't think it would be *now*. Not today! Not"—interrupting herself—"You! You . . ."

I froze, worried I'd spoken aloud or my less-than-charitable thoughts were apparent on my face. "Ma'am?"

"You have the *worst* job in the world!" she declared, then sobbed again.

"I'm sorry? How—"

She looked up at me, tears rimming her eyes. "You do this a lot, don't you? You have to tell people their loved ones are dead, then stand there while they scream and cry and yell at you. Your job is to watch people suffer. You can't fix it. It isn't your fault, but here you are, and I'm crying and yelling and blaming you. What a horrible job."

I tried not to smile. She was the first person in nearly twenty years to make that connection. *Damn, lady,* I thought. "That's very kind of you, ma'am. Yes, it is something. It is a strange job. But that's okay. It's what we do. I'm sorry we couldn't do more for him, for you."

We spoke of what would happen next, and her now-dashed holiday plans, and how happy they had been together. A young police officer arrived. I walked him back to the room, gave my perspective. I watched his face as he studied the room. *He's a rookie,* I thought. I took a few moments longer to explain more and to ask if he had questions. When we were done, my crew was dismissed. Before leaving, I went to the widow and took her hand. I gave her my condolences and told her this was one of the most love-filled homes I'd had the honor to be in; no matter how hard the death of her husband was, nothing could touch the decades of love and the loving children they had created together. I meant every word.

//

If we cannot hold steady in the suffering, see ourselves as part of something both essential and existential, accept our roles as tiny pieces in a large system, own our complicity and our connection, we will be lost. We cannot hide from it; nothing remains buried forever. Although he's referring to this nation's racial history and sickness in *Begin Again*, Eddie Glaude Jr. nails what I'm suggesting: "We dig trenches to redirect the memories and to get them to flow away from us. But, like the waters of the Mississippi River, the memories always return, flooding everything no matter how high we build the stilts."

I mentioned at the outset a conversation I had with a journalist friend, who argued that our job was dangerously abnormal—owing to our frequent exposure to death and trauma—and I countered that, in fact, I found it reinforced the biological and behavioral normalcy of life. Meaning: I *know* that all around us people are dying or already dead, that most people are making any number of compromised life choices that will eventually bring them to suffering.

Throughout their childhoods, I'd tell my daughters this: My job requires that I deal with tough things. Right away, no matter what— hard tasks, dirty toil, all stripes of people (generally not in good moods), bad hours, extremes of weather, anger and anguish and grief. I must, we must, handle whatever it is, whether it's a station chore, a gruesome medical, a tedious non-emergent call, or a dangerous fire. We deal with whatever we find. No matter what. I'm not always gracious, but I muster something approximating grace or gentle bemusement most of the time.

I deeply appreciate the ethos of emergency response: *Do what needs to be done. Work together. Appreciate how bad some people have it. Be nice to folks: it's free. Do right. Be kind.*

We are not really special. Certainly not superheroes or even regular heroes. Maybe it takes something extra to face the risks, wade through the mess, keep one's soul and courtesy and humor mostly healthy and intact. I am inured to puke, piss, shit, viscera, blood, and crying. I respond reasonably well to crises. It isn't rocket science: find the fire, disrupt the chemical reaction, extinguish the fire, clean up the debris. Give sick people bandages and oxygen; stop the bleeding and restart their hearts. But the shades of gray are deeper than most civilians can ever imagine. Too, we are encountering chaos and, within seconds, making tactical, safety, and critical decisions despite that chaos.

Every day I go to work, I see the unpretty, unpleasant, unsimple consequences of living, of life. Victims of gravity, bad timing, or bad luck. Mostly we get the sick and the poor, those who for a constellation of causes rely on emergency services. Every one of us, however, will lose the race in the end. Sometimes the only thing we can do, despite our training, equipment, and experience, is bear witness to a person's lowest or last moments. Stand silently before a family's wretched anguish. We try to bring compassion to those we serve, to bear witness. That's our duty, our honor, our meager gift. And then we go home, to our families, our dogs and cats, our empty rooms, our haunted memories. Sometimes we think it all over. Sometimes we bury it deep within. Either way, the sun will rise again, and, while we can, we get to start the next shift, to see what the world will bring us.

CONCLUSION
Burnt Norton

The final trial of the officers charged in the killing of George Floyd approached. I reviewed my notes from May 25, 2020, preparing for the punishing, racking process of testifying. I watched—once again—the horrible footage, beginning to end, from each officer's body camera. It is brutal, so brutal. And I must watch it with ruthless clarity and focus. I could not leave it on Mute, as the timeline and the dialogue matter. I met with the prosecution team for trial prep, going over what to expect, what to focus on. My nights were jagged with stress dreams. My days had intrusive flashes of worries: about the trial's heightened stakes and stress, about the vulnerability of testifying, about looking over my shoulder for hostile police officers. My small piece in this felt significant. I was, and am, one of the only badged responders who could challenge the police claims about a riotous crowd, who could speak from experience about what the officers did wrong and all they did not do right.

The day jury selection was to begin, I flew to D.C. to care for my parents. As I waited to board, I learned that J. Alexander Kueng had pled guilty. By the time I landed, Tou Thao had requested the judge decide his fate. That night, I received an email from the prosecutors, releasing me from my subpoena.

Was I relieved? Not at first. I had rewatched the footage and relived it all: I had done all the reagitating, upsetting parts; I was consumed with stress and worry again. Testifying would allow an imperfect gesture toward justice and finality for me. But I was damn glad that everyone—Mr. Floyd's family and the witnesses—would be spared the galling indecency of the trial.

//

What is wild about emergency response work is how ceaseless it is. While I was revising this book, significant and poignant incidents kept occurring. How many types of heart attacks or suicides or car wrecks need I work to convey their essence to a reader? I see so many more connections, deeper meanings, and big-picture issues than I did when I was "merely" documenting the early calls. While I've been editing, more incidents have occurred to reinforce (to me) all the connections I have tried to make clear to you.

I will close this out with two vignettes. They separately reflect different and profound aspects of the work and how I carry it. Together, they offer insights that are, typically, grim and absurd. Someone asked about a denouement. I guess this might be it.

July 2022, Northside

I worked an overtime shift on Engine 14 in July 2022. As 14s goes, it was not a bad Sunday. No one fell out in church; no one started a beef at the parks or at a backyard gathering; no stolen car wrecks or deadly carjackings. No shootings or fatal overdoses. A mellow shift.

At 2:45 a.m., we were dispatched to a commercial fire alarm, just our engine. This is usually a faulty battery or a power surge, not a fire. Middle of the night, we were groggy, dressing on autopilot. As the durgan and I were gearing up, the driver saw a man waving frantically outside the bay doors. He opened the door slightly and the man rushed in, racing past me into the middle of the apparatus area. He was frenetic and breathless, muttering, "They're after me. They're trying to get me. They're gonna kill me."

I looked back toward the street, scanning outside the station. Much as I wanted to help the man, I did not want to be collateral damage if someone started shooting at him. The driver checked outside, then retreated from the (big, wide, revealing) glass windows. "No one's out there."

As we tried to calm the man, offering him a chair and asking him what was going on, it became clear he was incoherent. He was jittery and manic, his eyes rolling about. He bobbed and weaved, muttering, "They're after me" over and over. "Got to get away. Help me! Help me!" I tried to calm him, to steady him, to hold his focus. I put my hand on his shoulder and asked him "Who?" He started, as if suddenly aware of me, and skittered away across the apparatus floor. I nodded to the durgan to head him off and try to get him settled. We were still dispatched to the fire alarm, and I needed to ask Dispatch for help or to substitute for us. I grabbed my radio and, as it was turning on, I heard the man yelling at my partner, "People? What people, man? A big-ass dog's trying to eat me! A wolf-dog! You gotta help me!"

As I radioed Dispatch, the other captain at the station entered the floor. He's calm; he's also a wrestler. I wasn't worried about him. I asked if he and his two durgans could handle getting the man to settle down or leave the station. He nodded. *Sure.*

No menacing strangers, no wolf-dogs, no dog-dogs, no dog-men, nothing outside the station. The man was loopy. High and paranoid, it seemed. We mounted the rig, figuring the other three could manage.

I looked back in the rearview as we started to drive and saw—

The man flailing as the captain was trying to guide him toward the rear doors. Not attacking our guys, but flailing wildly. I told the driver to hold on. I looked again and saw—

The man, now naked, his pants at his ankles, throwing himself to the ground.

"Holy shit!" I yelled. The driver stopped the rig, and I ran to help the other captain. The man was sprawled on the cement floor, swinging his arms and legs as if swimming. My co-captain was trying to keep the man from grabbing the other firefighters or squirming under Ladder 10. I joined him, as did my durgan.

We held him in place, preventing him from smashing his head on the cement or hurting us with his wild kicks. We turned him face up, the durgan controlling his left arm, the captain on his right arm, and me straddling his legs. He ranted and raved, called us names, threatened to kill us, begged us to help him, told us he was going to kick our asses. Straddling him, I caught a lot of homophobic guff. We maintained the passive restraints: no joint locks, no knees to his bones. He was on his back, not prone. He could breathe. But he fought against us madly, wildly, incoherently. We could not penetrate the mania.

He tired himself out. He was less agitated, less aggressively strug-gling, when the police and the medics arrived. He was mostly lucid, able to answer questions. He consented to go to the hospital and prom-ised he was good. He apologized for the fuss. He'd been smoking too much PCP, he said. We were not surprised. We helped him up, wrapped him in a sheet, got him on the stretcher, and the medics wheeled him away.

A good resolution, no?

No. When our man burned himself out and quit fighting against even our passive control, he was not simply "coming to his senses"; he was on the verge of a respiratory or cardiac collapse. He had strained so hard, become so hypoxic, that he was in danger of causing himself permanent damage—even death. His blood pressure was 220/160 when we were finally able to take it. Dangerously high.

So, the guy (me) who has been studying and writing about emer-gency response and altered mentation is involved trying to safely con-tain a man who is loopy and incoherent. The guy (me) who has read extensively, written lengthily, watched hours of video on the topic—this guy got suckered by a drug-addled man's paranoid frenzy. And in the brief, hectic seconds it took to go from trying to passively engage the man to putting hands on him to stop him from lurching wildly at us (and in the stunningly fast moments in which he ripped off his clothes, revealing himself to be the naked, sweaty man of our misguided old training videos) to collapsing with him onto the concrete floor as he writhed, squirmed, and kicked blindly, I missed the telltale indications of drug incoherence.

No, wait. I did *not* miss the signs.

As I wrote in chapter 12, "Ketamine or Kill a Man," knowing he was that high did not offer us any solutions. The fact remains that we encounter people who are out of control, who are dangers to themselves and others. We don't carry sedatives. If we'd shooed him out into the night, and he'd run into traffic, or accosted someone (whom he hurt accidentally, or who shot him reactively): that was on us. Had it not been me and the other captain, a very calm, skilled grappler, we might have escalated further, or taken the man's frenzy as "attacking us" and responded aggressively. We might have taken personally his rantings and nakedness, pinning him face down (prone) and sitting on him to "keep everyone safe." We could easily have killed him, unknowingly and unintentionally.

I tell you this because it illustrates how little information we have to go on, how quickly things escalate, and how messy the human factors can be. We did not overlook or dismiss the man's crisis. We were not deliberately rough to "get through to him." There was *no* getting through to him. That was the danger. In a matter of minutes, the man could have hit respiratory collapse or failure. His heart might have stopped. A dead man on the floor of a firehouse, with eight firefighters, two cops, two medics standing right there, "doing nothing to save him." The thinnest of margins, indeed.

August 2022, Southside

It is not my story to tell you how the events of the past two-plus years have eaten at my coworkers, and especially not my crew. But it has been hard on us, in multiple ways; each of us differently but also challenging us collectively, as a crew. What I see and understand and want, in terms of racial justice and specific approaches to our patch of south Minneapolis: I can argue endlessly but if my crew does not wholly agree or share the vision, I cannot force them. Even when we want the same things, *how* the work and the world affect us varies and alters our responses. Tracy and Steve, my core crew, and then Jenn and Dan, and now Evan, have been stalwart and engaged, but it has been hard and messy and unending. The layered, shifting tensions have strained us.

There are complicated social and historical dynamics at play, and real-time human attempts at forging solutions. My default perspective, which I have bludgeoned my crew with, is that we should not blame individual citizens' reactions to the city's (the system's) protracted, more powerful manipulations and status quo protections. I cannot blame the protesters or the activists more than I blame those in positions of power. So, for me, the issues at George Floyd Square pale in comparison to the city's ongoing failures to address racial inequality, protracted police violence, and disingenuous approaches to the square itself.

We have argued and disagreed at 17s about this, because theories are one thing, but constantly driving through or around what has felt at times like a chaotic mess cuts the shiny rhetoric to shreds. I insist that we must not get captured by Alpha News hyperbole about a "violent, drug-infested gangland." That is bullshit, empirically and statistically. Across the nation, there have been upticks in carjackings, group shootings, youth crime. There have been *more* shootings in the Uptown area of Minneapolis than at GFS, but the reactionary narrative has juice. It is reductive and dishonest to paint the entire area—which is really a region of our minds—as a single entity. The activists and artists have created a powerful memorial, one that exists in a historically gang-infected area, where the locals are activists, regular citizens, church folk, gang members. Black (and white) people of contrasting ilks. I refuse the default conflation of all of it into one abstract thing. I counter it all I can. But my crew has their own perceptions and feelings. How each of us responds to the uncertainty and the hurt varies. I ask a lot for them to follow me and trust my cynical resolve to do right.

Thus, this final tale is my happy ending. Given the job, it is grim, and my "happy" is absurd. *And* it is an honest summation.

Three Sundays after the incident involving the man on PCP, mid-August 2022, we were working our regular shift at 17s. The crew had spent the morning talking over the damage of the past two-plus years, how we'd been hurting and not recognizing clearly what was happening inside ourselves. How we'd taken it out on each other or been shut down. It was a good conversation: raw, vulnerable, clarifying. Cleansing. We had been bottling up our messy, complicated feelings. Our frustrations, our fears, our anger, our stress coming out sideways at those who were closest. This was a conversation that was certainly overdue, a deep and honest purging of our respective feelings and worries. It is the beauty of this job, how nakedly honest we can be with each other, when we allow ourselves, when we are open.

Late morning, we were called to a "possible heart" at the church kitty-corner from Cup Foods on George Floyd Square. This church has been a cornerstone of the neighborhood for years and has deep roots in the community. Again, all those who say *George Floyd Square is a no-go zone . . . a drug market . . . a gang haven* miss (ignore) how many residents do right and stand up together. This church is a beaming example. Fortunately, the man asked for help promptly, and we arrived swiftly, and the medics arrived shortly afterward. We got him onto the stretcher and out to the ambulance, and the medics started treatment before transporting him. He was having a significant cardiac event and needed immediate help. That is what he got. No delays, no staging, no low-balling. After the medics cleared us, we chatted with the church folks—it was early and the service had not started in earnest. They were holding their session outdoors, as a Covid stance and a way to proselytize to the neighborhood. It was a gorgeous Sunday, and the streets were filling with people.

Two hours later we were called to a shooting. The first 911 caller put it "behind 37xx Columbus Avenue" [just around the corner from GFS], then someone else said "in the Speedway parking lot" [now the People's Way parking lot, across the street from Cup Foods], then someone else called and said "on the sidewalk *by* the Square." As I've written repeatedly, the work dispatchers do in receiving, parsing, interpreting, and transmitting information to us—when it comes in frantically, screamed and shouted, from people who are reacting and panicked or hurt—is phenomenal. And it entails a lot of guesswork. It's also a hectic game of telephone: are there five victims or one victim called in by five people? The salient points for me were *Was the shooter gone?* and *How many victims? (approximately)* because that allows us to formulate a realistic, safe response plan.

The update from Dispatch indicated there was one shooter, who had run north. I radioed that we were responding and would assess before entering the scene. As we approached, I saw someone down on the sidewalk, with several people kneeling beside him. This was not an active shootout. I radioed Dispatch to inform medics that the scene was safe for medical and that we were going to the patient. Steve and I got to the man as he took his final breaths. He had been shot in the chest. One of the primary caretakers of GFS held the man up, holding his hand and praying for him. I felt the victim's pulse fade then stop.

As Steve was getting our medical supplies out, someone yelled there was a second victim in the alley across the street. I left the first man with Steve and Tracy and ran past the church's parking lot service and down the alley. The minister was praying aloud over their PA for the wounded; the congregation stopped midservice, looking grave. Several people were surrounding the second victim. An MPD officer was helping him, and one of the other primary caretakers of GFS was using a towel from her house to stanch the man's bleeding. The victim, also a young man, was awake. He had also been shot in the chest and had other non-life-threatening bullet wounds. Another MPD officer joined, giving us her own trauma dressing. I radioed for a second ambulance, repeating that the scene was safe for medical. I said we had one critical with a gunshot wound and another unresponsive. The MPD officers were helpful and focused, and together with the lead activist we worked to calm the man, treat his wounds, and then got him loaded onto the medics' stretcher when they arrived. I rode with my patient down to the STAB room. He remained alive and went directly into surgery.

The paramedic told me as we were standing outside afterward that it was six minutes from when they arrived, got through the crowd to the patient, we got him loaded, and drove to County. That was incredible service. *Incredible.*

We talked about the call afterward, the details and weird human aspects. It had been an intense, upsetting call. Our shift continued; we had other calls and we had downtime. Another Sunday. I followed up with my crew the next day, once we'd had time to sleep on it. They were both saddened—the dead man was theirs. He was young, in his early twenties. A life cut short, over what? Men arguing; pride, ego, insecurity. It's a shame.

As I checked in with Steve and Tracy that next day, one of them asked how I was doing. I paused a bit before responding. "Honestly, I'm good. It went great. Really fucking great. I'm so psyched by our response. And not just us: the cops were there fast, and there to help—not messing with people. Those first officers were awesome! And the medics—holy hell! We got two ambulances to the scene in minutes!" *Sure,* I thought, *it's easy for me to be psyched: my guy survived—I'd left them with the dead man . . .* But, seriously. This was the call I have been dreading for over two years, since they killed George Floyd.

And that was it, that was the truth. Since May 25, 2020, this has been precisely the call that has caused me such inchoate stress. I have carried profound worry about the human factors on calls like these: the police, the medics, the crowds. The police killing of Mr. Floyd haunts me not solely for the horror of the act; the systemic issues consume me: *Why weren't we dispatched sooner? What might we have done, had we arrived sooner? What has the city done to prevent another such murder? What can I do to prevent another such murder? Will the police kill another person as we're arriving? Will the city erupt? Will there be warfare on the streets? Will anyone in power understand what America does to its citizens?* My traumatic stress is not the dead bodies, it is the system and the structural refusal to open our eyes, hearts, and minds to what we continue to do.

There is so much structural crap that gunks up the wheels, when really, all of us *want* to help others. We have lost the narrative. My fears on a call like this one—a shooting in public, at or near GFS—concerned medics refusing to enter (for "safety"), police staging until they could amass a platoon (for "safety"), my bosses ordering us to wait (for "safety"). Meanwhile the people I've come to know and respect, the various citizens who dedicate their lives to a vision of racial justice and a better America embodied by the scrappy enterprise of George Floyd Square, those good folks would be kneeling helplessly in a dying man's blood while we, the city's official emergency responders, wait idly for some sign that our fear of Black America has abated (for "safety").

I pointed out to Steve and Tracy, genuinely, that about five hundred people passed through the intersection of Thirty-eighth and Chicago that Sunday morning: going to church, seeing friends, checking out the memorial, newcomers doing the tourist-and-educational component, getting food at the restaurants, buying souvenir T-shirts, taking photos, being human. One asshole with a gun stole a man's life and damaged another's. But the community jumped to care for the injured and help us. *Don't let one man ruin all the good of the other four hundred and ninety-nine,* I said.

I realized as I sifted through thousands of calls, pondered so many unnecessary deaths, considered all I have encountered, that a significant amount of our work comes directly from men acting like the wrong type of man. Men who answer taunts or slights or challenges with guns. Men who see challenges everywhere. Men who think they will not die, no matter how they eat, drink, smoke, drive. Men who hurt the women and children in their lives. Similarly do my macho coworkers act like the wrong type of men: men who bully the junior firefighters; who persist in flogging the dead *fireman* mythos; who persist with misogynist, racist, and homophobic bigotry; who act too cool about everything and then fall through a hole in the floor of a building they shouldn't have entered; or who die when their hearts cannot carry their bulk and girth. If we could freeze time and help each guy see—really perceive—the costs of whatever foolish machismo he was perpetrating, I think our calls for service would plummet. And the world would be a safer, happier place.

We cannot stop men from fighting, from shooting each other, from making reckless choices. We cannot force people to jump the tracks of their ingrained habits, their contexts, their upbringings. That's not how humans work. When the consequences of life happen, I want to get there fast and provide the best care I can, to give each person their best shot at survival. I'm proud of my crew, of the medics and police, and of the citizens of our patch of Southside. It is only together that we can find our way home.

//

My career is winding down. Soon, I will no longer sling my gear aboard the big red truck and race through the streets to unknown emergencies. I will hear sirens or see the rigs gathered around wrecked cars or burning houses. I might feel the impulse to go toward it, to jump in. But I won't. It will not be my duty to enter strangers' lives, to put myself at risk.

There's a new youth brigade in the department, just as my cohort was at the turn of the century (*gasp*—2000, not 1900). I do not fret for the department's future. As I wrote of myself at the outset, "typically atypically," I do not look upon the next generation and shudder or cry. The kids are all right. The new durgans will learn, the newly promoted will take charge. I don't blame the newbies. Whatever they lack is a reflection of the ongoing dysfunction of the system: the city, the administration, the firefighter culture. They are better prepared than we were, and we made it—more or less. The tones will sound, and they will go out to help the public. Are things different from how they used to be? Sure. But life is nothing but our movement through time. *All fires go out—eventually.* And thus we stumble onward. *You must go on. I can't go on. I'll go on.*

ACKNOWLEDGMENTS

Thank you to Michael Croy and Northstar Literary Agency for being willing to read the manuscript *and* get back to me about it. Quinton Skinner gets a big hug for connecting us. Profound gratitude to the team at the University of Minnesota Press for believing in and fighting for (and with) this manuscript: Laura Westlund, Jason Weidemann, Emily Hamilton, Heather Skinner, Matt Smiley, Maggie Sattler, Shelby Connelly, and Emma Saks. Erik Anderson deserves his reputation as a genius editor and shaper of ideas. Mary Byers whipped this beast into shape, despite my far-flung references and some dubious syntax. This book is far better for your wise guidance.

Gratitude to my coworkers, especially those who taught me well, and the good people I was fortunate to work with. The majority of us serve our fellow citizens with dedication, compassion, and rough-edged humor. The best firefighters have shown it is more important to do right than to follow strict rules. Equally, I give my profound respect to the many, many paramedics who run high-stakes operating theaters inside rolling delivery trucks. Y'all rock.

In a profession that still clings to the mantle of *firemen,* I was inspired, taught, mentored by, and enjoyed some of my best crews with many badass *fireladies.* Nowhere does "Don't Let the Bastards Grind You Down" ring truer. My love and gratitude to you all, especially:

Jen Cornell, the reason I'm here, who taught me to be both smart and humble in my approach to the essence of firefighting; who led by example, endured the laziest misogyny and chauvinistic devaluing, and was always smarter than everyone else in the room.

Kath Mullen, for being more stubborn and principled than I am—

by miles—and fighting to the end despite the slings and arrows of indignant poltroons. A true, dedicated, and caring leader.

Tracy Terbell: our decades of steady friendship, medical problems, bad funnies, and good times amid the bad shit. Thank you for everything.

Rita Juran, for providing bighearted leadership, love, dutiful engagement, and motivation.

Shana York, for being a good friend, rare vessel of common sense, and inspiring peer.

Kalimba Edwards, for growing up and unapologetically becoming herself since rookie school, sharing her struggles and keeping her grace, wit, humor. Tough as nails, indeed.

The Colonel (ahem, General) Christie Nixon, who taught me greatly about duty, dedication, and unimpeachable integrity.

Carla McClellan, who maintains an infectious positivity and dedication to finding the light and love in this broken world.

Bridget Bender, who assumed Jen Cornell's unwanted mantle as the most overqualified and underappreciated woman on the job.

A. K. Baumtrog: for walking the righteous path and bearing more than any of us should.

All the early MFD women, the Mary M.s and Vickies, Jean K., Stubbs and Stepan, Cherié; our list: Siobhan, Amy P., Helena, Sherri, Susan M. (RIP), and the rest, thank you for holding fast amid the petulance. Captain Brenda Berkman (FDNY, Ret.) fought so many battles on so many levels, then forged a path for the women who followed.

This is a book emphasizing EMS, and I must give deep thanks for Deputy Chiefs/Paramedics Charlotte Holt and Amber Lage, and Captain Steve Pleasants, for their tireless efforts on behalf of far too many recalcitrant firefighters. Firefighter/Medic Bill Schaetzel (Burnsville FD, Ret.) started me off wanting to learn more and do well as an EMT. Also, Erin and Jill and the educators at HCMC have thrown pearls before swine too often, but their labors have not been in vain: thank you.

A hearty shout-out to the cats who have ridden on my rigs, especially Ben Peña, the Colonel, Nick Quinn, Garrett Nelson, Daramorah Hill, the Unicorns. If we don't get there safely, we can't do good work: FMOs Andre Rush, Mark McClun, Tbell, Kris Larson, Chris Ellison,

Brook Kabanuk have made me better by doing their jobs well. Deep respect and gratitude for Jenn Hall and Genevieve Hansen—through the crucible and into history—and my crew for the past several years of Southside Magic: Tracy Terbell, Steve Mudek, Dan Bellis, Evan Graning, and for Chief J.R. Klepp, as we navigated Covid-19 and the period following the riots. I am grateful for the friendship and support of Dan Casper (Skinny Norton), the Good Jeremy Howard, Linda Sone, Richard Heim, Bad Brad Brautigam, Doug Gilbert, Joe Lompart, and Zen Master Jeff Ostberg. Chris Weltin made the wise decision to skip out on the couch-hero lifestyle and actually help people as a nurse. We miss her but that's cool.

A great many of my coworkers have shaped my appreciation for this profession and our membership. There are too many fireboys to list, but I'm grateful to have learned so much, whether the instruction was positive or cautionary. Props to the Andres Rush and Sewell, Mike Terry, Sean Thomas, and Bilal Atiq. Chief Ulysses Seal inspired me to look beyond the clichés, to seek How and Why we do things. Captain Paul Baumtrog (Emeritus) blended schools old and new. Gratitude to the good folks at Minneapolis Firefighters Local 82 for their efforts on our behalf. I thank every good firefighter, medic, and police officer who has worked to keep the public safe.

Recognition and respect to Captains Mark Olson (Ret.), Bridget Bender, and Linda Sone, along with Dr. Margaret Gavian and Frankie Jo McNallan (of the Minnesota Firefighter Initiative), for their dedication to firefighters in need of healing and help.

Movement, sweat, connection: they heal and power us. My dear friends Bekah and Jeff Metzdorff opened Mill City Running and brought people together, creating a vibrant community; more than simply running and athleisure, their mission is meaningful human connection. The lovely maniacs of November Project Minneapolis also pursue connection and community through sweat and joy: *Fuck yeah!* Doctors Kevin Schreifels and Ryan Jones of Lyn Lake Chiropractic, and their awesome staff, have cared for many of our bodies, which helps heal our spirits and mind. *Drive fast; take chances.*

The following readers provided invaluable encouragement and advice, willing ears and eyes: Stephen Belber, Susanna Bernstein, Annie

Enneking, Flannery Enneking-Norton, Marya Hornbacher, Hank Lewis, Mimi O'Donnell, Nick Quinn, Leslie Morgan Steiner, Arwen Wilder. You each helped and encouraged me through that long sojourn in the wilderness.

Gratitude to my parents, Amanda and Jerry Norton, for enduring me being me and supporting me throughout. My siblings Liza Jordan and Adam Norton, for providing a looking glass and support. The Belber family was a warm second home for me, and I owe so much to all of you. Mrs. B. offered years of principled engagement with the world; Henry instilled a love of jazz, the pleasure of a good book, and the virtues of weekday movie matinees. Lucie Tiberghien and Steve B. have provided inspiration through their creative careers and embrace of human connection. Cheri Jendro has always cheered wildly, no matter what I say: that loving enthusiasm should be bottled. The Enneking–Dorn family has been unconditionally welcoming, despite my spotty attendance at holiday gatherings. My eminently practical brother-in-law Jason Jordan gave me freeing advice when I was overwhelmed with the scope of this project: "Just write two books. Write one about firefighting. Write the other about EMS or whatever." And so I did.

There was a time, when I stopped flogging the corpse of my fiction-writing dreams, that I dove into dog training. I learned a great many lessons about myself, communication and process, humans (and dogs). Things were bumpy at work and home, and the friendship and guidance from Michael and Carol Ellis, Sam Mannion, Francis Metcalf, Irina Shimko, Ed Frawley and Cindy Rhodes, Donna Matey, and Maureen Haggerty gave me a place to put so much want and desire. Good things happened in the far-flung fields.

Steady-handed and principled reporting is rare and necessary in this land. I thank Katie Grace Nelson, Andy Mannix, and Libor Jany for their courageous and dogged work to shine light on the local messy things. Gratitude to Jesse Ross, the Whisperer of Whites, whose heart and mind do great things for us all. Much respect to my fellow D.C. native Greg Taylor for his decades of leadership and inspiration as an educator and a man. Christin Crabtree has inspired and educated me, #ttbt.

The following have each and together created a powerful, visionary location for healing, remembrance, and learning at George Floyd Square and Memorial, serving as witnesses, activists, caretakers, educators, and engaged community members: Jeanelle Austin (executive director, George Floyd Global Memorial), Marcia Howard, Angela Harrelson and Paris Stevens (codirectors, GFGM), Jay Webb, Mileesha Boh Smith, Marquise Bowie, Heather Doyle (Chicago Avenue Fire Arts Center). Thank you for standing tall since the get-go.

Big kudos to Carly Danek, photographer extraordinaire and carrot cake plug. Thanks to the great folks at Peace Coffee and Five Watt Coffee, as well as Kat Naden and Duck Duck Coffee, for keeping our minds sharp, our hearts hammering, and our breath sour.

Of all the great professors I've been fortunate to learn from and study with, I was most profoundly influenced by Professor Lee Edelman (literature) and the late Dr. Gerald R. Gill (history). I thank Jill McCorkle, Ian Graham Leask, Susanna Kaysen, Ralph Lombreglia, and Leslie Epstein for their time and tutelage in fiction writing classes. Professor Alan Leibowitz performed double duty, literature *and* writing.

When I stopped drinking cold, Will Wilson was a boon friend and the clearest voice of support I had. As I re-formed myself in Chattanooga, Hank Lewis, Dr. David Feldman, Cindy H. Carlson, and Paco and Ann Watkins were instrumental in supporting, loving, and inspiring me. So many years ago, yet so dear.

Gratitude to the inner chambers of my dented heart: Annie Enneking, profoundly, for twenty-five-plus years of love and encouragement—and having to listen to me process over and over and over again. Steve Belber, my common-law brother, inspiring mensch, bighearted boon companion, whose love, counsel, and support have been unwavering since before we could underage drink at the Zebra Room. Arwen Wilder, my trusted litmus and wise, grounded compass. Jen Cornell, for being a sister-friend, mentor, and inspiration. Abigail Cerra, for moral support, legal advice, and feisty inspiration. My fellow mordant Capricorn, Nora McInerny, whose brave and funny Widow+ work (like Google+ but longer lasting, and sadder) taught me much about the death, dying, and grieving processes. Hank Lewis, a righteous friend, an inspiration, a compass, a living rebuke to the rigged game and casual cruelty of the system: thank you.

Gratitude above all for my Devil Dolls, Harper Lux and Flannery, who motivated me to always do right and hold steady. You provided solace, motivation, and joy when the jagged pieces of work and life dug too close to my heart. A childhood spent listening to my barely edited work tales of "Bad Life Choices and Ugly Consequences" seems not to have ruined you.

And my beloved Auntiest, Lindsay Ralphs: she saved my life over the course of a nondescript lunch on Santa Monica Pier in 1989, and then has spent the next thirty-plus years being a cosmic connection, endlessly loving, mirthful and bemused side-parent. While it would likely have been messy for both of us had she adopted me in 1969, the end result has been so much deeper and sweeter. My thanks to Linds and to Shelley Glazer for their love, support, and open arms (and providing my Lake Merritt escape, where I did a major early revision of this book).

I'd like to express deep appreciation for the nurses, doctors, and staff at the UM–Fairview Pediatric Rheumatology and Journey Clinic, especially Dr. Shawn Mahmud. Their care and treatment of Lux, as well as the multitude of truly sick children, make the hard things so much better.

LUCK WON'T SAVE YOU BUT THESE BOOKS MIGHT

A Reading List

The following writers and thinkers shaped me, and thus this book. Had I not read Joseph Heller's *Catch-22*, Claude Brown's *Manchild in the Promised Land*, and the *Autobiography of Malcolm X: As Told to Alex Haley* in junior high, I might not have begun to understand that there is a structural con, a veritable machine against which the individual can and ought to rage—as well as glimpsing the reality that Black people exist outside the white gaze.

My debt to Martin Luther King Jr.'s "Letter from Birmingham Jail" and to James Baldwin's multitudinous essays is profound. They broke open my understanding of America's protracted racial sickness. Baldwin and Greg Tate (RIP) were powerful correctives to white American unthinking. Baldwin's ornate prose, lucid reasoning, and sustained fury, coupled with Tate's nimble, wry signifying in *Flyboy in the Buttermilk*, freed my mind from the fetters of Chattanoogan propriety (not that I ever fit in). Then I found Cornel West's *Prophetic Thought* and my mind cracked open. Had I not read them in my early twenties, I doubt I would have been able to see through the multiple layers of our lies and misconceptions, nor seen the potential to flow between "serious" theorizing and "lowbrow" casual convo. Audre Lorde's and Toni Morrison's respective dismantling of heteronormative and white-presumptive cultural mindset pushed me to question more, learn more, dig deeper. In the mid-2000s, Hank Lewis told me to check out this cat Tim Wise. He is White Like Me, smarter and better skilled, and thankfully still swinging at the Fortresses of Caucacity.

Charles D'Ambrosio's *Loitering* emboldened me to try something more than just scary fire stories, to aim for hybridity of essay and memoir, and to trust people to use dictionaries. Retired firefighter/medic Roger Huder's *Gutter Medicine* was the first memoir I found that addressed the scope and span of a career (rather than those glorious and antic rookie years), as well as identifying the weight that immersion in trauma that we all carry. Dr. Frank Huyler's two memoirs reassured me that what I was trying to write was in fact doable: that I didn't have to write a Minneapolis version of *Backdraft* or *Rescue Me*, that I could aim for something larger, deeper, more nuanced.

Speaking of location: I read Michael Perry's wonderful *Population 485* when it debuted, and, while I bought copies for several of my rookie classmates, I was miffed that he had "cornered" what I hoped would be my significant advantage over most fire writers: unlike Oxford, Mississippi's other literary son, Larry Brown, and the atypically lyrical FDNY vet Dennis Smith, I had hoped that my depictions of fire/EMS work in the cold and snowy northland would be singular. And then Perry dropped *Population 485* on us. "Damnit! He writes about the cold, about the Midwest—he 'stole' my small angle."

I wrote him a congratulatory and fanboy email. He responded with genuine humility and encouragement. He is a good man. Twenty years later, I've produced a far better, deeper, more interesting book than anything I imagined writing back then, and Mr. Perry continues to write, work, sing, create. I am happy for his well-earned successes, and grateful for his works. There is always room for more good thinking and writing.

Courtney Maum's *Before and after the Book Deal* contains generous and savvy advice for newbie authors. I read it late in this process, but I came away with oodles of good insights and practical guidance. Check it out if you're writing your own book—which I encourage you to do.

The following is a list of recommended books and articles that have shaped my understanding of this work, this world. I also include sources and resources I mention in the book.

Firefighting

Larry Brown, *On Fire*

Sabrina Cohen-Hatton, *The Heat of the Moment: Life and Death Decision-Making from a Firefighter*

David Halberstam, *Firehouse*

Peter M. Leschak, *Ghosts of the Fireground: Echoes of the Great Peshtigo Fire and the Calling of a Wildland Firefighter*

Michael Perry, *Montaigne in Barn Boots: An Amateur Ambles through Philosophy* and *Population: 485. Meeting Your Neighbors One Siren at a Time*

Dennis Smith, *Report from Engine Company 82*

EMS

Anthony Almojera, *Riding the Lightning: A Year in the Life of a New York City Paramedic*

Marjorie L. Bomben, *It's Not the Trauma, It's the Drama: More Stories by a Chicago Fire Department Paramedic*

Shannon Burke, *Black Flies* and *Safelight*

Peter Canning, *Paramedic: On the Front Lines of Medicine*

Maggie Dubris, *Skels*

Kevin Hazzard, *A Thousand Naked Strangers: A Paramedic's Wild Ride to the Edge and Back*

Roger Huder, *Gutter Medicine: Twenty-Six Years as a Firefighter/Paramedic*

Michael Morse, *City Life* and *EMS by Fire: The Making of a Fire Medic*

Medical Machine and Death

Caitlin Doughty, *From Here to Eternity: Traveling the World to Find the Good Death* and *Smoke Gets in Your Eyes: And Other Lessons from the Crematory*

Thomas Fisher, *The Emergency: A Year of Healing and Heartbreak in a Chicago ER*

Atul Gawande, *Being Mortal*

Michele Harper, *The Beauty in Breaking: A Memoir*

Terrence Holt, *Internal Medicine: A Doctor's Stories*

Frank Huyler, *The Blood of Strangers: True Stories from the Emergency Room* and *White Hot Light: Twenty-Five Years in Emergency Medicine*

Adam Kay, *This Is Going to Hurt: Secret Diaries of a Junior Doctor*
Daniela Lamas, *You Can Stop Humming Now: A Doctor's Stories of Life, Death, and in Between*
Thomas Lynch, *The Undertaking: Life Studies from the Dismal Trade*
Robert Meyer and Dan Koeppel, *Every Minute Is a Day: A Doctor, an Emergency Room, and a City under Siege*
Sunita Puri, *That Good Night: Life and Medicine in the Eleventh Hour*
Victoria Sweet, *God's Hotel: A Doctor, a Hospital, and a Pilgrimage to the Heart of Medicine*
Sally Tisdale, *Advice for Future Corpses (And Those Who Love Them): A Practical Perspective on Death and Dying*
Damon Tweedy, *Black Man in a White Coat: A Doctor's Reflections on Race and Medicine*
Bessel van der Kolk, *The Body Keeps the Score: Brain, Mind, and Body in the Healing of Trauma*

Cultural Studies

Carol Anderson, *White Rage: The Unspoken Truth of Our Racial Divide*
James Baldwin, *The Cross of Redemption: Uncollected Writings*; *The Fire Next Time*; *Notes of a Native Son*; and *The Price of the Ticket*
Alison Mariella Désir, *Running While Black: Finding Freedom in a Sport That Wasn't Built for Us*
Robin DiAngelo, *White Fragility: Why It's So Hard for White People to Talk about Racism*
Melissa Febos, *Body Work: The Radical Power of Personal Narrative*
Henry Louis Gates, editor, *"Race," Writing, and Difference* and *Reading Black, Reading Feminist: A Critical Anthology*
Eddie Glaude Jr., *Begin Again: James Baldwin's America and Its Urgent Lessons for Our Own*
Laurence Gonzales, *Deep Survival: Who Lives, Who Dies, and Why*; *Everyday Survival: Why Smart People Do Stupid Things*; and *Surviving Survival: The Art and Science of Resilience*
Christopher Hitchens, *God Is Not Great: How Religion Poisons Everything* and *Mortality*
bell hooks, *Black Looks: Race and Representation* and *Outlaw Culture: Resisting Representation*
Mira Jacob, *Good Talk: A Memoir in Conversations*

Leslie Jamison, *The Empathy Exams: Essays* and *Make It Scream, Make It Burn: Essays*

Frederick Joseph, *Patriarchy Blues: Reflections on Manhood*

Ibram X. Kendi, *How to Be an Antiracist*

Nora McInerny, *The Hot Young Widows Club*; *It's Okay to Laugh (Crying Is Cool Too)*; and *No Happy Endings: A Memoir*

Toni Morrison, *Playing in the Dark: Whiteness and the Literary Imagination*

Ijeoma Oluo, *Mediocre: The Dangerous Legacy of White Male America*

Liz Plank, *For the Love of Men: From Toxic to a More Mindful Masculinity*

Jess Row, *White Flights: Race, Fiction, and the American Imagination*

Greg Tate, *Flyboy in the Buttermilk: Essays on Contemporary America*

Jesmyn Ward, *The Fire This Time: A New Generation Speaks about Race*

Kenneth W. Warren, *Black & White Strangers: Race and American Literary Realism*

Cornel West, *Prophetic Reflections: Notes on Race and Power in America* and *Prophetic Thought in Postmodern Times*

Tim Wise, *Dispatches from the Race War*; *Speaking Treason Fluently: Anti-Racist Reflections from an Angry White Male*; and *White Like Me: Notes on Race from a Privileged Son*

Malcolm X, *The Autobiography of Malcolm X: As Told to Alex Haley*

Damon Young, *What Doesn't Kill You Makes You Blacker: A Memoir in Essays*

Covid-19

Julianne Viviano, "All Quiet on the Eastern Front," *Medium*, June 1, 2020, https://medium.com/@jnviviano/all-quiet-on-the-eastern -front-407b702eec94.

The coverage of *The Atlantic* was searing and thorough. These three offer a master class.

Elaine Batchlor, "I'm a Black Doctor. My Mom Still Won't Get Vaccinated," *The Atlantic*, September 1, 2021, https://www.theatlantic .com/ideas/archive/2021/09/im-a-black-doctor-i-cant-persuade -my-mom-to-get-vaccinated/619933/.

Katherine J. Wu, Ed Yong, and Sarah Zhang, "Omicron Is Our Past Pandemic Mistakes on Fast-Forward," *The Atlantic*, December 23, 2021, https://www.theatlantic.com/health/archive/2021/12/omicron-mistakes/621112/.

Ed Yong, "How Did This Many Deaths Become Normal," *The Atlantic*, March 8, 2022, https://www.theatlantic.com/health/archive/2022/03/covid-us-death-rate/626972/.

Policing and Systemic Violence

Trone Dowd, "Cops and Paramedics Involved in Elijah McClain's Death Charged with Homicide," Vice.com, September 1, 2021, https://www.vice.com/en/article/epn9em/elijah-mcclain-death-homicide-charges-police-parademics.

Phillip Atiba Goff and Katie Porter, "A Mental Health Crisis Is Not a Crime," *New York Times*, July 6, 2021, https://www.nytimes.com/2021/07/06/opinion/mental-health-police-violence-congress.html.

Joe Hernandez, "A Deaf Man Who Couldn't Hear Police Commands Was Tased and Spent 4 Months in Jail," NPR.org, September 29, 2021, https://www.npr.org/2021/09/29/1041562502/deaf-man-tased-police-colorado-lawsuit.

Libor Jany, "Mother of Travis Jordan Sues MPD Officers Who Fatally Shot Her Son," *Minneapolis Star Tribune*, November 11, 2021, https://www.startribune.com/mother-of-travis-jordan-sues-city-officers-who-fatally-shot-mentally-ill-man-in-2018/600115208/.

A. Mannix, "At Urging of Minneapolis Police, Hennepin EMS Workers Subdued Dozens with a Powerful Sedative," *Minneapolis Star Tribune*, June 15, 2018, https://www.startribune.com/at-urging-of-police-hennepin-emts-subdued-dozens-with-powerful-sedative/485607381/.

A. Mannix, "Minneapolis Police Still Teaching 'Excited Delirium Syndrome'—Despite Claiming It Stopped," *Minneapolis Star Tribune*, February 22, 2022, https://www.startribune.com/minneapolis-police-still-teaching-excited-delirium-syndrome-despite-claiming-it-stopped/600146112.

"New AMA Policy Opposes 'Excited Delirium' Diagnosis," *AMA Journal*, June 14, 2021, https://www.ama-assn.org/press-center/press-releases/new-ama-policy-opposes-excited-delirium-diagnosis.

M. O'Hare, J. Budhu, and A. Saadi, "Police Keep Using 'Excited Delirium' to Justify Brutality. It's Junk Science," *Washington Post*, July 17, 2020, https://www.washingtonpost.com/outlook/chokehold-police-excited-delirium/2020/07/17.

Neena Satija, "How Minneapolis Police Handled the In-Custody Death of a Black Man 10 Years Before George Floyd," *Washington Post*, August 29, 2020, https://www.washingtonpost.com/investigations/2020/08/29/david-smith-death-minneapolis-police-kneeling/.

David Stout, "Inquiry into Reporter's Death Finds Multiple Failures in Care," *New York Times*, June 17, 2006, https://www.nytimes.com/2006/06/17/washington/inquiry-into-reporters-death-finds-multiple-failures-in-care.html.

E. Strömmer, W. Leith, M. Zeegers, and M. Freeman, "The Role of Restraint in Fatal Excited Delirium: A Research Synthesis and Pooled Analysis," National Institutes of Health, National Library of Medicine, August 22, 2020, https://www.ncbi.nlm.nih.gov/pmc/articles/PMC7669776/.

A. Truscott, "A Knee in the Neck of Excited Delirium," *Canadian Medical Journal*, March 11, 2008, https://www.cmaj.ca/content/178/6/669.

George Floyd, the Brief Racial Justice Reckoning, and Our Systemic Dysfunction

T. Eldridge, "Cops Could Use First Aid to Save Lives. Many Never Try," Marshall Project, December 15, 2020, https://www.themarshallproject.org/2020/12/15/cops-could-use-first-aid-to-save-lives-many-never-try.

E. Hill et al., "How George Floyd Was Killed in Police Custody," *New York Times*, May 31, 2020, https://www.nytimes.com/2020/05/31/us/george-floyd-investigation.html.

A. Mannix, "Weeks Before Pinning George Floyd, Three of the Same Officers Roughly Detained the Wrong Man," *Minneapolis Star*

Tribune, February 2, 2021, https://www.startribune.com/video
-weeks-before-pinning-george-floyd-three-of-the-same-officers
-roughly-detained-the-wrong-man/600018251/.

Body camera from Officer T. Thao: RAW: Court-released George Floyd
bodycam footage from former officer Tou Thao, https://www
.youtube.com/watch?v=f5eYvDToQgQ.

Body camera from Officers T. Lane and J. A. Keung: RAW: Released
George Floyd bodycam footage from former officers Thomas Lane
and J. Alexander Kueng, https://www.youtube.com/watch?v=0g
QYMBALDXc; https://www.youtube.com/watch?v=NjKjaCvXdf4;
https://www.youtube.com/watch?v=kFojaNbJLCA.

Footage from Cup Foods' camera: https://vimeo.com/541882648/
da884ed63e.

JEREMY NORTON has been a firefighter/EMT with the Minneapolis Fire Department since 2000. A proud native of D.C., he has lived in the Colorado mountains, the Tennessee mountains, and the Minnesota not-mountains. He taught middle school and high school literature and has taught creative writing at the Loft Literary Center in Minneapolis. He has a strong stomach and grim sense of humor.